The Call of Abraham

Christianity and Judaism in Antiquity Series

Gregory E. Sterling, Series Editor

Volume 19

The University of Notre Dame Press gratefully acknowledges the generous support of Jack and Joan Conroy of Naples, Florida, in the publication of titles in this series.

THE CALL of ABRAHAM

ESSAYS ON THE ELECTION OF ISRAEL IN HONOR OF JON D. LEVENSON

edited by
GARY A. ANDERSON
and
JOEL S. KAMINSKY

University of Notre Dame Press
Notre Dame, Indiana

Copyright © 2013 by University of Notre Dame
Notre Dame, Indiana 46556
www.undpress.nd.edu
All Rights Reserved

Manufactured in the United States of America

Library of Congress Cataloging-in-Publication Data

The call of Abraham : essays on the election of Israel in honor of
Jon D. Levenson / edited by Gary A. Anderson and Joel S. Kaminsky.
    pages   cm. — (Christianity and Judaism in antiquity)
Includes bibliographical references and index.
ISBN 978-0-268-02043-9 (cloth : alk. paper) — ISBN 0-268-02043-4
(cloth : alk. paper)
1. Jews—Election, Doctrine of. 2. Election (Theology)   I. Levenson, Jon
Douglas.   II. Anderson, Gary A., 1955–   III. Kaminsky, Joel S., 1960–
BM613.C35   2013
221.6—dc23
                                                    2013022743

∞ *The paper in this book meets the guidelines for permanence and durability of the Committee on Production Guidelines for Book Longevity of the Council on Library Resources.*

Contents

List of Abbreviations   ix

Introduction   1

Part I
THE HEBREW BIBLE

1	Election in Genesis 1 RICHARD J. CLIFFORD, S.J.	7
2	Abraham's Election in Faith W. RANDALL GARR	23
3	Can Election Be Forfeited? JOEL S. KAMINSKY	44
4	Election and the Transformation of *Ḥērem* R. W. L. MOBERLY	67
5	Job as Prototype of Dying and Rising Israel KATHRYN SCHIFFERDECKER	99

Part II
RECEPTION OF THE HEBREW BIBLE

6	Does Tobit Fear God for Nought? GARY A. ANDERSON	115
7	Divine Sovereignty and the Election of Israel in the Wisdom of Ben Sira GREG SCHMIDT GOERING	144
8	The Chosenness of Israel in the Apocrypha and Pseudepigrapha MATTHIAS HENZE	170
9	"A House of Prayer for All Peoples" (Isaiah 56:7) in Rabbinic Thought MARC HIRSHMAN	199
10	The Descent of the Wicked Angels and the Persistence of Evil JAMES KUGEL	210
11	The Election of Israel Imperilled: Early Christian Views of the "Sacrifice of Isaac" KEVIN MADIGAN	236
12	The Salvation of Israel in Romans 9–11 MARK REASONER	256
13	*Populus Dei:* Luther on Jacob and the Election of Israel (Genesis 25) BROOKS SCHRAMM	280

Part III
THEOLOGICAL ESSAYS

14	Election and Affection: On God's Sovereignty and Human Action LEORA BATNITZKY	309
15	Christ and Israel: An Unsolved Problem in Catholic Theology BRUCE D. MARSHALL	330

Publications by Jon D. Levenson — 351

Doctoral Dissertations Supervised by Jon D. Levenson — 357

List of Contributors — 359

Index of Sources — 361

Index of Modern Authors — 388

Abbreviations

HEBREW BIBLE/OLD TESTAMENT

Gen	Genesis
Exod	Exodus
Lev	Leviticus
Num	Numbers
Deut	Deuteronomy
Josh	Joshua
Judg	Judges
1–2 Sam	1–2 Samuel
1–2 Kgs	1–2 Kings
1–2 Chr	1–2 Chronicles
Ezra	Ezra
Neh	Nehemiah
Ps/Pss	Psalms
Prov	Proverbs
Eccl	Ecclesiastes
Isa	Isaiah
Jer	Jeremiah
Lam	Lamentations
Ezek	Ezekiel
Mic	Micah
Hab	Habakkuk

Hag   Haggai
Zech   Zechariah
Mal   Malachi
Tob   Tobit
Sir   Sirach/Ecclesiasticus

NEW TESTAMENT

Matt   Matthew
Rom   Romans
1 Cor   1 Corinthians
Gal   Galatians
Eph   Ephesians
Phil   Philippians
2 Thess 2 Thessalonians
Heb   Hebrews
Jas   James
Rev   Revelation

POST-BIBLICAL JEWISH TEXTS

Pseudepigrapha

Apoc. Ab.   *Apocalypse of Abraham*
2 Bar.   *2 Baruch (Syriac Apocalypse)*
1 En.   *1 Enoch (Ethiopic Apocalypse)*
4 Ezra   *4 Ezra*
Jub.   *Jubilees*
3 Macc   *3 Maccabees*
4 Macc   *4 Maccabees*
Pss. Sol.   *Psalms of Solomon*
Syr. Jub.   *Syriac Jubilees*
T. Ash.   *Testament of Asher*

T. Levi	Testament of Levi
T. Zeb.	Testament of Zebulun
T. Mos.	Testament of Moses

Dead Sea Scrolls and Related Texts

1QpHab	Pesher Habakkuk
1QS	Serek Hayahad or Rule of the Community
4QEn^g	4QEnoch^g
4QpNah	Pesher Nahum
4QpPs^a	4Q Psalms Pesher^a
4QpsJub^a	4QpseudoJubilees^a
4QpsJub^b	4QpseudoJubilees^b

Josephus

Ant.	Jewish Antiquities
J.W.	Jewish War

Rabbinic Writings

b.	Babylonian Talmud
B. Bat.	Baba Batra
Ber.	Berakot
Deut. Rab.	Deuteronomy Rabbah
Exod. Rab.	Exodus Rabbah
Gen. Rab.	Genesis Rabbah
Lev. Rab.	Leviticus Rabbah
m.	Mishna
Mek.	Mekhilta d'Rabbi Yishmael
Pesiq. Rab.	Pesiqta Rabbati
Qidd.	Qiddushin
Sanh.	Sanhedrin
Sifre Deut.	Sifre Deuteronomy
Sifre Num.	Sifre Numbers

S. 'Olam Rab.   *Seder 'Olam Rabbah*
Sotah   *Sotah*
t.   *Tosefta*
Tanh.   *Tanhuma*
Ter.   *Terumot*

POST-BIBLICAL CHRISTIAN TEXTS

Barn.   *Barnabas*
1 Clem.   *1 Clement*
Did.   *Didache*

Clement of Alexandria
Strom.   *Stromata*

Eusebius
Hist. Eccl.   *Historia Ecclesiastica*

Irenaeus
Haer.   *Adversus Haereses*

Jerome
Vir. Ill.   *De viris illustribus*

Origen
Hom. Gen.   *Homilies on Genesis*

Tertullian
Praescr.   *De praescriptione haereticorum*
Pud.   *De pudicitia*

Thomas Aquinas
In IV Sent.   *S. Thomae Aquinatis Scriptum Super Sententiis*, vol. 4
STh   *Summa Theologiae*

VATICAN II TEXTS

AG	*Ad Gentes*
GS	*Gaudium et Spes*
LG	*Lumen Gentium*
NA	*Nostra Aetate*

TEXTS AND VERSIONS

LXX	Septuagint
MT	Masoretic Text
NAB	New American Bible
NJPS	Tanakh: The Holy Scriptures: The New JPS Translation according to the Traditional Hebrew Text
NRSV	New Revised Standard Version
Sam. Pent.	Samaritan Pentateuch
Syr.	Syriac

SECONDARY SOURCES: JOURNALS, PERIODICALS, MAJOR REFERENCE WORKS, AND SERIES

AB	Anchor Bible
AB	*Assyriologische Bibliothek*
ABD	*Anchor Bible Dictionary*. Edited by D. N. Freedman. 6 vols. New York, 1992.
ABS	Archaeology and Biblical Studies
ACCS	Ancient Christian Commentary on Scripture
AnBib	Analecta biblica
AOAT	Alter Orient und Altes Testament
BDB	Brown, F., S. R. Driver, and C. A. Briggs. *A Hebrew and English Lexicon of the Old Testament*. Oxford, 1907.
BFCT	Beiträge zur Förderung christlicher Theologie

Bib	*Biblica*
BibInt	*Biblical Interpretation*
BIOSCS	*Bulletin of the International Organization for Septuagint And Cognate Studies*
BJS	Brown Judaic Studies
BZ	*Biblische Zeitschrift*
BZAW	Beihefte zur Zeitschrift für die alttestamentliche Wissenschaft
CBQ	*Catholic Biblical Quarterly*
CBQMS	Catholic Biblical Quarterly Monograph Series
CC	Continental Commentaries
CEJL	Commentaries on Early Jewish Literature
CRINT	Compendia rerum iudaicarum ad Novum Testamentum
CTR	*Criswell Theological Review*
CTU	*Cuneiform Alphabetic Texts from Ugarit*
DB	*Dictionnaire de la Bible*. Edited by F. Vigouroux. 5 vols. 1895–1912.
DJD	Discoveries in the Judean Desert
DSD	*Dead Sea Discoveries*
FAT	Forschungen zum Alten Testament
GKC	*Gesenius' Hebrew Grammar*. Edited by E. Kautzsch. Translated by A. E. Cowley. 2d. ed. Oxford, 1910.
HALOT	*The Hebrew and Aramaic Lexicon of the Old Testament*. By L. Koehler, W. Baumgartner and J. J. Stamm. Translated and edited under the supervision of M. E. Richardson. 4 vols. Leiden, 1994–1999.
HBT	*Horizons in Biblical Theology*
HSM	Harvard Semitic Monographs
HSS	Harvard Semitic Studies
HTR	*Harvard Theological Review*
HTS	Harvard Theological Studies
HUCA	*Hebrew Union College Annual*
IBC	Interpretation: A Bible Commentary for Teaching and Preaching
ICC	International Critical Commentary
JBL	*Journal of Biblical Literature*

JJS	*Journal of Jewish Studies*
JQR	*Jewish Quarterly Review*
JRS	*Journal of Roman Studies*
JSJ	*Journal for the Study of Judaism in the Persian, Hellenistic, and Roman Periods*
JSJSup	Journal for the Study of Judaism in the Persian, Hellenistic, and Roman Periods Supplements
JSOT	*Journal for the Study of the Old Testament*
JSQ	*Jewish Studies Quarterly*
JTIS	Journal of Theological Interpretation Supplements
Judaism	*Judaism*
KAT	Kommentar zum Alten Testament
L.A.B.	Liber Antiquitatum Biblicarum
LCL	Loeb Classical Library
LHBOTS	Library of Hebrew Bible/Old Testament Studies
NCB	New Century Bible
NETS	*A New English Translation of the Septuagint*. Edited by Albert Pietersma and Benjamin G. Wright. Oxford, 2007.
NovT	*Novum Testamentum*
NTS	New Testament Studies
OTL	Old Testament Library
OTP	*Old Testament Pseudepigrapha*. Edited by J. H. Charlesworth. 2 vols. New York, 1983.
RES	*Répertoire d'épigraphie sémitique*
RES	*Revue des etudes sémitiques*
RevQ	*Revue de Qumran*
RRJ	*The Review of Rabbinic Judaism*
SBLDS	Society of Biblical Literature Dissertation Series
SBLEJL	Society of Biblical Literature Early Judaism and Its Literature
SBLSCS	Society of Biblical Literature Septuagint and Cognate Studies
SC	*Sources chrétiennes*. Paris: Cerf, 1943–
SHR	Studies in the History of Religions
STDJ	*Studies on the Texts of the Desert of Judah*

SVTP	Studia in Veteris Testamenti pseudepigraphica
Tarbiz	*Tarbiz*
TDOT	*Theological Dictionary of the Old Testament.* Edited by G. J. Botterweck and H. Ringgren. Translated by J. T. Willis, G. W. Bromiley, and D. E. Green. 8 vols. Grand Rapids, 1974–.
TLOT	*Theological Lexicon of the Old Testament.* Edited by E. Jenni, with assistance from C. Westermann. Translated by M. E. Biddle. 3 vols. Peabody, Mass., 1997.
VT	*Vetus Testamentum*
VTSup	Vetus Testamentum Supplements
WBC	Word Biblical Commentary
WC	Westminster Commentaries
WMANT	Wissenschaftliche Monographien zum Alten und Neuen Testament
WTJ	*Westminster Theological Journal*
ZAW	*Zeitschrift für die alttestamentliche Wissenschaft*
ZBK.AT	Zürcher Bibelkommentare. Altes Testament
ZTK	*Zeitschrift für Theologie und Kirche*

Introduction

This volume of essays is a Festschrift for Professor Jon D. Levenson, the Albert A. List Professor of Jewish Studies at Harvard Divinity School in honor of his sixty-fifth birthday. Unlike similar volumes, which tend to be collections of loosely related essays, we have opted to focus on one theme that we believe animates much of Jon Levenson's scholarship: the theological meaning of Israel's election. Thus we asked each contributor for an essay in his or her discipline focused as squarely as possible on that theme. Furthermore, we encouraged the authors to emulate the clear and concise style characteristic of both Levenson's scholarly and his more popular writing, in the hope of making this book accessible to lay readers and useful in the classroom setting. We think that the resulting volume not only engages the lifelong work of Jon Levenson but sheds new light on a topic of great import to Judaism and Christianity and contributes to the ongoing dialogue between these two faith traditions.

Perhaps a brief historical overview is in order here. Up until the last decades of the twentieth century, much of modern biblical scholarship portrayed Judaism as an inherently particularistic religion that could never fully embrace the type of universalism that many claimed to have pervaded Christianity from its origins. That assumption was animated by a number of factors, but especially by the belief that Judaism's affirmation of Jewish election impeded its ability to break free from the confines of nationalistic particularism. In such a reading, Jesus and even more so Paul are understood to be the towering figures who created a new religion by opening election to everyone and thus universalizing biblical religion. This view was undergirded by a tendency to confuse Enlightenment universalism with certain universalist strands of biblical thinking and to assume that modern universalism was indeed identical with the biblical strands of universalism found in a Christian approach to scripture.

This problematic understanding of Judaism and Christianity has been critiqued from differing angles by scholars in a number of fields. One of the most important and theologically incisive voices on this topic has been that of Jon D. Levenson. His careful but very wide-ranging scholarship on the Hebrew Bible and its theological reuse in later Judaic and Christian sources has influenced a generation of Jewish and Christian thinkers. Levenson's seminal book, *The Death and Resurrection of the Beloved Son,* demonstrated that both Judaism and Christianity equally embraced the notion of election, even if they understood the meaning of their elect status in unique ways. Rather than rejecting the Hebrew Bible's election theology, Christianity amplified it, as seen most clearly in the way that Jesus's life, death, and resurrection mirror major narrative and ritual texts from the Hebrew Bible. Levenson went on to demonstrate that those who understood Jesus and Paul as universalists were imposing a set of modern and wrongheaded assumptions on these figures, both of whom loudly affirmed the notion of Israel's special election.

To be clear, Levenson does not go on to argue that the shared affirmation of election theology means that the fundamental truth claims of these two religions can be easily reconciled. On the contrary, he demonstrates that in many ways Judaism and Christianity are divided by a common heritage because their understandings of biblical election theology are at once structurally analogous and unique. While this might be a cause for despair, Levenson's thinking has actually laid the groundwork for a more authentic Jewish-Christian dialogue inasmuch as he has helped both Jewish and Christian thinkers understand their deepest theological claims more clearly and cogently.

Focusing on the theme of Israel's election, this volume seeks to present to a broad audience the rich theological dialogue that Professor

Levenson's thoughtful and wide-ranging scholarship has given rise to over the last three decades. These essays span a host of fields including: Hebrew Bible (Clifford, Garr, Kaminsky, Moberly, Schifferdecker), apocryphal and pseudepigraphic literature (Anderson, Goering, Henze, Kugel), New Testament (Reasoner), rabbinics (Hirshman), history of Christian exegesis (Madigan, Schramm) and modern theology (Batnitzky, Marshall). They are penned by Jews, Catholics, and Protestants. A number of essays take up particular insights in Levenson's work, thus illuminating them from a range of disciplines and perspectives. All the contributors to this volume have had their thinking deepened by Levenson's thoughtful scholarship, and our lives have been enriched by our personal and professional interactions with Jon.

We write this with the knowledge that Professor Levenson is still hale and healthy and busy working on more contributions to the study of the Hebrew Bible. We wish him many more productive years and the traditional blessing that he reach a hundred and twenty years!

Gary A. Anderson and Joel S. Kaminsky

PART I

The Hebrew Bible

CHAPTER 1

Election in Genesis 1

RICHARD J. CLIFFORD, S.J.

Genesis 1:1–2:4 (hereafter Gen 1) is a composition of the Priestly source (P), a source that has among its interests Israel's distinctive public worship and the chronology of events in the story of the human race and of Israel. The P preamble to the Pentateuch, Gen 1, narrates the coming into being of heaven and earth (the Hebrew idiom for the universe), an event that took place long before the origin of Israel in the person of its ancestors Abraham, Isaac, and Jacob. One would expect therefore that P, given its care for chronology, would in Gen 1 have studiously avoided anachronistic references to Israel, and especially to its liturgical life, which for P began at Mount Sinai (Exod 19–Num 10). This article explores the surprising fact that Gen 1 contains covert references to several defining features of Israel, viz., the Sabbath, the temple, the dietary laws, and the conquest. Despite its care for proper chronology, P evidently shared the ancient conviction that important elements of the world "were there from the beginning" and acquired their significance at their origin. If one may borrow from computer language, P's references to Israel are "locked" in the disk of Gen 1 and are accessible only to those possessing the required code.

If allusions to Israel are indeed locked in Gen 1, the fact has implications for the meaning of election in the Bible. The Gen 1 allusions to Israel have been read in at least two ways. According to the first, Gen 1 is communicating to insiders that God's real interest in creating the world was Israel; others nations are mentioned, but they are present only as backdrop and audience for God's business with Israel. According to the second, the foreshadowing means that from the beginning there existed a complementarity between the elect nation and the other nations. The tasks and hopes of Israel and the nations, respectively, might be differently expressed and differently timed, but they are closely related. Israel is an example of a nation doing important things in its own way while sharing the experience and aspirations of other nations.

TWO PRELIMINARY COMMENTS ON THE GEN 1 COSMOGONY

Genre and Structure

Like many ancient Near Eastern cosmogonies, Gen 1 is introductory, preparing readers to appreciate the great literary work that follows. As Mark Smith points out, "the placement of Genesis 1 at the very beginning of the Bible stakes a claim, asserting the primary status of its account over and above other biblical versions of creation."[1] Given the pronounced theocentrism and traditionalism of the ancient Near East, scribes assumed that the meaning of a reality was clearest at the moment of its creation, when God's imprint, so to speak, was freshest and most visible. Gen 1 lets the reader know what to look for in the vast and compendious Pentateuch, not only in the primeval history, but in Gen 12–50, and indeed in the entire Pentateuch.

One of the most striking features of Gen 1 is its seven-day structure. That structure can help us see the introductory function of Gen 1. The six days on which God works are arranged in matching panels (days 1–3 and 4–6), with God's day of cessation from work placed outside the series in the climactic seventh spot. (See table below.) With qualifications that we will discuss below, days 1–3 depict the creation of the *domains* of sea, sky, and earth, and days 4–6, the creation of *their mobile inhabitants*, classified according to their means of locomotion— wings flapping in the sky, fins propelling (*rāmaś*) through the sea, animals crawling with legs (*rāmaś*) or walking on all fours on land. In the perspective of Gen 1, life is concretized as movement; what moves on its own power is alive. Days 4–6 display the energy permeating the universe. Day 7, however, is a reminder of the text's profound theocentrism, drawing attention to the creator rather than the creation.

The Pre-creation State (1:1–2)

Panel I: Creation of Static Domains	Panel II: Creation of Their Mobile Occupants
Day 1. 1:3–5	Day 4. 1:14–19
[1] Light/darkness	[5] Luminaries
Day 2. 1:6–8	Day 5. 1:20–23
[2] Water/dome/sea	[6] Fish and birds
Day 3. 1:9–13	Day 6. 1:24–31
[3] Water/dry ground (vv. 9–10)	[7] Land animals (vv. 24–25)
[4] Plant life (vv. 11–13)	[8] Human beings (vv. 26–31)
Day 7: Post-creation Rest. 2:1–3	

Though appearing at first reading to be rigid, the text actually alternates between fixed and flexible. The "two-panel" scheme (vv. 3–13 // 13–31) conflicts with the act-oriented scheme in days 1–4. God's shaping of "heaven and earth" is completed on the fourth day, not the third, for only on the fourth day is the sky hung with the greater and lesser lights. The panels therefore overlap: the making of domains (the chief work of days 1–3) is completed only on day 4, whereas the populating of the domains (the chief work of days 4–6) gets underway on day 3.

"Heaven and earth" is the Hebrew idiom for the universe in which each noun is qualified by the other. As Luis Stadelmann notes, "the term *ʾrṣ* means primarily the entire area in which man thinks of himself as living, as opposed to the regions of heaven or the underworld."[2] "The heavens" in Gen 1 is more accurately rendered "sky." God's heaven is a completely different reality, existing prior to any creation, and inhabited by the perennially existing *běnê ʾĕlōhîm,* lit. "sons of God," heavenly beings. The universe depicted in Gen 1 is best described in Shakespeare's phrase, "O brave new world, That has such people in't!" (*The Tempest* 5.1). The new world is deliberately put in parallel to the heavenly world and its inhabitants while remaining quite distinct from it. In this new heaven and earth, earthly beings will play a role analogous to the role played by beings in the heavenly world. Earth's inhabitants are even called *ṣābāʾ,* "host," in Gen 2:1, a term that elsewhere refers to the heavenly host (e.g., 1 Kgs 22:19; Pss 103:21, 148:2). Psalm 115:16 catches both the parallelism and the difference: "The heaven of heavens belong to YHWH, but earth he has given to human beings." The priority of the heavenly beings and their respectful relationship to earthlings is nicely expressed by the divine assembly's decision to create human beings "in our image, after our likeness" (Gen 1:26).

Many ancient Near Eastern cosmogonies have as their purpose to ground present-day realities in the primal moment when the gods laid down the fundamentals of the universe. Several cosmogonies describe the ordering of heavenly bodies that determine the reckoning of time and thus of feast days honoring the gods. In other cosmogonies, the construction of a temple is part and parcel of creation. In still others, kingship is an original feature of the primordial world. Many cosmogonies lay down the basic features that constitute a particular people, e.g., they mention the particular land on which the people will live.

Dating and Original Context

The Pentateuch reworks many preexilic traditions and presents them in a new synthesis for an exilic audience. "Exilic" can refer both to those actually suffering exile in the sixth century B.C.E. and to those experiencing the crisis of meaning that came in its wake decades after the physical event. Such audiences needed to hear Gen 1 highlight relevant themes in order to restore their faith and and sense of hope. Among the relevant themes would have been God's sovereign power and free commitment to "heaven and earth," the extraordinary worth of human beings, the divine intent that the species of "man" continue in existence through progeny and through possessing land to sustain itself, and the reaffirmation of the importance of key Israelite institutions such as the Sabbath, the temple, and dietary laws. To all of these issues Gen 1 has something to say, for as we shall see, the Pentateuch was designed in part to help anxious and displaced exiles reread their traditions as promise and assurance. Gen 1 directs them to read their traditions in just that way.

THE SABBATH

> And since God finished on the sixth[3] day the work he had been doing, he ceased (*šābat*) on the seventh day from all the work he had been doing. God blessed the seventh day and made it holy, for on it he ceased (*šābat*) from all the work he had done in creation.[4] (Gen 2:2)

The most obvious connection between Gen 1 and later Israelite institutions is God's six-day work week followed by a seventh day of cessation from work. Elsewhere in the Bible, and especially in the P source in the Pentateuch, the seventh day of the week is called the Sabbath (*haššabbāt*), but the word does not occur in Gen 1. Genesis 1 twice uses the similar-sounding verb *šābat*, "to cease (doing an act)," to characterize the seventh day (Gen 2:2, 3). There is debate on whether *šābat* and *šabbat* are etymologically related and, if they are, whether the noun comes from the verb or the verb from the noun. To be precise, Gen 1 does not describe the institution of the Sabbath, but simply shows God working six days and ceasing from work on the seventh. The NRSV and NABRE render *šābat* in Gen 2:2, 3 "rested," but LXX and NJPS render more accurately "ceased (working)," for the primary meaning of *šābat* is to cease doing something, not to rest. Nonetheless, Gen 2:2–3 provides a basis for the later institutionalization of seventh-day rest.

The first occurrence of the word Sabbath in the Pentateuch is in the P verse, Exod 16:23, in which Moses tells the people: "This is what the Yhwh meant: Tomorrow is a day of rest, a holy Sabbath (*šabbātôn šabbat qōdeš*) of Yhwh." In the largely P narrative in Exod 16, Israel encounters for the first time, it seems, God's way of acting in a six-plus-one day mode, for the people had not yet been commanded to observe the Sabbath. They only came to know the six-plus-one manner of acting through their experience of receiving the manna. Each day they gathered the day's yield. Gathering more did not increase the yield, nor did storing up manna for the next day prove useful, for stored-up manna became maggoty and foul smelling (vv. 17–20). On the seventh day, the Sabbath, things were different. On the day before Sabbath, the people were told to lay in a two-day supply and were guaranteed that the stored portion would not become foul. They were "to stay where they were," i.e., not go out and gather. "So the people remained inactive (*šābat*) on the seventh day" (vv. 29–30 NJPS). Through their formative experience in the wilderness, the people came to learn God's rhythm in working and dealing with them.

The people's wilderness experience prepared them for the next stage of "learning the Sabbath." It was at Sinai, according to P, that Israel came to be a nation with a law. In the Decalogue (Exod 20:8–11), the people's wilderness experience of the manna distribution becomes concretely expressed as a commandment. In Exod 25:1–31:17, Moses gives seven speeches detailing how the people are to build the tabernacle. Six of the speeches concern its construction, and the seventh (Exod 31:12–17, P) concerns the Sabbath: "You shall nonetheless keep my Sabbaths, for this is a sign between me and you throughout your generations, given in order that you may know that I, Yhwh, sanctify you" (NSRV). ("Nonetheless (*ʾak*)" in the sentence indicates that the Sabbath is to be observed even while the tabernacle is constructed.) Six days of work plus one of rest follows the order of creation. Israel's observance of that order in the Sabbath makes known to other nations that they are God's special people. Sabbath observance is thus a sign of the "covenant for all time" (Exod 31:16): "It shall be a sign for all time between Me and the people of Israel. For in six days Yhwh made heaven and earth, and on the seventh day he ceased from work and was refreshed" (Exod 31:17 NJPS).

In Priestly theology, God brought the world into being in a particular rhythm of work and cessation from work. Israel has the great privilege of knowing that rhythm through experience and commandment. Their observance of it becomes a sign that they are God's people, imitating his manner of acting by the way they structure their week. In the course of time, Israelite thinkers reflected further on the meaning of Sabbath observance. Exod 20:8–11 applies it to the need of all animals—beasts and humans alike—to have a day of rest. No work is to be done on that day; it is set apart from profane use; it is holy. Deut 5:12–15 develops God's work and rest in a slightly different direction: observing the Sabbath means cessation of work for all humans and their animals, with a particular concern for slaves that was based on the fact that Israel was once enslaved. Now freed by God's power, it has an obligation to care for slaves' welfare.

As is widely recognized, Sabbath observance became a distinctive feature of Early Judaism, evidenced particularly in Neh 9:14, 10:31 (Heb 10:32), and 13:15–22. In a period when Jewish identity had to be clear, Sabbath observance was one way of effectively differentiating Jew from Gentile and of proclaiming God's sovereignty to the Gentile world. The Sabbath is therefore an important theme in the Pentateuch, which is addressed to exiles.

THE TEMPLE

In a number of Near Eastern cosmogonies, the creator god builds a palace for himself or is provided with one by the other gods, sometimes at the conclusion of the process of creation.[5] The palace (or temple) provides a site for ceremonies to honor the god's great deed, thus commemorating the creation. The Akkadian epic *Enūma eliš* offers two illustrations of the phenomenon. In i.67–74, Ea dons the royal regalia of the sleeping Apsu, slays him, and sets up his own dwelling (Akkadian *šubtum*) on the surface of Apsu (the underground freshwater ocean); in verses 109–39, after Marduk's victory over Tiamat, the grateful gods build him a dwelling (Akkadian *šubtum*) in Babylon and acclaim him king. Three other Akkadian cosmogonies explicitly connect temple and creation: In the composition entitled "When Anu created the heavens," Ea creates the brick-god Kulla for the restoration of the temples and creates the reed marsh and forest to supply materials for the construction; in a temple dedication prayer, the gods "prepared in the land a pleasant dwelling"; and in the Chaldean Cosmogony, Marduk creates and builds temples in sacred cities.[6] In the Ugaritic texts, Baal's palace concretely symbolizes his kingship; in *CTU* 1.4.v–vi, he builds a palace and proclaims his kingship (though it is not clear in the text whether the palace is the result of a cosmogonic victory). In the biblical Psalm 93, Yhwh defeats the Floods and Mighty Waters (*nĕhārôt, mayim rabbîm*), and the psalm ends with a verse celebrating Yhwh's powerful decrees and construction of a palace: "Your decrees are indeed enduring; / holiness befits (MT *nāʾăwāh qōdeš*) your house, Yhwh, forever" (NJPS); or, slightly emending MT: "Your house is a holy dwelling (*nāwēh qōdeš*) forever."[7] In Ps 29:3 and 10, Yhwh defeats Mighty Waters and makes his throne on Flood (*mabbûl*), and in Ps 89:6–38 Yhwh defeats Sea, establishes the cosmos, and appoints a king. Several Songs of Zion (Pss 46, 48, and 76) speak of Yhwh's cosmic battle at the site of the Temple. Psalm 48:13–15 urges visitors to contemplate the buildings of the temple, which by themselves seem to proclaim that "this is God, our God forever."

Does Gen 1, which is a creation account, refer to the temple or to its forerunner, the tabernacle in the wilderness? The answer is similar to the answer given about the Sabbath, viz., Gen 1 does not mention explicitly the institution of the temple, but it indirectly alludes to the tabernacle. In the P account of the construction of the tabernacle in Exod 25–31, the seven speeches of Moses (each initiated by a divine command) obviously imitate the seven-day construction of the universe in Gen 1. Though of widely varying lengths, the speeches are recognizable by their common introduction, "Yhwh spoke to Moses": 25:1–30:10; 30:11–16; 30:17–21; 30:22–33; 30:34–38; 31:1–11; 31:12–17.[8] Moses's seventh speech harks back to Gen 2:2–3: "For in six days Yhwh made heaven and earth, and on the seventh day he ceased and was refreshed" (Exod 31:17 NJPS). Jon Levenson, our honoré, developing observations made by Joseph Blenkinsopp, points out characteristic P formulas ("X saw . . . and blessed"; "he/they completed the work") and finds that they cluster around certain topics: the etiology of the Sabbath, the construction of the tabernacle, and the division of the land under Joshua. Space permits giving only one example: "And God saw all that he had made and, behold, it was exceedingly good" (Gen 1:31). // "And

Moses saw all the work and, behold, they did it as YHWH had commanded; so they did (it) and Moses blessed them" (Exod 39:43). Other instances of similarity between Gen 1 and Exodus are Gen 2:1 // Exod 39:32; Gen 2:2 // Exod 40:33b–34; Gen 2:3 // Exod 39:43; Gen 2:3 // Exod 40:9–11.[9]

Another indication of a link between creation and the temple is the pervasiveness of the number seven, which structures Gen 1. In addition to the seven divine speeches directing the construction of the tabernacle and the institution of the Sabbath, the lampstand has seven candles (Exod 25:37) and Aaron wears seven sacred vestments (28:1–39). As Levenson has noted,[10] seven is the number of days in the New Year feasts of Israel–Passover in the spring and the Feast of Tabernacles (Booths) in the fall. Each feast has connections with creation.[11] Pre-exilic Israel likely celebrated the New Year festival in the fall, and then, during the exile, under the influence of the Babylonian calendar, shifted it to the spring. Both Passover and Tabernacles were seven-day festivals, which suggests that the time-unit was well known even before P's use of it in Gen 1. New Year festivals provided the community with an opportunity to celebrate the ordering and rejuvenation of the universe, especially palpable at the beginning of the agricultural year, and to respond through rituals. Closely linked to the life-imparting creation victory was the temple, the palace of the victorious god, which symbolized his victory and kingship over the cosmos. It is probably no coincidence that the erection of the tabernacle in Exod 40:2[7] took place in the spring New Year's Day and that on the same day Noah first sighted the drying earth after the flood (Gen 8:13).

Though it does not mention the tabernacle or the temple, Gen 1 foreshadows its construction, thereby managing to ground it in creation and giving it legitimation. It also aligns the construction of the temple with the construction of the universe, making the Jerusalem temple a memorial of creation.

DIETARY LAWS

Most cultures and religions, e.g., Judaism, Islam, and Hinduism, have dietary rules that were developed over centuries to guide adherents to eat or not eat various foods. Eating is essential to all living creatures, and it is thus not surprising that religious concerns should come to bear on so basic a human activity. Dietary laws unite a people by providing them with common practices and differentiate them from other peoples by a unique code. By making a people distinctive, dietary laws make the people a more visible representative of their patron deity. Judaism stands out among religions for its detailed dietary laws, and the basis for many of them are found in the Priestly source of the Bible.

The dietary laws are closely related to holiness, a persistent concern of P: "You shall be holy because I am holy" runs through Leviticus (11:44, 45; 19:2; 20:7, 26; 21:8). "Holy," in the biblical understanding, is "separateness," a quality of God vis à vis human beings. Yet the "separate God" wants close fellowship and union with human beings, who are by their nature profane, and often even sinful. Dietary laws are a means of overcoming humans' distance from God and gaining the purity such nearness requires.

The basis of the dietary laws, like those of the Sabbath and the temple, are ultimately rooted in the created order depicted in Gen 1, but the laws' connection to Israel, the elect people, is only implicit and allusive. The explicit connection is made clear in other Priestly texts, which develop the Genesis-rooted features into a means for maintaining the holiness that God demands of his people.

Some of the systematizations and analogies in the dietary laws are found in Gen 1. During the first three days of creation in Gen 1, the three static domains of the universe—sky, sea, and earth—came into being. They were populated during the second set of three days by the life forms proper to each domain—birds, fish, and land animals. As we have already seen, the P writer defines life concretely by self-movement: the animals are described by their means of locomotion through their proper spheres—birds flying through the air with their wings, fish swimming (*rāmaś*, lit. "creep") through the waters with their fins and scales, and land animals creeping with their many legs (*rāmaś*) on the ground or (one may suppose) walking on their legs. Limiting ourselves for the moment to the P dietary laws in Leviticus 11, we can see that many of the criteria refer to animal means of locomotion, including hoofs (Lev 11:2–8), fins and scales (Lev 11:9–12), wings (Lev

11:20–23), paws (lit. "hands," Lev 11:27), ways of creeping on the ground (Lev 11:29), ways of crawling on the belly, and ways of walking on four legs (Lev 11:41–42). Genesis 1 classifies animals by their locomotion and Lev 11 develops the classification into criteria. Genesis 1 and Lev 11 also share vocabulary, e.g., *šāraṣ, rāmaś, ḥāyāh,* and *lĕmînāh.*

The dietary laws in Lev 11 (and Deut 14:1–21) are too complex and diverse to be linear developments of the systematizing of Gen 1. It is likely, for example, that the double criteria for determining acceptable animals in Lev 11:3 (cleft hoofs and chewing the cud) were derived from the animals long used in sacrifice—cattle, sheep, and goats—and then extended to animals resembling them. And ancient custom must be the reason why locusts were permitted food despite the prohibition on winged swarming things that walk on all fours (Lev 11:20–23).

One can, nonetheless, identify principles operative in the divisions visible in Gen 1. Jacob Milgrom notes that "those animals are permitted that move in a way that is natural to their environment: land animals walk (on feet, not paws), water animals swim (not crawl), and air animals fly."[12] Mary Douglas, the anthropologist who did so much to teach modern scholars to appreciate the dietary laws of Leviticus, articulates a principle that is at the heart of Gen 1: "The underlying principle of cleanness in animals is that they shall conform fully to their class. Those species are unclean which are imperfect members of their class, or whose class itself confounds the general scheme of the world." She roots this conception in the three-fold classification of Gen 1. "In the firmament two-legged fowls fly with wings. In the water, scaly fish swim with fins. On the earth four-legged animals hop, jump, or walk. Any class of creatures which is not equipped with the right kind of locomotion in its element is contrary to holiness." "Four-footed creatures which fly (11:20–26) are unclean. Any creature which has two legs and two hands and which goes on all fours like a quadruped is unclean (11:27)."[13]

In sum, Israel's dietary laws, which set it apart from its neighbors, are rooted in the distinctions and separations that characterized creation. Its laws concerning eating are aligned with the way God created the universe and are therefore closely aligned with the divine will. By observing them, the people become holy, overcoming the barriers that separate a profane people from their all-holy God.

LAND TAKING

In Gen 1:28, God blesses "them" (ʾōtām refers to hāʾādām, male and female, in v. 27) and gives the human race a two-fold defining imperative: "Be fertile and multiply, fill the earth and subdue it" (NABRE). A typical example of a biblical defining imperative is the appointment of judges in Deut 16:18–19: "[18]You shall appoint judges and officials in all your tribes ... and they shall render just decisions for the people. [19]You must not pervert justice; you must not show partiality and you must not take a bribe." Instead of employing, as a modern writer would, third-person verbs stating that honest judges should be appointed, the biblical text uses an imperative verb directly commanding judges to act justly. The imperative verb defines what a judge is by what God commands the judge to do. This manner of speaking serves to highlight the divine will in the functioning of society. The imperatives addressed to the freshly created hāʾādām in Gen 1:28 seem to function in the same way. The divine will is, first, that hāʾādām continue in existence by begetting progeny, and second, that they acquire the land that God wishes to give them. Two comments are called for. First, land, especially arable land, had an importance in antiquity that moderns easily underestimate. In an age when storing and transporting food was well nigh impossible on a large scale, families depended directly on their land for the necessities of life, food, and clothing. Without adequate land for crops and herds, a family or a nation could not long survive. To live in any meaningful sense required land, territory. Second, the context of Gen 1:28 shows that hāʾādām is not a monadic individual, but "them," i.e., "man" as male and female, and, it is important to note, "man" as *grouped*, i.e., belonging to a people or nation. Given the individual's "embeddedness" in the group in biblical anthropology, it would be highly unlikely that the text addresses an isolated individual. Rather, the text has in view "man" embedded in a people or nation, just as the Table of Nations in Gen 10–11 has in view a nation even as it speak of its individual ancestors. Looking at chapters 2–11 as a whole, one can say that chapters

2–9 focus on the first defining imperative, "be fertile and increase," whereas chapters 10–11 focus on the second imperative, "fill the earth and subdue it." God in 1:28 commands each nation to continue through progeny and to take the territory on which they are to live.

The interpretation just given is far from being the *opinio communis* of verse 28, which must now be subject to critique. Common opinion has gone in two directions. The vast majority of commentators correctly take *kābaš* in a violent sense as "to subdue, tread down," and take *ʾereṣ* (incorrectly) as the earth and its animals that humans are meant to subdue as part of their commission to "rule over" it (*rādāh*, v. 26, 28).[14]

A second, minority view, represented most recently by Ute Neumann-Gorsolke, rids the verb *kābaš* of its violent meaning of subdue and tread down and interprets it as (peacefully) receiving territory through the legal gesture of walking upon it to indicate ownership.[15] Arguing from Akkadian texts in which *kabāsu* means "to set foot (upon a land)" in a gesture of sovereignty, Neumann-Gorsolke proposes that Heb. *kābaš* in Num 32:22, 29, and Josh 18:1 should be similarly interpreted. Numbers 32:20–22, where Moses tells the Reubenites and Gadites they must fight against the inhabitants of the land with their fellow Israelites, is thus rendered: "[20]if you will indeed take up arms to get in the presence of Yahweh for the war, [21]and every armed man of you will indeed pass over the Jordan in the presence of Yahweh, until he has driven out his enemies from before him, [22]and the land can be stepped upon (*nikbĕšāh hāʾāreṣ*) in the presence of Yahweh . . . ." She translates Num 32:29 and Josh 18:1 in similar fashion.

The interpretation is unconvincing. Even in Akkadian, the meaning "to oppress, tread upon" (human enemies) is more frequently attested for *kabāsu* than is "stand on." The latter meaning, it should be said, has the nuance of "standing majestically upon" a land in a manner befitting a king or noble. The Akkadian examples, however, do not indicate that standing upon a land is a *legal* gesture. Hebrew *kābaš*, on the other hand, in its thirteen other occurrences always means to subdue; it never means "to step upon." Despite assertions to the contrary, the context of Num 32:20–22, 29 is unquestionably violent. Moses's whole point is that the Reubenites and Gadites, understandably eager to avoid battle and return to their farms, must join their fellows in battle (*lĕmilḥāmāh*, v. 20) against the inhabitants of Canaan. Yʜᴡʜ will fight with them in holy war, but they must join in the battle. They cannot go home until the native inhabitants of the land are defeated and the land is subdued (*nikbĕšāh hāʾāreṣ*).

The most satisfactory solution to the problem of *kābaš* in Gen 1:28 is to take *ʾereṣ*, its object, as territory, not earth. The proposed translation of "subdue (your) land" is given support by the parallel verb to *kābaš*, *milĕʾŭ*, "fill." "Fill" in the G-stem masculine plural imperative mood occurs in v. 22 commanding the newly created fish to fill, to populate, the waters of the seas, and again in v. 28 commanding the newly created *ʾādām* to fill, to populate, the earth. "Earth" here is the land on which man lives, as in Gen 10–11. Note especially Gen 10:10, "the land of Shinar," and 10:20 (P): "These are the descendants of Ham, by their clans and languages, and by *their lands* and nations."

But why would Gen 1:29 use a violent verb, "to subdue, to tread down" (*kābaš*), to describe the nations who, according to Gen 10–11, will presumably move peacefully into their unoccupied territories? Taking a cue from the foreshadowing in Gen 1 of the Israelite Sabbath, temple, and dietary laws, one can conclude that *kābaš* in coded fashion alludes to Israel's later taking of the land of Canaan. Because Canaan was already occupied (unlike the territories of the other nations), Israel had to invade and subdue its inhabitants.

In short, God's word in Gen 1:28, "fill the earth and subdue it," commands human beings, seen as nations, to take the territory given to them. At the same time, the command in Gen 1:28 uses a verb that foreshadows Israel's later taking of its land by force.

— This article has sought to demonstrate that Gen 1, in describing God's creation of the world and the human race, subtly alludes to constituent features of Israel that will be expanded and articulated at Sinai and beyond. By doing so, Gen 1 places the origin of Israel "in the beginning," gaining the prestige that comes with antiquity. Though its actual emergence came later than that of the nations, Israel actually predated them all, existing in the divine mind from of old. By this move, the biblical author is able to affirm the honor of his people in the commonwealth of nations and affirm as well their kinship with all peoples.

NOTES

It is a pleasure to dedicate this study to Professor Jon D. Levenson, who has contributed significantly to our understanding of the Bible in elegant and perceptive books, essays, and commentaries. He has instructed Jews and Christians alike in the perennial relevance of the Bible for living rightly today. One of his scholarly interests has been the distinctiveness of Israel as revealed in Tanak and in Jewish commentary, as well as in Jewish and Christian theological reflection over the centuries. It is my hope that this essay will further this interest of his as well as recognize Professor Levenson's distinguished contribution to this central biblical topic.

1. Mark S. Smith, *The Priestly Vision of Genesis 1* (Minneapolis: Fortress, 2010), 2.

2. Luis. I. J. Stadelmann, *The Hebrew Conception of the World: A Philological and Literary Study* (AnBib 39; Rome: Pontifical Biblical Institute, 1970), 127.

3. MT *hšbyʿy*, "the seventh (day)." Sam. Pent., LXX, Syr., *Jub* 2:16 have, *hšsy*, "the sixth (day)." For the textual problem, see Ronald Hendel, *The Text of Genesis 1–11: Textual Studies and Critical Edition* (New York: Oxford University Press, 1998), 32–34.

4. All translations are the author's unless otherwise noted. When using other translations, the term LORD has been replaced with YHWH.

5. Hebrew *hêkāl*, like Akkadian *bītu(m)*, has the meaning "palace" and "temple." A god's dwelling in the heavenly world is appropriately termed a "palace" and in the earthly world a "temple." The fluidity of the terms is a reminder that the temple on earth is a reflection or copy of the real palace in the heavens. The ceremonies in the earthly temple enable human worshipers to participate in the heavenly worship of the deity.

6. For translations and comment, see Richard J. Clifford, *Creation in the Ancient Near East and in the Bible* (CBQMS 26; Washington, DC: Catholic Biblical Association, 1994), 59–65.

7. Cf. Exod 15:13, *nĕwēh qodšekā*, "your holy dwelling."

8. Peter Kearney, "Creation and Liturgy: The P Redaction of Ex 25–40," *ZAW* 89 (1977): 375–87 was one of the first to explore the parallel. His further attempts to match each day of Genesis creation with each speech are, except for the last day, unpersuasive.

9. Joseph Blenkinsopp, "The Structure of P," *CBQ* 38 (1976): 276–78; Jon D. Levenson, *Creation and the Persistence of Evil: The Jewish Drama of Divine Omnipotence* (San Francisco: Harper and Row, 1988), 82–86. See also M. Weinfeld, "Sabbath, Temple, and the Enthronement of the Lord: The Problem of the

Sitz-im-Leben of Genesis 1:1–2:3," in *Mélanges bibliques et orientaux en l'honneur de M. Henri Cazelles* (AOAT 212; ed. A. Caquot and M. Delcor; Kevelaer: Butzon and Bercker; Neukirchen-Vluyn: Neukircherner Verlag, 1981), 501–12.

10. Levenson, *Creation and the Persistence of Evil*, 66–99.

11. Levenson, *Creation and the Persistence of Evil*, ch. 6, "Creation in Seven Days."

12. Jacob Milgrom, "The Dietary Laws," *Leviticus: A Book of Ritual and Ethics* (CC; Minneapolis: Fortress Press, 2004), 117.

13. Mary Douglas, *Purity and Danger* (London: Routledge and Kegan Paul, 2007; repr. of the 1966 edition), 69–70.

14. Here is a sample of opinions: A. Dillmann, *Genesis Critically and Exegetically Expounded* (trans. Wm. B. Stevenson; Edinburgh: T & T Clark, 1887), 1–84; Hermann Gunkel, *Genesis* (trans. Mark E. Biddle; Macon: Mercer University Press, 1997), 114: "the people were promised dominion over the earth and all animals in harsh terms (*kābaš, rādāh*)."; S. R. Driver, *The Book of Genesis* (London: Methuen, 1916), 16; Gerhard von Rad, *Genesis* (rev. ed.; trans. John H. Marks; Philadelphia: Westminster, 1972), 60; Leonard Greenspoon, "From Dominion to Stewardship? The Ecology of Biblical Translations," in *Journal of Religion and Society Sup. Ser. 3* (2008), 162, states that "human actions in subduing the 'chaos' of wild animals would mirror God's action in his initial chaos-quelling acts of creation."

15. Ute Neumann-Gorsolke, "'And the Land Was Subdued before Them . . .'? Some Remarks on the Meaning of *kbš* in Joshua 18:1 and Related Texts," in *The Land of Israel in Bible, History, and Theology: Studies in Honor of Ed Noort* (SVT 124; Leiden: Brill, 2009), 73–85. The article draws on her dissertation done under Bernd Janowski, *Herrschen in den Grenzen der Schöpfung: Ein Beitrag zur alttestamentlichen Anthropologie am Beispiel von Psalm 8, Genesis 1 und verwandten Texten* (WMANT 101; Neukirchen-Vluyn: Neukirchener Verlag, 2004).

CHAPTER 2

Abraham's Election in Faith

W. RANDALL GARR

Drawing on earlier material, the prayer recorded in Neh 9 explicitly confers elected status on Abraham.

> You solely are the LORD God, who *bāḥartā bě'aḇrām* chose Abram, brought him out of Ur of the Chaldeans, and made his name Abraham. You found him (lit., "his heart") *ne'ĕmān* faithful to you, making the covenant with him to give the land of the Canaanite, Hittite, Amorite, and the Perizzite, and the Jebusite, and the Girgashite—to give (it) to his descendants. (Neh 9:7–8a)

With the exception of the change in the patriarch's name (Neh 9:7b < Gen 17:5), that earlier material is drawn from Gen 15. The Lord called the patriarch from Ur of the Chaldeans (Gen 15:7bα), promised land to him and his descendants (vv. 7bβ, 18b–21), and confirmed the promise with a covenantal ritual (v. 18a, interpreting vv. 9–11, 17). Likewise, the patriarch's merit for elected status—*neʾĕmān*—is "an interpretive paraphrase of Gen 15:6":[1] viz., *wĕheʾĕmin ba-Yhwh* "He believed in the Lord."

As Jon Levenson has demonstrated, the contents of the patriarch's "faith" vary both within and across the three Western religious traditions that claim him as archetype.[2] For the apostle Paul, faith is neither action nor deed; it is an attitude or disposition (e.g., Rom 4:5, Gal 5:6). The author of James's letter holds a different view: faithful attitude and obedient conduct go hand in hand; the former is incomplete without the latter (e.g., Jas 2:22–24, 26; see also Heb 11:8–11, 17–18). In contrast, Ben Sira narrows the definition to obedience alone, as exemplified in Abraham's response to the "test" of Genesis 22 (Sir 44:20; see also 4QpsJub[a] ii 8 and perhaps 4QpsJub[b'] 7 1). The author of 1 Macc goes a step further, tying Abraham's faith to both the Akeda and a version of the meritorious assessment of his (prior) faith in Gen 15:6b (1 Macc 2:52; see also Jas 2:21).[3] According to these interpretations, Abraham's faith is a state of mind and/or active behavior.

Inasmuch as Nehemiah traces Abraham's elected status to his faith, first recorded in Gen 15:6, this essay investigates the verb that expresses this laudable trait: *heʾĕmin* "believe."[4] It begins with verbal morphology and what that morphology might—or might not—suggest for the verb's semantic content. Next, it discusses the meaning of the verb in several of its idioms: as an absolute form, as an auxiliary followed by an infinitive, and as a matrix verb followed by a subordinate clause; and in combination with *lĕ-* and *bĕ-*.[5] The discussion then returns to Gen 15:1–6, an analysis of its conversational structure, and the role that v. 6a plays in that context. This journey, though, is not without its landmine. In Levenson's words: "[I]t makes sense that each of the three self-styled Abrahamic traditions would sometimes portray their founder as practicing that tradition."[6] More pointedly, characterizations of Abraham or, in this case, Abraham's faith can be self-serving. This essay presents a particular type of scholarly Abraham.

HE'ĔMÎN, MORPHOLOGY, AND SEMANTICS

Linguists have long noted that "markedness is iconically motivated";[7] an item that is morphologically marked should be semantically marked as well. In that context, James Barr poses the relevant question bearing on this study: "[W]hat is the force of, or the reason for, the fact that the verb 'trust, believe' in Hebrew is in the form or theme known as *hiphʿil?*"[8] Among the credible suggestions, some diagnose the verb as a declarative *hiphil*, whether it originates in the responsive affirmative particle *ʾāmēn* (i.e., "say Amen [and thereby endorse the speech act at hand]"[9]) or in the *niphal* participle *neʾĕmān* (i.e., "declare someone or something faithful").[10] Others judge it to be an inchoative *hiphil* which expresses the entry into (and attainment of) a state expressed by the root (i.e., "become faithful [and remain in that state]; believe").[11] These proposals, though, respond to only part of Barr's question. In fact, since they address the issue of semantic categorization within the *hiphil* stem, these analyses are arguably of minor concern. Of greater importance is the issue of morphological assignment itself. Does the *hiphil* form of *heʾĕmîn* bear on any of the interpretations of Abraham's faith promoted by the "self-styled Abrahamic traditions"?

It certainly bears on the Pauline interpretation of faith as a state of mind, at least as conventionally understood. For among more than nine thousand instances of *hiphil* forms in the biblical corpus, not a single *hiphil* verb form has an uncontestable stative meaning. Bergsträsser offers potential counterexamples: e.g., *heʾĕrîk̠* "be long" (e.g., Exod 20:12 = Deut 5:16), *heḥĕrîš* "be silent" (e.g., Exod 14:14), *heḥšîk̠* "be dark" (e.g., Ps 139:12), *himtîq* "be sweet" (Job 20:12), and *himrā* "be rebellious" (e.g., Deut 9:24).[12] Upon examination, however, none of these stative interpretations is compelling. For instance, *heʾĕrîk̠* and *heḥšîk̠* are part of an established *hiphil* subcategory whose underlying root expresses a property concept. This subcategory, including verbs such as *hilbîn* "turn white" (e.g., Isa 1:18) or *hišpîl* "fall down" (lit., "become low") (Job 22:29), is semantically inchoative and therefore active. *Heʾĕrîk̠* and *heḥšîk̠* are better translated "become long, lengthen" and "become dark, darken," respectively. *Heḥĕrîš* and *himrā* have a different explanation. Since their subject is always human or, in the case of *heḥĕrîš*, divine, these verbs are always controlled by a willful agent who chooses to initiate and/or perpetuate the situation expressed by the verb (e.g., Judg 18:19 and Ps 106:43). Once the subject's agency is recognized, *heḥĕrîš* is no longer adjectival and stative; it means "keep still, silent." Likewise, *himrā* is an activity: "act rebellious." *Himtîq* is different still. Despite translations such as "though wickedness is sweet in their mouth" (NRSV) and "though evil is sweet to his taste" (NJPS), only a minority of scholars suggest that the verb is stative in *'im tamtiq běp̄îw rā'ā* (Job 20:12). The majority correctly associate the *hiphil* verb with already recognized semantic categories such as inchoative ("become sweet"), effective ("produce sweetness"), or intransitive ("taste sweet").[13] All told, Bergsträsser's evidence for a stative *hiphil* is not persuasive. Or, to apply this discussion to Paul's interpretation of faith, the morphology of *he'ĕmîn* cannot express a human state, attitude, or disposition.

HE'ĔMÎN AS AN ABSOLUTE, AUXILIARY, OR MATRIX VERB

A small group of attestations sets the semantic stage for understanding *he'ĕmîn*. These attestations involve neither religious devotion nor an explicit appraisal of truth. They do not involve dependent objects, either.

One example appears in Job 29. In this idealized and hyperbolic self-assessment, Job first lists his many magnanimous deeds to the disenfranchised. Then, he speaks of the reception he noticed in return.

> I would smile in their direction, *lo' ya'ămînû* they could hardly believe; they showed no displeasure at my radiant face. (Job 29:24)

The issue here is not one of trust, confidence, or verifiable truth. Job asserts the opinion that his favorable gestures were unexpected, welcome, and comforting. Belief/disbelief is an issue of subjective expectation based on observation or experience.[14]

On two occasions, *he'ĕmîn* is followed by an infinitive.

> *lo' ya'ămîn šûḇ* He does not believe (he'll) come back from darkness; he is targeted for the sword. (Job 15:22)

> *he'ĕmantî lir'ōṯ* I do believe (I'll) experience the LORD's goodness in the land of the living. (Ps 27:13)

In the former passage, the wicked man faces a problem similar to that presented in Job 15:23b: *yāḏa* "He knows that the day of darkness is set by his own doing." He cannot expect or even hope to escape. In the latter passage, the situation is very different. Though the speaker may come under attack (Ps 27:2–3), he is confident of divine protection (vv. 1, 4–5); he may feel threatened (v. 12) and anxious of divine neglect (v. 9), but he has hope (see v. 14). Informed perhaps by his own experience (vv. 2–3), he claims that God will further his survival (v. 13). When *he'ĕmîn* is followed by an infinitive, "believe" expresses the subject's cognitive evaluation of a future situation.[15]

The same evaluation can occur when *he'ĕmîn* is followed by a complement clause.

> If I summoned (God) and he responded, *lo' 'a'ămîn* I do not believe *kî* that he'd pay me attention. (Job 9:16)

> *lo' he'ĕmînû* The kings of the land, as well as all the inhabitants of the world, did not believe *kî* that foe or enemy could enter Jerusalem's gates. (Lam 4:12)

> Take a look among the nations, analyze (the situation) (lit., "have a glance"), and be completely astounded. For something is taking effect in your time. *lo' ta'ămînû* You wouldn't believe (it) *kî* should it be told. (Hab 1:5)

Job's experience, for example, convinces him that God would ignore his grievance (see Job 9:17–18). In Lamentations, onlookers are dumbfounded that God would change course and not defend Jerusalem (cf., e.g., Ps 48). In Habakkuk, God warns his audience of a tactical recalibration to punish Judah by means of the Chaldeans (Hab 1:6–11). Each time, *(lo') he'ĕmîn* has an epistemic interpretation. But unlike its use as an absolute or auxiliary verb, the epistemic force of *he'ĕmîn* here varies with the context. It may be relatively weak ("expect, anticipate") or relatively strong ("believe [to be true]"). Regardless, it is an assessment based on prior knowledge—common or personal—and/or experience.

HE'ĔMÎN LĔ-

The combination of *he'ĕmîn* and indirect object is more specific.

> [Joseph's brothers] informed [their father Jacob], "Joseph is still alive. (*We can report*) that he is ruler over the entire land of Egypt." He (lit., "his heart") went cold, because *loʾ heʾĕmîn lāhem* he did not believe them. (Gen 45:26)

Jacob's assessment is based upon evidence. He had seen Joseph's bloody tunic and drew the only possible conclusion: Joseph was dead, mauled by an animal (Gen 37:33). In the absence of credible evidence or convincing argumentation to the contrary, he judges ("believed") the information carried by his sons ("them") untrue ("not").

Heʾĕmîn lĕ- involves evidence, whether implicitly or explicitly. For instance, an uncritical person may accept anything as truth.

> Someone naive *yaʾămîn lĕkol dābār* believes everything. (Prov 14:15a)

In this case, evidence is not required. Alternatively, there may be evidence of an oral nature.

> Who *heʾĕmîn lišmuʿātēnû* believes what we've heard? To whom has the power (lit., "arm") of the LORD been revealed? (Isa 53:1; see also Ps 106:24)

Sometimes, however, word alone may not suffice.

> *wĕloʾ heʾĕmantî laddĕbārîm* But I didn't believe the reports until I came and saw with my own eye. (1 Kgs 10:7aα; see also 2 Chr 9:6aα)

The queen of Sheba had to conduct her own test to "see" that Solomon's famed wisdom and wealth were indeed *ĕmet* "true" (1 Kgs 10:6 = 2 Chr 9:5).

Heʾĕmîn lĕ- always denotes a cognitive exercise.

> They said to [Gedaliah], *hăyādoaʿ tēdaʿ* "Do you have any knowledge that Baalis, king of the Ammonites, has sent Ishmael b. Nethaniah to strike you down?" *wĕloʾ heʾĕmîn lāhem* But Gedaliah b. Ahikam did not believe them. (Jer 40:14)

> Now don't let Hezekiah deceive you, don't let him entice you in this way, *wĕ'al ta'ămînû lô* and don't believe him. For every god of every nation or kingdom has been unable to save his people from my grip or from my fathers' grip. All the more, your god will not save you from my grip. (2 Chr 32:15)

Informed of the contracted assassination, Gedaliah both ignores the warning and denies truth to the rumor. Sennacherib, in contrast, makes an argument attempting to reverse public opinion, and works to convince the Jerusalemites that Hezekiah misled them when he advised calm in face of probable attack (2 Chr 32:7). Specifically, in light of the counterevidence of many failed attempts to escape Assyrian control, he argues that Hezekiah lied; the claim that Israel's God will protect or save them (v. 8a) can only be wrong-headed, dangerous, and false (see also v. 17). In both passages, then, belief/disbelief involves an assessment of truth. Whether the indirect object is inanimate or human, the verb phrase *he'ĕmîn lĕ-* expresses a mental act that evaluates propositional truth.

The same is true when the indirect object is God.

> When the LORD sent you from Qadesh Barnea, "Go up and reclaim the land that I gave you," you rebelled against the command of the LORD your God to you. *wĕlō' he'ĕmantem lô* You didn't believe him or obey him. (Deut 9:23)

> You are my witnesses—oracle of the LORD—and my servant, whom I have chosen, so that you may come to know, *wĕta'ămînû lî* believe me, and fully comprehend that I solely am he. Before me no god was formed, and after me none will exist. (Isa 43:10)

Isaiah's oracle makes the point clearly; God, in a courtroom scene with an impaneled jury, contends that his divinity is unique (see also Isa 43:11–13). It is an assertion whose truth, he argues, his addressees must understand completely. Moses's assertion is somewhat different. The Israelites, he says, failed to follow God's directive and thus disobeyed.

But the basis of this disobedience lay in a cognitive assessment; the phraseology signals that, in Moses's judgment, they did not accept what God said as true—viz., that the land was already theirs (see also Num 13:2) because God promised them victory (Deut 9:3–5). Disbelief fed disobedience (cf. 1:32, below).

Finally, *he'ĕmîn lĕ-* appears several times in Exod 4. It begins with Moses's prediction that the Israelites will not accept his claim of witnessing God.[16]

> Moses said in response, "Fact is, *lo' ya'ămînû lî* they won't believe me or obey me. For they'll say, 'The LORD did not appear to you.'" (Exod 4:1)

Interestingly, his conversational partner, God, does not respond with a counterargument designed to persuade the skeptical Israelites that Moses truly saw a divine apparition (cf. Gen 45:27–28a). God instead addresses the Israelites' need for tangible proof and offers three controlled supernatural omens. Each omen, in fact, should provide increasingly convincing demonstration that Moses's claim is true and, by implication, that his proxy to rescue Israel is true as well.

> If *lo' ya'ămînû lāk* they don't believe you or pay attention to the former sign, *wĕhe'ĕmînû lĕqol hā'ot hā'aḥărôn* they should believe the latter sign. But if *lo' ya'ămînû gam lišnê hā'otōt hā'ēllê* they don't believe even these two signs or pay attention to you, you should take some of the Nile's water and pour (it) on the ground. Then, the water that you take from the Nile will then turn into blood on the ground. (Exod 4:8–9)

By God's logic, cumulative evidence has a specific demonstrative goal[17]

> that *ya'ămînû kî* they believe that the LORD, God of their fathers, God of Abraham, God of Isaac, and God of Jacob, appeared to you. (Exod 4:5)

Evidence, then, can overcome (reverse) doubt. In Exod 4, it should convert a skeptic into a believer, acknowledging Moses's claims as true.

HE'ĔMÎN BĔ-

From a semantic perspective, *he'ĕmîn bĕ-* is considerably different from *he'ĕmîn lĕ-*.[18] One measure of that difference is the nature of the nominals governed by each preposition. With *he'ĕmîn lĕ-*, seven cases (50 percent) are followed by nominals that express visible phenomena (Exod 4:9), audible phenomena (1 Kgs 10:7 = 2 Chr 9:6, Isa 53:1, Ps 106:24), or a combination of the two (Prov 14:15; see also Exod 4:8b); the other seven (50 percent) are nominals referring to God (Deut 9:23, Isa 43:10) or humans (Gen 45:26, Exod 4:1, 8a, Jer 40:14, 2 Chr 32:15). This division, though, is more apparent than real. The dative object marks either the evidence subject to cognitive evaluation or the conveyor of such evidence.[19] With *he'ĕmîn bĕ-*, the object nominals are more varied. A fraction (8 percent) express visible (Ps 78:32) or audible phenomena (106:12). The majority (72 percent) signify God (Gen 15:6, Exod 14:31, Num 14:11, 20:12, Deut 1:32, 2 Kgs 17:14, Jonah 3:5, Ps 78:22, 2 Chr 20:20), angels (Job 4:18, 15:15), or human beings (Exod 14:31, 19:9, 1 Sam 27:12, Jer 12:6, Mic 7:5, Prov 26:25, 2 Chr 20:20). The remainder (20 percent) include a wild ox (Job 39:12) and nonconcrete nouns such as "life" (Deut 28:66, Job 24:22), "commandments" (Ps 119:66), and "nothing" (Job 15:31). This profile points to a significant contrast: unlike *he'ĕmîn lĕ-*, the majority of objects marked with the locative preposition are intrinsically capable of affecting the subject of *he'ĕmîn*.[20]

He'ĕmîn bĕ- also has a behavioral component.

> The LORD spoke to Moses, "Take the rod and assemble the community—you and Aaron your brother. You should speak to the rock in eyeshot of them. It'll produce its water. You'll extract water from the rock for them, and you'll provide the community and its animals water." Moses took the rod from before the LORD. . . . Moses and Aaron assembled the group in front of the rock. One of them (lit., "he") said to them, "Rebels, please listen. Will we extract water for you from this rock?" Moses raised his hand and struck the rock twice with his rod. Out came a lot of water, and the community and its animals drank. The LORD said to Moses and Aaron, *lo' he'ĕmantem bî* "You didn't believe in

me. . . . Accordingly, you won't bring this group to the land that I give you." (Num 20:7–12)

On the one hand, the Lord instructs Moses to speak to the rock within the people's field of vision. On the other hand, Moses addresses the community, poses a question of inherent uncertainty, implies human responsibility for the miracle to come, and hits the rock with the rod twice. The number of discrepancies between instruction and execution is impressive. Moses does not act in conformity to God's will and, with his brother, is roundly punished. Their infraction: They "did not believe in" the Lord. More than incredulity (*loʾ heʾĕmîn lĕ-*), *loʾ heʾĕmîn bĕ-* here is tantamount to disobedience.

For this reason, *loʾ heʾĕmîn bĕ-* can be coupled with other verbs and idioms expressing defiant conduct.[21]

> Because *ḥāṭĕʾû* the Israelites sinned against the Lord their God, . . . *wayyîrĕʾû ʾĕlōhîm ʾăḥērîm* feared other gods, *wayyēlĕkû bĕḥuqqôt* conformed to the protocols of the nations . . . , *wayyibnû* built themselves *bāmôt* shrines . . . , *wayyaṣṣibû* erected themselves *maṣṣēbôt waʾăšērîm* stelae and asherim . . . , *wayqaṭṭĕrû* performed sacrifices there, on all the shrines, like the nations . . . , *wayyaʿăśû* and performed *dĕbārîm rāʿîm lĕhakʿîs* wicked deeds to provoke the Lord's anger . . . , the Lord warned Israel and Judah . . . , "Quit your wicked ways . . ." *wĕloʾ šāmēʿû* But they did not obey (lit., "hear"). *wayyaqšû ʾet ʿorpām* They were obstinate (lit., "made their neck hard[er]"), like their ancestors who *loʾ heʾĕmînû ba-Yhwh* did not believe in the Lord their God. (2 Kgs 17:7–14)

Loʾ heʾĕmîn bĕ- can even express conduct that defies a reasonable interpretation of evidence.

> The Lord said to Moses, "How long *yĕnaʾăṣunî* will this people treat me with contempt? How long *loʾ yaʾămînû bî* will they not believe in me despite all the signs that I have performed in their midst?" (Num 14:11)

> *wayyôsîpû ʿôd laḥăṭōʾ* They kept on sinning against [God], *lamrôt* rebelling against the Most High in the dry land. *waynassû* They deliberately tested God . . . *waydabbĕrû bēʾlōhîm* and spoke against God, "Can God

arrange a feast in the wilderness? Yes, he struck the rock, water flowed, and streams flooded. Can he also provide bread?" . . . Accordingly, having heard (the speech), the LORD turned furious . . . because *lo' he'ĕmînû bē'lohîm* they did not believe in God. (Ps 78:17–22a)

The same issue appears in Deut 1 where, in Moses's reiteration of the scout episode (Num 13–14), the Israelites are squarely blamed for losing the opportunity to reclaim the land. God assured their success (Deut 1:8); the scouts delivered a positive report (v. 25b); and God's prior deeds on their behalf prefigured his deeds to come (vv. 30–31). Nonetheless, the Israelites deliberately refused (*wĕlo' 'ăḇîtem*), defied the order (*wattamrû 'et pî* YHWH), and thereby failed to enact his command (*ênĕḵem ma'ămînim ba-*YHWH) (vv. 26, 32).

The behavioral dimension of *(lo') he'ĕmîn bĕ-*, though, is an expression of more fundamental semantic concepts.

> *hăṯa'ămîn bô* Do you believe in [a wild ox] to bring in the seed and collect (it from) your threshing floor? (Job 39:12)

> Your life ahead will be hanging. You will live in terror night and day. *wĕlo' ṯa'ămîn bĕḥayyêḵā* You will not believe in your life. (Deut 28:66; see also Job 24:22)

Those concepts involve the will of the grammatical subject. In the case of Job, for example, the Lord notes the foolishness of choosing and expecting a wild animal to perform domestic work (see also Job 39:9a); uncontrollable by nature, such an animal is undependable (see also v. 11a). For the Deuteronomist, the failure to uphold Yahwistic prescriptions will jeopardize one's own life. One should have no confidence of survival (cf. Ps 27:13; see also 116:9–10a). *(Lo') he'ĕmîn bĕ-* is more than a choice or mental act; it entails a degree of personal involvement and reliance on a projected outcome.

In other words, the situation expressed by the verb phrase *he'ĕmîn bĕ-* includes a chain of events.

> *wayya'ămēn* Achish believed *bĕḏāwiḏ* in David. "He has become thoroughly noxious among his people Israel. He can become my vassal forever." (1 Sam 27:12)

> Jonah started to enter the city, one day's walk. He announced, "Forty more days, Nineveh's transformed." *wayyaʾăminû* The Ninevites believed *bēʾlōhîm* in God, announced a fast, and, from greatest to least, put on sackcloth. (Jonah 3:4–5)

For Achish, the chain began when he accepted (believed) David's account of killing Judeans on his Philistine raids (1 Sam 27:8–11). Then, with this "evidence" at hand, Achish places trust in David, adopts him into his entourage, and appoints him as bodyguard (28:2). Achish therefore acts on his belief in David. The Ninevites act, too. For a reason unknown to the reader, and despite its ambiguity, the Ninevites judge God's oracle true. They then initiate mourning rituals that include the king (Jonah 3:6) and animals (v. 7), and perform "deeds" signifying a renunciation of their wicked ways (v. 10a). In both episodes, an assertion is made, it is assessed to be true, and a decision is made to act in conformity with that assessment.[22]

The situation portrayed in Exodus 14 is similar. Seeing the Egyptians on their tail terrifies the Israelites (v. 10). Moses counsels calm and promises an alternative conclusion to what they presently expect: the Israelites will witness (lit., "see") both the Lord's victory as well as the disappearance of the Egyptians (v. 13). As evidence, the divine cloud shifts position (vv. 19–20), and Moses channels the Lord's power over the sea (v. 21): the cloud sends the Egyptians into panic (v. 24b) and instills the recognition of the Lord's responsibility in the affair (v. 25b; see also v. 14a); the Lord's power through Moses drowns the Egyptians (v. 27; see also v. 28). The outcome is narrated according to plan: "On that day, the LORD saved Israel from the grip of Egypt. Israel saw Egypt dead on the seashore" (v. 30). Moreover, these demonstrations move the Israelites beyond visual awareness of divine power or Mosaic instrumentality (v. 31aα; see also 19:9).

> The people feared the LORD. *wayyaʾăminû ba-YHWH* They believed in the LORD *ûbmōšê ʿaḇdô* and in his servant Moses. (Exod 14:31aβ–b)

The Israelites' great fear of the Egyptians has faded (v. 10); prompted by God's overwhelming display of power, the Israelites now fear the

Lord. They are also prepared to act in keeping with the directives of God and his authorized deputy. More than an acceptance of evidence, *he'ĕmîn bĕ-* signals personal investment and a decision to abide by the locative object (e.g., Jer 12:6, Mic 7:5; Prov 26:25, Job 4:18, 15:5 [all negated]) or, when that object is inanimate, its immediate implications (e.g., Pss 78:32, 106:12, 119:66; see also Job 15:31).

On occasion, however, *he'ĕmîn* lacks an overt object. Yet, unlike Job 29:24, in these cases the verb does not register a simple epistemic assessment. It implies something more.

> *wayya'āmēn* The people believed. They heard that the LORD had taken note of the Israelites and that he had seen their plight. They bowed in reverence. (Exod 4:31)

> If *lo' ta'ămînû* you do not believe, (*know*) that *lo' tē'āmēnû* you will not endure. (Isa 7:9b)

The former passage, in fact, has a double meaning. It signifies that the people accept the evidence of the signs performed by Moses, judge the signs true, and even acknowledge Moses's commission (Exod 3:17). It also signifies their obedience. By an act of gestural deference, they show their willingness to follow his lead (v. 31bβ). The latter passage is famously elliptical and enigmatic (cf. 2 Chr 20:20). Under attack by a coalition of Aramaeans and Israelites (Isa 7:1; see also 2 Kgs 16:5), Ahaz faces a dilemma:[23] He can form a political-military alliance with Assyria (2 Kgs 16:7–9), or he can abide by Isaiah's oracle not to panic (Isa 7:4; see also 28:16). The oracle also comes with a divine promise that the attack will not succeed (v. 7) because the Lord fights for and saves his people from foreign harm (see, e.g., Deut 20:3–4). Ultimately, though, Isaiah warns Ahaz that he and his royal house hang in the balance. Failure to accept the truth of Isaiah's oracle (7:7) and a concomitant failure to act in accordance with the implications of that oracle (v. 4)—including the formation of an Assyrian alliance—will decertify God's promise of *bayit ne'ĕmān* an enduring Davidic dynasty (see 2 Sam 7:16 or Ps 89:4–5, 29, conditionalized in 1 Kgs 9:4–5) and, by implication, the kingdom itself.²⁴ Even in the absence of explicit objects, then, the meaning of *heʾĕmîn* is retrievable from the immediate context.

GENESIS 15:6

Genesis 15 follows a significant crisis. There was a large regional war in which Abram's nephew Lot got entangled and captured (Gen 14:12). Abram responded. He led a sizable homegrown posse against the captors, extricated Lot, and retrieved all of Lot's property (vv. 14–16). Upon his return home, two officials greeted Abram: Melchizedek, who blessed him and received a tithe offering of loot; and the king of Sodom, Lot's residence (v. 12b < 13:12), who offered to let Abram keep the nonpersonnel trophies of war but whose offer Abram solidly rejected in an oath sworn to the Lord (14:21–24). "In Abram's view, the true hero of the victorious campaign [wa]s not himself, but the LORD."²⁵

Another crisis arises when the Lord next addresses Abram.

> Don't be scared (lit., "fear not"), Abram. I am your shield. Your reward will be very much more. (Gen 15:1b)

At first blush, this crisis is another military threat of some kind, as signaled by the verb phrase "fear not" (e.g., Exod 14:13, Deut 3:2, 20:3).²⁶ Mention of the Lord's protective "shield" just after would in fact insure such an interpretation (see, e.g., Deut 33:29, 2 Sam 22:3, Ps 3:4).²⁷ But the verb phrase "fear not" is not restricted to military contexts. It is an idiomatic offer of assurance and/or a bid for calm in a general crisis, including a crisis of confidence, or a "presumed state of anxiety."²⁸ And as Abram himself soon volunteers (Gen 15:2a), that crisis comes from his considerable frustration that he remains childless.

The frustration is intense enough to affect Abram's speech. On the surface at least, he descends into gibberish.

> *ûḇen mešeq bêtî hûʾ dammeśeq ʾĕlîʿezer. Ben-mesheq*'s my family; that is, Damascus Eliezer. (Gen 15:2b)

The terms *bēn* "son" and *bêtî* "my household, family" suggest his topic of concern. But the other words add nothing of clear meaning and, if the history of interpretation is any gauge, are a pointless detour. Nevertheless, Abram collects himself, begins another turn at speech, and restates his position in unambiguous terms. Despite earlier promises (Gen 12:2, 13:15–16), he has no children and, as he sees it, will be leaving his estate to someone in his employ (15:3).

The Lord's rebuttal is incremental and successful. First, he denies that Abram's heir will be an employee and reasserts the promise that Abram's heir will be his own genetic legacy (Gen 15:4). Then, he shows Abram the innumerable stars in the sky (v. 5a). Finally, he draws an analogy, promising that Abram's children will be just like the stars—innumerable (v. 5b). Abram, for his part, is convinced: *wĕheʾĕmin ba-YHWH* "He believed in the LORD" (v. 6a).

Hermisson, Lohse, and Moberly recognize a problem at this narrative juncture. Hermisson and Lohse state the problem in brief: "Why does he *believe*? Neither the text nor its continuation offers an answer. Abraham's faith is not motivated."[29] Moberly elaborates:

> It is highly doubtful that Abraham's believing response to the promise of Gen. xv 4–5 should be seen as a deeper or truer response than his response to the initial command to leave home, family and country (Gen. xii 1–4). Likewise, it is doubtful that his response to the promise of Gen. xv 4–5 should be seen as in any way different to his response to the promise of xiii 14–17. The promise of xiii 14–17 is in fact more amazing than that of xv 4–5, for it not only promises countless descendants in a similar way . . . but also promises land at the same time . . . . [I]t sharply poses the question why Abraham's faith and Yahweh's response should be specified at xv 6 rather than elsewhere.[30]

Hermisson, Lohse, and Moberly all provide answers to the question. Hermisson and Lohse defer to the perspective of the narrator who "knows about Israel's long history with its God" and who works to align "often historically incomprehensible" religious experiences with historical time.[31] Moberly finds the answer in the covenantal ritual of Gen 15 and an effort "to link Israel's existence as a people in the land (i.e. the concern of Gen xv as a whole) to Abraham's trust in Yahweh. It was not only the promise of Yahweh that gave existence to Israel ... but also the faithful response of Abraham."[32]

These answers, though, underestimate the crisis faced by Abram in Gen 15. Abram has emerged from a military victory in chapter 14; some time has passed (v. 15:1a); the Lord tells him not to be scared (v. 1bαα). The Lord's words are suspicious. They may be intended to assure or reassure the patriarch. Perhaps they are meant to console, calm, or encourage. But the context gives no clue. God's statement of protection (v. 1bαb) could narrow the possibilities. Yet the following promise of numerically abundant compensation (v. 1bβ) only aggravates the situation. For Abram, it recalls the divine promises of nationhood (12:2) and countless offspring (13:15–16) which have *both* gone unfulfilled.[33] Whether intentionally or inadvertently, the Lord's words provoke Abram's crisis.

Abram's fears are justified, too. He knows that he has neither child nor blood heir (Gen 15:2aβ). That is, he has no evidence that God's promise is still in effect or will come true. More than skepticism, Abram has empirical doubts.[34]

The Lord addresses these doubts and provides evidence from the natural world. That evidence is preexisting and, as already mentioned, analogical. It also addresses Abram's problem directly, at least from a canonical viewpoint.[35] For in the course of his encounter with Melchizedek, Abram learned of—and received a blessing in the name of—the creator deity El Elyon (Gen 14:19). More importantly, he drew two new theological conclusions from this encounter: (1) El Elyon is identical to the deity he had known as Yhwh (v. 22bα < 12:8, 13:4); and (2) like El Elyon, Yhwh is "creator of heaven and earth" (14:22bβ < v. 19bβ). In this light, then, Abram is prepared and even disposed to processing the Lord's astral presentation as an analogical lesson: Just as the "creator of heaven and earth" created a starry infinity in the world, that same creator can create a comparable genealogy from him. The evidence sufficiently convinces Abram. He overcomes (reverses) doubt, invests in the Lord, and chooses to abide by him.[36]

But it would be wrong to infer that, once achieved, "faith" is a permanent state. The Israelites themselves, for example, are accused of changing course. More generally, the grammatical category of *hiphil* verbs does not express states, qualities, or conditions (see above). In fact, some *hiphil* verbs which Bergsträsser identifies as semantic statives require a continuing input of energy to maintain: e.g., *heḥĕrîš* "keep still, silent" and *himrā* "act rebellious." The agentive *hiphil* verb *heʾĕmîn* must follow suit.

In this context, Abram's next conversational move finds at least a partial explanation. Addressing God by title and name (Gen 15:8bα; see v. 2aαb), Abram poses a second *mâ*-question (v. 8bβ; see v. 2aαb): "How (lit., "by what [means]") will I know that I'll inherit the land?" It is a move whose implication often troubles scholars, for "Abraham's question in v. 8 seems to contradict the affirmation of his faith in v. 6."[37] Abram's position, though, improves in comparison to that of Ahaz. In that latter case, Ahaz receives an oracle from Isaiah (Isa 7:4–9) but rejects the prophet's offer of a collateral, demonstrative "sign" (vv. 11–12). Ahaz disengages and retreats. But in the former case, Abram persists. He remains committed, engages God, and triggers a covenant that also explicitly extends the promise of land to his genetic heirs (Gen 15:18–21; cf. *lĕkā* in 13:17). True, the Lord does not inform the patriarch how he will attain or recognize the fulfillment of the promise. But Abram receives much more than he requested, too.[38]

For the patriarch Abraham, faith is a conversion experience. Unlike earlier episodes where he accepts God's promises in silence, in Gen 15 Abraham is in crisis. At first, he betrays considerable doubt; ultimately, he accepts the divine promise of offspring. The intervening evidence of God's creative activity in the sky convinces Abraham that the promise is true. But his is more than an empirically driven judgment (*heʾĕmîn lĕ-*). He decides to abide by his judgment and conduct himself accordingly. He decides to invest himself in, and rely on (trust), the promising deity.[39] From that agentive vantage point, he then persists and engages God on the other unresolved promise given him—that of land. He behaves in a manner consistent with the *hiphil* verb form and maintains as much involvement and effort as (he feels) the situation requires. Perhaps his faith is not perfect or flawless. It is nonetheless exemplary enough to earn him elected status in the Hebrew Bible and beyond.

NOTES

I thank the editors for commenting on an earlier draft of this paper. I also thank Tremper Longman, J. J. M. Roberts, and Hugh Williamson for advice and references. All translations are those of the author unless otherwise indicated.

1. Jon D. Levenson, *The Death and Resurrection of the Beloved Son: The Transformation of Child Sacrifice in Judaism and Christianity* (New Haven: Yale University Press, 1993), 175. Cf. Manfred Oeming, "Der Glaube Abrahams: Zur Rezeptionsgeschichte von Gen 15,6 in der Zeit des zweiten Tempels," *ZAW* 110 (1998): 23–24.

2. Levenson, "The Conversion of Abraham to Judaism, Christianity, and Islam," in *The Idea of Biblical Interpretation: Essays in Honor of James L. Kugel* (ed. Hindy Najman and Judith H. Newman; JSJSup 83; Leiden: Brill, 2004), 3–40; idem, *Monotheism and Chosenness: The Abrahamic Foundation of Judaism and Roman Catholicism* (Joseph Cardinal Bernardin Jerusalem Lecture, March 26, 2009; Chicago: Presto Press, 2009); idem, "The Idea of Abrahamic Religions: A Qualified Dissent," *Jewish Review of Books* 1 (2010): 40–42, 44; idem, *Abraham Between Torah and Gospel* (Père Marquette Lecture in Theology 2011; Milwaukee: Marquette University Press, 2011); and idem, *Inheriting Abraham: The Legacy of the Patriarch in Judaism, Christianity, and Islam* (Princeton, N.J.: Princeton University Press, 2012).

3. Ultimately, the notion of Abraham as exemplary Torah practitioner (*m. Qidd* 4:14) may also be an interpretive judgment based on Gen 15:6. See, in this context, Otto Kaiser, "Traditionsgeschichtliche Untersuchung von Genesis 15," *ZAW* 70 (1958): 117; and Lloyd Gaston, "Abraham and the Righteousness of God," *HBT* 2 (1980): 48.

4. I omit Isa 30:21 and Job 39:24 from consideration, where *heʾĕmîn* seems to be a verb of (non-) motion.

5. For the verb phrase *heʾĕmîn ʾet*, see n. 20, below.

6. Levenson, "The Idea of Abrahamic Religions," 44b. See also R. W. L. Moberly, "Abraham's Righteousness (Genesis xv 6)," in *Studies in the Pentateuch* (ed. J. A. Emerton; VTSup 41; Leiden: Brill, 1990), 109.

7. John Haiman, "The Iconicity of Grammar: Isomorphism and Motivation," *Language* 56 (1980): 528.

8. James Barr, *The Semantics of Biblical Language* (Oxford: Oxford University Press, 1961; repr., London: SCM/Trinity International, 1991), 176.

9. E.g., Meredith G. Kline, "Abram's Amen," *WTJ* 31 (1968): 1–11, using the term "delocutive."

10. E.g., Gerhard Ebeling, "Jesus and Faith," in *Word and Faith* (trans. James W. Leitch; Philadelphia: Fortress, 1963), 209 (one option).

11. E.g., GKC §53e; and Alfred Jepsen, "*āman; ʾᵉmûnāh; ʾāmēn; ʾᵉmeth*," *TDOT* 1:309. See also Otto Procksch, *Theologie des Alten Testaments* (Gütersloh: Bertelsmann, 1950), 604.

12. G. Bergsträsser, *Hebräische Grammatik* (2 vols.; Leipzig: Vogel/Hinrichs, 1918–29; repr., Hildesheim: Olms, 1986), 2:§19d. See also Joshua Blau, *Phonology and Morphology of Biblical Hebrew: An Introduction* (Linguistic Studies in Ancient West Semitic 2; Winona Lake, Ind.: Eisenbrauns, 2010), §4.3.5.7.1 (p. 234).

13. E.g., Samuel Rolles Driver and George Buchanan Gray, *A Critical and Exegetical Commentary on the Book of Job* (2 vols.; ICC; Edinburgh: Clark, 1921), 2:137 (one option); BDB 608b (despite itself); and Norman C. Habel, *The Book of Job* (OTL; Philadelphia: Westminster, 1985), 317, respectively.

14. See also Harry Torczyner, *Das Buch Hiob: Eine kritische Analyse des überlieferten Hiobtextes* (Vienna: Löwit, 1920), 205; or NJPS, on v. 24b.

15. See Hans Wildberger, "'Glauben': Erwägungen zu האמין," in *Hebräische Wortforschung. Festschrift zum 80. Geburtstag von Walter Baumgartner* (VTSup 16; Leiden: Brill, 1967), 384; repr. in *Jahwe und sein Volk. Gesammelte Aufsätze zum Alten Testament. Zu seinem 70. Geburtstag am 2. Januar 1980* (ed. Hans Heinrich Schmid and Odil Hannes Steck; Theologische Bücherei 66; Munich: Kaiser, 1979); and, somewhat differently, *HALOT* 1:64a (no. 1).

16. See U. Cassuto, *A Commentary on the Book of Exodus* (trans. Israel Abrahams; Jerusalem: Magnes, 1967), 45.

17. Ludwig Bach, *Der Glaube nach der Anschauung des Alten Testamentes: Eine Untersuchung über die Bedeutung von* האמין *im alttestamentlichen Sprachgebrauch* (BFCT 4/6; Gütersloh: Bertelsmann, 1900), 57; in conjunction with Brevard S. Childs, *The Book of Exodus* (OTL; Philadelphia: Westminster, 1974), 77–78.

18. E.g., Moberly, "Abraham's Righteousness," 105 with nn. 7–8; and Joseph P. Healey, "Faith: Old Testament," *ABD* 2:745. Cf. Bach, *Der Glaube*, 31; and Horst Dietrich Preuss, *Old Testament Theology* (trans. Leo G. Perdue; 2 vols.; OTL; Louisville: Westminster John Knox, 1995–96), 2:362 n. 459.

19. See Tzvi Novick, "האמין in Jud 11,20 and the Semantics of Assent," *ZAW* 121 (2009): 579.

20. Contrast the idiom *heʾĕmîn ʾet*, in which *ʾet* marks a completely affected object: *wĕlōʾ heʾĕmîn sîḥôn ʾet yiśrāʾēl ʿăbor* (Judg 11:20). By all accounts, Sihon denies Israel passage through his territory (see, recently, ibid., 577–83, on a different grammatical basis).

21. See Wildberger, "'Glauben' im Alten Testament," *ZTK* 65 (1968): 153–54; repr. in *Jahwe und sein Volk;* and idem, "*ʾmn* firm, secure," *TLOT* 1:145.

22. See Bach, *Der Glaube*, 91–92.

23. See Levenson, *Sinai and Zion: An Entry into the Jewish Bible* (New Voices in Biblical Studies; Minneapolis: Winston Press, 1985), 158. For an excellent study of this episode, see Ernst Würthwein, "Jesaia 7, 1–9. Ein Beitrag zu dem Thema: Prophetie und Politik," in *Theologie als Glaubenswagnis: Festschrift zum 80. Geburtstag von Karl Heim* (Hamburg: Furche-Verlag, 1954), 47–63; repr. in *Wort und Existenz: Studien zum Alten Testament* (Göttingen: Vandenhoeck & Ruprecht, 1970).

24. Ibid., 59–60; and J. J. M. Roberts, "The Context, Text, and Logic of Isaiah 7.7–9," in *Inspired Speech: Prophecy in the Ancient Near East; Essays in Honour of Herbert B. Huffmon* (ed. John Kaltner and Louis Stulman; London: Clark, 2004), 169. Cf. Artur Weiser, "Glauben im Alten Testament," in *Festschrift Georg Beer zum 70. Geburtstage* (ed. Artur Weiser; Stuttgart: Kohlhammer, 1935), 93; and idem, "πιστεύω κτλ. B. The Old Testament Concept," 6:189.

25. Levenson, "Genesis," in *The Jewish Study Bible* (ed. Adele Berlin and Marc Zvi Brettler; Oxford: Oxford University Press, 1999), 35 (ad Gen 14:21–24).

26. E.g., Gordon J. Wenham, *Genesis* (2 vols.; WBC 1–2; Waco/Dallas: Word, 1987–94), 1:327.

27. Kaiser, "Genesis 15," 113. Cf. Peter Weimar, "Genesis 15. Ein redaktionskritischer Versuch," in *Die Väter Israels. Beiträge zur Theologie der Patriarchenüberlieferungen im Alten Testament. Festschrift für Josef Scharbert zum 70. Geburtstag* (ed. Manfred Görg and Augustin R. Müller; Stuttgart: Katholisches Bibelwerk, 1989), 392 n. 109.

28. Driver, *The Book of Genesis* (12th ed.; WC; London: Methuen, 1926), 174.

29. Hans-Jürgen Hermisson and Eduard Lohse, *Faith* (Biblical Encounters Series; trans. Douglas W. Stott; Nashville: Abingdon, 1981), 19 (italics original).

30. Moberly, "Abraham's Righteousness," 118–19.

31. Hermisson and Lohse, *Faith*, 20.

32. Moberly, "Abraham's Righteousness," 119.

33. See Ernst Haag, "Die Abrahamtradition in Gen 15," in *Die Väter Israels*, 105–6; and, in the same vein, Levenson, *Monotheism and Chosenness*, 4.

34. See Horst Seebass, *Genesis* (4 pts. in 3 vols.; Neukirchen-Vluyn: Neukirchener Verlag, 1996–2000), 2/1:70.

35. Cf. Jean-Louis Ska, "Some Groundwork on Genesis 15," in *The Exegesis of the Pentateuch: Exegetical Studies and Basic Questions* (FAT 66; Tübingen: Mohr Siebeck, 2009), 71.

36. See Procksch, *Die Genesis* (2nd–3rd ed.; KAT 1; Leipzig/Erlangen: Deichert/Scholl, 1924), 296; Hermisson and Lohse, *Faith*, 27; and Levenson, *Abraham*, 39, each differently.

37. John Ha, *Genesis 15: A Theological Compendium of Pentateuchal History* (BZAW 181; Berlin: Walter de Gruyter, 1989), 42. See also Walther Zimmerli, *1.Mose 1–25* (2 vols.; 3rd/1st ed.; ZBK.AT 1/1–2; Zurich: Theologischer Verlag, 1967–76), 2:53. Cf. Franz Delitzsch, *A New Commentary on Genesis* (2 vols.; trans. Sophia Taylor; 1888; repr., Minneapolis: Klock & Klock, 1978), 2:8; Seebass, *Genesis*, 2/1:73; and, differently, Wenham, *Genesis*, 1:329.

38. Gary Anderson (personal communication) also includes the "dark codicil" of quadricentary slavery in Egypt under this rubric. The forecast is a counterchallenge to the patriarch; as Abram's faith develops, the more is God willing to risk and let Abram risk as well.

39. For an ironic interpretation of this response, see Weimar, "Genesis 15," in *Die Väter Israels*, 369.

CHAPTER 3

Can Election Be Forfeited?

JOEL S. KAMINSKY

Of late, the biblical theme of chosenness has begun to receive increasing attention after a long period in which this important theological idea was rarely discussed. Aside from Jon Levenson's seminal monograph *The Death and Resurrection of the Beloved Son*, several other books touching upon various aspects of election in the Bible have been recently published. These include Frank Spina's *The Faith of the Outsider*, Lawrence Wills's *Not God's People*, my own *Yet I Loved Jacob*, and more recently Joel Lohr's *Chosen and Unchosen*.[1] Each of these studies explores in its own way the notion of God's special favor toward some and its implications for those not chosen.

One area of election theology that still has not been examined in a sustained manner concerns whether a chosen individual or group can lose their chosen status, and if so, under what circumstances. In this essay I hope to map out some of the complexity of the biblical evidence, for one cannot give a simple yes or no answer to this type of question. Differing biblical texts reveal a range of views on this subject and certain passages leave some ambiguity about the possibility of the elect forfeiting their lofty position.

When we look at the many stories of sibling rivalry found in Genesis, these narratives suggest that although a chosen person may be punished for acting wrongly, those who are favored by God seem to retain their status. This is true even when a chosen person or group acts in a questionable or even immoral manner. One need only think about a character like Jacob, who somewhat regularly acts in ethically or religiously troubling ways and yet remains divinely favored. Jacob does at times suffer the consequences that flow from his problematic actions. Thus he is forced to flee before Esau's wrath after deceitfully obtaining the blessing reserved for the firstborn son. In addition, one senses that Laban's substitution of Leah for Rachel may be a form of divine payback for Jacob's usurpation of Esau's position. But the fact that Jacob suffers certain punishments for his behavior does not mean that he is not blessed. Upon realizing that Jacob had obtained the blessing he intended for Esau, Isaac exclaims, "Yes, and blessed he shall be" (Gen 27:33).[2] We might speculate that this is because blessings, once issued, cannot be retracted. But this explanation is less satisfying when one reads the larger Jacob story in a holistic manner. Immediately after Jacob's deceit, Isaac once more blesses Jacob, and in the following verses God appears in a dream vision and bestows a version of the Abrahamic blessing on Jacob. Additionally, the birth of Jacob's many children and the multiplication of his own flocks as well as those that he tends for Laban all point to God's continuing favor toward Jacob. Laban acknowledges this fact when he tells Jacob: "I have learned by divination that the LORD has blessed me because of you" (Gen 30:27).

Although not a case of sibling rivalry, Abraham too engages in occasional unsavory behavior when he twice attempts to pawn off his wife as his sister. Yet in these instances those who took possession of Sarah suffer, rather than Abraham. Pharaoh's household experiences plagues (Gen 12:17) and the women in Abimelech's house become infertile because each man had unknowingly and illicitly taken the married Sarah as a potential wife (Gen 20:18).[3] Abraham not only remains untouched, but in the first instance he gains great wealth through his questionable behavior.

The one possible instance of a specific character in Genesis losing his chosen status is Reuben's apparent demotion in the wake of his sexual liaison with Bilhah, Jacob's secondary wife (Gen 35:22; 49:4).[4] But Reuben's special position in Genesis flows from his being Jacob's firstborn son, which throughout Genesis is generally a marker of being unfavored. While Reuben's immoral behavior helps to explain his fall from Jacob's favor, the thrust of the Joseph story requires that Joseph displace him. It is far from clear that Reuben was ever a divinely favored child whose behavior led to his diselection.

When we look elsewhere in the Pentateuch, we find little evidence that favored Israel can lose her special place in the divine economy. That is not to say that Israel never encounters adversity or judgment, because she regularly experiences each. Of course, suffering itself is strongly correlated with being chosen by God. One witnesses this correlation between chosenness and suffering in the lives of Abel, Isaac, Jacob, and Joseph, and more broadly in the experience of the whole people of Israel during their Egyptian bondage. In terms of judgment, not only are the elect not immune from punishment, but as I will discuss in more detail below, God's favor toward Israel frequently means that she is held more accountable for her misdeeds than others who are not favored.

Still, there are a few passages in the Torah that appear to entertain the total diselection of Israel. One thinks particularly of the golden calf episode, when God informs Moses that if God's wrath were left unchecked, he would destroy Israel and seek to build a new nation from Moses and his descendants (Exod 32:10). Even here, however, it is not clear that God is proposing to diselect Israel. Rather, God seeks to punish guilty Israel, which in at least one strand of the narrative includes everyone but Moses, who was absent when Israel manufactured and worshiped the golden calf.[5] In truth, this is not all that different from God's actions in Genesis of saving only Noah's family and then later saving only Lot's family.

Even more to the point is God's initial suggestion that failing prophetic intervention he would annihilate all Israel except for Moses and then build a new nation from Moses's descendants. That is close to what eventually occurs in the Torah when the spies bring back a negative report in Num 13–14. In the wake of Israel's refusal to conquer Canaan, God announces that the whole exodus generation except for Joshua and Caleb must die in the wilderness due to their rebellion. There, God actually does build a new Israel out of old Israel's descendants, but he punishes the exodus generation almost to a person (Num 14:20–38, 26:63–65). Of course, preserving the descendants of old sinful Israel is much more merciful than destroying all sinful Israelites and their future descendants. But even if God had pursued the most radical option and started over with Moses, God's commitment to start over with Moses suggests that God's promises to Israel remain in force. Furthermore, the actual story we have in Exod 32–34 highlights not Israel's potential loss of her elect status, but just the opposite! The text not only emphasizes the continuing persistence of Israel's chosenness inasmuch as God's relationship to Israel is in the end fully restored, but also heightens the unconditionality of Israel's election in that it now rests upon an even more radical act of divine mercy than it did before the golden calf story.

Similarly, Deuteronomy affirms Israel's chosen status even while proclaiming that her behavior up to this point demonstrates that she has not yet acted commensurately with God's special divine favor. Deuteronomy 9 contains an exposition of Israel's sins reaching back to the Sinai encounter. Moses informs the Israelites that God's gracious treatment toward them does not stem from their meritorious behavior. In fact, Israel is a stubborn and rebellious people. God is allowing Israel to take possession of the land only because the Canaanites have behaved so sinfully and because of God's special attachment to the patriarchs. Since Israel did not earn her elect status, one could suggest that she cannot lose her elevated position by means of wrongful actions.

Both Exod 32 and Deut 9, which narrate the story of the golden calf, raise the following hypothetical question: if Moses had not been successful at interceding, then might those Israelites who had been annihilated in the ensuing punishment have been diselected? This is a hypothetical question precisely because the unfolding story of the Hebrew Bible tells of God's continuing commitment to Israel in spite of her sins, even when those sins bring some level of punishment in their wake.⁶ Nevertheless, entertaining such a query is revealing. Even if God had opted to destroy the vast majority of the Israelites in the wake of their idolatry, it is not at all certain that this radical action would have signaled that those so punished were in effect diselected. One might argue that diselection should result in God no longer regarding Israel as his chosen people and simply sending them on their way. The very punishment God was planning to inflict on Israel points to the persistence rather than the loss of her special status. Exactly this point is underlined by prophetic texts such as Amos 3:2 and Ezekiel. While various prophetic texts receive further attention below, here we briefly note that in Ezekiel, God's punishment does not signal an end of God's unique relationship with Israel. Rather, God finds that his punishment of Israel, which itself stemmed from Israel's chosenness, has in turn led to the profanation of his own name. The result is that God will have to redeem Israel and restore her to the Holy Land in order to stop his name from being profaned. In short, Israel's punishment underlines her continuing special status, all the more so once God realizes that his own reputation is permanently tied to Israel's fate.

A final Torah narrative worthy of consideration is that of Balaam and his oracles in Num 22–24. Dennis Olson has persuasively argued that Numbers is framed by the two census lists, one at the start of the book, and the other in Num 26. Olson goes on to show how time and again the narratives found in Num 1–25 depict a rebellious and distrusting Israel. This point extends even to Moses, whose failure to heed God's exact instructions results in God prohibiting him from entering Canaan. On the other hand, the stories found in Num 26–36 portray an obedient Israel.⁷ Yet Balaam's oracles occur in the first section of Numbers, in which Israel's disobedience is highlighted, and these very oracles proclaim God's special favor toward Israel in soaring and highly unconditional terms:

> God is not a human being, that he should lie, or a mortal, that he should change his mind. Has he promised, and will he not do it? Has he spoken, and will he not fulfill it? See, I received a command to bless; he has blessed, and I cannot revoke it. He has not beheld misfortune in Jacob; nor has he seen trouble in Israel. (Num 23:19–21a)

The Balaam materials are placed near the end of a section in which we find bad behavior not only on the part of Israel as a nation, but also on the part of various subgroups and individuals within Israel. The text therefore strongly suggests a purposeful canonical move to demonstrate the unbreakable nature of God's special relationship to Israel.[8]

There are many other places in the Hebrew Bible that we might look at to learn whether election can be forfeited. In Joshua, we find the case of Achan, a person with a lineage going back to Judah himself. Despite his special lineage, Achan and his whole family are put to death for violating the war ban by taking booty from Jericho. The severity of this punishment suggests that he has removed himself from Israel and in some sense become equivalent to a Canaanite.[9]

Another locus worthy of attention is 1 Samuel, which contains the stories of Eli and Saul, both of whom appear to have been chosen, and both of whom also fall from grace. Note the language surrounding God's relationship to Eli in 1 Sam 2:27–31:

> A man of God came to Eli and said to him, "Thus the Lord has said, 'I revealed myself to the family of your ancestor in Egypt when they were slaves to the house of Pharaoh. I chose him out of all the tribes of Israel to be my priest, to go up to my altar, to offer incense, to wear an ephod before me; and I gave to the family of your ancestor all my offerings by fire from the people of Israel. Why then look with greedy eye at my sacrifices and my offerings that I commanded, and honor your sons more than me by fattening yourselves on the choicest parts of every offering of my people Israel?' Therefore the Lord the God of Israel declares: 'I promised that your family and the family of your ancestor should go in and out before me forever'; but now the Lord declares: 'Far be it from me; for those who honor me I will honor, and those who despise me shall be treated with contempt. See, a time is coming when I will cut off your strength and the strength of your ancestor's family, so that no one in your family will live to old age.'"

Here we learn that God chose Eli's ancestral family as the group from which he would draw the priests who would be in charge of his sanctuary. In fact, 1 Sam 2:30 states that Eli's family was to serve in this special priestly position in perpetuity. Yet, we are told in the following verses that Eli's descendants would all die young and that those who survived would now have to beg for food and for priestly work from a newly established priestly lineage (1 Sam 2:35–36). This seems to be an instance in which a chosen family who receives a promise of special status manages to lose their elevated position through sinning against God. Yet even in this instance, Eli himself is never stripped of his special office during his lifetime. Rather he dies in old age when he hears of the loss of the ark and the death of his two sons. While his descendants lose the special privileges granted to Eli and his father's house, the fact that he is not deposed in his lifetime means that whatever loss of divine grace he experienced primarily affected his progeny and is only fully glimpsed seconds before he dies.[10]

Still, Eli's case demonstrates that God's favor toward a family can be taken away, even when that favor is granted in terms of a promise that *sounds* unconditional and perpetual. I have used the qualifier "sounds" because we must be cautious about the nuances of the expression ʿad ʿôlām in 1 Sam 2:30, an expression frequently translated as "forever" (see NRSV and NJPS). Nearly fifty years ago M. Tsevat argued that this term and certain related expressions found in promise and covenantal texts such as 2 Sam 7 have been misunderstood because later Western ideas of infinitude and absoluteness were wrongly being read into the ancient biblical context. Such expressions "qualify a thing within its proper limits" and thus, according to Tzevat, 1 Sam 2:30 is simply saying that because of the sinful behavior of Eli's sons "the end of the time designated by ʿad ʿôlām has arrived."[11] Even in our culture, unconditional-sounding language often carries implicit conditions. Wedding vows are characteristically of an unconditional sort, but they presume the fidelity of each partner to the other. Thus, we should not be shocked to find that God can nullify an apparently permanent promise issued in unconditional language when the other party utterly violates their relational duties.

On the surface, Eli's case appears to be analogous to the golden calf episode. In the golden calf episode, however, God merely entertained the possibility of punishing all Israel in a way that might have suggested her diselection. In this more limited case, God actually follows through and does so in a way that implies that the favor experienced by

Eli and his ancestral house has now come to an end, or perhaps more accurately, that it has been transferred to another, more worthy party. Eli is in fact told that God will raise up someone else as his faithful priest (1 Sam 2:35). This latter point needs to be highlighted not only in this instance, but all the more so in the case of Saul, where God's promise remains in force, but with a change concerning which specific Israelite family will now be the recipient of this divine promise. I will discuss this matter further below.

One other issue deserving attention is that the disinheritance of Eli's house is accompanied by the destruction of the shrine at Shiloh. This fateful event is portrayed in both Jer 7 and Ps 78 (vv. 56–67) as an example of God's ability to undo a choice he once made. Shiloh's destruction comes to be viewed not only as a larger rejection of the North in favor of the South (Jer 7:12–15; Ps 78:67–68), but at least in Jeremiah 7, as an explanation for the later defeat and exile of the northern tribes. The dismissal of Eli's extended family from their privileged position and its linkage to God's rejection of Shiloh and to the later exiling of the northern tribes constitutes some of the strongest evidence that election can in certain circumstances be taken away from those people or places that had initially been the recipients of said divine favor. Here, too, in the case of Shiloh we find the idea that God's special favor is not entirely nullified, but is rather transferred elsewhere, in this instance to Mount Zion, Judah, and David (Ps 78:68–72). One caveat concerning Shiloh is that neither Ps 78, nor Jer 7, nor any other passage I can think of ever clearly indicates that Shiloh had been chosen in perpetuity at one time.[12] In this sense the rejection of Shiloh may be less analogous to the case of Eli's family, which involved the negation of a seemingly perpetual promise, and more in keeping with Saul's fate, to which we now turn.

The possibility of an individual or family losing divine favor is seen once again in the yet more complicated case of Saul. There is little doubt that Saul has the markings of chosenness. He has physical beauty and height (1 Sam 9:1–2), he is anointed by Samuel (1 Sam 10:1), he is prophetically possessed (1 Sam 10:10), he is confirmed by the casting of lots (1 Sam 10:20–21), and he earns kingship through heroic military action (1 Sam 11). But the text also portrays Saul as having fallen out of

God's favor in a number of ways. His disobedience to Samuel's sacrificial instructions is linked to the fact that his son would not rule after his death (1 Sam 13:13–14) and his failure to kill Agag and put the Amalekite animals to the ban is tied to God's wish to replace him with David (1 Sam 15). We are also told that God's spirit was removed from him and that an evil spirit haunted him at times (1 Sam 16:14), that God was no longer willing to communicate with him (1 Sam 28:6), and finally we learn that after he was mortally wounded in a battle with the Philistines he commits suicide rather than be mocked and killed by the enemy (1 Sam 31:4). Clearly Saul was once divinely favored, but later in his life he is marked out as having lost his chosen status.

However, in spite of Saul's fall from grace, certain markers of his chosen status persist. Immediately after Saul is told that God will take the kingship from him and give it to an associate of his who is better than he (1 Sam 15:28), Saul gets Samuel to accede to his request that Samuel accompany him as Saul leads a communal worship service (1 Sam 15:31–32). Now perhaps this is done for the sake of decorum, but other texts suggest something more may be at stake. In spite of Samuel's anointment of David in 1 Sam 16, Saul remains king until his death. David himself recognizes the legitimacy of Saul's claim to the kingship as long as Saul is alive. Note the language of 1 Sam 24:7 (Eng. 24:6) expressing David's regret at having covertly cut off the edge of Saul's garment: "The Lord forbid that I should do this thing to my lord, the Lord's anointed, to raise my hand against him; for he is the Lord's anointed." Not only does he refer to Saul as "my lord," but twice he affirms that Saul is "the Lord's anointed" or more literally, the "messiah of the Lord." If Saul's failure to obey Samuel's command to put the Amalekites to the ban in 1 Sam 15 resulted in the loss of his chosen status, why does David regularly indicate that Saul remains God's anointed one? In fact, David maintains this attitude of respect even at the time of Saul's death, as we can see by his treatment of the Amalekite lad who (likely falsely) claims to have killed Saul at Saul's request. Here again David twice refers to Saul as "the Lord's anointed" (2 Sam 1:14, 16), both times indicating that Saul's status as such means that anyone who raises a hand against the reigning monarch is guilty of a capital crime.

What are we to make of the fact that the text portrays Saul as having fallen out of God's favor, but affirms that as long as he lives he is the legitimate king and remains God's anointed? Perhaps what we have here is simply a recognition that in ancient Israel, short of death, a king once anointed could not be unanointed or step down. If so, we might argue that one must separate God's favor toward an individual from the fact that certain individuals inhabit permanent offices such as that of kingship. This may explain why Eli, too, retains his office. But it is also possible that certain offices cannot be resigned partly because they are initiated by God's choosing, making at least some aspect of this kind of divine favor irrevocable.

In actuality, the eternal dynastic promise that God makes to David and his descendants in 2 Sam 7 is premised on the very notion that in some instances God's favor toward certain individuals, households, or peoples is irrevocable. The destruction of Jerusalem and the dethroning of the reigning Davidic monarch posed a challenge to this theological notion, but not an insurmountable one. Psalm 89, which may well have been penned in the wake of the destruction of Jerusalem and the deposing of the Davidic king, proclaims God's promises to David and his future household in its most unconditional form, even while recognizing the full challenge that these historical events posed to maintaining such a belief. The persistent affirmation of God's promises to David and his descendants gave rise to a number of important eschatological forms of thinking, one of the most well known being the hope for the eventual restoration of a Davidic monarch on the throne of Israel.[13] It is this idea that sits at the root of all biblical messianism, most especially Christian messianism. There would be no eschatologically oriented messianism without the belief that the eternal divine promises to David in particular, and to Israel in general, could never be fully negated. If the exile proved that these promises were now void then no one would have ever expected a messianic figure to arise in the future.

Furthermore, the theological notion that certain promises of divine favor are permanent and not negated by a judgment of exile, recurs in other texts that are not messianic in orientation. One only needs to look at the synthesis of various covenantal streams found in Deut 4. In this passage, God requires Israel to observe the commandments of his covenant or face exile. But as Deut 4:29–31 makes clear, Israel's failure to observe God's commandments and the punishment that may follow upon such disobedience still does not abrogate the eternal covenant between God and Israel, which according to this text endures because of God's oath to the patriarchs.

Let us summarize our findings up to this point. Even when it seems that God's promises appear to be in danger of being abrogated due to human failings, the received form of the Torah consistently and without exception proclaims that God's promises of special favor toward Israel persist in spite of any disobedience and can be fully reactualized after God's judgment and Israel's repentance. In contrast to the Torah, there are materials in the Former Prophets indicating that the special divine favor extended to select individuals or households in Israel can be abrogated in some circumstances (e.g., Eli and Saul). But such cases are rather exceptional and even in these instances elements of God's favor once extended, seem to persist. Whatever we make of the cases of Eli and Saul, when it comes to Israel as a whole, Joshua–2 Kings affirms the Torah's viewpoint that God's election of Israel remains intact in perpetuity. One need only look at the framework of Judges or of the larger Deuteronomistic history to see that Israel's disobedience does not negate her divine election.

Turning to the Latter Prophets, we discover an equally complex portrait of this issue. Much of the prophetic corpus is concerned with trying to get Israel to see that her special status does not insulate her from God's coming judgment. But it is hard to argue that the prophets are in fact telling Israel that her behavior will result in her diselection. As noted earlier, Amos directly links Israel's coming punishment to God's unique relationship with Israel (Amos 3:2). While it is possible that the historical prophet Amos may never have envisioned a restoration of the fallen North, the prophetic corpus as a whole, as well as the editorial framework of Amos, affirm the future restoration of Israel. The oracles of hope, which regularly punctuate the prophetic corpus, demonstrate that the oracles of woe are not to be read as God's last word to Israel or as proof that Israel has lost her elect status. Furthermore, rather than viewing the harshness of Israel's punishment as proof of her diselection, the prophets do just the opposite. Thus Second Isaiah opens with an acknowledgement that Israel has suffered double for her sins, but this functions as a notice that Israel's slate has been wiped clean, enabling God to announce his program of coming restoration (Isa 40:2).

While Israel's election is widely seen as irrevocable, there is the possibility that not everyone who is a living descendant of Jacob will continue to receive the divine favor directed toward Israel. Sometimes Israel as a whole is judged and those who are found most guilty are then purged. We see something of this theology operative already in the golden calf episode, in which the Levites act as a vanguard who purify Israel of idolaters (Exod 32:25–29). Similarly, Ezek 20:33–38 speaks of a postexilic judgment of Israel, followed by the elimination of the most egregious rebels and sinners. What we see most clearly in Ezekiel is that God cannot disown Israel because doing so will profane God's name inasmuch as Israel's fate directly affects God's reputation. Note the language used in Ezek 36:22–28:

> Therefore say to the house of Israel, Thus says the Lord God: It is not for your sake, O house of Israel, that I am about to act, but for the sake of my holy name, which you have profaned among the nations to which you came. I will sanctify my great name, which has been profaned among the nations, and which you have profaned among them; and the nations shall know that I am the Lord, says the Lord God, when through you I display my holiness before their eyes. I will take you from the nations, and gather you from all the countries, and bring you into your own land. I will sprinkle clean water upon you, and you shall be clean from all your uncleannesses, and from all your idols I will cleanse you. A new heart I will give you, and a new spirit I will put within you; and I will remove from your body the heart of stone and give you a heart of flesh. I will put my spirit within you, and make you follow my statutes and be careful to observe my ordinances. Then you shall live in the land that I gave to your ancestors; and you shall be my people, and I will be your God.

This excerpt underlines the permanency of God's connection to Israel. It also highlights the fact that if this relationship needs Israel's obedience to endure, God can accomplish this difficult feat, even if it requires a spiritual heart transplant.

Using very different logic, the oracles of hope from Jeremiah's Book of Consolation as well as many passages from Second Isaiah time and again speak of the irrevocability of God's election of Israel. Unlike Ezekiel, who explores the impact on God's name caused by Israel's disobedience, Jeremiah and Second Isaiah stress God's eternal love toward Israel and the temporariness of God's anger. While various prophetic texts affirm the enduring nature of Israel's election, they substantiate this claim by different arguments. It is worth citing some of this language to give the reader a fuller sense of these powerful passages.

> Thus says the LORD, who gives the sun for light by day and the fixed order of the moon and the stars for light by night, who stirs up the sea so that its waves roar—the LORD of hosts is his name: If this fixed order were ever to cease from my presence, says the LORD, then also the offspring of Israel would cease to be a nation before me forever. Thus says the LORD: If the heavens above can be measured, and the foundations of the earth below can be explored, then I will reject all the offspring of Israel because of all they have done, says the LORD. (Jer 31:35–37)

While earlier parts of Jer 31 openly acknowledge Israel's sinfulness and the suffering that it brought in its wake (vv. 18–19), the overarching message of this passage is of an unbreakable loving bond that endures in perpetuity between God and his special people Israel.

Finally, Second Isaiah, arguably the locus of the most potent expressions of God's special relationship to Israel, uses soaring poetic language to proclaim that Israel's election is irrevocable:

> For your Maker is your husband, the LORD of hosts is his name; the Holy One of Israel is your Redeemer, the God of the whole earth he is called. For the LORD has called you like a wife forsaken and grieved in spirit, like the wife of a man's youth when she is cast off, says your God. For a brief moment I abandoned you, but with great compassion I will gather you. In overflowing wrath for a moment I hid my face from you, but with everlasting love I will have compassion on you, says the LORD, your Redeemer. This is like the days of Noah to me: Just as I swore that

the waters of Noah would never again go over the earth, so I have sworn that I will not be angry with you and will not rebuke you. For the mountains may depart and the hills be removed, but my steadfast love shall not depart from you, and my covenant of peace shall not be removed, says the LORD, who has compassion on you. (Isa 54:5–10)

Building on the marriage metaphor first found in Hosea, this anonymous prophet of the exile puts Israel's exilic suffering into perspective. While Israel's sinfulness may have caused God to break off relations for a short time, Isa 54 envisions God's covenantal relationship to Israel as being as unconditional as, or possibly even less conditioned than, God's covenant with Noah in Gen 9. Here we are told that even if the earthly order partially collapses, God's steadfast loyalty toward Israel will endure.

It is important to highlight that texts like these recognize that not all Israel survived the exile. Jeremiah 31:7 speaks of God having saved a remnant of Israel. The notion of a surviving remnant is already implicit in the story of Noah's ark (Gen 6–9), and was picked up by prophets such as Elijah (1 Kgs 19:18), and in Isa 6:13 given a strong eschatological twist. In Jer 31, this remnant seems to be equivalent to those who survived the exile. In certain late biblical texts, however, we start to see expressions of the theological idea that membership in the people of Israel was no longer just a matter of genealogy, but rather required one to maintain certain behaviors and practices or risk losing one's place among the elect. In such texts, only a subset of those born to Israel— that is, those who were properly observant and pleasing to God— constitute the chosen people. Note the following excerpt from Isa 65:13–15:

> Therefore thus says the Lord GOD: My servants shall eat, but you shall be hungry; My servants shall drink, but you shall be thirsty; My servants shall rejoice, but you shall be put to shame; My servants shall sing for gladness of heart, but you shall cry out for pain of heart, and shall wail for anguish of spirit. You shall leave your name to my chosen to use as a curse, and the Lord GOD will put you to death; But to his servants he will give a different name.

Earlier verses in Isa 65 condemn those Judeans who engage in improper religious behaviors. Many scholars see this passage as expressing the anger felt by a sectarian group against more mainstream societal forces. Whatever the exact sociological locus of verses 13–15, they suggest a division between true Israel and others who have gone astray.

The growing emphasis on proper behavior as an essential component of election may illuminate why other texts in Trito-Isaiah, such as Isa 56:1–8, envision a growing number of non-Israelites, who observe proper ritual and ethical norms, joining in the worship Yhwh in Jerusalem.[14] It is overstated to say that these foreign Yhwh worshipers become part of the people of Israel. Rather, as Isa 56:7 notes, these foreigners are able to join themselves to the Lord because his house is now a house of prayer for all peoples. The point is that there was an increasing emphasis upon maintaining certain behavioral norms for all those who wished to participate in Jerusalem's Yhwh community, whether one was a native, elect Israelite, or an alien or foreigner drawn to Israel's God. The inverse side of such thinking sometimes engages in rhetoric that appears to split Israel in a dualistic manner into the righteous who are saved and the wicked, who are not only punished but seem to be removed completely from the people of Israel. Perhaps such rhetoric was primarily aimed at motivating sinners to return to the fold. In any case, over time it led to a situation in which certain groups within the wider people of Israel linked election to highly specific behavioral norms, thus producing the very real possibility that the majority of Israel might be viewed as being diselected. This is exactly what occurs in the highly charged apocalyptic dualism found in the Dead Sea Scrolls as well as in certain early Christian texts, as succinctly stated by Lawrence Schiffman:

> For the sectarians, the renewed covenant was the indication of their particular relation with God—what made them the true Israel and disqualified the rest of the Jewish people. In this respect, some affinity does exist between the Qumran "new covenant" and that of the early Christians.[15]

Note that Schiffman uses the qualifier: "some affinity." One can find a number of differing New Testament views on whether the historic people of Israel have forfeited their election. For example, texts like the parable of the wicked tenants in Matt 21:33–44 can and indeed often have been read in a supersessionist manner as suggesting that the Gentile church will displace the Jews. In a similar vein, one thinks of the speech in John 8:39–59 in which Jews who fail to recognize Jesus as the Christ not only lose their status as the children of Abraham but are now seen as the devil's spawn. In certain ways these texts are extensions of prophetic critiques of unfaithful Israel found widely in the Hebrew Bible. Such texts do not abrogate Israel's election theology, but rather heighten the importance of this theology. Nevertheless, they seem to push us closer to the possibility that God might replace the historic people of Israel with a different group. These New Testament passages build on the notion that certain eternal divine promises can be transferred, as occurs in the case of Eli, but apply this idea more broadly to Israel as a whole. While drawing on ideas found within the Hebrew Bible, this theology goes a step beyond what one finds in the Hebrew Bible by envisioning a situation in which the vast majority of the descendants of Abraham, Isaac, and Jacob are no longer considered part of the chosen people.

Of course, any discussion of the New Testament's views of Israel's chosenness would be deficient without some attention to Rom 9–11. As anyone knows, who is familiar with this complex passage or the vast secondary literature it has spawned, it contains major tensions. On the one hand, Rom 9:6–18 moves in a supersessionist direction by decoupling chosenness from Jewish genealogical descent. Paul does this by reading one part of Genesis into another later part of the story in an imaginative and somewhat hypothetical manner. The narrative of Genesis clearly recognizes that from Jacob forward, all Jacob's children are part of the one people of Israel, inheritors of the promises made to Abraham, Isaac, and Jacob. But Paul notes that Abraham and Isaac both had some offspring who were not chosen, thus allowing him to argue that physical descent from Abraham, Isaac, and Jacob is not what determines one's elect status. While Paul's focus is on God's freedom, his reading of Genesis strongly obscures the importance of physical descent as a marker of chosenness even in the cases of Isaac and Jacob, and all the more so from Jacob forward. In fairness, Paul is consistent in his assertion that election can be taken away from those to whom it was once given: he warns his Gentile audience that should they become haughty or fall away from their faith they, too, can lose their lofty position (Rom 11:20–21).

Paul's larger argument in Rom 9–11, however, backs away from this radical idea inasmuch as he views Israel's unbelief as a temporary state of affairs that will be reversed at a later point in time. He even gives theological meaning to Israel's temporary hardening by viewing it as a boon for those Gentiles who wish to join the elect through affirming a belief in Jesus as the Christ (Rom 11:11–12, 25–27). In any case, this section of Romans opens and closes with declarations that affirm the special place of the people of Israel in the divine economy (Rom 9:1–5; 11:28–29). In summary, while parts of Paul's argument in Rom 9–11 suggest that God, if he so wills it, can abrogate Israel's election, the framework of this passage can be read as affirming the viewpoint found throughout the Hebrew Bible that God's favor toward Israel endures in perpetuity. It may be that the tensions one senses between various parts of Rom 9–11 reflect the fact that Paul is delivering a sermon, not a systematic theological statement. One possibility is that perhaps Paul is envisioning Israel's election as having been suspended until such a time as they turn from their disobedience and accept Jesus as the Christ (Rom 11:23). The notion that Israel's disobedience might lead to God's temporary suspension of her chosen status has an analogue in texts such as Hosea or Isa 54, in which God, like a wronged husband, separates himself from Israel for a time.

However one seeks to explain these tensions in Paul's thinking, it is unsurprising that in the end Paul seems to affirm that Israel's election is irrevocable. After all, if God were to utterly dispossess historic Israel, the basis of Paul's claims concerning Jesus would be called into question. According to Paul and the authors of all four gospels, Jesus is the fulfillment of the temporarily suspended Davidic promises. If the judgment of the exile is read as a permanent voiding of God's promises to Israel in general and to King David and his descendants in particular, then there is little reason to hope for a coming messiah who will institute a new order. Similarly, if Paul left no room for the physical descendants of Abraham to be grafted back onto his metaphorical olive tree, then not only would God's fidelity to his past promises be called into question, but so would Paul's theological beliefs that are grounded upon these previous promises. In fact, in Rom 8 Paul invokes the unconditional language surrounding Israel's chosenness to reassure the nascent Christian community, now envisioned as God's elect, of the reliability of God's promises (Rom 8:28–39).

Our brief tour through the biblical text has revealed the following: the vast bulk of relevant texts in both the Hebrew Bible and the New Testament affirm that God's promises to Israel are unbreakable and persist in perpetuity. However, both corpora contain some passages that point to the possibility of election being forfeited. Within the Hebrew Bible this is generally limited to a few instances in which the special favor shown toward an individual or a larger household, or in the case of Shiloh toward a place, is taken away due to disobedience or sin. In all these cases, God's special favor appears to be transferred to more worthy parties, rather than simply abrogated. Some prophetic texts, too, imply the possibility of certain parts of Israel losing their elect status, while a faithful remnant is preserved. In passages that mention this latter possibility, it is difficult to tell whether the text imagines the actual loss of election by some part of Israel; or rather is speaking about a punishment that may be inflicted upon those among the chosen people who disobey God; or is primarily a rhetorical device used to motivate sinners to repent from their wicked ways so that they may once again experience the blessings offered to God's people.

Within the New Testament, some passages appear to affirm the possibility that almost all of the historic Jewish people may be diselected and replaced by Gentile believers in Christ. As noted above, a few passages in the Hebrew Bible indicate that God may transfer his favor from one family or group to another within Israel (1 Sam 2:27–36 and Isa 65). Although the New Testament passages discussed here are likely drawing on theological currents found in earlier Hebrew Bible texts, they also push this theology in a more radical direction. Like their Hebrew Bible counterparts, these New Testament passages may be more rhetorical than is commonly understood. Furthermore, even the most radical passages are qualified by other New Testament texts such as the strongly worded conclusion of Rom 11, which is unequivocal when it states of God's commitment to the Jewish people: "but as regards election they are beloved, for the sake of their ancestors; for the gifts and the calling of God are irrevocable" (Rom 11:28b–29). Finally, we must recognize that the New Testament is itself part of a larger Christian Bible that includes the Old Testament, which time and again affirms God's unbreakable commitment to his beloved people Israel and his wish to restore the historic people of Israel to their former glory.

Nevertheless, we must acknowledge that the history of much post-biblical Christian interpretation reveals a supersessionist tendency, which asserts that God abrogated his promises to Israel and applied them to the now predominantly Gentile church.[16] This might be a misreading of scripture, but it is not difficult to see how this line of thinking developed. The fact is that the New Testament does appear to go further than the Hebrew Bible in envisaging the very real possibility that not only could certain individuals or households lose their chosen status, but so could the whole people of Israel. Unfortunately, the latter, more troubling reading gained extra traction because of the Christian tendency to value the New Testament above the Old. More pernicious yet, many Christians subscribe to a Marcionite outlook that drives a wedge between the two testaments, in effect relegating much of the content of the Old Testament, including the notion of God's election of Israel, to the theological scrap heap of history.

The differences between the views of the Hebrew Bible and those of the New Testament concerning the forfeiture of election may explain in part certain features of later Judaism and Christianity. Rabbinic Judaism maintains the unusual belief that someone who is born a Jew cannot really leave Judaism. The community might view someone as a bad Jew or even a heretic, but from a Jewish standpoint that person is still a Jew. One does not make a decision to be Jewish unless one converts into the religion, nor can someone who is Jewish make a decision to stop being a Jew. While certain streams of intertestamental literature envision Israel as only a small subgroup of those genealogically descended from the patriarchs, the rabbis tended to emphasize that God's relationship is with the whole people of Israel, both its sinners and its saints, its wise teachers and its ignoramuses.

Of course, Judaism's distinct religio-cultural orientation is due in part to the fact that the rabbis maintained certain familial and tribal dimensions of ancient Israelite religion. But make no mistake about it, the Jewish idea of chosenness is itself heavily tied to these very familial ideas. It is extraordinarily difficult for humans to fully disconnect themselves from parents, siblings, or children whatever their behavior. Similarly, Israel recognizes that the divine favor she experiences is not grounded in her behavior but rather stems from being part of an extended family that has a unique relationship with God. This is not to say that her behavior is irrelevant, because in certain ways it is strongly relevant. In actuality, the bad actions of an individual Jew may bring negative consequences upon the larger community and can, in the language of Judaism, lead to a profanation of the divine name (an idea drawn from Ezekiel's theology). Still, even a sinning Jew who may endanger the larger community remains a Jew, just as one's relative who commits a crime and brings disgrace on the entire family still remains part of that same family.

It is simplistic to say that Christianity is belief-based while Judaism is not. Nevertheless, in a very major stream of Christian tradition one needs to accept certain agreed-upon beliefs to become a Christian. This makes it possible for someone who had once been a Christian to fall away morally and theologically in a manner that moves them outside of the Christian community. An important nuance is that someone who has fallen away does not lose all marks of his or her original baptized state, as seen by the fact that adherents are not usually rebaptized when they repent and return to the community.[17] Even so, it would seem that one can enter and exit Christianity more easily than is the case in Judaism.

It is somewhat ironic that many Christians have portrayed Judaism negatively by casting it as a works-oriented religion in contrast to Christianity's emphasis on grace. In actuality, Judaism's understanding of election theology may be more radically grace-oriented than that of certain major streams of Christian thinking. Thus both the Tanakh and later Jewish tradition categorically affirm God's unbreakable bond to his people Israel in perpetuity, while some New Testament texts introduce into election the equivalence of a kind of works righteousness by making it contingent on certain human dispositions, most particularly on the acceptance of Jesus as the Christ. It is interesting to note that those Calvinist streams of Christianity that see election as unconditional and not able to be lost push quite close to a Jewish view of *this aspect* of election theology.[18] This commonality did not necessarily result in a less supersessionist stance among denominations that draw upon Calvin, but one wonders whether Calvin's deep interest in the Old Testament led him to deemphasize some New Testament passages that see election as something that might be lost.

In any case, it seems probable that for both Judaism and Christianity, the various views on how one joins or leaves the group may have influenced, and been influenced by, each religion's notion of election and of whether Israel's chosen status can or cannot be abrogated. This set of reflections on whether chosenness, once granted, can be forfeited underlines both the centrality of the concept of election to Judaism and Christianity and the fact that the two traditions have appropriated the Hebrew Bible's election theology in unique but related ways. As Jon Levenson has demonstrated throughout his scholarly career, true religious dialogue is not only about identifying what we share in common, but also about realizing that ideas shared by these two traditions can illuminate both subtle and not so subtle theological differences between Judaism and Christianity. Levenson has helped us see that understanding our distinct, respective religious claims more clearly actually creates an environment for a richer dialogue between various faith traditions. With humility, I offer this essay in honor of my mentor Jon Levenson's sixty-fifth birthday and hope that it does justice to his thoughtful approach to both biblical studies and Jewish-Christian dialogue.

NOTES

1. Jon D. Levenson, *The Death and Resurrection of the Beloved Son: The Transformation of Child Sacrifice in Judaism and Christianity* (New Haven: Yale University Press, 1993); Frank Spina, *The Faith of the Outsider: Exclusion and Inclusion in the Biblical Story* (Grand Rapids: Eerdmans, 2005); Lawrence Wills, *Not God's People: Insiders and Outsiders in the Biblical World* (Religion in the Modern World; Lanham, Md.: Rowman and Littlefield, 2008); Joel Kaminsky, *Yet I Loved Jacob: Reclaiming the Biblical Concept of Election* (Nashville: Abingdon, 2007); Joel N. Lohr, *Chosen and Unchosen: Conceptions of Election in the Pentateuch and Jewish–Christian Interpretation* (Winona Lake, Ind.: Eisenbrauns, 2009).

2. All translations in this chapter are from the NRSV unless otherwise noted.

3. For an insightful article on the theology of chosenness in relation to the three wife-sister stories in Genesis, see Mark E. Biddle, "The 'Endangered Ancestress' and Blessing for the Nations," *JBL* 109 (Winter 1990): 599–611.

4. There is one legally oriented passage in Gen 17:14 that mentions the possibility of an individual Israelite cutting himself off from the community of Israel by ignoring God's command to be circumcised. It is likely that this injunction and other laws in Leviticus that contain similar terminology employ this extreme language in order to stress the importance of obeying these specific commandments (see Lev 17:4, 9; 18:29; 20:18 et al.). Interestingly, these Priestly texts share an outlook with certain late prophetic passages such as those found in Isa 56–66, in that both sets of texts imply that membership in Israel is at least partially based on behavior. I discuss this theological development in more depth toward the end of this essay.

5. Exod 32:25–29 implies a much lower number of truly guilty people; there the Levites purge about three thousand sinners from the camp.

6. In fact, Gary Anderson questions whether Moses could have actually failed at this task and even more radically whether God would have annihilated Israel if Moses had not intervened. See his provocative essay "Moses and Jonah in Gethsemane: Representation and Impassibility in Their Old Testament Inflections," in *Seeking the Identity of Jesus* (ed. Beverly Gaventa and Richard Hays; Grand Rapids: Eerdmans, 2008), 215–31.

7. Dennis Olson, *The Death of the Old and the Birth of the New: The Framework of the Book of Numbers and the Pentateuch* (BJS 71; Chico, Calif.: Scholars Press, 1985).

8. On this point, see Joel Lohr, *Chosen and Unchosen*, 125–47.

9. This becomes clearer when one realizes that the early chapters of Joshua contrast the fidelity of the Canaanite prostitute Rahab with the treachery of Achan, as noted in Spina, *The Faith of the Outsider*, 52–71.

10. In what appears to be Deuteronomistic comment, 1 Kgs 2:27 sees Solomon's exile of Abiathar to Anathoth as a fulfillment of God's rejection of Eli and his household.

11. Matitiahu Tsevat, "The Steadfast House: What was David Promised in II Sam. 7:11b–16?," Studies in the Book of Samuel III, *HUCA* 34 (1963): 71–82, here at 76–77.

12. The language in Ps 78:67 likely indicates that Shiloh and Ephraim were previously specially favored by God. Note that this verse pairs the verb "to reject" (*māʾas*) with the words "he did not choose" (*lōʾ bāḥar*), which may well be how an ancient Israelite writer would have expressed the idea of unchoosing (cf. 2 Kgs 23:27 and Jer 33:24). While it could be argued that the favor of God, once extended, was intended to be permanent, neither this text nor Jer 7 actually use

the explicit language of perpetuity in reference to God's previous favor toward Shiloh and Ephraim.

13. Not all eschatological uses of the Davidic covenant are messianic in the classical sense of envisioning a descendant of David taking the throne of Israel. In Isa 55:1–5 God's covenant with David has been reworked and "democratized" so as to apply to the whole people of Israel.

14. There are many other texts, some which may well predate Isa 56, that recognize the possibility of non-Israelites wishing to worship Yhwh. Here one thinks of 1 Kgs 8:41–43; 2 Kings 5; and Jon 1. Isaiah 56 is thus likely building upon earlier precedents.

15. Lawrence Schiffman, "The Concept of Covenant in the Qumran Scrolls and Rabbinic Literature," in *The Idea of Biblical Interpretation: Essays in Honor of James L. Kugel* (ed. Hindy Najman and Judith Newman; Leiden: Brill, 2004), 257–78, here at 276.

16. Jeffrey S. Siker, *Disinheriting the Jews: Abraham in Early Christian* (Louisville, Ky.: Westminster/John Knox Press, 1991).

17. Since not all groups recognize every form of baptism (for example, infant baptism is rejected by some Christians), adherents moving between certain Christian denominations may be required to go through a new baptism because their original one is not recognized as valid.

18. I wish to emphasize that both the Hebrew Bible and later Jewish thought openly reject other aspects of Calvin's election theology, particularly the Calvinist doctrine of double predestination. I argue at length in my book *Yet I Loved Jacob* that the Hebrew Bible and postbiblical Jewish thought do not equate election with salvation and do not think that only the elect stand in God's good graces.

CHAPTER 4

Election and the Transformation of Ḥērem

R. W. L. MOBERLY

In his book *The Death and Resurrection of the Beloved Son: The Transformation of Child Sacrifice in Judaism and Christianity*,[1] Jon Levenson memorably and persuasively sets the biblical concept of election in a fresh light. The presenting issue is child sacrifice. Contrary to then-predominant scholarly opinion, Levenson argues that it was practiced in ancient Israel, where it was understood to be a requirement of Yhwh, as specified in Exod 22:28b. Over time, however, this practice was substituted by certain rituals. These retained the idea of the donation of the firstborn son and the impulse underlying it, but reworked them in metaphorical mode. Levenson further argues that the recurrent pattern in Genesis of the firstborn son being endangered to the point of death, but then being astonishingly restored to his father, constitutes a narrative analogy to the ritual practices. Child sacrifice in Israel was not

67

so much abolished as transformed: "Though the *practice* was at some point eradicated, the *religious idea* ... remained potent and productive," and a "barbaric ritual" metamorphosed into "a sublime paradigm of the religious life."[2]

Levenson crucially associates the favored, yet imperilled, status of the firstborn son with an understanding of chosenness or election in general, so as to offer a searching account of what it means to be God's chosen. As he puts it, in the context of commenting on a midrash on the Akedah but simultaneously (if I read rightly) expressing his own thesis:

> The larger theological point is that the trials of the righteous serve to demonstrate not God's injustice, as many think to be the case, but quite the opposite, the fairness of his choices. For those choices are not mere whims, evidence of the arbitrariness of providence, and the proof is that those chosen, like Abraham, for exaltation, are able to pass the brutal tests to which God subjects them and thus to vindicate the grace he has shown them. The trials that appear to be their humiliation are, in fact, the means of their exaltation, proof positive that their special destiny is based on other than caprice. The trials of the righteous mediate the contradiction between God's grace and his justice. They also make sense of the combination of humiliations and exaltations in the lives of the chosen.[3]

With this argument Levenson takes one of the most problematic features of the religion of ancient Israel, child sacrifice, and sees its history of development as a key to a constructive account of a central feature in the theological self-understandings of those faiths, both Jewish and Christian, that are rooted in the Bible. Thus, if one can overcome knee-jerk tendencies to recoil from or dismiss that which appears offensive and learn to work patiently with the specifics of the biblical text, one can gain from the developing biblical construal of child sacrifice a better understanding of the nature of election.

The thesis of this essay is that another highly offensive feature within Israel's scriptures, the apparent requirement that Israel put to death—carry out *ḥērem* upon—all the occupants of Canaan, can be seen to undergo a process of development analogous to that of child sacrifice, and that correspondingly the biblical construal of *ḥērem* illuminates the meaning of election. In this essay I can sketch out the shape of my argument, but not develop it with the thoroughness, depth, and subtlety that Levenson displays in his monograph. Nonetheless I hope that my hypothesis will not only be a tribute to the fertile potential of Levenson's argument in *Death and Resurrection,*[4] but will also be a not inappropriate token of my intellectual indebtedness to Levenson's oeuvre more generally. I have learned from him, and am indebted to him, more than I can say.

ḤĒREM WITHIN SCHOLARLY ACCOUNTS OF ISRAEL'S HISTORY

The nature of *ḥērem* and of its practice in ancient Israel is a complex and contested historical matter, where evidence is limited and hypotheses, conjectures, and surmises abound. So as to set the context for my argument, it is necessary to note only two matters on which there is reasonably widespread scholarly consensus: first, the practice of *ḥērem*, and secondly, the nonpractice of *ḥērem*.

The first point of consensus is that certain biblical narratives give the prima facie impression that *ḥērem* was indeed a practice that was, in certain circumstances in Israel's early history, expected to be carried out on the field of battle,[5] and that it was so carried out. Apart from the narratives of the book of Joshua (to be considered below), the most famous story is that of Saul, Agag, and Samuel in 1 Sam 15. As it stands, this is a rich text with numerous significant concerns, not least its resonance with prophetic theology. Nonetheless, the premise of all dimensions within the narrative is Saul's failure to fulfil the requirement of *ḥērem* with regard to Agag and everything Amalekite (esp. vv. 3, 9)—a failure which, at least with regard to Agag, is ultimately resolved by Samuel (vv. 32–33).

Whatever the traditio-historical and redactional complexities of this story in relation to its role within the Deuteronomistic History,[6] there has been a widespread consensus, at least until the advent of fashionable "minimalism," that an ancient, and most likely historical, tradition is represented in this text; for myself, I can see no good reason to doubt this. On any reckoning, the narrative attests that in Israel's collective memory *ḥērem* was envisaged as a military practice on the battlefield in at least certain circumstances.[7]

There is reason also to see *ḥērem* as a practice of war beyond the context of ancient Israel. Most famously, the language of *ḥērem* has been found in a rare surviving text from one of Israel's immediate neighbors: the ninth-century Moabite stone.[8] Here Mesha, king of Moab, tells of how, among other things, "Kemosh said to me, 'Go seize Nebo from Israel'"; subsequently, he was victorious and killed seven thousand Israelite prisoners "for I devoted [*ḥrm*, in a verbal form analogous to the *hiphil* verbal form in Deut 7:2, 20:17] it [sc. Nebo] to Ashtar-Kemosh" (line 17). There is also a usage in a Sabaean text from South Arabia, RES 3945, possibly seventh-century, which can be interpreted as depicting the military action of a Sabaean king, Karib-ilu, who "devoted the city of Nashan to the *ḥērem* by burning."[9] It would be unwise, however, to generalize on the basis of such evidence and suggest that *ḥērem* was part of the common cultural coinage of the ancient Near East ("the general spirit of the *ḥerem* coincided with the accepted ethics of the Ancient Near East"[10]). There is no evidence that *ḥērem* was ever practiced in the two major centers of civilization of the ancient Near East, Mesopotamia and Egypt, still less that it was linked to their peoples' own self-understandings as peoples (as we will see is the case for Israel in Deuteronomy). No doubt armies and cities were regularly wiped out in ancient warfare by Assyrians, Babylonians, and Egyptians, but in terms of the available evidence, these were not conceived, or prescribed, in the category of *ḥērem*.[11] As such, the practice of *ḥērem* must be seen as characteristically, although not uniquely, Israelite.[12]

On a point of terminology (which is inseparable from major interpretive issues), it is important initially to note the difficulty of finding a good translation of *ḥērem* in such military contexts. In particular, we should be wary about too easy use of the contemporary term "ethnic cleansing," which has come into common parlance through atrocities committed during the collapse of Tito's Yugoslavia in the 1990s. Deuteronomy prescribes *ḥērem* against fellow Israelites who renounce allegiance to Yhwh (13:16, ET 15), which clearly shows a prime concern not for ethnic identity but for religious identity and allegiance. In contemporary Western culture, which has generally marginalized and privatized religious identity and practice, it is hard to take issues of religious identity and allegiance with anything like the seriousness with which Israel's scriptures take them,[13] and it is correspondingly tempting to transpose the issues into more readily accessible categories. Yet for all that it is desirable ultimately to bring together ancient and modern horizons in the understanding of the biblical text, there are numerous hard issues and texts where premature fusion of horizons makes the task of comprehending the biblical text impossible; the disciplines of patient philological and historical understanding remain indispensable.

The second point of consensus is that the fullest biblical account of the need for Israel to practice ḥērem, that found within Deuteronomy—especially 7:1–5, 20:16–18 (which will be discussed below)—in fact depicts something that was not actually realized within Israel's history. A representative voice is that of Moshe Weinfeld, who has discussed this issue in various contexts.[14] He consistently contends that "the law of ḥērem in Deuteronomy . . . is a utopian law that was written in retrospect."[15] Further, "in reality, the Canaanites were neither expelled nor exterminated, as may be learned from Judg 1:21–33 and 1 Kgs 9:20–21, so that the whole question [sc. of ḥērem] was a theoretical one, especially raised by the Deuteronomic movement." Deuteronomy's conception of ḥērem "is an a priori decree that belongs more to theory than to practice."[16] The consensus nature of Weinfeld's thesis is concisely articulated by Jeffrey Tigay: "Modern scholars hold that this law is purely theoretical and was never in effect."[17]

Why this consensus as to the nonimplementation of Deuteronomy's prescription of ḥērem? It is inseparable from the question of Deuteronomy's likely context of composition, which a general modern scholarly consensus, to which Weinfeld and Tigay belong, has set in the late seventh century, in some kind of relation to Josiah's reform. In a late seventh-century context—and equally in later contexts (if, as some propose, one lowers the date of Deuteronomy or of elements within it)—it is most unlikely that extensive military action against non-Israelite peoples within the land of Canaan with a view to wiping them out could have been considered as in any way a meaningful option. The kingdom of Judah did not have the resources, and in any case people from other nations had long since been assimilated within Israel.[18]

These two points of scholarly consensus can surely appear somewhat paradoxical to the nonspecialist, for if *ḥērem* was practiced in Israel, why should the major injunction to practice *ḥērem* have no bearing on that practice? Might not one point of consensus or the other be mistaken? To be sure, this is possible. Nonetheless, the complex relationship between Israel's scriptures and a history of Israelite religion and practice can lead to paradoxes that may in fact be fruitful. Not least, they can lead one to rethink familiar assumptions about the nature of those scriptures, and perhaps thereby discover purposes on the part of their authors and preservers other than that of providing what has so often appeared to be a kind of ancient history manqué.

In any case, we are brought to a clear specific question: Why should Deuteronomy use the language of *ḥērem* as a way of depicting warfare against the inhabitants of Canaan? This question becomes sharper when we compare Deut 7:1–5 and 20:16–18 with other, probably older, pentateuchal laws, especially those of Exod 23:23–33 and 34:11–16, whose content is similar but which do not use the terminology of *ḥērem* and typically speak of Yhwh's "driving out" (*gāraš*) the Canaanites.[19] It seems likely to me that Deuteronomy deliberately introduced the term into older law, even though questions of traditio-historical and literary dependence in the legal material of the Pentateuch can increasingly be argued any which way. Why should Deuteronomy do so? Why should it promote and prioritize *ḥērem* if it "was never in effect?"

There are various answers to this question. Many scholars see the issue as illustrative of the "theoretical" or "idealistic" nature of Deuteronomy in general. As Susan Niditch puts it: "Much in Deuteronomy is of a theoretical nature, like the second-century Jewish law code, the Mishnah, often planning for a reality that no longer or does not yet exist."[20] Alternatively, Moshe Weinfeld, as we have already noted, uses terminology such as "utopian," "theoretical," "a priori." Others, however, try to imagine some more concrete scenario or purpose. Jeffrey Tigay, for example, envisages Deuteronomy's *ḥērem* as conceived "when the Canaanites had ceased to exist as a discernible element of the population in Israel, to account for their disappearance."[21] By contrast, Rainer Albertz sees the *ḥērem* legislation ("fortunately purely theoretical") as demonstrating "fear of a cultural and religious swamping in the time of the exile."[22] Philip Stern considers that the Deuteronomic writers restricted the use of the ḥērem to certain primordial nations who had ceased to exist, so as "to eliminate the possibility of using the ḥērem against others."[23] Not infrequently, scholars see Deuteronomy's promotion of ḥērem to be indicative of a problematic shadow side within its author's mindset. Keith Ward, for example, confidently affirms that the call for ḥērem

> is an excessively vindictive and ultra-nationalistic expression of the frustration and anger of a much later writer [sc. than Moses], who wishes that all the Canaanites, in his own day causing so much conflict in his country, had been exterminated long ago.... It is wishful thinking by a very intolerant and zealous writer.[24]

It is striking, however, that diametrically opposed assumptions are made about the challenges facing Israel/Judah and/or the impact of whichever Canaanites, if any, were contemporary to the Deuteronomic writer(s). The paucity of genuine historical evidence means of course that such scenarios can be neither confirmed nor disproved. They remain hypothetical imaginative constructs, whose persuasiveness, or otherwise, depends on our judgment of their ability to explain the puzzle already outlined: why should Deuteronomy promote ḥērem at a time when ḥērem could not have been practiced?

DEUTERONOMY'S INJUNCTIONS THAT ISRAEL SHOULD PRACTICE ḤĒREM

By way of pursuing an answer to this question, we should turn to Deuteronomy itself and consider afresh its relevant primary texts. First we have Deut 7:1–5, where Moses, the speaking voice, continues his general exposition of the requirements of the covenant, subsequent to the Shema:

> [1] When the LORD your God brings you to the land that you are about to enter and possess, and He dislodges many nations before you—the Hittites, Girgashites, Amorites, Canaanites, Perizzites, Hivites, and

> Jebusites, seven nations much larger than you²—and the LORD your God delivers them to you and you defeat them, you must doom them to destruction [*haḥărēm taḥărîm*, a *hiphil* verbal form of the *ḥērem* root]: grant them no terms and give them no quarter. ³ You shall not intermarry with them: do not give your daughters to their sons or take their daughters for your sons. ⁴ For they will turn your children away from Me to worship other gods, and the LORD's anger will blaze forth against you and He will promptly wipe you out. ⁵Instead, this is what you shall do to them: you shall tear down their altars, smash their pillars, cut down their sacred posts, and consign their images to the fire.[25]

At the outset, it is important to recognize the rhetorical nature of the text, and to take this rhetoric seriously without taking it woodenly. On the one hand, the seven nations of Deut 7:1 are impossible to place on a map of Canaan in terms of historical geography. "Seven" in Hebrew idiom often functions to indicate "many" rather than a precise number, as in "your enemies ... shall come out against you one way, and flee before you seven ways," (Deut 28:7).[26] Moreover, comparable lists of the peoples of Canaan in other contexts (e.g. Gen 15:20–21; Exod. 3:8,17; 13:5), lists which vary both in the number and identity of those mentioned, suggest that the function of the lists is more rhetorical than geographical. In other words, the seven nations less represent particular targets for warfare than they do generalized symbolic opponents.[27]

On the other hand, the strongly rhetorical character of Deut 7 as a whole is evident in its depiction of the seven nations as "mightier and more numerous" than Israel, such that they make Israel afraid as to how they can succeed against them (7:1,17). Such rhetoric is intended to induce Israel to have confidence not in themselves but in YHWH, who can again deliver Israel from superior opposition as he delivered them from Egypt (7:17–19, cf. 9:1–3). It stands, however, in obvious tension with the rhetoric elsewhere, that YHWH has made Israel "as numerous as the stars of heaven" (Deut 1:10, 10:22), whose purpose is to induce gratitude to YHWH for fulfilling his promises to their ancestors (cf. Gen 15:5, 22:17, 26:4). One consequence of a recognition of these rhetorical tensions is, I suggest, that the historical specificity both of Israel and of the Canaanites recedes in favor of their being envisaged more symbolically as imaginative types.

Besides these issues of rhetoric, the biblical text poses interesting issues of translation and interpretation. First, despite the frequency with which the verbal form of *ḥērem* (7:2b) is translated with a straightforward English verb that signifies the taking of life—"destroy" (KJV, NRSV); "exterminate" (REB); although NJPS uses "doom to destruction" in 7:2, the rendering of the parallel usage in 20:17 is "annihilate"— I suggest that such a translation may beg the interpretive question. Deuteronomy has two other verbs to express a straightforward sense of "destroy." Most common is *hišmîd*, which, strikingly, is used frequently for Yhwh's bringing an end to Israel if they are faithless (7:4, 9:8,14, etc), though it is also used for Yhwh's actions on Israel's behalf against other nations (2:21, 9:3) and can be used for the actions of one nation against another (2:12). The other verb, apparently synonymous, is *heʾĕbîd* (7:10, 24; 8: 20; 9:3). On any reckoning, the conceptuality of *ḥērem* is more complex than "destroy," even if in certain contexts destruction might be entailed. A translation such as "put under the ban" or simply "ban" is surely preferable,[28] as it has the merit of being somewhat opaque in the kind of way that prevents the contemporary reader from too readily assuming that the meaning of the word is understood.[29]

There is also one obvious contextual difficulty with the translation "destroy." If the seven nations are to be "destroyed" (v. 2), why should intermarriage need to be prohibited (vv.3–4)? Since, to put it bluntly, corpses present no temptation to intermarriage, the text surely envisages the continuance of living non-Israelites in close proximity to Israel.[30]

In the light of this I propose that one should read Deut 7:1–5 as a particular definitional exposition of the practice of *ḥērem*, where its requirement of the absolute nonuse by Israel of that which is designated *ḥērem* is given a specific focus. First, there is a specification that Israel is to practice *ḥērem* with regard to the seven nations (7:1–2a,bα), which means refusing normal practices of treaty making or being moved to pity for the vanquished (7:2bβ). The content of this *ḥērem* is then given in what immediately follows, in terms of two specific practices. Negatively, Israel is to avoid intermarriage (7:3–4), for this would entail religious compromise, since intermarriage as a rule entails acceptance and incorporation of the religious culture of the non-Israelite.[31] Positively, Israel is indeed to carry out destruction—but the specified destruction is not of people but solely of those objects that symbolize and enable allegiances to deities other than Yhwh (7:5). Thus *ḥērem* is being presented as a metaphor for unqualified allegiance to Yhwh. On this reading *ḥērem* is not a "mere" metaphor, for it envisages specific and demanding practices. These practices, however, do not entail the taking of life on the battlefield, but rather the rejection of that which could compromise Israel's covenantal allegiance to Yhwh: intermarriage and the presence of alien religious symbols within Israel's promised land. When referring to Israel vis-à-vis the "seven nations of Canaan," Deuteronomy uses the language and imagery of warfare in a metaphorical mode, so as to depict the real conflicts over identity and allegiance that confront Israel in engagement with her neighbors.

The second instance of *ḥērem* being enjoined against the inhabitants of Canaan appears in Deut 20. After permission is given, in the case of warfare against distant nations, for Israel to take plunder and captives, the text continues:

> [16] But as for the towns of these peoples that the Lord your God is giving you as an inheritance, you must not let anything that breathes remain alive. [17] You shall annihilate them (*haḥărēm taḥărîm*, as in 7:2)—the Hittites and the Amorites, the Canaanites and the Perizzites, the Hivites and the Jebusites—just as the Lord your God has commanded, [18] so that they may not teach you to do all the abhorrent things that they do for their gods, and you thus sin against the Lord your God.

Again, the purpose of the *ḥērem* is unambiguous—it is to preserve undiluted allegiance to Yhwh. It should, of course, be noted that here the language of *ḥērem* is prefaced by an explicit requirement not to "let anything that breathes remain alive," and it could be argued that such specificity overturns the metaphorical sense for which I have argued in 7:1–5 in favor of a "literal" reading of *ḥērem*. Conceivably this could be so. It is unlikely that this text envisages anything different from 7:1–5; "not let remain alive" (20:16) is probably envisaged as the same as "grant them no terms and give them no quarter" (7:2), both being variants of "take no prisoners."[32] Moreover, the final words of 20:17, "as the Lord your God has commanded," indicate that the specification of 20:16–18

Election and the Transformation of *Ḥērem* 77

is to be read as a restatement of 7:1–5 (assuming that the words of Moses represent the will of Yhwh, as in 5:22–31, esp. 27, 31). One can argue that if a metaphorical meaning is sufficiently clear in 7:1–5 then it should be carried over here, but the opposite could also be argued—that a "literal" sense in 20:16–18 should be carried over to 7:1–5. The real point, however, is not whether the text uses the language of warfare, defeat, and killing, for it clearly and consistently does. The point is rather to recognize the genre of the text and the register of the language, and to ask whether the overall proposal to construe metaphorically is cogent. Such cogency will depend cumulatively on all the elements in the proposal.

ḤĒREM AND ELECTION

In essence I have already proposed an answer to the question of why Deuteronomy promotes and prioritizes *ḥērem* even if it "was never in effect": I have suggested that to speak of its being "never in effect" misrepresents the issue. It is not that Deuteronomic *ḥērem* was not envisaged as an actual practice, but rather that the nature of the practice that the text envisages is no longer military. My contention is that, although it appears that there was once an actual practice of *ḥērem* on the battlefield, Deuteronomy uses, and indeed privileges, the notion of *ḥērem* only because it was seen to lend itself to a particular metaphorical usage for practices appropriate to enabling Israel's everyday allegiance to Yhwh within a world of conflicting allegiances.

The next factor to consider is what else is said in Deut 7. For arguably the best known and most cited passage about Israel as the chosen people of Yhwh occurs in Deut 7:

> [6] For you are a people consecrated to the Lord your God: of all the peoples on earth the Lord your God chose (*bāḥar*) you to be His treasured people. [7] It is not because you are the most numerous of peoples that the Lord set His heart on (*ḥāšaq*) you and chose (*bāḥar*) you—indeed, you are the smallest of peoples; [8] but it was because the Lord favored (*ʾāhab*) you and kept the oath He made to your fathers

that the LORD freed you with a mighty hand and rescued you from the house of bondage, from the power of Pharaoh king of Egypt.

Here we see one of the conceptually foundational uses of the specific verb "choose" (*bāḥar*) that has led to "election" becoming a mainstream theological concept in both Judaism and Christianity. Earlier biblical traditions portray YHWH's singling out of Abraham and his descendants, but it is Deuteronomy that uses a specific term for this, which then passes into the theological lexicon. YHWH's delight in, and commitment to, Israel is formulated strongly: the idea of Israel as a "treasured people" conveys the image of Israel as the object of YHWH's special delight, and the verb "set his heart on" (*ḥāšaq*) is used elsewhere for the passionate emotion of a man's falling in love with and desiring a woman (Deut 21:11, cf. Gen 34:8). The nature of election as rooted in, and expressive of, the act of divine loving is thus clear.

It is perhaps the theological depth of Deuteronomy's construal of divine election in terms of the logic and dynamics of love that has given rise to a curiosity in standard accounts of biblical theology: Deut 7:6–8 must be a prime candidate (at least among Christians) for the passage in Israel's scriptures that is most frequently cited without reference to its literary context; i.e., it is interpreted out of context. Whatever might be the reason for this—there are various tempting conjectures—the fact is that in mainstream scholarly literature this prime account of Israel as a chosen people is routinely read without reference to the material that both immediately precedes and follows it. Just about every recent significant work on Old Testament theology—including those of Eichrodt, von Rad, Zimmerli, Clements, Childs, Preuss, Brueggemann, Gerstenberger, Goldingay, Rendtorff, and Waltke[33]—mentions the theological importance of this passage for understanding election, while saying nothing about its immediate context, as though it can and should be understood on its own in an axiomatic way.

Yet this passage immediately follows the injunction that Israel should practice *ḥērem* on the inhabitants of Canaan in 7:1–5. Indeed, the fact that verse 6 begins with "for" makes unambiguous that *election is specified in verses 6–8 so as to underwrite the just-mentioned practice of ḥērem*. Even if one were attracted to the hypothesis that 7:1–5 is a "later accretion" and that the "for" of 7:6 originally justified the observances in 6:20–25[34]—a hypothesis that, like many comparable hypotheses that fill discussions of the tradition-history and composition of Deuteronomy, mainly serves to show that it is easy to imagine differing linkages between the various constituent elements of Moses's discourse—one would still need to give an account of the logic of the text in its received form.[35] The text of Deuteronomy as it stands is clear: Israel's status as elect provides the rationale for *ḥērem* toward the "seven nations" who reside in the land that Yhwh is giving to Israel.

This brings us to the heart of my thesis. It is not only that Deuteronomy has preserved the ancient practice of *ḥērem* by construing it metaphorically—which in one form or other is a not uncommon proposal.[36] It is also that the theological logic underlying this reconstrual is that of election. It is, I propose, because Deuteronomy wishes to highlight and develop the ancient understanding of Yhwh's call of Abraham and his descendants, and also undergird the requirement for Israel to be "holy" (*qādoš*) with the specific conceptuality and terminology of Yhwh's "choosing" (*bāḥar*), that *ḥērem* is seen as a prime vehicle for articulating the implications of choice/election. One can then also appreciate the significance of the fact that the prescription of *ḥērem*, as warranted by Yhwh's election of Israel to be a holy people, should come so soon after the Shema (Deut 6:4–9).[37] For Israel's election is surely the counterpart to their recognition of Yhwh as "one," most likely in the sense of "the one and only," such that the practice of *ḥērem*, in the metaphorical sense outlined, becomes a primary working out of Israel's covenantal love of Yhwh.

To put the emphasis on divine election as the reason for promoting a reconstrued *ḥērem* does not, to be sure, rule out other possible factors that may have been influential in Deuteronomy's religio-historical context. As Mark Brett suggests, "the quest to formulate an exclusivist worship of Yhwh was itself shaped, it seems, by a mimetic logic which is both borrowing from Assyrian culture while resisting foreign influence, appropriating the imperial discourses of loyalty, violence and punishment."[38] In historical terms, such may have been the case (though of course we can never be sure). Nonetheless, whatever may be the contextual factors that influenced those responsible for Deuteronomy, the theological logic of election as the warrant for *ḥērem* is on any reckoning clear and primary within the text.

This reading of Deuteronomy moves in a different direction from the classic rabbinic preference to construe the *ḥērem* legislation as addressed to one specific generation in such a way that it does not apply also to subsequent generations. As Moshe Greenberg puts it:

> Now, had there been any inclination to generalize this law, it would have been easy for the talmudic sages to perform an appropriate hermeneutical exercise to that end.
>
> But in fact the sages left the ancient *ḥerem* law as they found it: applying to seven extinct nations, while radically meliorating other terms of the obsolete law. The rabbis adjusted its meaning to their moral sentiment. Since Deuteronomy expressly grounded the *ḥerem* in the warning "lest you learn their evil ways and they cause you to sin to the Lord," the rabbis concluded, reasonably enough, that if the Canaanites reformed they should be allowed to remain. The moral sensibility of postbiblical Judaism cancelled the indiscriminate, inevitable application of the *ḥerem* (which is the plain sense of Scripture).[39]

This move is readily understandable, and reflects a sure-footed moral sensibility. Nonetheless, my question is whether the "plain sense of Scripture" is really so plain, and whether the "appropriate hermeneutical exercise" which the rabbis declined to perform might not already have been performed by those responsible for Deuteronomy. And of course, the retention of community identity and allegiance through strong disapproval and discouragement of marrying outside the community has in fact been common among both Jews and Christians down the ages, even if it has not been understood as an appropriation of *ḥērem* legislation.

The present thesis might also claim support from the earliest explicit interpretive engagement with Deut 7 that has been preserved: the narrative about Ezra's dissolution of mixed marriages in Ezra 9–10. Here the narrative is set in motion through the citation of Deut 7:1,3 in Ezra 9:1–2:

> ... The officers approached me, saying, "The people of Israel and the priests and Levites have not separated themselves from the peoples of the land whose abhorrent practices are like those of the Canaanites, the Hittites, the Perizzites, the Jebusites, the Ammonites, the Moabites, the Egyptians, and the Amorites. They have taken their daughters as wives for themselves and for their sons . . . .

Ezra's list of the various nations differs from that in Deuteronomy and seems to embody a contemporizing of the text, in conjunction with other portions of Torah. This fits well with what has been argued to be the intrinsic significance of Deut 7:1 as a general symbolic depiction of problematic other nations. As the narrative develops, the issues are posed entirely in terms of Israel's separation from other peoples, so as to preserve holiness through the abolition of intermarriage. It is striking that there is no hint of any notion that other peoples should be put to death, or that Deuteronomy requires anything other than separation through rejecting intermarriage. Moreover, the one use of a verbal form of *ḥērem* depicts the "forfeiting" of property by the noncompliant (Ezra 10:8). To be sure, one might observe that any action more warlike than dissolving marriages would not have been a feasible option in the Persian context. Nonetheless, it is striking that there is no hint within the narrative that anything other than full compliance with the Deuteronomic prohibition is what is being enacted, or that separation is in any sense a compliance that is second best because of the constraints of the situation. Such a reading of Deut 7 may stand much closer to the intrinsic sense of Deut 7 than has generally been recognized.

ḤĒREM IN JOSHUA

A final element in my construal of Deut 7 and 20 must be a proposal for reading the narratives in the book of Joshua which depict Israel as fighting the Canaanites and practicing *ḥērem*. It has long been recognized that the book of Joshua is closely related to Deuteronomy. How then should its narratives of warfare and *ḥērem* be read?

This issue has been set in a new light by recent scholarship. Indirectly, there are well-known debates about the paucity of archaeological evidence to support the historicity of a conquest under Joshua, as well as debates about the nature and purpose of Joshua as a book that was apparently composed near the time of Deuteronomy (either seventh or sixth century). Both controversies sharply pose the problem of what sort of text Joshua is and how it ought to be read. More directly, there have been close readings of the text of Joshua which show that the narrative of Joshua is much more surprising than one might have imagined,[40] at least if one were expecting a depiction of Yhwh's being on Israel's side and enabling them to defeat and destroy the wicked Canaanites. For Yhwh is not straightforwardly on Israel's side, nor are the Canaanites depicted as wicked.

Yhwh's relationship to Israel's war effort is perhaps most explicitly addressed in a brief and intriguing episode that prefaces the overthrow of Jericho (Josh 5:13–15). Even if it were a latecomer within the history of the text's formation, it nonetheless now serves as an interpretive key:

> Once, when Joshua was near Jericho, he looked up and saw a man standing before him, drawn sword in hand. Joshua went up to him and asked him, "Are you one of us or of our enemies?" He replied, "No,[41] I am captain of the Lord's host. Now I have come." Joshua threw himself face down to the ground and, prostrating himself, said to him, "What does my lord command his servant?" The captain of the Lord's answered Joshua, "Remove your sandals from your feet, for the place where you stand is holy." And Joshua did so.

Joshua responds to this figure as Moses does to Yhwh at the burning bush. He is commanded to perform an act of reverence that has no apparent connection with warfare, although as such it anticipates the ritual actions that replace military actions around Jericho. Most importantly, the direct question about being "for us" or "for them" is straightforwardly rebutted: despite expectations, Yhwh is not "on Israel's side."

Something of what is involved in this unsettling of expectations can be seen in the two most developed depictions of a Canaanite and an Israelite within the wider narrative. The most developed depiction of a Canaanite introduces the main narrative action. Rahab is prima facie a maximally unpromising figure—she is a Canaanite, a woman, and a prostitute. Yet she assists the Israelite spies, she acknowledges Yhwh in language that resonates with Israel's primary affirmations ("the Lord your God is the only God in heaven above and on earth below" [2:11]), and she practices the primary divine quality of "loyalty" (*ḥesed*, 2:12). Both her words and her deeds are exemplary from the perspective of Israel's faith. She is thus exempted from *ḥērem*, despite the lack of exemption clauses in Deuteronomy, and enabled (with her family) to become part of Israel (6:23,25)—in rabbinic tradition she even marries Joshua and becomes the ancestress of prophets.[42] Conversely, Achan is a Judahite of impeccable pedigree (7:1). Yet he is disobedient, and he (with his family) dies (7:1–26). If these two narratives problematize any straightforward notion of the identity of Israel, the subsequent narrative of the altar beyond the Jordan makes problematic any easy notion of what territory constitutes that land which Yhwh gives to Israel (22:7–34).

When we read Joshua as a sequel to Deuteronomy, the uncompromising allegiance to Yhwh that is represented by *ḥērem* is seen to involve no simplistic account of what qualifies as allegiance, but rather a searching exploration of what the maintenance of Israel's identity in relation to Yhwh really entails, more searching than that in Ezra.

ON APPROPRIATING DEUTERONOMY'S CONSTRUAL OF *ḤĒREM*

Even if we allow the thesis that *ḥērem* is construed metaphorically in Deuteronomy, we have by no means resolved all the problems for Jews and Christians if and when they seek to appropriate the content of Deuteronomy today.

In December 2010 some senior Israeli rabbis issued a religious ruling that prohibits Jews from selling or renting property to non-Jews, based on an appeal to "You shall make no covenant with them" (Deut 7:2, "grant them no terms" in NJPS). Despite the apparently "literal" appeal to "no covenant" as a basis for "no legal agreement," the recontextualization of the language, together with an unconcern for warfare, constitutes this as in effect a metaphorical reading of Deut 7.

Unsurprisingly, this ruling has proved controversial, not just within its own primary frame of reference of the principles and practice of halakah,[43] but also for more general reasons. Emma Klein, writing in *The Times*, reported that "the Israeli President, Shimon Peres . . . cited a key biblical tenet, intrinsic to Judaism, 'Every person is created in God's image' (Gen 1:27), while Binyamin Netanyahu, the Prime Minister, voiced the principle: 'You shall love the stranger,' found in various verses in the books of Leviticus and Deuteronomy." Klein herself casts the issue as "the contrast between affinity with the plight of fellow human beings and fundamentalist enmity."[44]

There is obvious force to such critiques. Nonetheless, to polarize the notion of particularity over against what Klein terms "universal Jewish values" may be undialectically to privilege the "universal" over the "Jewish." Such a generalized ethical humanitarianism may come to be seen as trumping religion and theology. In other words, it is possible to lose sight both of Israel's election and of the possible enduring significance of election, even without construing it in the mode of the Israeli rabbis.

We might recall that Jon Levenson managed not long ago to bring down upon his head the wrath and indignation of not a few senior Jewish scholars for his critique of the 2000 "Jewish Statement on Christians and Christianity" entitled *Dabru Emet*. His measured critique provoked a torrent of astonishing misrepresentation.[45] Among other things, Levenson responded to the seventh thesis of *Dabru Emet*, that "a new relationship between Jews and Christians will not weaken Jewish practice," by raising the issue of "soaring rates of intermarriage" between Jews and Christians. Given the welcome disappearance of older hostilities between Jews and Christians, it becomes harder to justify resistance to intermarriage, for such resistance "will come to seem increasingly retrograde and parochial, even racist," even though "the risks are higher for the smaller community—that is, the Jews." Thus, he notes that "the maintenance of Jewish identity has become correspondingly more dependent on the religious dimension."[46] In that context he did not articulate what the religious dimension might be. Yet I do not think it unreasonable to suggest that election and its implications would play a fundamental role in any such articulation, whatever the halakic working out.

To conclude. Whether or not my reading of Deuteronomy—as displaying a transformation of *ḥērem* into a metaphor for two specific practices, the first of which is the avoidance of intermarriage—will commend itself to the honorand is not for me to say. Nonetheless, I hope that my proposal about the theological logic of Deuteronomy in relation to election and *ḥērem* is at least congruous with the profound thinking about election and the maintenance of particularity which features prominently in the writings of Jon Levenson.

NOTES

1. Jon D. Levenson, *The Death and Resurrection of the Beloved Son: The Transformation of Child Sacrifice in Judaism and Christianity* (New Haven: Yale University Press, 1993).

2. Levenson, *Death and Resurrection*, ix, x.

3. Levenson, *Death and Resurrection*, 139. Comparable is the account of God's favoring Joseph (167–68).

4. This essay develops a thesis first outlined in my "Toward an Interpretation of the Shema" in *Theological Exegesis: Essays in Honor of Brevard S. Childs* (ed. Christopher Seitz and Kathryn Greene-McCreight; Grand Rapids, Mich.: Eerdmans, 1999), 124–144, written after I had read *Death and Resurrection of the Beloved Son*. I have also sketched it out in my "Is Election Bad for You?" in *The Centre and the Periphery: A European Tribute to Walter Brueggemann* (ed. Jill Middlemas, David J. A. Clines, and Else K. Holt; Sheffield, UK: Sheffield Phoenix Press, 2010), 95–111.

5. *Ḥērem* can also occasionally be used in other, nonmilitary contexts, several of which are noted in Lev 27; e.g. a unredeemed field may become *ḥērem* at the jubilee (27:20–21), or an individual may dedicate to Yhwh an object that has become *ḥērem* (27:28). The dating of these conceptions, and their relation to other conceptions of *ḥērem*, is unclear.

6. See e.g. Antony F. Campbell and Mark O'Brien, *Unfolding the Deuteronomistic History* (Minneapolis: Fortress, 2000), 254–56.

7. The peculiarly negative significance attaching to the Amalekites within Israel's scriptures makes it unwise to generalize about early Israelite practice on the basis of 1 Sam 15 alone.

8. For a detailed analysis of the text and language see Kent Jackson and Andrew Dearman, "The Text of the Mesha Inscription," and Kent Jackson, "The Language of the Mesha Inscription" in *Studies in the Mesha Inscription and Moab* (ed. Andrew Dearman; ABS 2; Atlanta: Scholars Press, 1989), 93–130.

9. See Lauren A. S. Monroe, "Israelite, Moabite, and Sabaean War-ḥērem Traditions and the Forging of National Identity: Reconsidering the Sabaean Text RES 3945 in Light of Biblical and Moabite Evidence," *VT* 57 (2007): 318–41, esp. 333.

10. So Yair Hoffman, "The Deuteronomistic Concept of the Herem," *ZAW* 111 (1999): 196–210 (197).

11. To be sure, in a biblical account the Rabshakeh speaks of Assyria practicing ḥērem (2 Kgs 19:11//Isa 37:11), but the Rabshakeh's speeches are Israelite compositions, full of rhetoric which in narrative terms is meant to be (a) representative of what an Assyrian might consider persuasive to people in a besieged city, and (b) deeply ironic from the perspective of an informed reader who understands Deuteronomic theology. Such language should not be taken as evidence for Assyria's own understanding of its military practices.

12. For a survey of other possible ANE uses of, or analogues to, the ḥrm root, see Philip D. Stern, *The Biblical "Ḥerem": A Window on Israel's Religious Experience* (BJS 211; Atlanta: Scholars, 1991), 5–87.

13. A suggestive example of the kind of imaginative rethinking that may be appropriate is Rob Barrett, *Disloyalty and Destruction: Religion and Politics in Deuteronomy and the Modern World* (LHBOTS 511; New York: T and T Clark, 2009).

14. Moshe Weinfeld, *Deuteronomy 1–11* (AB 5; New York: Doubleday, 1991), 357–84; Moshe Weinfeld, "The Ban on the Canaanites in the Biblical Codes and its Historical Development" in *History and Traditions of Early Israel: Studies Presented to Eduard Nielsen* (ed. André Lemaire and Benedikt Otzen; SVT 50; Leiden: Brill, 1993), 142–60; Moshe Weinfeld, "Expulsion, Dispossession, and Extermination of the Pre-Israelite Population in the Biblical Sources" in his *The Promise of the Land* (Berkeley: University of California Press, 1993), 76–98.

15. Weinfeld, "Expulsion," 91.

16. Weinfeld, *Deuteronomy 1–11*, 384.

17. Jeffrey H. Tigay, *The JPS Torah Commentary: Deuteronomy* (Philadelphia: Jewish Publication Society, 1996), 471.

18. One of the most famous of those assimilated is the loyal soldier Uriah the Hittite (2 Sam 11); Hittites are the first of the proscribed peoples in Deut 7:1.

19. See e.g. Weinfeld, *Deuteronomy*, 382–84, or his "Ban," 142–55, 159.

20. Susan Niditch, *War in the Hebrew Bible: A Study in the Ethics of Violence* (New York: Oxford University Press, 1993), 63.

21. Tigay, *Deuteronomy*, 471.

22. Rainer Albertz, *A History of Israelite Religion in the Old Testament Period*, vol. 2 (trans. John Bowden; London: SCM, 1994), 391.

23. Philip Stern, *Biblical "Ḥerem,"* 102–3 n. 12.

24. Keith Ward, *The Word of God? The Bible after Modern Scholarship* (London: SPCK, 2010), 39.

25. All biblical translations are NJPS.

26. Similarly the idiom "seven times" means "many times" (e.g. Gen 4:15; Ps 79:12; Prov 6:31, 24:16).

27. There is a fuller discussion in Stern, Biblical "Ḥerem," 89–103.

28. I strongly disagree with Lohfink's contention that "the usual translation, 'ban,' is and always has been false and misleading" ("ḥāram; ḥērem" in *TDOT* V, 180–99, at 188).

29. The noun *ḥērem* has a long postbiblical history. In due course it came to be the term for expulsion and exclusion from the synagogue—"excommunication," to use the common Christian term. The historical development and use of the term is complex and controverted. For an entrée, see William Horbury, "Extirpation and Excommunication," *VT* 35 (1985): 13–38.

30. This point is commonly recognized by interpreters who argue for the "ideal"/"utopian" nature of Deuteronomy's legislation; e.g. A. D. H. Mayes, *Deuteronomy* (NCB; Grand Rapids, Mich.: Eerdmans, 1979), 183. For a concern, however, that this might be overly pressing the terminology in a manner insensitive to its rhetoric, see Joel N. Lohr, *Chosen and Unchosen* (Siphrut 2; Winona Lake, Ind.: Eisenbrauns, 2009), 167–70.

31. I say "as a rule" because Deut 21:10–14 envisages an Israelite soldier taking a non-Israelite wife from among those whom Israel have defeated. This exception has long puzzled interpreters, and is hardly resolved by arguing that she would not be a Canaanite and so would not come under the prohibition of 7:3–4—for the basic logic of the prohibition is that *any* non-Israelite spouse would entail religious compromise because of the intrinsic social and familial, and so religio-cultural, dimensions of regular marriage. Some scholars simply argue that this must be an earlier law that was formulated prior to the distinctive Deuteronomic development of *ḥērem* and was preserved unchanged despite the tensions it now creates (e.g. Michael Fishbane, *Biblical Interpretation in Ancient Israel* [Oxford: Clarendon, 1985], 199–200). Most likely the marriage is permitted because a captive woman would have in effect forfeited her original religio-cultural context and her wider familial context, and so she would no longer represent a religious compromise (whatever her own individual inclinations). The assumption would be that she would be obliged to conform to her new husband's frame of reference and mode of life, religious and otherwise, or at least not actively dissent from it.

32. The language of Deut 20:16 is also used in a stereotypical way in the summary account of Joshua's victories (Josh 10:28, 30, 33, 37, 39, 40; 11:11, 14).

33. Walther Eichrodt, *Theology of the Old Testament* (2 vols.; trans. J. A. Baker; London: SCM, 1961, 1967), 1:256, 2:299, 372; Gerhard von Rad, *Old Testament Theology*, vol. 1 (trans. D. M. G. Stalker; London: SCM, 1975), 178; Walther Zimmerli, *Old Testament Theology in Outline* (trans. David Green; Edinburgh: T and T Clark, 1978), 45; R. E. Clements, *Old Testament Theology: A Fresh*

Approach (Basingstoke, UK: Marshall, Morgan, and Scott, 1978), 87–89; Brevard S. Childs, *Old Testament Theology in a Canonical Context* (London: SCM, 1985), 44; Brevard S. Childs, *Biblical Theology of the Old and New Testaments* (London: SCM, 1992), 426; Horst Dietrich Preuss, *Old Testament Theology*, vol. 1 (trans. Leo Perdue; Edinburgh: T and T Clark, 1995), 31–33, 38, 40; Walter Brueggemann, *Theology of the Old Testament: Testimony, Dispute, Advocacy* (Minneapolis: Fortress, 1997), 415–17, 497; Erhard Gerstenberger, *Theologies in the Old Testament* (trans. John Bowden; Minneapolis: Fortress, 2002), 86; John Goldingay, *Old Testament Theology*, vol. 1: *Israel's Gospel* (Downers Grove: InterVarsity Press, 2003), 215, cf. 498; Rolf Rendtorff, *The Canonical Hebrew Bible: A Theology of the Old Testament* (trans. David Orton; Leiden: Deo, 2005), 90, 461; Bruce K. Waltke, *An Old Testament Theology* (Grand Rapids: Zondervan, 2007), 509.

34. So Hoffman, "Deuteronomistic Concept," 202. See also n. 10 above.

35. Curiously, there is something of a parallel to those scholars who consider 7:6–8 in isolation from 7:1–5 in the good number of the scholars who take *ḥērem* as their topic and discuss *ḥērem* in 7:1–5 largely or wholly without reference to 7:6–8; the tendency is to cite 7:1–5 (in whole or part) as the relevant text, which is then quickly set alongside 20:16–18 and/or other texts in which *ḥērem* appears, in such a way that the literary context of *ḥērem* in 7:1–5 in relation to the divine election and holiness which warrants it (7:6), recedes from view.

36. See especially Christa Schäfer-Lichtenberger, "JHWH, Israel und die Völker aus der Perspektive von Dtn 7," *BZ* 40 (1996): 194–218, with whose reading of Deut 7 my own thesis has significant resonances.

37. This linkage between the *Shema* and *ḥērem* within Deuteronomy also tends to remain below the horizon in scholarly discussions, especially those concerned with the enduring signficance of the Shema.

38. "Genocide in Deuteronomy: Postcolonial Variations on Mimetic Desire" in *Seeing Signals, Reading Signs* (ed. Mark O'Brien and Howard Wallace; London: T and T Clark, 2004), 75–89 (84).

39. Moshe Greenberg, "On the Political Use of the Bible in Modern Israel: An Engaged Critique" in *Pomegranates and Golden Bells: F/S Jacob Milgrom* (ed. D. P. Wright et al.; Winona Lake, Ind.: Eisenbrauns, 1995), 461–71 at 469–70.

40. See especially Ellen Davis, "The Poetics of Generosity" in *The Word Leaps the Gap: Essays on Scripture and Theology in Honor of Richard Hays* (ed. J. Ross Wagner, C. Kavin Rowe, and A. Katherine Grieb; Grand Rapids, Mich.: Eerdmans, 2008), 626–45, esp.630–39; and, more fully, Douglas S. Earl, *Reading Joshua as Christian Scripture* (JTIS 2; Winona Lake, Ind.: Eisenbrauns, 2010). I am particularly indebted to Earl's work.

41. There is a textual variant, *lô* ("to him") rather than *lōʾ* ("no") which is probably an error.

42. See Louis Ginzberg, *Legends of the Jews*, vol. 2 (Philadelphia: JPS, 2003), 843, 844.

43. See the thoughtful halakic critique by Rabbi Aharon Lichtenstein. Online: http://kolharav.blogspot.com/2010/12/rabbi-aharon-lichtensteins-response-to.html.

44. "When the Hardest Thing to Do Is To Love the Stranger," *The Times*, April 9, 2011, 88.

45. See Jon D. Levenson, "How Not to Conduct Jewish-Christian Dialogue," *Commentary* (December 2001): 31–37. Responses and Levenson's response to the responses can be found in "Jewish-Christian Dialogue: Jon D. Levenson and Critics," *Commentary* (April 2002): 8–21. A fuller account of Levenson's critique is his "The Agenda of *Dabru Emet*," *Review of Rabbinic Judaism* 7 (2004): 1–26.

46. Citations from Levenson, "How Not to Conduct," 37, and "Levenson and Critics," 18.

CHAPTER 5

Job as Prototype of Dying and Rising Israel

KATHRYN SCHIFFERDECKER

The election of Israel is a theme that pervades the Hebrew Bible, occasioning consternation on the part of many a modern reader. In the Pentateuch course that I teach nearly every semester (a required course for all first-year students at my seminary), we encounter the scandal of election first in the story of Cain and Abel. Why, my students wonder, would God choose Abel's sacrifice over Cain's? Why would God—the God who created everyone in the divine image—play favorites?

The perceived problem is only amplified when we get to the election of Abram just a few chapters later in Gen 12. In this story the "problem" of election is mitigated somewhat by the closing statement of God's call to the patriarch: "Through you all the families of the earth will be blessed" (Gen 12:3b).[1] Abraham, in a phrase popular in American Christian circles, is "blessed to be a blessing." He is indeed chosen by God, but his election is primarily for the purpose of being a conduit of blessing for the entire world. Such an understanding of Abraham's election serves to moderate the scandal of election for my students, and there is indeed biblical warrant for such an understanding.[2] Abraham and Israel have a special responsibility to be bearers of God's blessings to the world. As other scholars have argued, however, Abraham's (and Israel's) election cannot be reduced simply to its instrumental function. Jon Levenson puts it this way:

> There is, then, a duality in the Bible's concept of election. On the one hand, election is at times articulated in terms of larger purposes that it is to serve, and, of necessity, those purposes extend beyond the confines of the chosen people. On the other hand, God bears with Israel even when it fails in its mission . . . The specialness of Israel is neither altogether self-sufficient nor altogether instrumental.[3]

In other words, to say that Abraham (or Israel) is "blessed to be a blessing" is most certainly true, but it is not the whole story. There is something irreducibly distinctive about the election of Israel, something that has more to do with God's love for Israel than with Israel's role vis-à-vis other nations.[4]

Of course, as one travels through Genesis the "problem" of election becomes more acute. Why Isaac and not Ishmael? Why Jacob and not Esau? Why is Joseph singled out for special favor by his father and by God? What do we (self-proclaimed enlightened and egalitarian) readers do with these texts?

Even as my students struggle with these questions, they also begin to notice something else about these stories; that is, they notice that it is not an easy thing to be one of the elect. In fact, it may not even be, on the face of it, a *desirable* thing to be one of the elect.

The examples abound, beginning in Genesis: Abel is killed by his own brother; Abraham and Sarah all but give up hope of having a child; Isaac is nearly sacrificed by his God-fearing father; Jacob is in exile for twenty years from his homeland and suffers the loss of his beloved son; Joseph himself is sold into slavery by his jealous brothers and is in exile for all his adult life. And none of the patriarchs ever really possess the land promised to Abraham in Gen 12. These stories of the patriarchs and matriarchs of Israel adumbrate what the people of Israel themselves will go through: slavery, hostility from the nonelect, exile, and diaspora. It is not an easy thing to be chosen.

These stories in Genesis participate in what Levenson describes as "the ancient, protean, and strangely resilient story of the death and resurrection of the beloved son."[5] Each of the beloved sons in Genesis—Abel, Isaac, Jacob, Joseph—goes through a near death and resurrection.[6] Being the beloved, chosen son is not an easy thing: "The beloved son is marked for both exaltation and humiliation. In his life the two are seldom far apart."[7] In this movement of death and resurrection, the beloved sons of Israel's foundational narratives prefigure what the nation itself will be, "the ever-dying, ever-reviving people of Israel."[8] Indeed, it is Israel's election as the "firstborn" of God (Exod 4:22; cf. Jer 31:9) that marks it for both humiliation and exaltation: "The story of the humiliation and exaltation of the beloved son reverberates throughout the Bible because it is the story of the people about whom and to whom it is told. It is the story of Israel the beloved son, the firstborn of God."[9]

As Levenson has so clearly demonstrated, this story of the death and resurrection of the beloved son, of Israel itself, permeates the Hebrew Bible and is closely connected with the theology of election. One sees the story played out communally particularly in those two momentous events in Israel's salvation history: the exodus and the Babylonian exile, the latter spoken of in language reminiscent of the former,[10] and both spoken of in terms of election theology.[11] In both instances, Israel/Judah comes back to life from an experience of near annihilation through the miraculous intervention of God. The exodus and the exile describe the humiliation and the exaltation of God's beloved, a movement that accompanies the election of Israel throughout the Bible. We see this movement from death to life also, however, in biblical texts which do not speak explicitly of the election of Israel or of anything specifically Israelite. In this latter category, the preeminent example is the book of Job.

JOB THE RIGHTEOUS GENTILE

It may seem odd to speak about Job in a collection of essays about the election of Israel. Job is, after all, part of the corpus of biblical Wisdom literature, which is decidedly nonnationalistic. The book never speaks of Israel's election or, indeed, of Israel. Moberly's comment about Job may be taken as characteristic of most scholars' thinking on the matter: "*Job stands outside the specific context of God's election of Israel,* and so seems to represent something about humanity as such which may be valid independently of God's special revelation to Israel (although it is Israel which recognizes and characterizes it)."[12]

There is warrant for characterizing Job as standing "outside the specific context of God's election of Israel." Job is not designated an Israelite. In fact, he is introduced as "greater than all the sons of the East" or perhaps "the greatest of all the sons of the East" (Job 1:3).[13] His homeland, Uz, is connected in other biblical passages with the land and people of Edom.[14] In fact, the LXX book of Job ends with a genealogy that identifies Job with the Jobab of Gen 36:33–34, an Edomite king and descendant of Esau.[15]

The book of Job shows no concern with the particular events, people, and places associated with Israel. There is no mention of Abraham (or any of the patriarchs or matriarchs) in Job. There is no mention in the book of the exodus, Sinai, the temple, or the land of Israel itself. The names for God which populate the poetic core of the book—El, Eloah, Elohim, and Shaddai—are not the covenant name of God, Yhwh, peculiar to the revelation to Israel.

For all these reasons, the person of Job is often understood by both ancient and modern commentators as an exemplar of the "righteous Gentile." Patristic biblical exegetes understood him as such, and claimed him as a sort of proto-Christian: one who, though outside the covenant with Israel, had faith in God and was counted righteous.[16] Gregory the Great, in his *Moralia on Job,* writes: "It is not without cause that the life of a just pagan is set before us as a model side by side with the life of the Israelites. Our Savior, coming for the redemption of Jews and Gentiles, willed also to be foretold by the voices of Jews and Gentiles."[17]

Many rabbinic commentators also identified Job as a Gentile, though whether he was righteous or not was a matter of debate. One tradition makes Job a Canaanite and places him in the land of Canaan at the time of the spies sent by Moses (Num 13).[18] Other rabbis count Job, along with Jethro and Balaam, as one of Pharaoh's counselors.[19] Still others list him as one of seven Gentile prophets who prophesied to the nations before the Torah was given to Israel.[20]

In contrast to the patristic writers and the rabbis cited above, there is in rabbinic commentary on Job a strong minority opinion that identifies him as an Israelite. Rabbi Johanan and Rabbi Eleazar both argue that Job was one of the people who returned from the Babylonian exile.[21] Against the idea that Job was a Gentile prophet, it is argued that he was instead an Israelite who prophesied *to* the Gentiles.[22] Rabbi Johanan, after reading the book of Job, comments: "Blessed is he who was brought up in the Torah and who has given delight to his Maker."[23]

The disagreements between rabbinic writers about Job's identity are possible because of the ambiguities in the book of Job itself. Job is not identified as an Israelite. Nor is he identified as a non-Israelite. Though the lack of references in the book to anything specifically Israelite would seem to suggest that Job is a Gentile, there are facets of his story that point to his identification as one of the elect. The first of these is the strong resemblance of Job to the patriarchs of Genesis.

JOB THE PATRIARCH

It has long been noticed that the Job of the prologue and the epilogue bears a striking resemblance to the patriarchs of Genesis. Several rabbinic traditions compare Job with Abraham, some favorably, some unfavorably. One tradition compares God's love for Job with God's love for Abraham.[24] Another maintains that if Job had not complained, his name would have been included in the daily prayers along with the names of the patriarchs: "If he [Job] had not cried out, as we now say in the *Tefillah*, 'God of Abraham, God of Isaac, and God of Jacob,' we would also say, 'and God of Job.'"[25]

Some rabbinic traditions place Job in the time of Abraham.[26] Others contend that Job married Dinah, Jacob's daughter.[27] As noted above, the LXX book of Job ends with a genealogy that identifies Job as a grandson of Esau, a direct descendant of Abraham. The pseudepigraphical *Testament of Job* and most of the patristic writers also hold to this tradition.[28]

These interpreters of the book noticed what most modern commentators also note—the many connections between the story of Job and the stories of the Israelite patriarchs.[29] Job's wealth of flocks and herds is reminiscent of that of the patriarchs (Gen 26:13–14/Job 1:3; Gen 30:29–30/Job 1:10). So is his wealth of children reminiscent of Jacob's (Job 1:2). The currency in Job is the *qĕśîṭâ* (Job 42:11), which is mentioned nowhere else in the Hebrew Bible except in stories about Jacob (Gen 33:19; Josh 24:32). The death of Job is described in the same terms as the deaths of Abraham and Isaac. All three patriarchs die *zāqēn ûśĕbaʿ yāmîm*, "old and full of days" (Gen 25:8, 35:29; Job 42:17).[30] Both Abraham and Job are described as God-fearers (Gen 22:12; Job 1:1).[31] Both Jacob and Job are designated *tām*, "blameless, wholehearted" (Gen 25:27; Job 1:1, 8; 2:3).[32] Job, like the patriarchs, acts as a priest (Gen 12:7, 13:18, 22:13, 26:25, 31:54, 35:14; Job 1:5, 42:8–9), even praying, like Abraham, for his enemies (Gen 20:7, 17; Job 42:8–9). Finally, two of the most common names for God used in the book of Job—El and Shaddai—are associated with the patriarchal narratives: "I appeared to Abraham, to Isaac, and to Jacob as El Shaddai, but by my name Yhwh I did not make myself known to them" (Exod 6:3).[33]

The author of the book of Job places his protagonist in the time and circumstances of the Israelite patriarchs, using allusive language and images to connect his story to those of Genesis. So evocative was this characterization that at least one Second Temple Jewish interpreter read the Genesis narratives in light of the later narrative of Job.[34] The author of *Jubilees* retells the story of the Akedah in Gen 22 by referring to the prologue of the book of Job.[35] Why would God demand from Abraham the terrible sacrifice of his son? Because Prince Mastema—the Satan figure in *Jubilees*—places doubts in God's mind, claiming that Abraham loves Isaac more than he loves God. Abraham, like Job, passes the test and Mastema is put to shame. In both cases, God tests his faithful servants because of the assertions of the Accuser against them, and God rewards them when they prove the Accuser wrong.

The connection that *Jubilees* draws between Abraham and Job underscores not only the patriarchal characterization of the latter, but also a deeper correlation between the stories of the two men. Namely, both Abraham and Job are chosen by God, and both experience great suffering precisely because of that election.

JOB THE ELECT

To call Job one of the elect is not to circumvent the debate about whether he is to be identified as an Israelite or not. It is to assert, however, that he is described in terms reminiscent of Israel's own election.

At the very beginning of the book of Job, we are introduced to Job as a man "whole-hearted and upright, one who feared God and turned from evil" (Job 1:1). He is an exemplary figure even by God's own reckoning, as we learn a few verses later: "Yhwh said to the Satan, 'Have you noticed my servant Job? There is no one like him on earth, a man whole-hearted and upright, one who fears God and turns from evil'" (Job 1:8, 2:3).

This commendation of Job by God is remarkable for several reasons. First, it must be noted that the deity who speaks here is identified as Yhwh, the God of Israel. We have had occasion to note above that Job and his companions in the dialogue do not use this covenant name of God.[36] Yet here, at the very beginning of the book, we find out that the God who acts in the book of Job is none other than the God of the patriarchs, the God known by his people as Yhwh. The deity is so named several times in the prologue, the divine speeches, and the epilogue of Job. Whether Job is an Israelite is unclear. What is clear is that he is in relationship with the God of Israel.

Another remarkable thing about this passage is the designation of Job by God as "my servant" (ʿabdî). Yhwh repeatedly calls Job "my servant" to the Satan and to Job's three companions (Job 1:8, 2:3, 42:7–8), three times in one verse alone (42:8), as if to emphasize Job's special relationship with God. The phrase "my servant(s)" in the mouth of God is not particularly rare in the Hebrew Bible; it occurs several dozen times. In all but one case, however, the people so designated are the elect, either the people of Israel themselves, or specific individuals from Israel: Abraham, Moses, David, Isaiah, Zerubbabel, the prophets, the Davidic king.[37] The only exception to this rule is the designation by God of Nebuchadnezzar as "my servant" in Jeremiah, a role the Babylonian king is given not because he is one of the elect, but because God is using him as an instrument to punish the elect (Jer 25:9, 27:6, 43:10). Once he fulfills that role, God will punish him in turn (Jer 25:12–14).

The divine commendation of someone as "my servant" occurs several times in the Bible in conjunction with language of election, particularly with the root *bḥr*, "to choose": "You, Israel, *my servant*, Jacob, whom *I have chosen*, seed of Abraham, my friend; you whom I have taken from the ends of the earth and have called from its farthest corners—I said to you, 'You are *my servant. I have chosen you.* I have not rejected you'" (Isa 41:8–9).[38]

Job, then, is in an extraordinary company. That God identifies him several times as "my servant" is no small matter. He is not, like Nebuchadnezzar, an instrument used by God for punishing the elect. He is himself one of the elect, a servant of God in the company of such notables as Abraham, Moses, David, and Isaiah. Like these chosen ones, Job has a relationship with Yhwh and he is singled out for special commendation by the deity.

This commendation is itself a kind of choosing. Out of all the people on earth, God chooses Job as the exemplar of righteousness, integrity, and piety: "There is no one like him on earth." God singles out Job for the Satan's attention. Whether that is a desirable thing or not is beside the point. God singles out Job for the Satan's attention and thereby God inevitably chooses Job for the test the Satan proposes. The commendation and the test are, in the logic of the book, inseparable, given the personage to whom God speaks. The Satan, the Accuser, will not take God's praise of Job at face value: "Does Job fear God for nothing? Have you not put a fence around him and around his house and around all that he has? You have blessed (*bēraktā*) the work of his hands (*maʿăśēh yādāyw*) and his possessions overflow (*pāraṣ*) in the land" (Job 1:9–10).

The Satan is describing Job's situation in terms reminiscent (again) of the stories of the patriarchs. God has blessed Job as he blessed the patriarchs, so that they (and those with whom they associate) acquire abundant wealth, wealth that "overflows" or "breaks out" across the land.[39] These blessings also echo the blessings promised in Deuteronomy to Israel itself, when they keep covenant with God. God will bless (*ûlĕbārēk*) the work of their hands (*maʿăśēh yādekā*).[40]

There are differences between Job and the patriarchs, of course. There is, for instance, no explicit call or covenant ceremony described in the book of Job. Nevertheless, the echoes of election language in the story of Job seem to indicate that when we meet him he is already chosen, already elect, already in a covenant relationship with God.

These allusions to Job as one of the elect cluster primarily in the prose framework of the book, the story of the so-called "patient Job."[41] There are parts of the poetic core of the book, however, which also depict Job as one of the elect. Job's own self-descriptions in chapters 29 and 31 are particularly instructive.

In chapter 29, Job describes his former life, before calamity struck. He refers to his wealth only obliquely, but in terms evocative (again) of election. Describing his former existence, Job wishes for the days "when my steps were bathed in butter, and rocks (*ṣûr*) poured out for me rivers of oil (*šemen*)" (Job 29:6). The only other place in the Hebrew Bible where rocks pour out oil is in Deut 32, in an account of God's election of Israel:

> But Yhwh's portion is his people; Jacob his allotted inheritance. He found him in a wasteland, in an empty, howling wilderness. He encompassed him and cared for him. He kept him as the apple of his eye.... He set him on the heights of the land and he ate the produce of the field. He nursed him with honey from the rock and oil (*šemen*) from the flinty rock (*ṣûr*). (Deut 32:9–10, 13)[42]

Job, like Israel, is beloved of God, chosen by God. Indeed, even more instructive than Job's description of his status or wealth is his description of his relationship with God: "Oh, that I were as in months gone by, as in days when God kept me; when his lamp shone upon my head and by his light I walked through darkness; when I was in the days of my prime, when the friendship of God graced my tent, when Shaddai was still with me and my children were around me" (Job 29:2–5). Job was in God's circle of intimates. God guarded him, watched over him, guided him. This is not the first time Job has spoken of his close relationship with the Almighty. In the midst of an anguished cry earlier in the dialogue, Job, like the psalmist of Ps 139, recalls the intimate care with which God "knit" (*sākak*) him together in his mother's womb (Job 10:11; Ps 139:13). God gave him life and showed him steadfast love (*ḥesed*) (Job 10:12). Job hopes against hope for a time when God might again care for him: "You would call and I—I would answer you. You would yearn for the work of your hands" (Job 14:15).

Job is in relationship with the God of Israel. Though this relationship is not spoken of explicitly in terms of covenant, Job seems to know and follow God's *mitzvot:* "I have followed in his footsteps. I have kept his way and have not turned aside. From the commandment (*mitzvat*) of his lips I have not departed. I have treasured the words of his mouth more than my daily bread" (Job 23:11–12).[43] His long oath in chapter 31 describes in detail how he has followed God's *mitzvot,* including such biblical mandates as caring for the widow and the orphan (Job 31:16–19), dealing justly with slaves/servants (Job 31:13–15), welcoming the stranger (Job 31:32), and not committing idolatry (Job 31:26–28). There is no explicit mention of covenant in Job, but the book describes a relationship between Job and God that in many respects mirrors the covenant relationship of Israel and God. It is a relationship marked by fidelity, obedience, *ḥesed,* and a certain amount of pain.[44]

The Satan's accusation against Job—that Job fears God only because he gets rewarded for such piety—leads, of course, to the testing of Job. Will he still fear God if he loses everything? In the space of two short chapters, Job loses wealth, health, and all his children. The children die as they feast at the home of the firstborn son. Janzen argues that the feast on "his day" is a birthday celebration.[45] If so, then it is during the commemoration of the birth of the firstborn son—an event dear to the heart of any Israelite parent—that all of Job's children suddenly perish.

The author of *Jubilees,* as noted above, connects this testing of Job with the testing of Abraham in Gen 22. The texts commend themselves to such a connection. Yhwh and the narrator extol Job as a God-fearer (*yĕrēʾ ʾĕlōhîm*) in the prologue (Job 1:1, 8; 2:3) and the Satan responds by questioning that very characteristic: "Does Job fear God for nothing?" At the end of Abraham's terrible test, God commends the same attribute in him: "Now I know that you are a God-fearer (*yĕrēʾ ʾĕlōhîm*), for you have not withheld your son, your only son, from me" (Gen 22:12). There are a number of other lexical connections between the Akedah and the prologue of Job that suggest the former may have shaped the composition or editing of the latter.[46]

There are, of course, significant differences between the two stories. It is Abraham's obedience that is tested as much as (or more than) his faith.[47] Will he carry out God's unthinkable command? Job, by contrast, is not asked to participate in the destruction of his children. At the same time, Abraham does not, in the end, lose his beloved son. Job does, along with all his other children. It is not Job's obedience to a command, but Job's reaction to these losses that will be the answer to the test.

Still, the connections between the two stories run deep. Both stories describe a fearsome part of life with God. For both Abraham and Job, being chosen by God leads not to a trouble-free existence, as the Satan asserts, but to terrible tests of their faithfulness. Do they fear God only for what they get out of the relationship? Do they fear God above all else? Will they trust God despite all evidence to the contrary?

The trials of Abraham and Job, then, point to an essential feature of the doctrine of election: those chosen by God bear a special responsibility—the responsibility to abide in relationship with God, to persevere in that relationship through good times and bad, not to give up or turn away even when God appears to be other than just, loving, and faithful. Davis writes of the designation of Job as *tām:* "The person of integrity [*tummâ*] is . . . humble and resilient in faith . . . responsive to the God who is free to change the terms of the relationship and the conditions under which faith must be practiced."[48]

To say that the elect are called to persevere in relationship with God is not to say that the elect are to be quietists. Job is anything but a quietist! He, like Jacob/Israel and the nation named for him, wrestles with God. Like the psalmists and the prophets, he laments. He holds on to God with one hand and shakes his fist at God with the other:

Am I the Sea or the Dragon, that you place a guard over me? . . . .
What is humanity, that you magnify them,
that you pay attention to them,
that you visit them every morning, that you test them every moment?
Will you not turn your gaze away from me?

Job as Prototype of Dying and Rising Israel 101

> Will you not leave me alone long enough for me to swallow my spit? (Job 7:12, 17–19)[49]

> Though he slay me, though I have no hope,
> I will defend my ways to his face! (Job 13:15)[50]

> Grant me two things, then I will not hide from your face.
> Remove your hand far from me,
> and do not make dread of you terrify me.
> Then call, and I will answer. Or I will speak, and you reply to me. (Job 13:20–22)

Job, like Israel, holds on to God. He does not let God off the hook, in a kind of misguided piety; but neither does he give up on God. Beginning in chapter 7, he addresses God directly, hurling harsh accusations at God while at the same time staying in relationship with him. For this, he is commended at the end of the book by Yhwh himself:

> After Yhwh had spoken these words to Job, Yhwh said to Eliphaz the Temanite, "I am angry with you and with your two friends, for you have not spoken to me rightly, as has my servant Job. Now take for yourselves seven bulls and seven rams and go to my servant Job and offer them as a burnt offering for yourselves. Job my servant will pray for you, for I will regard him and not deal with you according to your folly, for you have not spoken to me rightly, as has my servant Job." (Job 42:7–8)

The preposition *ʾēlay* in these verses is translated by all major English translations not as "to me," but as "about me." There are two problems with that translation. The grammatical problem is that *ʾēlay* is used two other times in verse 7 with verbs of speaking, and each time it plainly means to speak "to" someone, not "about" someone. The literary problem is that Job has just admitted a few verses earlier that he spoke "without understanding, of things too wonderful for me which I did not know" (42:3); and God earlier had chastised him for "darkening counsel with words lacking knowledge" (38:1). How is it that Job is now commended for speaking "about" God rightly? It may well be that this discrepancy is due to the combining of two different stories in the book, the story of Job the Impatient, who is chastised for his complaints, and the story of Job the Patient, who is commended in the prologue and epilogue.[51] If one takes seriously the final form of the book of Job, however, another explanation has to be found. I argue that Yhwh commends Job in the end not necessarily for what he said *about* God—Job admits that he spoke without understanding—but for the fact that he spoke *to* God, something his companions, for all their pious speaking *about* God, never did. They were enthusiastic theologians; they spoke at great length *about* God. They even advised Job to pray, but they themselves never spoke directly *to* God. They never once interceded for their suffering friend. For their folly, it is Job who finally intercedes for them.

The elect, including Job, are called to a relationship with God of integrity and faithfulness. Such faithfulness entails obedience, but it also demands a certain amount of *chutzpah*.[52] It involves neither passivity, on the one hand, nor apostasy, on the other. The long history of Israel's relationship with God makes that clear. Abraham, Jacob, Moses, the prophets, the psalmists—all are bold to argue with God, to wrestle with God, while always remaining in relationship with God. Job, with his bold claims against God, claims which are spoken directly *to* God, falls into that long line of the elect.

JOB AS DYING AND RISING ISRAEL

We have spoken of Job as patriarch and of Job as one of the elect. It remains to be seen how Job fits into the pattern of death and resurrection that so informs Israel's story of election.

Let us begin with two telling passages from the *Pesiqta Rabbati*. In the first (26:7), Jeremiah comforts "Mother Zion," who is in mourning: "Your chastisement is like Job's chastisement," says the prophet. Just as Job lost sons and daughters, silver and gold, so did Zion. Just as Job was cast on a garbage heap, so has Zion become a garbage heap. Nonetheless, just as God turned back and comforted Job, so God will do for Zion as well, restoring her children and her prosperity.

The second passage, too, compares Job and Jerusalem (*Pesiq. Rab.* 29/30A:7). The homily is based on Jer 30:14: "All your lovers have forgotten you. They do not seek you out, for I have struck you with the wound of an enemy." The homily goes on to say: "The words 'the wound of an enemy (*ʾôyēb*)' are to be read 'the wounds of Job (*ʾiyôb*).'" The rabbis then equate Jerusalem's troubles with Job's: both are attacked by Chaldeans; both are struck by fire; both are punished by the hand of God; neither is shown pity. Nevertheless, just as Job received in the end twice as much as he had lost, so Jerusalem will be given a double portion of comfort: "'Comfort, O comfort my people,' says your God" (Isa 40:1).

These two portions of the *Pesiqta Rabbati* trace the fundamental biblical story of death and resurrection in the life of Israel and in the life of one who may be seen as a personification of Israel: Job the elect, one who is chosen by God and who suffers precisely because of that chosenness; but one who is in the end restored to new life by that same God.[53]

That Job goes through a kind of death is abundantly clear in the book. "Naked I came from the womb of my mother and naked I shall return there. Yhwh gave and Yhwh has taken. May the name of Yhwh be blessed" (Job 1:21). Job frames his immense losses in terms of birth and death, for—as most scholars note—"there" (*šāmâ*) cannot, of course, be his mother's womb, but the womb of earth; that is, the grave. Job uses the same word (*šām*) for the grave in his first speech of the dialogue, the curse on the day of his birth: "*There* the wicked cease from turmoil, and *there* rest those whose strength is gone . . . . Small and great are *there,* and the slave is free of his master" (Job 3:17, 19).

Intermittently through the dialogue, Job continues to wish for the grave and/or describes his existence as though he were already there:

> My body is clothed with maggots and dust;
> my skin scabs over, then oozes again.
> My days pass faster than a weaver's shuttle;
> they come to an end without hope. (Job 7:5–6)

> Why did you bring me out from the womb?
> Would that I had died and no eye had seen me.

Would that I were as if I had never been,
carried straight from womb to tomb. (Job 10:18–19)

My spirit is broken; my days are extinguished.
The graveyard waits for me. (Job 17:1)

Job has lost everything. Death engulfs his life, and he is left naked, bitter, and despairing. Loss of family and possessions, physical affliction, the betrayal of friends, the (perceived) betrayal of God—all these lead Job into a kind of death, out of which he laments as bitterly as Zion bereft of her children.

And yet, there are moments in Job's speeches of inexplicable hope, or at least something akin to hope.[54] One of those moments is particularly striking, as in it Sheol plays a strangely positive role:

O that you would hide me in Sheol,
that you would conceal me until your anger has passed,
that you would appoint for me a time and then remember me!
If a man dies, will he live again?
All the days of my service I would wait until my release comes.
You would call and I would answer you;
you would yearn for the work of your hands. (Job 14:13–15)

This is a short-lived hope. A few verses later, Job bluntly says, "Water wears away stone, and torrents wash away soil. So you destroy a man's hope" (Job 14:19). Still, that Job can imagine a time, in or beyond the grave, when God might "remember" (*zākar*) him, is testament to a hope (however faint) that defies the evidence of his present circumstances. As it turns out, Job's hope is fulfilled. As with Noah, that other great paragon of righteousness, God's "remembering" of Job will lead to new life and a renewed relationship (Gen 8:1).[55]

The most famous expression of hope in Job's speeches is also one of the most difficult to translate. "I know that my Redeemer lives and at the last he will stand upon the dust," declares Job (Job 19:25). What follows in verses 26–27 has been taken by some scholars as a nascent belief in resurrection; by others as a desperate wish for vindication in this life. While the latter seems more likely in the context of the book, what is clear is that Job hopes to see God. "After my skin has been destroyed, in my flesh I shall see God, whom I shall see for myself. My eyes will see, and not another's" (Job 19:26–27a).[56] Again, though not in any way that he expected, his hope is fulfilled. After God speaks from the whirlwind, Job confesses, "By the hearing of the ear I had heard of you, but now my eyes see you" (Job 42:5).

In what way has he "seen" God in the whirlwind speeches? He has seen God's vibrant, wild, and beautiful creation, in which creatures indifferent and inaccessible to humanity are given a place in God's world and allowed to be what God has created them to be. He has seen the primal, inexorable power of procreation active in the world, contrary to his own curse on creation in chapter 3. He has seen God's obvious pride and delight in exactly those forces outside of humanity's control: the sea, the wild animals, Leviathan.[57] He has seen, in other words, life—life in all its many and varied forms, created and sustained by God.

This response by God to Job's situation has given rise to much discontent on the part of readers, and to doubts about the literary integrity of the book.[58] Nevertheless, in the final form of the book, it is clear that the divine speeches lead to a transformation in Job. He proclaims that he has seen God; he acknowledges that he did not speak with understanding; he offers sacrifices for his distinctly unhelpful friends. Most strikingly, he chooses to live again. Such might not have been the case, but in the end Job (and his wife) choose to live again. That is, they have more children, even knowing the pain that such an act entails.[59] Job chooses to live again, and to live in such a way that he mirrors God's way of ordering the world. He gives his daughters names to celebrate their incomparable beauty and he gives them an inheritance along with their brothers (Job 42:14–15). Davis writes of these verses:

> The anxious patriarch who once feared the possibility of his children's sin now takes revolutionary delight in their beauty. These final odd details are far from gratuitous—or, in a deeper sense, they are entirely gratuitous, and that is exactly the point. In this unconventional style of parenting we see how deeply Job has comprehended and adopted as his own the principle that underlies God's *mišpāṭ:* the freely bestowed

delight that is in fact the highest form of causality in the universe, the generosity that brings another into free being.[60]

Job chooses to live again. In the speeches from the whirlwind, God calls him out of his death-like existence into life again, with all of its risks and rewards. Such renewed life after unfathomable suffering can legitimately be spoken of in terms of resurrection.[61] Job's story participates in that fundamental biblical movement from death to resurrection. To be sure, the book does not speak explicitly of resurrection from the dead, as the later rabbis (and Christians) understood resurrection. Nevertheless, it speaks of reversal and restoration, "the possibility . . . of redemption after unspeakable tragedy."[62]

Job dies "old and full of days," surrounded by four generations of descendants. His earlier visions of a gloomy end in Sheol are not fulfilled. On the contrary, he is among those who die contented after a long and fulfilling life. In this, too, he mirrors the elect. Abraham and Isaac die "old and full of days." Jacob dies surrounded by his descendants. Such fortunate deaths are signs of God's favor.

Job's story of new life after terrible tragedy, a story that mirrors Israel's own, contributes to that trajectory in the Hebrew Bible that eventually leads to the doctrine of the resurrection of the dead. Levenson writes of the restoration of Job as envisioned by his friends; though not resurrection of the dead, "[i]t is a reversal nonetheless, the replacement of despair with hope, of gloom with shining light. It was such a reversal in the same direction, a restoration in the same direction, that the rabbis (along with their Pharisaic antecedents and Christian contemporaries) expected in the future resurrection of the dead."[63]

Given Job's story and the resonance it must have had with those steeped in the biblical tradition, it is perhaps not surprising that the LXX translator(s) of Job added this detail to the end of the book: "And Job died, old and full of days. *And it is written that he will rise again with those whom the Lord raises up.*"

According to this ending, Job—prototype of Israel, chosen of God—will, like Israel, be drawn finally out of death into life. Such an interpretation is true not only to this particular story of Job but also to the larger biblical narrative of which it is a part. It is not an easy thing to be one of the elect, to be sure. With election come severe trials, according to Job and to the whole biblical tradition. Nonetheless, with election comes also a relationship with the God of Israel; and that God—according to the faith communities born out of the biblical tradition—is a God of life, who is faithful even until death, and beyond.

NOTES

I have learned an inestimable amount—about the Bible, about theology, about teaching— from my former teacher and advisor, Jon Levenson. In particular, his erudite and profound exploration of themes of death and resurrection in the Hebrew Bible has informed my own reading of the biblical texts, including the book of Job. I count myself very fortunate to have been among his students, for whom he is not only a superb teacher, but also a wise and generous mentor. I am privileged to be among those offering essays in honor of him.

    1. All translations of the biblical text are the author's, unless otherwise noted. The niphal of *brk* can also be translated as a reflexive: "And by you all the families of the earth will bless themselves." For a fuller explication of the theological implications of each translation, see Joel Kaminsky, *Yet I Loved Jacob: Reclaiming the Biblical Concept of Election* (Nashville: Abingdon, 2007), 82–85.

    2. See Gen 18:17–19; Exod 19:5–6; Isa 2:2–4, 43:10, 60:3.

    3. Jon Levenson, "The Universal Horizon of Biblical Particularism," in *Ethnicity and the Bible* (ed. M.G. Brett; Leiden: Brill, 1996), 156.

    4. Deut 7:7–8 is a focal text for the theme of God's love for Israel. Levenson speaks of the text as describing "an affair of the heart" (ibid.).

    5. Jon Levenson, *The Death and Resurrection of the Beloved Son: The Transformation of Child Sacrifice in Judaism and Christianity* (New Haven: Yale University Press, 1993), 232.

    6. The exception, of course, is Abel, who does not go through a "near death" but a real death. Levenson argues that Seth is to be understood in the ancient Israelite narrative as "Abel redivivus, the slain son restored to his parents ... The death of the beloved son, even when it is not averted, can still be reversed." (*Death and Resurrection*, 78).

    7. Ibid., 59.

    8. Jon D. Levenson, *Resurrection and the Restoration of Israel: The Ultimate Victory of the God of Life* (New Haven: Yale University Press, 2006), 131.

    9. Levenson, *Death and Resurrection*, 67.

    10. Isa 43:14–21, 51:9–11.

11. Exod 4:22–23; 19:3–6; Lev 26:42–45; Deut 7:7–8; Josh 24:2–13; Ps 105; Isa 41:8–10; 44:1–3, 21–28; 45:1–7; Jer 33:23–26; Ezek 37:11–28; Amos 3:1–2.

12. R. W. L. Moberly, *The Bible, Theology, and Faith: A Study of Abraham and Jesus* (Cambridge: Cambridge University Press, 2000), 84–85. Emphasis added.

13. Notice the parallel phrase in 1 Kgs 5:10, where Solomon's wisdom is "greater than the wisdom of all the sons of the East." In this passage, of course, Solomon cannot be included in the "sons of the East." It is unclear whether Job is to be so designated.

14. The name Uz appears in genealogies of Esau (Gen 36:28; 1 Chr 1:42) and is connected with Edom/Esau also in Lam 4:21.

15. Job 42:17b–17c (LXX).

16. Judith R. Baskin, *Pharaoh's Counsellors: Job, Jethro, and Balaam in Rabbinic and Patristic Tradition* (BJS 47; Chico, Cal.: Scholars Press, 1983), 32–43. Manlio Simonetti and Marco Conti, eds., *Ancient Christian Commentary on Scripture: Job* (ACCS 6; Downers Grove, Ill.: InterVarsity Press, 2006), xviii, 1–2. Some patristic writers described Job as a type of the crucified and risen Christ (idem., 103–4, 159–60).

17. Gregory the Great, *Moralia on Job: Preface § 5*. Cited in Baskin, 35.

18. *b. B. Bat.* 15a. See also *b. Soṭah* 35a.

19. *b. Soṭah* 11a, *b. Sanh.* 106a, *Exod. Rab.* 1:9. In this tradition, Job is not considered righteous. He is punished because he does not speak up to defend the Israelites from Pharaoh's plans to destroy them.

20. *S. ʿOlam Rab.* 21; *b. B. Bat.* 15b. Cf. *Deut. Rab.* 2:4. The other Gentile prophets are Balaam and his father as well as Job's four interlocutors: Eliphaz, Bildad, Zophar, and Elihu.

21. *b. B. Bat.* 15a. See also *j. Soṭah* 20c and *Gen. Rab.* 57:4.

22. *b. B. Bat.* 15b.

23. *b. Ber.* 17a.

24. *b. B. Bat.* 16a.

25. *Pesiq. Rab.* 47:3. For other rabbinic comparisons of Job with Abraham, see *Gen. Rab.* 49:9; 57:4.

26. *Gen. Rab.* 57:4.

27. *b. B. Bat.* 15b. See also the *Testament of Job* 1:5–6 and *Gen. Rab.* 19:12.

28. The rabbis do not make this connection between Esau and Job, perhaps, as Baskin argues, because of the association in rabbinic times of Esau/Edom with Rome (Baskin, 29).

29. For a summary of many of these parallels, see Edouard Dhorme, *A Commentary on the Book of Job* (trans. H. Knight; London: Thomas Nelson, 1967), xx–xxi. I have added several parallels to Dhorme's list.

30. The MT of Gen 25:8 (Abraham's death) lacks the word *yāmîm*, "days," though the word (or its equivalent) appears in some Hebrew manuscripts, as well as in the LXX, the Samaritan Pentateuch, the Targums, and the Peshitta. The phrase is used only of Abraham, Isaac, Job, and David (1 Chr 23:1).

31. Being a God-fearer, of course, is not an unusual designation in the Hebrew Bible. Still, given the other parallels between the patriarchs and Job, it bears mentioning, especially because the particular phrase *yĕrē' 'ĕlōhîm*, which occurs in Gen 22:12 and Job 1:1, 8 and 2:3, is not common. For more on connections between Gen 22 and Job, see below.

32. Ellen F. Davis describes the literary and theological connections between Jacob and Job, including this designation of them as *tām*, in "Job and Jacob: The Integrity of Faith," in *The Whirlwind: Essays on Job, Hermeneutics, and Theology in Memory of Jane Morse* (ed. S. L. Cook et al.; New York: Sheffield Academic Press, 2001), 100–20. Note that *tām* and its cognates also occur in covenantal contexts (Gen 17:1; Deut 18:13).

33. See also Gen 17:1, 28:3, 35:11, 43:14, 48:3, 49:25; Job 5:17; 6:4, 14; 8:3, 5; 13:3, etc. The name Shaddai is used twenty-three times in the book of Job. The name El is used fifty-five times. The name Yhwh is used in the prologue, epilogue, and divine speeches of Job. For more on that topic, see below.

34. I am agreeing here with the majority of scholars who date Job no earlier than the Babylonian exile. For a discussion of scholarship on the dating of Job, see my book *Out of the Whirlwind: Creation Theology in the Book of Job* (HTS 61; Cambridge, Mass.: Harvard University Press, 2008), 13–20.

35. See Levenson's discussion of *Jubilees* and the prologue of Job in *Death and Resurrection*, 177–78.

36. The name Yhwh does appear once in the poetic dialogue, at 12:9, where it echoes a phrase from Isa 41:20.

37. See, among many examples, Gen 26:24; Lev 25:42; Num 12:7–8; 2 Sam 3:18; 1 Kgs 11:32–38; 2 Kgs 9:7; Isa 20:3; Ezek 34:23–24; and, of course, the "servant songs" in Isa 42, 49, 50, and 52–53.

38. For more examples of *'abdî* and *bḥr* used together, see 1 Kgs 11:34; Pss 78:70, 105:26; Isa 42:1, 43:10, 44:1–2, 65:9; Hag 2:23. Note that *bḥr* is used often by itself in contexts of election, to speak of God's "choosing" of Israel or of specific individuals from Israel. See, for example, Deut 7:6–7.

39. The instances of God blessing (*brk*) the patriarchs are too numerous to list. Note, however, the use of *prṣ* to speak of abundant wealth in Gen 28:14 (Jacob), 30:30 (Laban, because of his association with Jacob), and 30:43 (Jacob).

40. Deut. 28:12; cf. 28:8. For a discussion of the elements of covenant found in the book of Job, see Max Rogland, "The Covenant in the Book of Job," *CTR* 7 (Fall 2009): 49–62.

41. For a discussion of the two primary strata of the book discerned by many scholars (the original folktale of a "patient Job" and the addition of a story of an "impatient Job"), see the seminal study by H. L. Ginsberg, "Job the Patient and Job the Impatient," *Conservative Judaism* 21 (1967): 12–28.

42. Note that both passages also refer to ḥem'â ("curds, butter"), as a sign of blessing (Deut 32:14; Job 29:6).

43. I follow the NIV and the Tanakh in translating "my portion" as "my daily bread."

44. It is important to note that the suffering Job undergoes is not a result of sin. He does not break the covenant, as Israel is accused of doing. Indeed, God notes that "there is no one like him on earth" (Job 1:8). The book of Job is not Deuteronomistic. It explores, instead, the question of undeserved suffering, which, it may be argued, is also portrayed in other biblical stories of the elect (Abraham, Joseph).

45. J. Gerald Janzen, *Job* (IBC; Atlanta: John Knox, 1985), 36. Janzen connects *yômô* in Job 1:4, describing the sons' celebrations, with the same word in 3:1, the latter designating the day of Job's birth.

46. See Victoria Hoffer, "Illusion, Allusion, and Literary Artifice in the Frame Narrative of Job," in *The Whirlwind*, 84–99. Besides *yěrē' 'ělōhîm*, the other verbal connections Hoffer lists are: the mention of Uz (Job 1:1; Gen 22:21); *hiškîm babōqer* "rise early in the morning" (Job 1:5; Gen 22:3); *šālaḥ yād* "stretch out a hand" (Job 1:11, 12; 2:5; Gen 22:10, 12); *nāśā' 'ênayim mērāḥôq* "raise eyes from a distance" (Job 2:12; Gen 22:4).

47. Levenson makes this point strongly in *Death and Resurrection*, 125–42.

48. Davis, "Job and Jacob," 105.

49. For a similar sentiment, see Ps 39:10–13.

50. I am reading here the *ketib* (*lō'*) rather than the *qere* (*lô*). The NIV offers the alternate reading: "Though he slay me, yet will I hope in him; I will surely defend my ways to his face." The point is much the same in either reading: Job still clings to the God who has become, in his estimation, his enemy.

51. See Ginsberg, "Job the Patient."

52. Levenson speaks eloquently of this "dialectical theology" of the Hebrew Bible, in which "both arguing with God and obeying him can be central spiritual acts, although when to do which remains necessarily unclear." See *Creation and the Persistence of Evil: The Jewish Drama of Divine Omnipotence* (2nd ed.; Princeton, N.J.: Princeton University Press, 1994), 153.

53. Other scholars discern this correlation between Job and Israel. Note the comment by Ellen Davis: "Job is Israel in exile: radically alienated from God, and yet unable to separate himself from this God who seems bent on destroying him" ("Job and Jacob," 108). I am sympathetic to the argument that the book of Job was written as a response to the Babylonian exile, though of course there are

many times of suffering in the history of Israel to which Job could have been a response.

54. Here I want to nuance Levenson's characterization of Job's view in the dialogue. He says that Job, unlike his friends, "despair[s] of ultimate restoration," that his "lapse" lies in "his failure to see that the hellish suffering of his deathlike condition was not God's last word" (*Resurrection and Restoration*, 71). While this is certainly true of most of Job's speeches, there are moments when Job at least approaches a sense that there may be something more, something for which to hope. This hope is not for an afterlife, but for vindication and for God's renewed care in this life.

55. Note that Job and Noah (along with Daniel/Danel) are cited by Ezekiel as exemplars of righteousness (Ezek 14:14, 20). This is taken by most scholars as evidence of a well-known ANE folktale of Job, which was the basis for the prose framework of the book.

56. The phrase in 26a is difficult to translate, in part because the verb is 3cp and there is no subject for it. Most translators understand it as a passive verb, as do I. It is also unclear what "from/in my flesh" means.

57. For much more on this interpretation of the divine speeches, and how they provide a response to Job's situation and speeches, see my book *Out of the Whirlwind*, 63–127.

58. S. B. Freehof's statement about the divine speeches nicely summarizes the problem: "Job cries, 'I am innocent.' And God responds, 'You are ignorant.' The answer seems not only irrelevant but even unfeeling and heartless." See S. B. Freehof, *Book of Job* (New York: Union of American Hebrew Congregations, 1958), 236.

59. Though the "replacement" of the old set of children with the new set seems terribly inadequate to today's audience, another reading of the epilogue is possible. I find Ellen Davis's reading particularly edifying. She writes: "This book is not about justifying God's actions; it is about Job's transformation. It is useless to ask how much (or how little) it costs God to give more children. The real question is how much it costs Job to become a father again." (Ellen Davis, *Getting Involved with God: Rediscovering the Old Testament* [Lanham, Maryland: Cowley, 2001], 142.)

60. Davis, "Job and Jacob," 120.

61. Note the rabbinic midrash that Job "lived to see a new world" (*Gen. Rab.* 30:8).

62. Levenson, *Resurrection and Restoration*, 80.

63. Ibid., 70.

PART II

Reception of the Hebrew Bible

CHAPTER 6

Does Tobit Fear God for Nought?

GARY A. ANDERSON

I am delighted to offer this essay about the figure of Tobit in honor of Jon Levenson. For one, it is a piece of work that could not have been written had I not read and reread several times his marvelous book *The Death and Resurrection of the Beloved Son*.[1] In that work, he showed how the story of the binding of Isaac (the "Akedah") was not only important for postbiblical writers but also left a deep imprint on the formation of the book of Genesis itself.[2] To paraphrase a rabbinic dictum: Abraham is archetype; his descendants, the antitype.

But why Tobit? I cannot document all the reasons here, but suffice it to say that I agree with the thesis of George Nickelsburg that the figure of Tobit functions as a cipher for the elected nation as a whole.[3] In his descent to sheol through blindness and his ascent back to life through the restoration of his son and his eyesight, the paradigm for Israel's own plight and salvation was mapped out. Tobit, I would claim, was a "type" of the elected nation. And as type, it is fitting that the paradigm of the Akedah would be realized in his own life. A common assessment of Tobit is that the book reflects what biblical scholars have come to call the "Deuteronomic" retribution theology,[4] which means the penchant of the scroll of Deuteronomy, as well as the books that follow in its wake (the so-called Deuteronomic history, Joshua, Judges, and the books of Samuel and Kings), to attribute the rewards to a life of obedience to Torah and the suffering of sinners to the reverse. At first glance, this characterization of the theology of Tobit seems accurate, for the last chapter of the book makes it crystal clear to the reader that if you do good (sc. give alms), you will succeed (be saved from death); if you do evil, a horrible future awaits.[5]

Yet for all its similarity to the Deuteronomic theology, it would be a terribly facile to reduce the message of Tobit simply to a narrative rehearsal of a wooden deed-consequence theology. For this would be to overlook the central moment in the entire narrative: the divine testing of Tobit. In many respects, as scholars have noted, Tobit is very similar in plot and narrative detail to Job.[6] This aspect of the book conflicts with the supposed parallels to Deuteronomy. If, as many believe, Job is a critique of such a simple-minded retribution theology (do good and you will prosper), then how can Tobit be both dependent on that theology and also a critique of it? The answer to this puzzle, it seems to me, can be found in the book of Job itself. Though the principal narrative moment in that book is the test of Job's faithfulness—will he persevere in his righteousness even if it costs him everything?— the book closes with Job's being amply rewarded for the faith he demonstrated. In short, the book of Job questions the Deuteronomic model while reaffirming it at a deeper level. And so, I will contend, does the book of Tobit. The central narrative moment of Tobit's life (chs. 2–4) is a test that he must undergo; like Job he will lose nearly everything. But in the end he will persevere and inherit his just reward (ch. 14). The key to a sensitive reading of the book is to avoid letting its ending overly determine the texture of the test that occupies the heart of the story.

TOBIT'S HEROIC ACTS OF VIRTUE

My main interest will be the testing of Tobit's faith and the way that the test follows from the theology of almsgiving featured prominently in Wisdom literature. That theology could be reduced to a very simple formula: give alms and you will be delivered from all adversity. Yet, if we bracket for a moment the ending of Tobit, it does not appear that this formula holds true to Tobit's life. To be sure, it works for a while. When Tobit arrives in Nineveh and begins to give alms, he rises quickly in the administration of Shalmeneser and becomes so wealthy that he can afford to leave a sizable piece of currency on deposit while on a business trip:

> After I was carried away captive to Assyria and came as a captive to Nineveh, everyone of my kindred and my people ate the food of the Gentiles, but I kept myself from eating the food of the Gentiles. Because I was mindful of God with all my heart, the Most High gave me favor and good standing with Shalmaneser, and I used to buy everything he needed. Until his death I used to go into Media and buy for him there. While in the country of Media I left bags of silver worth ten talents in trust with Gabael, the brother of Gabri. But when Shalmaneser died, and his son Sennacherib reigned in his place, the highways into Media became unsafe and I could no longer go there.[7] (Tob 1:10–15)

When Shalmaneser dies, things take a terrible turn for the worse. Not only do the roads become unsafe, preventing any hope for a quick return to Media, but when Sennacherib becomes king, he launches what turns out to be an unsuccessful invasion of the province of Judah. He returns to Assyria enraged and unleashes a portion of his wrath upon the exiled Israelites. A number of Tobit's countrymen are executed and their corpses are left exposed to the elements. Tobit, however, persevered in his piety and bravely gathered the exposed corpses and prepared them for burial. Yet his good deeds won him no favor with the king. One of the Ninevites, Tobit tells us,

> informed the king about me, that I was burying them; so I hid myself. But when I realized that the king knew about me and that I was being searched for to be put to death, I was afraid and ran away. Then all my property was confiscated; nothing was left to me that was not taken into the royal treasury except my wife Anna and my son Tobias. (Tob 1:19–20)

Fortunately for Tobit, the trial was graciously cut short. Just forty days later, Sennacherib was murdered by his sons and Esarhaddon came to the throne. This king appointed Ahikar, a nephew of Tobit, to a high administrative post. From that vantage point Ahikar interceded for Tobit, who eventually returned to Nineveh and was restored to his home and family.

IS TOBIT STILL NOT AFRAID?

Yet, in the very next scene in the story, the other shoe drops and Tobit is plunged deeper into the abyss. As soon as Tobit returns home, he commences his works of mercy:

> Then during the reign of Esarhaddon I returned home, and my wife Anna and my son Tobias were restored to me. At our festival of Pentecost, which is the sacred festival of weeks, a good dinner was prepared for me and I reclined to eat. When the table was set for me and an abundance of food placed before me, I said to my son Tobias, "Go, my child, and bring whatever poor person you may find of our people among the exiles in Nineveh, who is wholeheartedly mindful of God, and he shall eat together with me. I will wait for you, until you come back." So Tobias went to look for some poor person of our people. When he had returned he said, "Father!" And I replied, "Here I am, my child."[8] Then he went on to say, "Look, father, one of our own people has been murdered and thrown into the market place, and now he lies there strangled." Then I sprang up, left the dinner before even tasting it, and removed the body from the square and laid it in one of the rooms until sunset when I might bury it. (Tob 2:1–4)

While out burying a corpse of a fellow countryman, he is mocked by his neighbors. "Is he still not afraid?" they ask. "He has already been hunted down to be put to death for doing this, and he ran away; yet here he is again burying the dead!" (2:8). Through it all Tobit remains unfazed. When he returns to his family, he decides not to enter the house but spends the night beside a wall in his courtyard.[9] But it happens to be unseasonably warm that evening and consequently Tobit falls asleep with his face uncovered. Unbeknownst to Tobit, there are sparrows perched upon that wall and "their fresh droppings fell into [his] eyes and produced white films." He visits several different doctors but they only make matters worse. "The more they treated me with ointments," Tobit reports, "the more my vision was obscured by the white films, until I became completely blind" (2:10). Though this tragic event seems to be a moment of terribly bad luck, we learn later in the book that the whole set of circumstances had been providentially arranged. Near the end of the book, after Tobit has been healed from his blindness, the archangel Raphael says: "I will now declare the whole truth to you and will conceal nothing from you. . . . [T]hat time when you did not hesitate to get up and leave your dinner to go and bury the dead, I was sent to you to test you" (Tob 12:11a, 14a).

Commentators have puzzled, however, over the exact parameters of the test.[10] And this confusion is understandable because unlike the book of Job; where God and the heavenly adversary (the "satan") discuss both the reason and the means of the test before anything happens, we only learn about the test of Tobit's faith retrospectively. It is clear that Tobit's blindness has provided the occasion, but what exactly is the test and what does God expect from Tobit as a sign that he has passed it?

TOBIT AND JOB

To understand better, let us recall the plot of the book of Job. There the issue on the table was whether Job would serve God for naught (Job 1:9). The test comes in two stages. It begins with a conversation between God and the adversary:

> One day the heavenly beings came to present themselves before the LORD, and Satan also came among them. The LORD said to Satan, "Where have you come from?" Satan answered the LORD, "From going to and fro on the earth and walking up and down on it." The LORD said to Satan, "Have you considered my servant Job? There is no one like

him on the earth, a blameless and upright man who fears God and turns away from evil." Then Satan answered the LORD, "Does Job fear God for nothing? Have you not put a fence around him and his house and all that he has, on every side? You have blessed the work of his hands, and his possessions have increased in the land. But stretch out your hand now, and touch all that he has, and he will curse you to your face!" (Job 1:6–11)

When Job's children and possessions are taken away, he is understandably disconsolate and gives voice to his grief:

Then Job arose, tore his robe, shaved his head, and fell on the ground and worshiped. He said, "Naked I came from my mother's womb, and naked shall I return there; the LORD gave, and the LORD has taken away; blessed be the name of the LORD." (Job 1:20–21)

Through it all, Job remains devout in his faith. "In all this," our narrator concludes, "Job did not sin or charge God with wrongdoing" (Job 1:22).

Once Job has passed this first test, the groundwork is laid for a second. God addresses the adversary with words of praise for Job's perseverance. "Have you considered, my servant Job?" God inquires. "There is no one like him on the earth, a blameless and upright man who fears God and turns away from evil. He still persists in his integrity, although you incited me against him, to destroy him for no reason" (Job 2:3). But the adversary remains unpersuaded. "Skin for skin! All that people have they give to save their lives," he responds. "But stretch out your hand now and touch his bone and his flesh and he will curse you to your face" (2:4–5). God accepts this challenge and Job is tested a second time, now with a hideous skin disease that repels his neighbors and brings him to the point of death.

The contours of the Joban narrative are picked up nicely in Tobit.[11] Let us recall that Tobit was also subjected to two different trials. In the first trial, King Sennacherib murdered various Israelites in Nineveh and left their corpses unburied. Tobit persevered in his works of mercy by continuing to bury the dead even when it violated an edict of the king. Tobit paid a high price for his integrity; he lost all he had. Yet through it all, Tobit remained steadfast in his faithfulness. As soon as he returned home, he resumed his generous ways even though he had to suffer the taunts of his neighbors—a trial that will be repeated shortly through the recriminations of his wife, Anna. But this first test, like that of Job, was limited to the loss of possessions. What if God went further and touched his very person? "Skin for skin," the adversary in Job had argued, "all that people have they will give to save their lives." So God permits a testing of Job that would involve his very person. Something very similar happens to Tobit. Though at first the reader believes that Tobit becomes blind due to the unhappy accident of having sparrow droppings fall in his eyes, at the end of the book we learn that there was nothing accidental about it. For just before he departs for heaven, Raphael reveals his angelic identity and discloses God's intention to test the faith of Tobit (12:13–14).[12]

The question we raised earlier about the purpose of the test now becomes clear. What the narrator wishes to explore is what will become of Tobit's distinctive form of righteousness: distributing alms to the poor. Does he serve God solely in light of the promised reward ("almsgiving keeps your from going into Darkness" [4:10]) or will he continue to persevere in this particular virtue even when it casts him into deepest darkness?

WHERE ARE YOUR ACTS OF CHARITY?

In the book of Job, the initial challenge to Job's faith is posed by his wife. While Job wallows in his sad condition, scraping the festering sores on his body with a potsherd, his wife approaches and says, "Do you still persist in your integrity? Curse God, and die." Job, however, is curt in his reply, "You speak as any foolish woman would speak. Shall we receive the good at the hands of God, and not receive the bad?" (Job 2:9–10). In the case of Tobit, a similar challenge is raised by his wife, Anna. Due to his blindness, Tobit has become dependent on his wife's income as a weaver. One day, when she is tipped for her efforts with a goat, Tobit interprets it as an act of thievery.[13] Insulted by Tobit's insistence that she stole the animal, Anna says, "Where are your acts of charity? Where are your righteous deeds? These things are known about you" (2:14b). Though Anna comes off far better than Job's wife—for the pointed barb she aimed his way was, in part, a legitimate riposte to the way Tobit had badgered her about the animal she received as a gift—she remains, like Job's wife, suspicious about the fruits of his piety. Rather than asking Tobit to curse God and die, she goes to the very heart of his religious life and highlights the dissonance between what Scripture has promised, "almsgiving delivers from death," and Tobit's present condition: "Where are your acts of charity?"

The question that she put to Tobit (and the reader) is a Joban one. If almsgiving is the very summit of Torah observance, and if the reason for that devotion lies in the promises God has made, then where are the good results that are your due? The implied answer is, of course, that those good deeds are nowhere to be found. They have been cast into the void and so are unnoticed by God. Put this way, Anna's question is not as innocent as it might appear at first. To be sure, unlike Job's wife she does not exhort Tobit to curse God, but she does imply that because the very core of his relationship with God has gone cold and sterile, it is worthy of reevaluation and perhaps repudiation. The question of the test, I would contend, is focused on Tobit's commitment to the commandment of almsgiving. Will he continue to hold to this commandment even though it not only has not provided the expected reward, but far worse, seems to have led to his personal demise?

TOBIT'S PROFESSION OF FAITH

Tobit's response to that test comes in two stages. First of all, immediately after his wife has declared that his acts of charity have produced no visible results and that God's abandonment of him is public knowledge, Tobit turns to God in prayer and declares his belief in God's trustworthiness, a habit that will become known in rabbinic prayer as *tsidduq ha-din*:

> You are righteous, O Lord,
>   And all your deeds are just;

> All your ways are mercy and truth;
>> You judge the world. (Tob 3:2)

The striking thing about this declaration of God's righteousness is that it provides a succinct reply to the theological challenge of his wife just two verses earlier. Her question had been: "Where are your acts of charity (*eleemosunai*)? Where are your righteous deeds (*dikaiosunai*)?" while his response to God is an unwavering declaration that "you are righteous (*dikaios*) and all your deeds are just (*dikaia*)." In the underlying Hebrew or Aramaic, the juxtaposition would have been even more striking, for all of the Greek words I have noted derive from a single root—*ts-d-q*. Tobit ends his prayer with a plea that God take his life for "it is better for me to die than to live, because I have had to listen to undeserved insults, and great is the sorrow within me" (Tob 3:6).

The second stage occurs when Tobit remembers the money that he had left on deposit with Gabael at Rages in Media earlier in the book. Calling to mind his request for death just a moment earlier, he asks, "Why do I not call my son Tobias and explain to him about the money before I die?" Then he called his son, Tobias, and when he came to him he said, "My son, when I die, give me a proper burial..." (Tob 4:2–3a). What is striking, however, is the Torah instruction that Tobit gives his son prior to sending him on this journey. In the middle of that instruction a strong emphasis is put on the need to give alms. As we have seen, Tobit grounds the reason for this in words that recall Prov 10:2: "So you will be laying up a good treasure for yourself against the day of necessity. For almsgiving delivers from death and keeps you from going into Darkness" (4:9–10). Though it has been suggested that the Torah instruction has been secondarily added to a chapter that originally would have included only the decision to send Tobias on this trip (4:1–3a) and his subsequent departure (4:20ff.), this seems very unlikely to me,[14] for the sending of Tobias and the instruction to give alms are inseparable themes in the structure of the book. Given the poverty that Tobit now finds himself in, the only way for his son to assume the role of an almsgiver (as opposed to an alms receiver) is to come upon a substantial sum of money.[15]

Another reason to understand the sequence of activity as a two-part response to Anna's query comes from the structure of the text itself. We could outline it in this fashion: The initial challenge is posed by Anna: "Where are your righteous deeds?" (2:13). Tobit responds by declaring that God is righteous (Tob 3:2), but asks as well that God take his life due to the terrible suffering he has undergone for his righteousness. Then the text makes a special point of declaring that several keys events transpire either simultaneously or within that very day:

1. *On the same day,* at Ecbatana in Media it happened that Sarah, the daughter of Raguel, was reproached by one of her father's maids (3:7).
2. *At that very moment,* she was grieved in spirit and wept [over the fact that seven potential suitors had been slain by the demon Asmodeus and proceeds to pray for God to take her life] (3:11).
3. *At that very moment,* the prayers of both of them [Sarah and Tobit] were heard in the glorious presence of God. So Raphael was sent to heal both of them: Tobit, by removing the white films from his eyes . . . and Sarah, daughter of Raguel, by giving her in marriage to Tobias son of Tobit and by setting her free from the wicked demon Asmodeus (3:16–17).
4. *On that same day,* Tobit remembered the money that he had left in trust with Gabel at Rages in Media, and he said to himself, "Now I have asked for death. Why do I not call my son Tobias and explain to him about the money before I die?" (4:2)

In effect the challenge of Anna's question—where are your deeds of righteousness?—sets in motion a cycle of related events. Tobit affirms that God is righteous but begs for his death. We learn of a similar trial that Sarah is undergoing due to the lack of a proper male suitor. But at the very moment that both pray for an early death, their cases are brought to the attention of God, who sends Raphael to deliver them. As is frequent for the Bible, God eschews direct intervention, preferring instead to work through the agency of the characters themselves. In this case, the answer to Tobit and Sarah's prayer hinges on the decision of Tobit to send his son on a journey to retrieve the money he has left on deposit. The logic of that decision is, in turn, dependent on the question that Anna had raised about the theological status of Tobit's almsgiving. Will Tobit persevere in his obedience to this commandment?[16] In sending his son to retrieve the money left on deposit, we can see that the answer to that question is decidedly in the affirmative. For it is those funds which will allow Tobias to escape the terrible penury that the family currently suffers from and emerge as a devoted almsgiver himself.[17]

TOBIT AND THE AKEDAH

Yet Tobit's decision to send his only son on such a trip was fraught with risk, an element not found, we should add, in the book of Job. Should Tobias not return, Tobit will have no one to remember him after he and Anna have died. His lineage, and so his memory, will come to an end. As Ben Sira had taught, and every one in the ancient Near East presumed, children are the primary means of providing a legacy after death (Sir 40:19). For this reason, Israelite culture took an extraordinary interest in making sure that one not die childless.[18] Many commentators have missed the significance of the risk Tobit assumes and the way this trial answers the central question of the story: will Tobit serve God for naught? In order to appreciate this central motif, I must briefly digress and consider the structure of Tobit's life compared with some significant parallels in the book of Genesis.

There is a clear parallel between the words of Anna and those of Jacob when they learn that their sons have survived their respective ordeals. In both cases, the dangerous journey that was undertaken resulted in gains that were unimagined by the fathers. When Tobit sent his son to retrieve the money he had left on deposit, his son returned with not only the money but also a bride, grandchildren to come, a very large inheritance, the means of restoring his father's eyesight, and so with the prospect for a new life (he lives to 112 rather than dying at sixty-two as he had thought). In Jacob's case, Benjamin is sent in order to free his brother, Simeon, and secure enough food to eke out a living for another year. But he ends up with far more: not only do Simeon and

Benjamin return with the food, but Jacob learns that his beloved son Joseph is still alive, married, and second in command over all of Egypt. Both stories end with restoration from sheol and what I have called the beatific vision in its Old Testament inflection: the opportunity to see and bless their sons and grandchildren before they die.

As Jon Levenson has shown, Jacob's sending of Benjamin on this dangerous journey to Egypt also has a number of parallels with the journey of Abraham and Isaac to Mount Moriah.[19] Both involve fathers who must put their beloved sons at risk very much against their better wishes, yet both result in gains their fathers could never have imagined. In the Akedah, the surprises include: the provision of a substitute for the son, a new grounding of the divine promise in the obedience of Abraham, and the restoration of a son ready for marriage.

THE AKEDAH AND MARRIAGE

This last theme is made evident in two ways. First, when Abraham is blessed by God, all the promises that are made, save one, are simply repetitions of what God had said earlier.

> The angel of the LORD called to Abraham a second time from heaven, and said, "By myself I have sworn, says the LORD: Because you have done this, and have not withheld you son, your only son, I will indeed bless you, and I will make your offspring as numerous as the stars of heaven and as the sand that is on the seashore. And your offspring shall possess the gate of their enemies, and by your offspring shall all the nations of the earth gain blessing for themselves, because you have obeyed my voice." (Gen 22:15–18)

The blessing that Abraham receives in this passage has three parts: first is the promise of numerous offspring ("I will make your offspring as numerous as the stars of heaven"); second, of power over one's enemies ("your offspring shall possess the gate of their enemies"); and finally, of the dissemination of blessing to the other nations of the earth ("by your offspring shall all the nations of the earth gain blessing for themselves").

The first part is simply a mild transformation of what had been stated earlier in Gen 13:16 and 15:5, whereas the third and final part was mentioned already at the call of Abraham in 12:2. What remains unaccounted for is the piece in the middle, "and your offspring shall possess the gate of your enemies." These lines do not come out of nowhere but are a literary anticipation of what Isaac will hear when his wife Rebekah is blessed by her family just prior to her departure for Canaan. They say to her: "May you, our sister, become thousands of myriads; may your offspring gain possession of the gates of your foes" (Gen 24:60). In addition to this, the story of the Akedah ends with what seems to be a complete non sequitur: the genealogy of Nahor, brother of Abraham. One might have thought that this genealogy should have been introduced at the end of Gen 11, when the genealogy of Abraham was first given. It would have served an excellent literary function there; it would have emphasized the surprise of God's election of Abraham and Sarah, for in contrast to this couple who was unable to have children, Nahor, his wife Milcah, and concubine Reumah were able to bear twelve sons between them, a symbolic number that bespeaks completeness and divine blessing. Yet, one item sticks out in this genealogy and certainly explains the reason for its inclusion here.

> Now after these things it was told to Abraham: "Milcah also has borne children, to your brother Nahor; Uz the first born, Buz his brother, Kemuel the father of Aram, Chesed, Hazo, Pildash, Jidlaph and Bethuel." *Now Bethuel also became the father of Rebekah.* These eight Milcah bore to Nahor, Abraham's brother. Moreover, his concubine, whose name was Reumah, bore Tebah, Gaham, Tahash, and Maacah. (Gen 22:20–24)

The surprise in this text is the narrative aside in the middle, "Now Bethuel also became the father of Rebekah." This brief excursus ties the theme of Isaac's marriage to his survival of the ordeal of the Akedah and supports the suggestion of Hugh C. White that the Akedah can be understood as a rite of passage for Isaac that marks his "passage into independence and manhood."[20]

It is striking to find a similar linkage of marriage to the survival of an ordeal when Sarah commands Abraham to cast Hagar and her son Ishmael out of the house.[21] As scholars have noted, this tale has multiple parallels with the Akedah. (See table 1.)

Table 1

Akedah of Ishmael	*Akedah of Isaac*
21:17. God heard the voice of the boy; and the angel of God called to Hagar from heaven.	22:11. But the angel of the LORD called to [Abraham] from heaven.
18. Come lift up the boy and hold him fast with your hand, for I will make a great nation of him.	17. I will indeed bless you and I will make your offspring as numerous as the stars of heaven.
19. Then God opened her eyes and she saw a well of water. She went, and filled the skin with water, and gave the boy a drink.	13. And Abraham looked up and saw a ram caught in a thicket by its horns. Abraham went and took the ram and offered it up as a burnt offering instead of his son.
20. God was with the boy, and he grew up; he lived in the wilderness, and became an expert with the bow. 21. He lived in the wilderness of Paran; and his mother got a wife for him from the land of Egypt.	20. Now after these things it was told Abraham, "Milcah also has borne children to your brother Nahor: 21. Uz the first born, . . . 22. . . . Pildash, Jidlaph, and Bethuel." 23. Bethuel became the father of Rebekah.

In each story there are four distinct movements: (1) an angel calls out just when the child is about to die, (2) the promise is repeated, (3) the means of deliverance are revealed, and (4) the child is prepared for marriage. The fact that both of these narratives end with references to marriage cannot be accidental. In Ishmael's case we learn of the fact that his mother secured him a wife from Egypt, whereas with Isaac we are pointed forward two chapters to the story of Abraham sending his servant back to Aram to secure a bride for his son from the household of Nahor, his brother.

I might mention one other theme that links the two stories. The ordeal in both cases is set in motion by a journey. As we have seen, the ordeal that Tobias will undergo is also linked to a journey. The danger of the trip itself is emphasized right from the start when Tobit commands his son to find a companion for the trip who will know the way. As luck would have it, Tobias bumps into and hires a man who goes by the name Azariah, but who in fact is none other than the archangel Raphael. Things take an ominous turn when Tobias learns from Raphael that the house they will stay at in Ecbatana belongs to Raguel and Edna, the parents of Sarah. "[Raguel] has no male heir and no daughter except Sarah only, and you, as next of kin to her, have before all other men a hereditary claim on her.[22] Also it is right for you to inherit her father's possessions. Moreover, the girl is very sensible, brave, and very beautiful, and her father is a good man" (Tob 6:12). One might imagine that this is a stroke of luck of such proportions (single, wealthy, sensible, and beautiful to boot!) that Tobias will leap at the possibility of acquiring such a bride. Yet, like Ishmael and Isaac, the bride will not be his until he has successfully completed his own ordeal. Sarah, it turns out, is not quite the lucky find that she might appear. Tobias responds to Raphael's proposal thus:

> Brother Azariah, I have heard that she already has been married to seven husbands and they died in the bridal chamber. On the night when they went in to her, they would die. I have heard people saying that it was a demon that killed them. It does not harm her, but it kills anyone who desires to approach her. So now, since I am the only son my father has, I am afraid that I may die and bring my father's and mother's life down to their grave, grieving for me—and they have no other son to buy them. (Tob 6:14–15)

The link to the Joseph story is made quite evident when Tobias remarks that he fears his death would "bring my father's and mother's life down to their grave, grieving for me" (cf. Gen 37:35, 42:38, 44:29). The link to the Akedah is equally clear. Tobias is quick to emphasize that he is an *only* son; his parent's future rests totally on his fate.

THE INSTRUMENTS OF THE PASSION

There are also other linkages to the Akedah, as Tzvi Novick has shown.[23] First of all, when Tobit is attacked by the fish, Raphael tells Tobias to grasp it firmly and bring it ashore. "Cut open the fish and take out its gall, heart, and liver," Raphael instructs. "Keep them with you, but throw away the intestines. For its gall, heart, and liver are useful as medicine" (Tob 6:4b–5). Curiously, Tobias asks no questions about the purpose for these peculiar instructions. Instead, we learn that "after cutting open the fish, the young man gathered together the gall, heart, and liver; then he roasted and ate some of the fish, and kept some to be salted" (6:6a). Only later, when they are on the road again, does he pose the question: "And the two continued on their way together until they were near Media. Then the young man questioned the angel and said to him, 'Brother Azariah, what medicinal value is there in the fish's heart and liver, and in the gall?'" (6:6b–7). As Novick notes, the peculiar delay of the question is paralleled in the story of the Akedah. There we learn that Abraham "rose early in the morning, saddled his donkey, and took two of his young men with him, and his son Isaac; he cut the wood for the burnt offering, and set out and went to the place in the distance that God had shown him" (Gen 22:3). After Abraham spotted the designated mountain for the sacrifice on the third day of the journey, he told his servants, "'Stay here with the donkey; the boy and I will go over there; we will worship, and then we will come back to you.' Abraham then took the wood of the burnt offering and laid it on his son Isaac, and he himself carried the fire and the knife" (22:5–6a). Curiously, Isaac poses no question about the significance of this ominous act. Only later in the story, once they have begun to make their way to Mt. Moriah, does he do so: "And the two continued on their way together. Isaac said to his father Abraham, 'Father!' And he said, 'Here I am, my son.' He said, 'The fire and wood are here, but where is the lamb for a burnt offering?'" (22:6b–7; trans. altered).

But it is not just the structure of the two stories that is similar. There is also evidence of direct citation of Gen 22 in the book of Tobit. Novick notes that the phrase "the two of them walked on together" is rare in the Bible; it occurs just three times and two of them are found in

Gen 22. It is certainly significant that the very same phrase is found in the book of Tobit: "*And the two walked on together* until they were near Media. Then the young man questioned the angel." Furthermore, the phrase is used to introduce a question that would have been voiced more naturally earlier in the tale.

I might add one other observation to the points that Novick has made.[24] In the Akedah of both Ishmael and Isaac, the apparent victims are asked to carry the items that signaled the ordeal they would have to undergo. For Ishmael, it was the skin of water that would give out and threaten a death of dehydration in the desert, whereas for Isaac it was the wood that was to be used for the pyre on which he would be sacrificed. Tobias joins this grouping by being asked to carry the heart and liver of the fish that would be used during his life-threatening encounter on his wedding night with Sarah. This encounter was thought to be so dangerous that Raguel ordered his household servants to dig a grave as soon as Tobias made his way to his marital bed.

AKEDAH AS A TEST OF FAITH

Finally, I should mention the interpretation found in the book of *Jubilees* regarding the Akedah. Building on the fact that Genesis describes the command to sacrifice Isaac as a divine test ("After these things, God *tested* Abraham" [22:1]), the author of *Jubilees* turns to the book of Job to provide further narrative details. Let's compare the text of Genesis with the expansion that is found in *Jubilees*. (See table 2.)

In the first half of this essay we spent a considerable amount of time showing the ways in which the book of Tobit was dependent on Job for a significant number of features in its story line. The fact that the central scene in the entire narrative—the decision to send Tobias to retrieve the money left on deposit in Media—follows from a question about the integrity of Tobit's faith from his wife, Anna, is hardly imaginable apart from the model provided in the book of Job. We then proceeded to show that the sending of Tobias has significant parallels with the story of the binding of Isaac in the book of Genesis. The book of *Jubilees* is an important intertext from this period because of the way it also links the Akedah to the trial of Job.[25]

Table 2

Genesis	Jubilees
22:1a. After these things God tested Abraham.	17:15. During [this time], there were voices in heaven regarding Abraham, that he was faithful in everything that he had told him, (that) the Lord loved him, and (that) in every difficulty he was faithful. 16. Then Prince Mastema came and said before God: "Abraham does indeed love his son Isaac and finds him more pleasing than anyone else. Tell him to offer him as a sacrifice on an altar. Then you will see whether he performs this order and will know whether he is faithful in everything through which you test him." 17. Now the Lord was aware that Abraham was faithful in every difficulty which he had told him. . . . 18. In everything through which he tested him he was found faithful. He himself did not grow impatient, nor was he slow to act; for he was faithful and one who loved the Lord .
1b. He said to him, "Abraham!" And he said, "Here I am."	18:1. The Lord said to him: "Abraham, Abraham!" He replied: "Yes?"
2. He said, "Take your son, your only son Isaac, whom you love, and go to the land of Moriah. And offer him there as a burnt offering on one of the mountains that I shall show you."	2. He said to him: "Take your son, your dear one whom you love—Isaac—and go to a high land. Offer him on one of the mountains which I will show you."

Novick has noted another point of similarity between *Jubilees* and Tobit: both allocate an important role to an angelic intermediary as the occasion for the test. In *Jubilees* it is the heavenly adversary, Mastema, who proposes the test. In Tobit, the matter is more complicated. We have already seen that it is a virtuous angel, Raphael, who is sent to test

Tobit, but perhaps it is significant that the demon Asmodeus makes an appearance as the cause of Sarah's tragic loss of seven male suitors. The test that Raphael sets in motion includes the encounter Tobias must experience with this fallen divine being. The linkage between Tobit and *Jubilees* becomes very close indeed.[26]

TOBIT PASSES THE TEST

Yet, as important as these parallels between Tobit and *Jubilees* are, they will add up to little if we don't tie them back to our central theme: the testing of Tobit's faith that began when he was struck blind. Given the linkages we have already established between Tobias's journey, the Akedah, the test of Tobit's faith, and the book of Job, I would contend that Tobit's decision to send his son on that fateful journey constitutes the completion of the test that Raphael set in motion.

We can put a bit more flesh on this comparison by tending to the words Tobit uses in what he thinks is his last opportunity to instruct his son in the ways of Torah. As we have noted, the center of the Torah for Tobit and the author of the book is the command to give alms which is formulated in terms that derive from the book of Proverbs: "[Give alms so that] you can lay a good treasure for yourself against the day of necessity. For almsgiving delivers from death and keeps you from going into the Darkness" (Tob 4:9–10). If we were to view this statement from the perspective of the last chapter of Tobit, its meaning would be clear. The one who is generous will, in the end, prosper. The book provides us with a classic narrative embodiment of the central claim of the book of Deuteronomy. But if we bracket the conclusion of the book for a moment and attend to Tobit's Torah instruction in its own context, it is anything but a simple recycling of Deuteronomy. Tobit transmits this piece of wisdom to his son with the full knowledge that its truth has not been reflected in his own life. The irony is breathtaking, and it is crucial to appreciate its full depth.

In order to appreciate the immensity of the contradiction, let's compare what Tobit says about almsgiving with what he says about his own life. In his paraphrase of Proverbs 10:2, Tobit not only asserts that almsgiving is a means of accumulating a heavenly treasury: he adds that this treasury will not only deliver one from death but that it will "keep you from going into the Darkness." Yet, just one chapter later when he hears Raphael's friendly words, "Joyous greetings to you!" he responds most bitterly, "What joy is left for me any more? I am a man without eyesight: I cannot see the light of heaven, but lie in darkness like the dead who no longer see the light. Although still alive, I am among the dead. I hear people but I cannot see them" (Tob 5:10). The reader is arrested by the disparity. How can Tobit, a man who has lost his eyesight due to his generosity and who now "lie[s] in darkness like the dead," teach his son that giving alms will deliver one from death and descending into darkness? Could Tobit not face the truth and admit that the truth was just the reverse?

The only possible way to understand Tobit's instruction is to presume that Tobit believes that although this piece of wisdom did not hold true within the temporal constraints of his own life, it will be vindicated in the future, most likely in the life of his son. There is a reason that the wisdom tradition held that only the elderly can truly be sages. You need the long view to put the events of life in their proper perspective. Sometimes not even one lifespan is sufficient; evidence of God's providence often requires a couple generations to pass. This is perhaps hinted at in a wisdom psalm that says: "I have been young and now am old, yet I have not seen the righteous forsaken, that is, their children begging bread. They are ever giving liberally and lending, and their children held to be blessed" (Ps 37:25–26).[27]

If we presume that Tobit has understood our proverb in this way and thus can convey its teaching in good conscience to his son, then the question naturally arises: how is Tobias to fulfill this commandment if he remains in penury? The only conceivable answer is to send his son to Media to collect the money he had left on deposit. Yet this is a radical act, for sending his son on a journey such as this is fraught with great risk. Anna appears to have sized up the situation in a far more rational manner. When Raphael and Tobias are about to embark on their journey, Tobit wishes them well but Anna begins to weep and cries out: "Why is it that you have sent our child away? Is he not the staff of our hand as he goes in and out before us? Do not heap money upon money, but let it be a ransom for our child. For the life that is given to us by the

Lord is enough for us" (Tob 5:18–19). Rather than putting their only child at risk, Anna is willing to forgo a vocation of charity, exchanging the privilege of wealth for a much lower standard of living.

In making such a proposal, Anna shows herself to be a prudent woman. In the ordinary course of human affairs it would be difficult to find fault with her reasoning. The health of an only child would seem to trump the demands of a (voluntary?) commandment. But risks such as the one that Tobit has proposed are what differentiate the heroes of faith in the Bible from ordinary folks.

Consider for a moment the two Moabite women, Orpah and Ruth. Both had been married to the sons of the Judahite, Naomi. Tragically, Naomi's husband and her two sons die, leaving all three women childless. For Naomi there is little point in remarrying because she is near the end of her childbearing years. Since agricultural conditions have improved in Judah, Naomi decides to return home. The two Moabite women are now in a quandary. What should they do in order to maximize their chances of finding a new husband? At first they both decide to follow Naomi on her trek back to Bethlehem, but Naomi finds this decision ill advised. "Go back," she urges, "each of you to your mother's house.... The Lord grant that you may find security, each of you in the house of your husband" (Ruth 1:8–9). But both daughters are unmoved by this plea and remain steadfast in their desire to migrate to Judah. Naomi must redouble her rhetorical efforts. "Turn back, my daughters," she exclaims,

> Go your way, for I am too old to have a husband. Even if I thought there was hope for me, even if I should have a husband tonight and bear sons, would you then wait until they were grown? Would you then refrain from marrying? No, my daughters, it has been far more bitter for me than for you, because the hand of the Lord has turned against me. (1:12–13)

After this second intervention, Orpah decides to return home, but Ruth remains steadfast in her desire to accompany Naomi on her journey. As commentators have long noted, behind Orpah's decision to return home lies a considerable degree of wisdom. In the ancient world, the chances of finding a spouse would be immeasurably greater within the confines of one's home village where parents and family members could assist in securing a mate. Naomi is altruistic in the very best sense of the word when she urges her daughters-in-law to remain in Moab. (Conversion, we must remember, was not a valued commodity at this time.) And there was not just the impediment of these societal variables to consider, for as Naomi notes, her own God has abandoned her ("the hand of the LORD has turned against me"). Why would Orpah or Ruth want to leave the comforts of their homeland in order to take a chance on a deity who had so heartlessly spurned Naomi?[28]

The author of the book of Ruth has set the situation up this way in order to accentuate the supernatural dimension of Ruth's decision to enter the land of Israel. By painting Orpah's choice to remain in Moab as eminently reasonable, the decision of Ruth to go up to land of Israel is put on a plane that is almost without parallel. Boaz acknowledges this fact when he meets Ruth for the first time. After Ruth had expressed her surprise that such a notable citizen as Boaz would take an interest in a lowly maiden such as herself, Boaz declares:

> All that you have done for your mother-in-law since the death of your husband has been fully told me, and how you left your father and mother and your native land and came to a people that you did not know before. May the LORD reward you for your deeds, and may you have a full reward from the LORD, the God of Israel, under whose wings you have come for refuge. (2:11–12)

What is striking about these words is the way in which they are little more than a verbal recycling of what God said to Abraham back in Gen 12. For that first patriarch was also one who left his parents and native land to set out for a land he had not known before. In return for the great risk he undertook to follow the command of a God who had not appeared to him before, Abraham was promised extraordinary things. And just so for Ruth. Though Boaz's words are not a promise of great things to come—after all, he is not God and has no such power—they are more like the words of a prayer that eventually achieve their aim. Ruth will find refuge under the wings of Boaz and will sire a son who will be part of the lineage of David himself. What the book of

Ruth adds to this picture, as Yair Zakovitch has shown, is a Joban dimension to Ruth's personal sacrifice. For certainly it is significant that Naomi has spoken of the fact that her God has made her life very bitter indeed, nearly to point of utter despondency. Yet, it is to this Joban God that Ruth wishes to attach herself. The reward that she will receive in the end is not based on any self-serving calculation—as if she had said: "because the God of Israel is the one true God, he will certainly reward my virtue in singling Him out for worship"—but is rather a desire to attach herself to Naomi and her God no matter what the future might portend. It is this selfless act that Boaz acknowledges and that God, in the end, rewards in a prodigal fashion.

If we return to the book of Tobit with all of this in mind, we can grasp more fully the nature of Anna's fears about parting with her son. Like Orpah, she takes the reasonable position. Her maternal worries hardly condemn her. Quite the reverse, they win our admiration. Her worries are, however, the necessary barometer against which we can measure the faith of Tobit: a faith that answers the test that Raphael had been charged with initiating and that was mediated by the remonstration of Anna herself: What are the results of your charity and righteousness? The fact that you have failed has become well known within the village. Had Tobit been satisfied with the logic of Anna's argument against sending Tobias to Media, not only would he have died a blind man but his son would have been deprived of marriage with Sarah and the many children and extraordinary wealth that came with it.

— We have traced a number of threads in this essay and it is time to make sure they have been woven into a suitable fabric. At issue when we began was the question of whether Tobit should be classified as a novella that inscribes within its story form the basic theological message of the book of Deuteronomy. At one level, the answer has to be yes. Tobit cleaves to the commandments and by the end of the tale we can see that the payoff is enormous. But the danger of attending to this aspect of the book alone is that we may fail to appreciate the significance of the most important event in the entire story: Tobit's decision to send Tobias on a journey to Media to retrieve the money that was left on deposit there. My central claim has been that this decision was fraught with terrible risk and it was precisely this risk that revealed the supreme faith Tobit had in the power of the commandments God had bequeathed to Israel. Tobit had come to see that his obedience to Torah was not going to be rewarded within the context of his own life, a point driven home by the biting question his wife, Anna, posed after he had been struck blind by God: "Where are the fruits of your charitable deeds?" Though Tobit's despair was made clear in his acerbic response to Raphael's greeting—"What joy is left for me anymore? I am a man without eyesight."—his persistent obedience in the face of such a trial was demonstrated in the instruction he gave had given his son, Tobias, just a moment earlier: "Almsgiving delivers from death and keeps you from going into the Darkness." This contradiction, we noted, creates a gap in our story that appears nearly unbridgeable. How could a man suffering in darkness as a "reward" for his charity continue to hold fast to the scriptural promise?

I suggested that the only way to make sense of the disparity was to presume that Tobit believed that although the commandment had not worked out in the course of his own life, this piece of divine teaching would be vindicated in the life of his son. And so Tobit passes the terrible Joban test to which he had been subjected. He will continue to serve his God for naught, that is, with no hope for a reward in the context of his own life. But it is precisely the faith he has in the eventual fulfillment of the divine promise that not only proves the mettle of his own devotion to the God of Israel but also enables the reward for that faith to take shape. Though the sending of Tobias on this journey would be considered foolhardy according to any sort of rational accounting (so Anna and, by extension, Orpah), in light of the divine promise there were supernatural reasons to believe it was the sole logical course worth following. Like Abraham and Ruth before him, Tobit makes a decision whose wisdom, in the moment of its being made, can be appreciated only in retrospect. The difference between a madman and a saint is narrow indeed, as the tradition has always taught. It is the appreciation of the Akedah-like character of the fateful fourth chapter of this book that allows us to see how Tobit passes the Job-like test he must endure and why the labeling of this book as a Deuteronomic novella so badly misses the mark.

NOTES

A slightly different version of this essay will appear in my book *Charity: The Place of the Poor in the Biblical Tradition* (New Haven: Yale University Press, 2013).

1. Jon D. Levenson, *Death and Resurrection of the Beloved Son: The Transformation of Child Sacrifice in Judaism and Christianity* (New Haven: Yale University Press, 1993).

2. Levenson notes in his preface that he first conceived of his book on the sacrifice of Isaac while teaching a course on the Joseph story. There it occurred to him "that the loss and restoration of Joseph to his father constitutes an analogy in narrative to the several Israelite rituals that substitute for the literal sacrifice of the first-born son.... Further reflection led to the conclusion that the analogy holds for other important sons in Genesis as well—Ishmael, Isaac, and Jacob—and for the man the Church believes to be the son of God" (*Death and Resurrection*, ix).

3. *Jewish Literature between the Bible and the Mishnah* (Philadelphia: Fortress Press, 1981), 33–35. See also R. Bauckham, "Tobit as Parable for the Exiles of Northern Israel," in *Studies in the Book of Tobit: A Multidisciplinary Approach* (ed. M. Bredin; London: T and T Clark, 2006), 140–64.

4. I must confess that I do not believe this to be an accurate description of the theology of the Deuteronomist, but here is not the place to make that argument. Given that this assessment is not only accepted by most scholars, but also applied to the book of Tobit, I will work within the parameters of this assumption for the purposes of this chapter.

5. For a general overview see Joseph Fitzmyer, *Tobit* (CEJL; Berlin: Walter de Gruyter, 2003), 47. Also worth consulting: A. A. Di Lella, "The Deuteronomic Background of the Farewell Discourse in Tob 14:3–11," *CBQ* 41 (1979): 380–89; Will Soll, "Misfortune and Exile in Tobit: The Juncture of a Fairy Tale Source and Deuteronomic Theology," *CBQ* 51 (1989): 209–31; Micah Kiel, "Tobit's Theological Blindness," *CBQ* 73 (2011): 281–98.

6. The links were already noticed by Jerome and accentuated in his Vulgate translation. On this see V. Skemp, *The Vulgate of Tobit Compared with Other Ancient Witnesses* (SBLDS 180; Atlanta: Society of Biblical Literature, 2000), 86–87, 93. But many moderns have noted the same thing. For example, see Robert Pfeiffer, *History of New Testament Times: With an Introduction to the Apocrypha* (New York: Harper and Bros., 1949), 267–68; A. Portier-Young, "'Eyes to the Blind': A Dialogue Between Tobit and Job," in *Intertextual Studies in Ben Sira and Tobit: Essays in Honor of Alexander A. Di Lella* (ed. J. Corley and V. Skemp; Washington, D.C.: Catholic Biblical Association of America, 2005), 14–27. See D. Dimant, "Use and Interpretation of Mikra in the Apocrypha and Pseudepigrapha," in *Mikra* (ed., M. J. Moulder and H. Sysling; CRINT, 2/1; Philadelphia: Fortress

Press, 1988), 417–19, and her more focused and detailed study, "The Bible through a Prism: The Wife of Job and the Wife of Tobit," [Hebrew] *Shnaton* 17 (2007): 201–11.

7. All biblical citations are from the New Revised Standard Version.

8. This exchange looks very similar to the story of Abraham's near-sacrifice of Isaac. In addition to the similarity to the angel's address to Abraham at the denouement of the episode (Tob 2:11), compare Isaac's exchange with his father when he notes the fire and the wood but no animal for a burnt offering: "Isaac said to his father Abraham, 'Father!' And he said, 'Here I am, my son'" (Gen 22:7). This parallel is not at all surprising in light of the other parallels we shall document below.

9. On the matter of Tobit's impurity after handling a corpse, see Beate Ego, "Death and Burial in the Tobit Narration in the Context of the Old Testament Tradition," in *The Human Body in Death and Resurrection* (ed. T. Nicklas, F. Reiterer, and J. Verheyden; Berlin: Walter de Gruyter, 2009), 89.

10. Joseph Fitzmyer, for example, asserts that the trial certainly centered around Tobit's blindness, but this takes place long before the arrival of Raphael (*Tobit*, 295). This leads him to wonder why Tobit had to be tested again and what that particular test would have amounted to. In my opinion, Fitzmyer has too narrowly centered his focus on the moment of blindness. The larger problem is the issue of theodicy that the blindness sets up. If almsgiving is to deliver one from the realm of darkness then why has it, in this instance, led to darkness? The larger problem, as I see it, is whether Tobit will stick to the truth of that piece of divine teaching or not. And to find the answer to that question, the matter of the sending of the son on the journey (and finding the requisite companion for the journey) becomes central.

11. Dimant does a very good job of assembling the parallels between Tobit and Job ("Use and Interpretation of Mikra").

12. One question that goes unanswered is *who* exactly orchestrates the test that Tobit must undergo. The text says that Raphael was the one sent to initiate the test: "And that time when you did not hesitate to get up and leave your dinner to go and bury the dead, I was sent to you to test you. And at the same time God sent me to heal you" (Tob 12:13–14a). Are we to presume that the angel of healing is the one responsible for Tobit's blindness? It seems that the shorter Greek text objected to such a view and restructured the verse to accentuate the beneficent characteristics of Raphael (italics mark the differences): "And that time when you did not hesitate to get up and leave your dinner and go and bury the dead, *your good deed did not escape me, but I was with you*. God sent me at the same time to heal you." The Vulgate solves the problem by keeping the idea of a test but leaving its originator unmarked: "And when you left your dinner and hid the dead by day in your house and buried them at night, I offered your prayer

to the Lord; because you were acceptable to God, it was necessary that temptation should test you." Clearly at some level, we must affirm that God allows the sparrows to blind Tobit. Whether our author understood Raphael as directly responsible for this test remains unanswered.

13. Dimant ("The Bible through a Prism") has observed an important development in the LXX of Job. Where as the MT has Job's wife rebuke him with few words and little explanation—"Then his wife said to him, 'Do you still persist in your integrity? Curse God, and die'" (2:9)—the LXX tells us much more (translation from *NETS*):

> Then after a long time had passed, his wife said to him, "How long will you persist and say, [9a] 'Look, I will hang on a little longer, while I wait for the hope of my deliverance?' [9b] For look, your legacy has vanished from the earth—sons and daughters, my womb's birth pangs and labors, for whom I wearied myself with hardships in vain. [9c] And you? You sit in the refuse of worms as you spend the night in the open air. [9d] *As for me, I am one that wanders about and a hired servant—from place to place and house to house, waiting for when the sun will set, so I can rest from the distresses and griefs that now beset me.* [9e] Now say some word to the Lord and die!"

According to the LXX, Job's physical illness required his wife to hire herself out as a day laborer, a motif very similar to what we see in Tobit (2:11–12). Dimant, however, goes too far when she asserts that the author of Tobit presumes we know one other detail from the *Testament of Job*, that is, that Job's wife supplemented her wages with sexual favors. In Dimant's view, that is the reason the author of Tobit has Anna bring home a goat as an extra wage from her employers. It is meant to recall the goat that Tamar receives from Jacob in exchange for sexual favors. As will become clear in my discussion below, I don't think that the book of Tobit shares this low opinion of Anna.

14. See Paul Deselaers, *Das Buch Tobit: Studien zu seiner Entstehung, Komposition, und Theologie* (Göttingen: Vandenhoek und Ruprecht, 1982), 27.

15. It is surprising to me how many readers of the book have missed this simple fact. In spite of the fact that everyone concedes that the command to give alms is a, if not the, major theme of the book. S. Van Den Eynde, for example, understands the trip to collect the deposit to be the result of Tobit's wish to "settle his financial affairs" before he dies ("One Journey and One Journey Makes Three: The Impact of the Readers' Knowledge in the Book of Tobit," *ZAW* 117 [2005]: 275). Would Tobit expose his son to such risk simply to put his books in order? That seems hard to imagine.

16. Jerome brings the matter into even sharper focus. Whereas the Greek simply records that Tobit had "left ten talents of silver in trust with Gabael" (Tob

1:14), the Vulgate records that Tobit "saw Gabelus [=Gabael] in want, a man of his own tribe, and taking a note from his hand, he gave the aforesaid sum of money." Because Gabael is thought to be a man stricken by poverty, the money that is given him is a loan and, as such, a form of charity which God has promised to reward: "He who assists the poor makes a loan to God and He shall surely repay him [Prov 19:17]." On this view, the sending of the son is nothing other than an act of faith in the promises of God.

17. So the logic of the conclusion of Tobit's testamentary instruction. After reiterating the matter of the deposit left with Gabael he says, "Do not be afraid, my son, because we have become poor. You have great wealth if you fear God and flee from every sin and do what is good in the sight of the LORD your God" (Tob 4:20–21).

18. Consider for example the institution of levirate marriage (Gen 38, Deut 25:5–10, and the book of Ruth), which mandates that a man have intercourse with the widow of his deceased brother if that marriage had produced no offspring in order to ensure that his brother's name endures.

19. Levenson observes that Jacob cannot abide the thought that his beloved Benjamin would die and thus will not at first accept the risk involved in sending him on the journey. The problem of course is that the famine that has gripped Egypt and spread through the world has threatened the survival of the chosen family. "[O]nly if life is risked," Levenson writes, "can it continue.... The irony is that when Jacob does finally surrender his beloved son Benjamin, he receives anew not only Simeon, but even Joseph, whom he has given up for dead. His courageous willingness to expose Benjamin to the risk of death restores Joseph to him alive" (*Death and Resurrection*, 162).

20. "The Initiation Legend of Isaac," *ZAW* 91 (1979): 17.

21. See the analysis of Levenson, *Death and Resurrection*, 104–110; and U. Simon, *Seek Peace and Pursue It: Topical Issues in the Light of the Bible, the Bible in the Light of Topical Issues* [Hebrew] (Tel Aviv: Yediot Achronot, 2002).

22. The fact that Tobias has a hereditary claim that precedes all other suitors recalls a similar theme in the book of Ruth (see 3:12). We will return to the similarities between Ruth and Tobit below.

23. Tzvi Novick, "Biblicized Narrative: On Tobit and Genesis 22," *JBL* 126 (2007): 755–64.

24. I should note that on page 757 n. 5, Novick also notes the similarity of Isaac's worry over what he must carry to the situation of Tobias. I do not wish to overstate my own originality.

25. The linkage between Job and Gen 22 is also evident in a text from Qumran. On the parallels between the two see J. VanderKam, "The Aqedah, *Jubilees*, and PseudoJubilees," in *The Quest for Context and Meaning: Studies in Biblical Intertextuality in Honor of James A. Sanders* (ed. C. Evans and S. Talmon;

Leiden: Brill, 1997), 241–61; J. Fitzmyer, "The Sacrifice of Isaac in Qumran Literature," *Bib* 83 (2002): 211–29; and J. Kugel, "Exegetical Notes on 4Q225 'PseudoJubilees,'" *DSD* 13 (2006): 73–98. On the roles of angels at the Akedah in particular, see M. Bernstein, "Angels at the Aqedah," *DSD* 7 (2000): 263–91.

26. Novick has noted that the name Asmodeus "is almost an anagram of the name Mastema" (760). If that is the case, then Asmodeus's character in the book of Tobit may be grounded in the figure of Mastema.

27. I have made some changes to the NRSV. It is also worth noting that even though punishment often skips a generation, it is the Bible's view that justice has been done.

28. On the Joban dimensions of Naomi's plight, see Y. Zakovitch, *Ruth: Introduction and Commentary* [Hebrew] (Mikra le-Yisrael; Tel Aviv: Am Oved, 1990).

CHAPTER 7

Divine Sovereignty and the Election of Israel in the Wisdom of Ben Sira

GREG SCHMIDT GOERING

In the Second Temple period, the notion of election as divine favor toward Israel became combined increasingly with notions of dualism and predestination. We can observe such a merger especially in those texts which combine wisdom and apocalypticism. While outside forces such as Zoroastrianism likely influenced dualistic notions within Jewish groups, the older Israelite wisdom tradition also classified human beings into two groups. According to the sapiential tradition, a person was either wise or foolish. This binary anthropology was easily combined with the idea that God favors some over others. In addition, many Second Temple Jewish groups came to see God's mastery over the world in increasingly absolute terms. Such strong notions of divine sovereignty led some Jews to posit that God had predetermined their election.

Divine Sovereignty and the Election of Israel

Like his predecessors in the Israelite wisdom tradition, the second-century B.C.E. sage Ben Sira also categorizes human beings into two groups. And despite the sage's nonapocalyptic framework, many scholars have assumed that he sees the world in dualistic terms. As I shall argue in this essay, however, Ben Sira distinguishes human beings based on a nondualistic understanding of election. His view of election emerges from his theology of creation, in which Yhwh, as wise and sovereign creator, dispenses wisdom to whomever he chooses. Ben Sira's notion of divine sovereignty, however, stops short of absolute mastery, a fact that tempers his interpretation of God's favor toward Israel. It is with great pleasure that I dedicate this essay to Jon Levenson, whose work has contributed greatly to understanding biblical notions of both election and divine mastery.[1]

WISDOM'S UNEVEN DISTRIBUTION

In the poem that opens his book, Ben Sira describes two apportionments of wisdom to humans:

> 1:9b [Yhwh] poured out [wisdom] upon all his works,
> 10a among all flesh according to his largess,
> b and he lavished her upon those who love him.[2] (Sir 1:9b–10b)

According to Ben Sira, Yhwh "poured out" a first allocation of wisdom upon *all* of his creations, including all human beings (vv. 9b, 10a). The deity then "lavished" a second allotment upon a *particular subset of humanity*, referred to here as "those who love him" (10b).

Ben Sira mentions these two apportionments of divine wisdom at the end of this opening poem, in which the sage recounts wisdom's origin. In the poem as a whole, he affirms that all wisdom originates with God (v. 1). Ben Sira considers Wisdom herself to be a creation of God, the first of all divine creations (v. 4; cf. v. 9a). In order to emphasize God's exceeding wisdom, Ben Sira uses a series of rhetorical questions (vv. 2, 3, 6), asking, for example, who can fathom "the height of heaven, the breadth of the earth, the abyss, and wisdom" (v. 3). The presumed answer to all these rhetorical questions is, of course, no one—except for God. As the original possessor of wisdom, God can dispense wisdom to whomever he chooses, and in whatever amount he chooses.

Ben Sira's language suggests that he views these two apportionments of wisdom to be uneven. Upon all his creations and upon all humanity Yhwh dispensed (ἐξέχεεν, literally "poured out [like water]") wisdom in a calculated amount. Thus, according to Ben Sira, all human beings receive a certain measure of wisdom by virtue of their created status. In the next colon, however, he indicates that God has granted wisdom profusely (ἐχορήγησεν, literally "furnished abundantly") to "those who love him." While the former verb suggests a deliberate, measured pouring of wisdom on all creation equally, the latter indicates that Ben Sira had in view a more bountiful outpouring of wisdom upon a select group of persons.

Ben Sira does not portray these two sets of human beings—"all flesh" and "those who love him"—along the lines of the traditional wisdom dichotomies between the foolish and the wise or the wicked and the righteous. Indeed, the second group is clearly a subset of the first, a select group of persons who also partake in the general outpouring of divine wisdom mentioned in Sir 1:9b–10a. For whatever reason, this second group receives an extra measure of divine wisdom.

Ben Sira's reference to these two apportionments of wisdom in a creation poem at the very beginning of his book suggests a connection between the uneven allocation of wisdom and Ben Sira's theology of creation. Before returning to this point, however, I shall describe Ben Sira's understanding of creation and then analyze further Ben Sira's view of the distinction that Yhwh draws in the human realm.

CREATION AND DIVINE SOVEREIGNTY

Johannes Marböck and Randal Argall describe the central feature of Ben Sira's creation theology as a "double aspect of reality" or "doctrine of opposites." Both Marböck and Argall ground their interpretation of Ben Sira's creation theology in Sir 33:7–15—a passage about which I will say more below—and suggest that Ben Sira observes in creation a system of polarities. According to Marböck, these polarities "form a structure of the whole creation." Moreover, this dual aspect observable in all God's works "is for Ben Sira a means for the discovery and explanation of the world order."[3] Like Marböck, Argall considers the "built-in polarity" something that is observable in the natural world. Argall defines the "doctrine of opposites" as the notion that "every element in creation obeys God and carries out the purpose for which it was designed, either good or bad."[4] I shall argue, however, that a doctrine of opposites does not lie at the heart of Ben Sira's view of the world.

The extended poem in Sir 42:15–43:33 is arguably the most important passage for understanding Ben Sira's creation theology, and thus I will focus my analysis on this passage. The poem contains four stanzas. The first introduces the entire hymn (42:15–25). The second surveys heavenly marvels (43:1–12), and the third reviews various phenomena that occur beneath the celestial realm (43:13–26). The fourth stanza concludes the hymn on a note of praise (43:27–33).

The Sovereignty of Yhwh

The poem takes the literary form of a hymn of praise, and stanza 1 expresses the hymn's subject as "the works of God" (42:15a), which is Ben Sira's way of referring to the created world. This phrasing of the hymn's subject indicates Ben Sira's premise that Yhwh is the creator of all. Indeed, the final verse of the entire hymn affirms that "Yhwh made *all* things" (43:33a). Ben Sira frequently employs the hymnic genre for didactic ends, and Argall argues that Ben Sira's didactic purpose in the present hymn is to illustrate a doctrine of opposites.[5] My analysis, however, will demonstrate that the doctrine of opposites is not in fact the main didactic point for the sage. Rather, the central idea communicated through the hymn is Yhwh's sovereignty over his creation.

Leo Perdue observes that the primary metaphor used by Ben Sira for Yhwh's creation of the world is that of the word.[6] Indeed, immediately after stating the subject of his poem, Ben Sira recounts that these works of creation came about "by Yhwh's word" (42:15c). Ben Sira elsewhere associates the creation of wisdom, Yhwh's first work, with the divine word—she emanated "from the mouth of the Most High" (24:3a).

The metaphor of the divine word, however, extends beyond Yhwh's initial creative activity. For example, "through his command" the moon "maintains its prescribed place" in the heavens (43:10a) and the waters stand "as in a heap" (39:17a; cf. Exod 15:8; Ps 33:6–9). "His word" controls the various winds (43:16b–17b). "His rebuke" guides the lightning as well as meteors (43:13). In Sir 43:26b, Ben Sira portrays individual elements of nature as messengers that fulfill Yhwh's will "at his commands." Once arranged in creation, Yhwh's works do not disobey "his word" (16:28; cf. 39:31). In Ben Sira's view, then, Yhwh also governs the *functioning* of nature by means of his word.

Based on this view of Yhwh's "continuing governance of reality," Perdue describes the purpose of Ben Sira's creation theology as the establishment of God's "providence."[7] The term "providence" connotes a divine engagement in history, but describes less well the assumption of divine mastery in the primordium. Thus, the royal term "sovereignty" better describes the core of Ben Sira's creation theology, both in its primordial and historical dimensions.

Wisdom's origin in the mouth of Yhwh indicates the close connection in Ben Sira's mind between wisdom and word. In connecting word and wisdom, Ben Sira combines two distinct creation traditions, both known from the Hebrew Bible. First, his notion of creation through the divine word parallels the Priestly account in Gen 1:1–2:4a. Second, his idea that Yhwh created the world "in wisdom" corresponds to Prov 3:19 (cf. Prov 8:30; Ps 104:24). Moreover, Ben Sira's creation theology merges these traditions of creation (Sir 1:5a, 24:3a). Together, the images of creation through divine word and divine wisdom serve Ben Sira's larger didactic purpose in his hymns on creation: the establishment of Yhwh's sovereignty.

The rhetorical questions contained in the conclusion to stanza 1 point to the beauty and awe-inspiring quality of God's works:

22a   Are not all his works desirable,
   b   delightful to gaze upon, and a sight to see?
25b   …who can be sated by gazing at their splendor? (Sir 42:22, 25b)

These cola set the stage for Ben Sira's overall discursive design of Sir 42:15–43:33. The sage aspires to demonstrate Yhwh's sovereignty over nature by employing a two-part rhetorical strategy of "amplification." First, he strives to instill marvel in his reader at the splendor of creation. Then he shifts the focus from the works of creation to the creator himself, in order to suggest how much more awe-inspiring Yhwh must be.

As a poetic commentary on Gen 1:14–19, stanza 2 surveys several heavenly phenomena: the sun, the moon, and the rainbow. Ben Sira describes the sun as an "awesome ($nôrā^{\flat}$) instrument" (v. 2b) that "scorches the surface of the earth" like a "blazing furnace" with its "fiery tongue." Humans can scarcely tolerate its intense heat and their "eyes are burned by its fire" (vv. 3–4). Ben Sira affirms that it is God who has made such a marvelous body:

> Great indeed is Yhwh who made it,
> at whose orders it urges on its steeds. (Sir 43:5ab)

This last bicolon supplies the point of Ben Sira's portrayal of the sun. While the sun is awesome in its display of power, it remains merely a creation of Yhwh, who must be more awesome still. For Ben Sira, the moon's magnificence derives from its role in regulating the religious calendar. The moon "makes the seasons travel" and determines the "sacred times" and the "pilgrimage feasts" (43:6–7). From the manner in which it changes throughout the month, the moon, like the sun, is described as "awesome" ($nôrā^{\flat}$; 43:8ab). Like the sun, the moon acts not by its own impulses, but by the command (literally "word," 43:10a) of Yhwh. In the closing cola of the stanza, Ben Sira turns to consider the splendor of the rainbow, which "the hand of God has stretched out" across the celestial vault. The "glory" of the rainbow, Ben Sira suggests, like the awesomeness of the sun and the moon before it, should lead the observer to "bless the one who made it" (43:11–12). Observation of these three heavenly phenomena, then, leads to a recognition of their awesomeness or splendor. Since Yhwh created them, and still controls them by his word, Ben Sira concludes, the creator must be greater still than his works.

A Doctrine of Opposites?

My reading of stanza 2 thus identifies its central theme as Yhwh's sovereignty. Argall, however, reads the portrayal of the sun and the moon in Sir 43:1–12 as a statement on the doctrine of opposites. In Argall's translation, Ben Sira calls the sun a "fearful (*nôrāʾ*) instrument" (Sir 43:2b). Argall interprets the scorching, blazing, fiery-tongued sun as "an instrument of wrath" that "has a punishing capacity as it carries out the word of the Lord."[8] Argall does not offer any positive role for the sun to complement its negative role.

In Argall's doctrine of opposites, the moon plays both a positive and a negative role. Positively, at least for the pious, the moon determines the religious festivals and sacred pilgrimages. Argall interprets the meteorological function of the moon to be both positive and negative. Sirach 43:8c describes the moon as "an army signal for the waterskins of the heights," that is, a military fire signal that controls the movements of an army, in this case the water-laden clouds. According to Argall, the resultant "rains can be either severe or gentle, they can curse or bless." To bolster his argument, he points to the fierce storms in stanza 3. In stanza 2, however, there is no hint that the rains resulting from the moon's direction are negative—or, for that matter, positive. Moreover, most of the meteorological phenomena in stanza 3 are directed by Yhwh, not by the moon. Only 43:22 does not mention the deity explicitly as the agent who rouses nature to act, and in this verse "dripping clouds" and "scattered dew"—not the moon—bring refreshment to a sun-scorched land.

Moreover, Argall's translation of *nôrāʾ* as "fearful" is misguided. Of the forty-five times that this Hebrew word occurs in the Bible, only seven times does it connote fright. More often, the term communicates the instilment of awe or reverence. Rather than portraying the sun, and to a certain extent the moon, as potential instruments of God's wrath, Ben Sira aims to demonstrate the awe-inspiring character of these heavenly creations. Additionally, Argall's recourse to the doctrine of opposites as an interpretive key for this passage fails to explain the role of the rainbow.

Divine Sovereignty and the Election of Israel

By showing the tremendous power and beauty of these celestial phenomena, Ben Sira attempts to inculcate in his reader an even greater appreciation for the majesty of Yhwh who created and controls the sun, the moon, and the rainbow. The real point is not how fierce the sun is or how the wise person can avoid its intense heat, as Argall suggests. Rather, Ben Sira is making a statement about God's status as creator and his sovereignty over nature.

Yhwh as Divine Warrior and Storm God

While Ben Sira portrays Yhwh's mastery over heavenly marvels in stanza 2, in stanza 3 he evokes the biblical motifs of the Divine Warrior and the storm god, in order to emphasize Yhwh's sovereignty over various natural phenomena that occur beneath the celestial realm. Sirach 43:13a–17b call to mind the theophany of the Divine Warrior:

13a		His rebuke marks a path for the lightning
	b	and directs meteors of judgment.
14a		For his own purpose he looses the storehouse
	b	and makes the clouds fly like birds of prey.
15a		His might strengthens the cloud-mass
	b	and chips off stones of hail.
17a		The sound of his thunder makes his earth writhe,
16a		and by his strength he shakes the mountains.
16b		His word causes reproach by means of the south wind,
17b		hurricane, whirlwind, and squall. (Sir 43:13a–17b)

In archaic biblical poetry, the Divine Warrior appears in the midst of a thunderstorm.[9] Thus, the older biblical materials already combine the Divine Warrior and storm god motifs to a certain extent. In this mythical motif that Israel adopted from traditions about the storm god Baal, Yhwh marches out to battle against an enemy (Hab 3:13–14). The clouds serve as Yhwh's battle chariot (Deut 33:26; Ps 18:10–13 = 2 Sam 22:10–13; Ps 68:5 [Eng. 4]). At Yhwh's presence, nature reacts: the earth trembles, the mountains quake, and the heavens pour down rain (Judg 5:4–5; cf. Hab 3:6; Ps 18:8 = 2 Sam 22:8; Ps 68:9 [Eng. 8]).

Natural phenomena are portrayed as attributes of the deity; a blast of wind, for instance, emanates from the deity's nostrils (Exod 15:8).

The vocabulary in the present passage from Ben Sira overlaps significantly with that of these Divine Warrior theophanies. Yhwh's "rebuke" (Sir 43:13a; cf. Ps 18:16 = 2 Sam 22:16) affects natural events. "Hail" (Sir 43:15b; cf. Ps 18:13), "thunder" (Sir 43:17a; cf. Ps 18:14 = 2 Sam 22:14), and "lightning" (Sir 43:13a; cf. Ps 18:15 = 2 Sam 22:15) serve as Yhwh's weapons. And Yhwh enters battle with an army that acts at his "command" (Sir 43:16b; cf. Deut 33:3).

Ben Sira's appropriation of the Divine Warrior theophany, however, exhibits some important differences from the original motif. For one, in Sirach there is no identifiable enemy against whom Yhwh fights. Second, Ben Sira plays down the frightful reaction of nature to the appearance of the deity. In Hab 3:10, for example, the mountains writhe at Yhwh's presence. In contrast, in Sir 43:17a, 16a, Yhwh *causes* the earth to writhe and the mountains to shake. Thus, these verses in Sirach do not indicate nature's fearful response to the appearance of the deity but rather his control over the natural elements.

In the next section of stanza 3, Argall perceives again a duality of punishment and blessing.

17c	He causes his snow to fly like birds,
17d	and like a locust swarm it settles in its descent.
18a	Its white form puzzles the eyes,
b	and the mind is astonished at its falling.
19a	Even frost he pours out like salt;
b	it shines like blackberry blossoms.
20a	The cold north wind he brings back,
b	and he solidifies the water-spring like a clod.
c	Over every pool of standing water he spreads a crust,
d	and the reservoir clothes itself as though with breast armor.
21a	When he burns the mountain growth with drought
b	and the flowering pasture as though with flame,
22a	a dripping cloud heals everything,
b	and loosed dew fattens the parched land. (Sir 43:17c–22b)

Interpreting this passage through a doctrine of opposites, Argall suggests that Ben Sira portrays "the meteorology of the south wind as a 'bad thing'" and the "fearful capacity" of the snow and north wind "as a tool of judgment."[10] In the last two verses of the stanza, Argall counterposes "the sun as an instrument of wrath" with "the clouds and dew as instruments of blessing" (43:21–22).

It is true that theophany can be a source of both fright and beneficence. But here, in a demythologized appropriation of the Divine Warrior theophany, Ben Sira's intent is not to frighten. The wintry images in verses 17c–20d and the refreshing waters of verses 21–22 are not generally associated with the motif of the Divine Warrior. These lines—in which Ben Sira further illustrates Yhwh's direction of natural elements—contextualize the Divine Warrior theophany in a larger passage about Yhwh's sovereign control over nature, thus indicating how far Ben Sira has strayed from the original motif. Rather than frighten, the sage aims to instill in his reader awe at the great power of nature. Moreover, through his technique of amplification, Ben Sira suggests that because Yhwh created and controls nature, he deserves even greater awe and respect than that elicited by nature.

Divine Mastery Over Primordial Chaos

In the conclusion to stanza 3, Ben Sira evokes one other biblical motif—Yhwh's primordial battle against chaos (*Chaoskampf*). In Ben Sira's didactic hymn, this motif stresses Yhwh's sovereignty. Yet, the particular way in which he appropriates the *Chaoskampf* motif indicates that Yhwh's mastery falls short of being absolute.

> 23a He quiets Rahab by means of his plan,
> b and he plants islands in the deep.
> 24a Those who go down to the sea recount its extent;
> b when our ears hear, we are astounded.
> 25a Within are wonders, marvels of his handiwork,
> b living things of every kind, and Rahab's mighty ones.
> 26a On his account the messenger succeeds,
> b and at his commands it accomplishes [his] will.
> (Sir 43:23a–26b)

Three terms in succeeding cola—Rahab (23a; cf. 25b), the deep (*tĕhôm*, 23b; cf. 42:18a), and the sea (*yām*, 24a)—all allude to biblical texts that intimate some sort of battle between Yhwh and the chaotic primordial waters. In Job 26:12, 38:8–11; Pss 65:7–8 [Eng. 6–7], 74:12–17, 89:10–15 [Eng. 9–14], 93:1–4; and Prov 8:29, *yām* refers to the primordial sea, which Yhwh brought under control in the creation of the world. In Ps 104:6–9, *tĕhôm* designates the primordial ocean, whose boundaries Yhwh circumscribes at the creation of the world. In Ps 89:11 [Eng. 10] and Job 26:12 (cf. 9:13), Rahab appears as a sea monster defeated by Yhwh at the time of creation.

Biblical texts that portray Yhwh's primordial battle against chaos as a conflict with the sea or a sea monster vary in their adaptation of the combat myth. Jon Levenson's continuum offers a useful heuristic tool for locating a given text in relation to others. At one end of the continuum lies Ps 74:12–17, in which the eradication of chaos results in the creation of the world. Levenson refers to this pole as the "full-fledged combat myth of creation." At the other end of the continuum lies P's creation story in Gen 1:1–2:4a. There the primordial sea (*tĕhôm*) is also connected to creation (Gen 1:2), but, as John Day notes, in this passage "all thought of conflict has disappeared" and "a process of demythologization has taken place."[11] Levenson calls this pole "creation through the unchallenged magisterial word of God."[12]

Ben Sira's appropriation of the combat myth lies at some intermediate point between these two ends of the continuum. As in Gen 1:1–2:4a, Ben Sira's poem evinces a certain amount of demythologization. The primordial waters "deep" and "sea" have no personality in Ben Sira's hymn, although the sea monster Rahab and her minions (Sir 43:25b) remain animated living things. Unlike Gen 1:1–2:4a, however, there remains more than a hint of the original conflict. Yhwh is said to "quiet" Rahab by means of "his plan" (43:23a), that is, his wisdom. As an agent of chaos, the sea monster Rahab is tamed but not, as in Ps 74, destroyed. In this sense, Ben Sira's position lies close to that of Job 40:25–32 [Eng. 41:1–8], where God contains the sea monster (in this case Leviathan) for his own pleasure. As Levenson notes, in texts such as Job 40:25–32 [Eng. 41:1–8]—and I would add Sir 43:23–26—the basis of creation lies not in the eradication of chaos but in its "confinement."¹³ In other words, Ben Sira's creation theology highlights Yʜwʜ's mastery over creation but stops short of describing it as absolute.

Stanza 4 concludes the hymn and states Ben Sira's main didactic point: the surpassing awesomeness of Yʜwʜ.

> 28b   He is greater than all his works.
> 29a   Very, very awesome is Yʜwʜ. (Sir 43:28b–29a)

Ben Sira uses the same adjective that he used earlier of the sun and moon to describe Yʜwʜ, but adds "very, very" (v. 29a) for emphasis. In order to underscore Yʜwʜ's awesomeness, Ben Sira declares that more marvels exist beyond those he has described (27a, 30b, 32a), and that some wonders remain unknown to human beings (28a, 30d, 31ab). By shifting his focus in this stanza from the magnificence of the works that he recounted in the previous stanzas to the one who made them, Ben Sira amplifies the creator's greatness (28b). And the creator's surpassing greatness indicates his sovereignty, even if it is not absolute.

Thus far, I have shown that the central idea in Ben Sira's theology of creation is the sovereignty of Yʜwʜ. In order to bolster his argument, Ben Sira creatively appropriates several biblical motifs—the Divine Warrior, the storm god, and the primordial battle against chaos—and employs a rhetorical strategy of amplification. Ben Sira's appropriation of the *Chaoskampf* motif shows that he views Yʜwʜ's creation of the world not in terms of the absolute defeat of chaos, but as divine containment of the sea monster. Moreover, from this primary principle of Yʜwʜ's sovereignty, and the notion that he alone possesses all wisdom, the sage derives the idea that Yʜwʜ can dispense wisdom to whomever he pleases. Indeed, the closing colon of the creation hymn reiterates the idea that I first observed in Sir 1:9b–10b:

> 33a   For Yʜwʜ made all things,
>   b   and to the righteous he gave wisdom. (Sir 43:33)

This verse associates Yʜwʜ's status as creator of the world with an apportionment of divine wisdom to a select group of persons. Skehan and Di Lella interpret the final colon to mean that "God 'gives wisdom' *only* 'to those who fear him.'"[14] But in light of other passages in which Ben Sira suggests that Yhwh gives wisdom to all humanity (17:6–7), indeed to all creation (1:9b–10a), Skehan and Di Lella overstate their case. In fact, like his predecessors in the Israelite wisdom tradition, Ben Sira affirms the principle that knowledge of the deity is universally available to all human beings through observation of the natural world (42:16). Yet, as I observed in 1:1–10, Ben Sira indicates that certain persons have been given an extra measure of wisdom, a fact that distinguishes them from other human beings. In the present verse (43:33), Ben Sira calls the special group to whom God grants wisdom "the righteous."

COSMOLOGY AND ANTHROPOLOGY

I shall now analyze more precisely Ben Sira's understanding of the distinction made by Yhwh in the human realm by the uneven distribution of wisdom. Scholars have generally interpreted the mechanism that expresses this distinction in Sirach in terms of opposition. They frequently cite Sir 33:7–15—in which Ben Sira contrasts evil with good, life with death, and the good person with the wicked—as the clearest expression of Ben Sira's doctrine of opposites. In contrast to this widespread view that Ben Sira sees the world in terms of opposites, I shall argue that the sage bases his anthropology on a nondualistic view of Israel's election, a notion he derives from his observation of the cosmos as well as from older biblical traditions.

Ben Sira's understanding of election is effectively illustrated in his distinction between ordinary time and festivals, which he associates with the sun and the moon, respectively. In Sir 33:7–15, Ben Sira draws an analogy between profane and sacred time, on the one hand, and two groups of human beings, on the other. He establishes the first half of the analogy as follows:

> 7a   Why is one day superior to another,
>   b   when all year long the light of every day comes from the sun?
> 8a   By Yhwh's knowledge they were distinguished,

> b   and he differentiated seasons and festivals.
> 9a   [Some he ex]alted and sanctified,
> b   and some he appointed as ordinary days. (Sir 33:7a–9b)

The terms of comparison in this half of the analogy are "ordinary days" (profane time), on the one hand, and those days which mark "seasons" and "festivals" (sacred time), on the other. Both sets of days—the ordinary and the festive—are alike in the sense that the light of the sun illuminates them both (33:7b). Yet, Ben Sira notes, Yhwh designates certain days out of the year to mark religious occasions. From his comparison of the respective functions carried out by the sun and moon in 43:1–12, it is clear that in Sir 33:7–15 Ben Sira alludes to the role of the moon in marking sacred time in the lunar version of the Jewish calendar that he recognizes. The distinction between ordinary days, illuminated by the sun, and exalted days, which are distinguished by the moon as well as illuminated by the sun, will prove an apt illustration for the way Ben Sira thinks about election.

The second half of the analogy is as follows:

> 10a   [All human beings are ve]ssels of clay;
> b   for from dust Adam was formed.
> 11a   Yet Yhwh's [understand]ing distinguished them;
> b   he set them upon their respective paths.
> 12a   [Some he blessed and exal]ted,
> b   and some he sanctified and [drew near to him]self.
> c   [Some he cursed and brought] low,
> d   and drove from the[ir pl]ace. (Sir 33:10a–12d)

Just as all days of the year partake in the light of the one sun, so too, Ben Sira suggests, all human beings share the same basic quality of being formed from the earth, a characteristic he traces to the creation of Adam (cf. Gen 2:7). Nevertheless, in the same way that Yhwh set apart certain days of the year to mark sacred occasions, so also he distinguished certain human beings from all others (33:11–12). Later in the poem, Ben Sira labels these two groups of people "the wicked" and "the good" (33:14c).

Most commentators identify correctly the terms of the analogy:

profane time : sacred time : : the wicked person : the good person.

They nonetheless misconstrue the nature of the analogy as one of opposition. Perdue's description of this passage is typical: "Here . . . Ben Sira proclaims that God has separated the components of reality into contrasting opposites. In this poem, the two categories of opposites are time (sacred and profane) and humans (the good and the bad)."[15] This widespread interpretation of the analogy as opposition likely results from the assumption on the part of commentators that Ben Sira views the wicked person and the good person as opposites. Scholars then project this perception of the distinction between the wicked and the good persons back onto the distinction between profane and sacred time. In Ben Sira's rhetoric, however, the analogy moves unidirectionally—*from* his observation of the distinction between profane and sacred time, which is rooted in the respective functions of the sun and moon, *to* the distinction made among human beings. In other words, Ben Sira uses a cosmological observation in order to make an anthropological classification. Thus, we must analyze the precise nature of the division between profane and sacred times in order to interpret the type of distinction Ben Sira wishes to communicate regarding human beings.

The nature of the relationship between profane time and sacred time is not opposition, as Perdue, Argall, and others have argued, since in Ben Sira's view the same sun illuminates every day of the year. Those days which mark festivals and seasons Yhwh has "exalted and sanctified" (*hērîm wĕhiqdîšô*) from the "ordinary days." The verb *hērîm* frequently means "to set one thing apart from a whole," such as an offering for dedication to Yhwh,[16] a holy district for the temple area,[17] spoils of war as tribute to Yhwh,[18] or a "chosen one" (David) to be king.[19] In each instance, a portion of the whole is set apart from the rest for a special purpose. The verb *hiqdîš* has similar connotations: to "sanctify" means to *set apart* human and animal firstborn,[20] the temple,[21] or a prophet[22] for special divine service. The item or person set apart does not become the opposite of those that remain members of the original group. Rather, the one that is set apart is "elected" for a special purpose.

Thus, the days designated as sacred by the function of the moon are not the opposite of all the other profane days. Rather, sacred time denotes those days of the year that are "set apart" from all others "through Yhwh's knowledge" (Sir 33:8a).

By analogy, then, Ben Sira suggests that Yhwh has similarly set apart certain people from all others for a special divine purpose even though all persons derive from the same basic substance, the dust of the earth. Indeed, Ben Sira applies the same two verbs—*hērîm* and *hiqdîš*—to describe the manner in which certain human beings have been set apart from the rest of humankind. The nature of this distinction, thus, is also one of election, not opposition.

Moreover, in the language he uses to describe the distinction among humans, Ben Sira alludes to instances of election in Israel's national traditions. In Sir 33:12a, for example, the verb "to bless" calls to mind references to the election of Abram and his descendants (cf., e.g., Gen 12:1–3, 22:17–18, 28:13–14; Exod 32:13; Deut 1:10). In Sir 33:12b, the verb "draw near" calls to mind the special function of the Levites and the priests as distinct from the rest of the Israelites: they are the ones who draw near to Yhwh for temple service (Ezek 40:46, 42:13, 44:15–16, 45:4). The verb *hiqdîš* ("set apart") alludes to the related adjective "holy" (*qādôš*) and noun "holiness" (*qōdeš*), terms that figure prominently in describing priests who are set apart for temple service (Lev 21:6–8; Num 16:5, 7; 2 Chr 23:6, 31:18, 35:3; Ps 106:16; Ezra 8:28). The evocation of these instances of election in Israel's history also suggests that the nature of the analogy in Sir 33:7–15 is election and not opposition.

Yet one might question whether the matter is as simple as I have suggested. At the end of the poem, Ben Sira contrasts three pairs of apparent opposites.

> 14a [Evil contrasts with] good,
> b and life contrasts with death,
> c so a [good] person [contrasts] with the wicked.
> 15a [Consider] every w[ork] of God;
> b all of them come in pairs, one corresponding to [the other].
> (Sir 33:14a–15b)

In verse 14, Ben Sira seems to compare the dyad good person/wicked person to the dyads life/death and good/evil. Should one not understand the elements of these dyads as opposites?

Saul Olyan notes the prevalence of binary oppositions throughout the discourse of the Hebrew Bible. Some binary oppositions in the biblical texts represent totalities, that is, they seek to classify all elements into one of two categories. These comprehensive dyads include male/female, clean/unclean, circumcised/uncircumcised, and whole/blemished. Such totalities permit no intermediate position. Olyan observes, however, that other dyads are not comprehensive and allow for intermediate categories. Take, for example, the pairs wise/foolish and good/evil. In the case of these noncomprehensive dyads, the two elements represent ends of a continuum, and it is possible for someone to be neither wise nor foolish, but somewhere in between.[23]

The present passage from Ben Sira contains the noncomprehensive dyad evil/good (33:14a). This dyad is common in the Hebrew Bible, particularly in the wisdom literature (Prov 11:27; 13:21; 14:19; 17:13, 20; Eccl 7:14). And while the wisdom tradition tended to articulate its view of the world using dyads such as wise/foolish and wicked/righteous, this simplistic way of portraying the world glossed over more complex realities in which gray areas existed. Yet even the book of Proverbs recognized that some persons belonged to neither category. The naïve or inexperienced person represents someone who is neither wise nor foolish, but who requires wisdom instruction in order to become wise (Prov 1:4, 32; 7:7; 8:5; 14:18; 22:3; 27:12). Given the correlation in wisdom literature of the wise and good persons, and of the foolish and the wicked persons, one should understand Ben Sira's pair wicked person/good person as a noncomprehensive dyad.

Indeed, despite the prevalence of dyads in biblical discourse, Joel Kaminsky has shown that the Hebrew Bible does not portray Israel's election in strictly binary terms. "The Israelite idea of election presupposes three categories," he argues, "rather than two: the elect, the anti-elect, and the non-elect." In general, the elect are the people of Israel. The anti-elect are those few groups of people considered unredeemable enemies of Yhwh, such as the Amalekites, Canaanites, and sometimes the Midianites. The nonelect consist in everyone else. Kaminsky notes that the last group, the nonelect, contains the vast majority of non-Israelites who "were always considered fully part of the divine economy."[24]

Olyan observes that in the Hebrew Bible, triadic constructions occur much less frequently than binary constructions. Examples of triadic constructions include priest/Levite/other Israelite (Num 18:1–7) and Israelite/resident outsider/nonresident alien (Deut 14:21). These triadic formulations, according to Olyan, "are generated out of and dependent upon binary oppositions." The triadic formulation priest/Levite/other Israelite, for example, represents a development from an underlying dyad priest/nonpriest. Olyan remarks: "One member of the initial opposition has itself been divided: the category nonpriest gives rise to the categories Levite and Israelite."[25] (See figure 1.)

Figure 1. Development of Priest/Levite/Other Triadic Construction

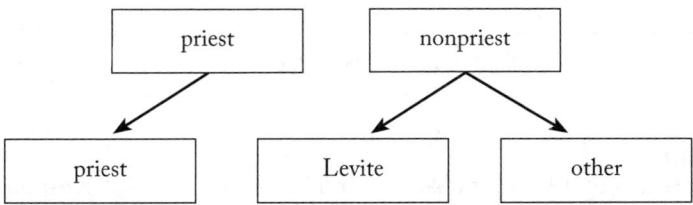

It seems plausible that the triadic construction of Israel's election tradition identified by Kaminsky also developed out of a binary construction which one might call elect/unelect. The second element of this binary construction was further divided into the nonelect and the anti-elect, resulting in the triadic construction. (See figure 2.) One could argue that, in one sense, the elect and anti-elect are opposites. The elect are "exalted" for special divine purpose while the anti-elect are "brought low" for special divine disfavor (see Sir 33:12). If, however, my hypothesis about the development of this particular triadic construction is correct, then the anti-elect are not the binary opposite of the elect. Rather, if the anti-elect are the opposite of any group, they are the opposite of the nonelect, since these two terms were generated as a secondary binary construction from what I have termed the unelect. By considering the triadic construction priest/Levite/Israelite, we can observe the nonoppositional relations among the elements of the triad: the Israelite priest and nonpriest are not opposites, since both elements share the larger identity "Israelite." Indeed, one cannot even affirm that the Levite and the Israelite are opposites. Rather, it seems, the nature of the secondary dyad Levite/Israelite originates in the selection of a subset of Israelites (the nonpriestly descendants of Levi) to serve in a special role. Thus, one should construe even this supposed binary opposition as a nonoppositional dyad. In terms of election, then, perhaps one should speak of the anti-elect as being selected from among the unelect for negative divine treatment.

Figure 2.   Development of Elect/Nonelect/Anti-Elect Triadic Construction

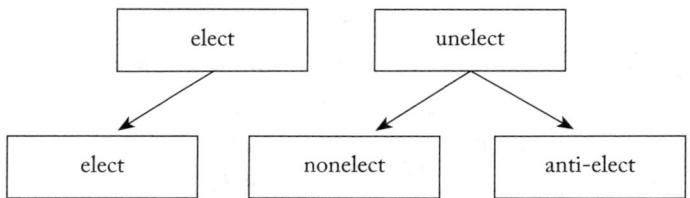

It seems that Ben Sira has in mind just such a group corresponding to what Kaminsky calls the anti-elect. Parallel to Ben Sira's allusion to the election of Israel from the other nations and of the priests from the rest of the Israelites, the sage alludes to a subset of humanity selected by Yhwh for divine disfavor. According to Ben Sira, Yhwh "cursed" this group (33:12c). This verb evokes the narrative regarding Abram's election in Gen 12:1–3, in which Yhwh promises to "curse" those who curse Abram (Gen 12:3a; cf. 27:29). It also calls to mind the curse of Canaan in Gen 9:25, a passage which likely represents a tradition in which Israelites considered as cursed the inhabitants of the land of Canaan—one group belonging to Kaminsky's anti-elect. Skehan and Di Lella suggest that "bring low" in 33:12c is a "reference to the Gentiles in general, who were not chosen as Israel had been." What Skehan and Di Lella call "the Gentiles in general" corresponds to my category of the unelect, however, and in light of the triadic construction of election in the biblical tradition, the verb more likely refers to the abasing of the anti-elect. The uncommon verb "drive away" (Sir 33:12d) is related to the verb "drive on, thrust down," which refers to the "wicked" who are "thrust down" by their own "evil" (Prov 14:32; cf. Ps 36:13 [Eng. 12]) or to the psalmist's enemies whom the angel of Yhwh like a wind "drives on" (Ps 35:5). It seems, therefore, that Skehan and Di Lella are correct in the second part of their assessment of Sir 33:12: namely, that Ben Sira refers "in particular [to] the Canaanites, whom the Lord had expelled 'from their place.'"[26]

While Ben Sira appears to have in mind the abasement of the anti-elect and the elevation of the elect in Sir 33:7–15, we should not assume that the sage views all persons as falling into one of these two categories. Like the biblical traditions on which he depends for his ideas about Israel's election, Ben Sira does not portray in a negative light the nonelect, that large intermediate group of non-Israelites (see Sir 17:1–10, 39:4).

ELECTION AND CREATION

Earlier I suggested that Ben Sira's reference to two apportionments of wisdom in a creation poem points to a connection between his creation theology and the uneven distribution of wisdom among humans. I am now in a position to describe more specifically the associations between Ben Sira's doctrine of election and his creation theology. The sage ties his doctrine of election to his creation theology in several ways.

First, as we have just seen, Ben Sira arrives at his doctrine of election through an observation he makes in nature. Ben Sira's contemplation of the different roles of the sun and moon leads him to consider a division among human beings. He infers that the distinction Yhwh made between human beings through the election of some over others—though not at the expense of others—has an analogue in the respective functions of the sun and moon in determining profane and sacred times.

Second, Ben Sira associates Israel's election with Yhwh's sovereignty and wisdom, that is, with Yhwh's divine prerogative to distribute wisdom to whomever he desires. As Ben Sira says, by means of his "knowledge" Yhwh set certain days apart from all the others to be special religious occasions (33:8a). Similarly, exercising his sovereignty, Yhwh distinguished among human beings through his "understanding" (33:11a). As I observed, Ben Sira associates Yhwh's sovereignty with creation, both in the sense of establishing divine mastery in the primordium and in his ongoing role in maintaining the operation of the universe.

Ben Sira goes further, however, and suggests that the election of Israel has its roots among the original acts of creation. In the Hebrew Bible, various sources portray Yhwh's election of Israel as a historical event. The juxtaposition of J's account of the call of Abram in Gen 12:1–3 with what scholars generally call the prehistory of Gen 1–11 illustrates the character of Israel's election as a historical event. The historical cast to Abram's election becomes apparent when viewed in conjunction with J's universal genealogy in the Table of Nations in Gen 10. The tradition contained in Exod 19:3b–8 portrays the election of the Israelite nation as a historical event that took place at Mount Sinai. The temporal reference which begins the pericope—"on the third new moon after the Israelites had departed from Egypt" (19:1a)—indicates the narrative's historical cast. For the most part the Deuteronomist, too, portrays Israel's election as a historical phenomenon. Deuteronomy 9:4–9 describes Israel's election as the fulfillment of a historical promise that Yhwh made to Israel's ancestors (cf. Deut 7:6–8, 10:15). These biblical traditions all portray Yhwh's election of Israel as unfolding at discrete moments in history.[27]

In the book of Sirach, however, the dominant biblical view of Israel's election as a historical phenomenon is eclipsed by the notion that Israel's chosenness originates in a primordial decision on the part of Yhwh. Whereas the biblical tradition generally roots election in historical providence, Ben Sira grounds election in primordial determinism.[28] In his commentary on Sir 33:12, Gerhard von Rad proposes that Israel's election results from "a primeval decision on God's part."[29] This may be an overinterpretation of the verse in and of itself. As I have shown, Sir 33:12 evokes biblical traditions regarding historical portrayals of Israel's election. Moreover, nothing in the verse links Israel's election explicitly to a divine decision in primordial times.

Nonetheless, von Rad's instincts are correct about Ben Sira's understanding of election in general. If one considers the first part of the poem (33:7–12) in conjunction with the last part of the poem (33:14–15), von Rad's assertion appears more accurate. As noted, verse 14 contrasts elements of three dyads, one of which (the good person and the wicked person) can be correlated with two of the three categories in the Bible's triadic construction of election: the elect and the anti-elect. In verse 15, Ben Sira includes these dyads among "all the works of God" (v. 15a), which he asserts "come in pairs, one corresponding to the other." From this verse, it appears that Ben Sira not only derives the doctrine of election from an observation about the sun and moon but locates the divine distinction among human beings in the very creation of the natural world.

Indeed, several other texts that I have already discussed confirm that Ben Sira grounds his doctrine of election in creation. The poetic structure of the creation poem in 1:1–10 connects the differential outpouring of wisdom in 1:9b–10b directly to the creation of wisdom herself in 1:9a. Similarly, in Sir 43:33 (cited above), Ben Sira associates the special divine dispensation of wisdom to a particular group with Yhwh's creation of the world. The chiastic structure of the underlying Hebrew text can be diagrammed. (See figure 3.)

Figure 3. Chiastic Structure of Sir 43:33ab

A All things
    B made
        C Yhwh
            D And to the righteous
  B' he gave
A' wisdom

The direct object of the second line, "wisdom" (A'), parallels the direct object of the first, "all things" (A'). Indeed, Ben Sira considers wisdom to be the first of Yhwh's creations (1:4, 24:9a). Individually, each line pivots around the verbs (B and B'), and the "giving" of wisdom in 33b parallels the "making" of the world in 33a. Finally, at the center of the chiasm stand Yhwh and the righteous (C and D). Although these elements are not parallel grammatically, their juxtaposition at the center of the chiasm signals that a special relationship exists between them. As in Sir 1:9b–10b, Ben Sira suggests that in conjunction with that relationship comes a special dispensation of wisdom. The parallelism between the direct objects and the verbs in verse 33 indicates that this special relationship, which I have shown should be understood in terms of election, is grounded not in history but in creation.

In other passages the sage also grounds Israel's election in a primordial decision of Yhwh. In Sir 24:1–12, for example, personified Wisdom recounts her origins in the mouth of Yhwh and her primordial journey through the created realm (vv. 4–5). While Wisdom acquired mastery over all creation during her primordial journey (v. 6), she nonetheless sought a particular location in which to dwell (v. 7). Yhwh chose Israel for Wisdom's ultimate dwelling place:

> Then the creator of all commanded me,
> the one who created me chose the spot for my tent;
> he said, "In Jacob pitch your tent,
> in Israel receive your inheritance." (Sir 24:8)

Although the temporal sequence of events in Wisdom's autobiography remains unclear, it seems as though Yhwh's election of Israel as the location for Wisdom's inheritance occurs as part of the process of creation.

For Ben Sira, then, Israel's election seems less a historical event than a cosmogonic phenomenon. In this sense, Ben Sira applies an assumption operative in the cosmogonies of Israel and her ancient Near Eastern neighbors—the beginning explains the present. For the sage, this "beginning" included Yhwh's creation of the cosmos and Israel's election by the deity, both through Wisdom (Sir 24:8, 33:11).

— By grounding his doctrine of election in his theology of creation, Ben Sira participated in a larger current in the late Second Temple period, in which authors understood election in terms of a primordial determinism. 4QInstruction and the *Book of Mysteries*, for example, view a person's fate as predetermined by God's plan (the *rāz nihyê*; 4Q417 1 i

10–18; 4Q418 81 20; 4Q299 3a ii–b). In the *Treatise on the Two Spirits*, God establishes the design of the entire cosmos, before it comes into existence, and implants a spirit of light or darkness in each person (1QS 3:18–26). In the book of *Jubilees*, during the creation of the world, God singles out Israel, along with the two highest orders of angels for Sabbath observance (*Jub.* 2:19–20). This general shift during the Second Temple period from historical to cosmogonic interpretations of Israel's election resulted from heightened notions of divine sovereignty.

Many Second Temple authors also linked their idea of election to notions of dualism. 4QInstruction distinguishes between "spiritual people" whom God accepts with favor and those of "fleshly spirit" whom God destroys (4Q416 1 10–13). In the *Treatise on the Two Spirits*, persons with the divinely implanted spirit of light receive their due reward in a postmortem existence while those with the spirit of darkness receive their just punishment (1QS 4:6–14). In *Jubilees*, the primordial decision to separate Israel from the nations corresponds to a heavenly distinction between higher and lower classes of angels. As a result, the author views Israel as radically holy and different in kind from other nations and therefore prohibits intermarriage (*Jub.* 25:1–12, 30:7–10).

In contrast to these dualists, other Jewish authors maintained more universal views. Philo, for example, understands Israel to mean "one who sees God" and therefore defines membership in the elect as those who pursue the philosophical quest to see God. In this way, he does not restrict membership in Israel to persons descended from Jews. Theoretically, anyone can embark upon the quest to see God and become a member of Israel.

Unlike most of these thinkers, Ben Sira resisted the temptation to merge his doctrine of election with a dualistic understanding of humanity. But neither did he take the universal approach of Philo. If *Jubilees* represents one extreme position, that of the particularist, and Philo embodies an opposing position, that of the universalist, Ben Sira exemplifies an intermediate position. He recognizes the inherent tension between universalism and particularism, and adapts the ancient Israelite notion of election as a device by which to mediate between the two extremes. He affirms that Israel is a particular people with a special relationship to God but recognizes that Israel's existence and behavior have universal implications.

No doubt Ben Sira's socio-historical context played some role in shaping this intermediate approach. Whereas the author of *Jubilees* may have experienced the turbulence of the Maccabean period and developed his radically particularist understandings of Israel in response to it, Ben Sira lived before the crisis brought on by Antiochus IV. Moreover, the relative benevolence of Seleucid policy toward Jerusalem in the sage's day lent itself to a more charitable attitude toward non-Jews. Ben Sira's social location also differed from Philo's. Whereas Philo was active in political affairs in the largely non-Jewish city of Alexandria, Ben Sira served the Jewish priestly ruling class in a predominantly Jewish Jerusalem.

In this relatively tolerant milieu, Ben Sira did not take the path of the dualist, as many modern interpreters have suggested. It is easy to imagine how a synthesis between the older wisdom dichotomies of wise/foolish and righteous/wicked, on the one hand, and the biblical election tradition, on the other, could have led to a strict dualism. But in Ben Sira's case, it did not. While Ben Sira saw the world in terms of Jew and non-Jew, he did not associate wisdom and righteousness entirely with the Jew, and folly and wickedness wholly with the non-Jew. Consequently, the widely held assumption among scholars regarding Ben Sira's supposed dualism must be abandoned.

NOTES

1. This essay draws upon my book *Wisdom's Root Revealed: Ben Sira and the Election of Israel* (JSJSup 139; Leiden: Brill, 2009), and I thank Brill for permission to reuse this material.

2. Unless otherwise noted, all translations are those of the author.

3. Johannes Marböck, *Weisheit im Wandel: Untersuchungen zur Weisheitstheologie bei Ben Sira. Mit Nachwort und Bibliographie zur Neuauflage* (BZAW 272; Berlin: Walter de Gruyter, 1999), 152–54. I have taken the liberty of translating Marböck's quotations from the German.

4. Randal A. Argall, *1 Enoch and Sirach: A Comparative Literary and Conceptual Analysis of the Themes of Revelation, Creation, and Judgment* (ed. William Adler; SBLEJL 8; Atlanta: Scholars Press, 1995), 135–36.

5. Ibid., 143.

6. Leo G. Perdue, *Wisdom and Creation: The Theology of Wisdom Literature* (Nashville: Abingdon, 1994), 289.

7. Ibid., 243–90.
8. Argall, *1 Enoch and Sirach*, 135, 145–47.
9. See, e.g., Exod 15:7–10; Deut 33:2–3, 26–9; Judg 5:4–5; Hab 3:3–15; Ps 68:7–8, 31–4 [Eng. 8–9, 32–5]; and 2 Sam 22:8–16 = Ps 18:8–16.
10. Argall, *1 Enoch and Sirach*, 148–50.
11. John Day, *God's Conflict with the Dragon and the Sea: Echoes of a Canaanite Myth in the Old Testament* (Cambridge: Cambridge University Press, 1985), 49.
12. Jon D. Levenson, *Creation and the Persistence of Evil: The Jewish Drama of Divine Omnipotence* (Princeton, N.J.: Princeton University Press, 1988), 7–8, 15.
13. Ibid., 17.
14. Patrick W. Skehan and Alexander A. Di Lella, *The Wisdom of Ben Sira* (AB 39; Garden City, N.Y.: Doubleday, 1987), 496. Italics added.
15. Perdue, *Wisdom and Creation*, 272–73.
16. Num 15:19–20; 18:19, 24, 26; 31:52; Ezek 45:13.
17. Ezek 45:1; 48:8–9, 20.
18. Num 31:28.
19. Ps 89:20 [Eng. 19].
20. Num 3:13, 8:17.
21. 1 Kgs 9:3, 7 = 2 Chr 7:16, 20; 2 Chr 30:8; 36:14.
22. Jer 1:5.
23. Saul M. Olyan, *Rites and Rank: Hierarchy in Biblical Representations of Cult* (Princeton, N.J.: Princeton University Press, 2000), 3, 124n6.
24. Joel Kaminsky, "Did Election Imply the Mistreatment of Non-Israelites?," *HTR* 96 (2003): 398–99, 401. For Kaminsky's more recent, book-length treatment of election in the Hebrew Bible, see Joel Kaminsky, *Yet I Loved Jacob: Reclaiming the Biblical Concept of Election* (Nashville: Abingdon, 2007), 109.
25. Olyan, *Rites and Rank*, 6–7.
26. Skehan and Di Lella, *Wisdom of Ben Sira*, 400.
27. Note, however, Richard Clifford's essay in this volume, which argues that Gen 1:1–2:4a represents P's attempt to inscribe Israel's election in the creation of the world.
28. One exception to the general portrait in the Hebrew Bible of election as a historical phenomenon is Deut 32:7–9, which implies that Yhwh selected Israel for his own "portion" (*ḥēleq*) and "inheritance" (*naḥălâ*) in the distant past (*yĕmôt ʿôlām*). This passage significantly influenced Ben Sira's thoughts about Israel's election; see Goering, *Wisdom's Root Revealed*, 67–68, 99, 179.
29. Gerhard von Rad, *Wisdom in Israel* (trans. James D. Martin; London: SCM, 1972), 267, 270.

CHAPTER 8

The Chosenness of Israel in the Apocrypha and Pseudepigrapha

MATTHIAS HENZE

The chosenness of Israel, God's inscrutable and mysterious election of Israel as the chosen people with whom God entered into a covenant, is a recurring theme in the work of Jon D. Levenson. In a number of publications Levenson has probed this central and seemingly obvious topic of biblical theology to uncover its complexities and to argue for its continuing relevance today. He has shown that the origins of the idea of chosenness reach back all the way to the book of Genesis.[1] He has followed the topic throughout the Hebrew Bible and into the New Testament to discuss its implications for Jewish-Christian relations.[2] And he has written eloquently against the modern detractors of this ancient biblical doctrine.[3]

This essay is intended as a supplement to this discussion. Rather than turning my attention to the biblical or rabbinic literature, as Levenson has already done with characteristic acumen, my task will be to trace the idea of chosenness through the Apocrypha and Pseudepigrapha—those Jewish texts that were composed as the biblical period was coming to an end and before rabbinic authority became widely accepted.[4] The texts I have selected cover a period of about three centuries, from the Apocalypse of Weeks of the second century B.C.E. to *2 Baruch* of the late first century C.E. Our brief survey shows that the election of Israel continued to be a topic of considerable interest at the time. It also shows that the idea of chosenness is a complex one and that it could be employed in a variety of contexts and used to different ends. In the midst of this variety of understandings we can detect three general interrelated themes, all linked to the chosenness of Israel, that tend to recur in the apocryphal and pseudepigraphic writings. First, several authors trace the election of Israel back to Abraham: God chose the patriarch out of love and entered into a covenant with him. Abraham's faithfulness, in return, is seen as a merit to which his descendants are eager to lay claim. Second, God freely determined that Israel should be the chosen people, the people whom God loves. We are frequently reminded that the initiative to elect Israel was God's. Over time, dissident groups claimed the title "the chosen" as a self-designation and assumed a new identity as God's chosen Israel. And third, chosenness does not imply that Israel has been blameless. Israel's unlawful acts, which in some texts are compared to those of her oppressors, are the reason why God delivered Israel into the hands of the enemy in the first place. Several authors express their longing for the eschatological reversal of fortunes, when Israel will be elevated and her enemies condemned.

1 ENOCH

The first text to be considered, the Apocalypse of Weeks, is part of the *Epistle of Enoch* (*1 En.* 91–105), the last of the five works included in the Ethiopic *Apocalypse of Enoch*, or *1 Enoch*. The Apocalypse of Weeks (*1 En.* 93:1–10; 91:11–17) offers a good point of entry into our discussion because of its early date of composition, the second century B.C.E., and because of its conspicuous use of language of chosenness.[5]

Following a brief introduction (*1 En.* 93:1–2), Enoch, the seventh antediluvian patriarch, gives his sons an overview of Israel's history from his own time to the *eschaton* (*1 En.* 93:3–10, 91:11–17). The overview takes the form of a "prophecy," in which Israel's history is structured in ten weeks.

Chosenness is mentioned no fewer than four times and at crucial junctures in the Apocalypse: first in the introduction (*1 En.* 93:2), and then in week three (*1 En.* 93:5, the time of Abraham), week six (*1 En.* 93:8, the preexilic period), and week seven (*1 En.* 93:10, from the exile to the second century B.C.E.). Enoch opens with a brief preview of what he is about to announce. He will speak

> concerning the sons of righteousness,
> and concerning the chosen of eternity,
> and concerning the plant of truth. (*1 En.* 93:2)[6]

The three parallel expressions all designate a distinctive group within Israel, whose election by God stands at the center of the Apocalypse in week 7. The first expression, "the sons of righteousness," makes clear that God has set the members of this group apart because of their righteousness, a sentiment further emphasized in verse 10. Next they are called "the eternally chosen ones" (Eth. *xeruyāna ʿalām*). This expression, which is not found in the Hebrew Bible or elsewhere in *1 Enoch*, entails two more of the group's attributes: they are the *chosen ones*;[7] and they are chosen *for eternity*, they will last forever.[8]

The third expression, finally, "concerning the plant of truth," anticipates the use of the same motif of the plant in week three (*1 En.* 93:5). There we read of Abraham: "A man will be chosen as the plant of righteous judgment." Abraham was chosen by God from among the Gentiles to be "the plant of righteousness" (Eth. *takla ṣedq*). This is the plant from which Israel will sprout. In the Bible, the chosenness of Abraham, using the verb *bḥr*, is made explicit only in Neh 9:7, though it may well be implicit much earlier.[9] The dual notion that the election of Israel has its origin in the chosenness of Abraham and that this election is eternal is also found in the book of *Jubilees*, another work from the second century B.C.E. In *Jub.* 19:18 Abraham says about Jacob, "I know that the LORD will choose him for himself as a people who will rise up from all the nations which are upon the earth."

Week six (*1 En.* 93:8) describes the preexilic age as a time during which "the whole race of the chosen root will be dispersed." Israel sprang from "the chosen root" (Eth. *šerw xeruy*) that is Abraham, hence the designation "the race of the chosen root." And yet, chosenness did not make Israel immune to divine punishment, it did not prevent the Babylonian exile. Loren Stuckenbruck comments: "While Israel is and remains God's special people, the fact that they descend from Abraham has not provided any guarantee that they would not be punished for their sins. Election must be confirmed through a further event of choosing."[10] That event is described in the next week.

With week seven (*1 En.* 93:9–10, 91:11) we have reached the central moment in Israel's history according to the Apocalypse, the period spanning from the exile to the real time of the author.

> And at its conclusion, the chosen will be chosen,
> as witnesses of righteousness from the everlasting plant of righteousness,
> to whom will be given sevenfold wisdom and knowledge. (*1 En.* 93:10)[11]

Week seven begins with a reference to "a perverse generation," that is, Israel during the exilic and early postexilic period. The deeds of the Israelites will be so wicked that God will intervene and choose anew, this time "the everlasting plant of righteousness." The Apocalypse thus distinguishes between "the chosen," i.e., all of Israel as the progeny of Abraham, and "the everlasting plant of righteousness," a group that will not include everybody but only "the chosen of the chosen," the community of the elect. Whereas Israel's chosenness stems from Abraham's special status, this group of the elect will be chosen only at the time of the Apocalypse's author. And whereas the rest of Israel is "perverse," this group will be endowed with wisdom and knowledge. The author does not further reveal the exact nature of this special knowledge, but the larger context of the *Epistle* makes clear that it concerns the proper understanding of the divine law and the eschatological lore, a secret knowledge about the end time that is deemed essential for obtaining salvation.[12]

A group called "the righteous and the chosen" also figures prominently in the *Book of Parables* (*1 En.* 37–71), the second and youngest in the collection of five books of *1 Enoch*, likely written at the turn of the c.e. It has long been recognized that the authors of the *Parables* drew their inspirations from earlier parts of *1 Enoch* and particularly from the *Book of the Watchers*.[13] There "the righteous and the chosen" are mentioned in the introduction to the book (*1 En.* 1:1–5:9). Enoch declares that he will speak "concerning the chosen" (*1 En.* 1:3; cf. 58:1): they will enjoy special protection during the final tribulations (*1 En.* 1:8), on judgment day their sins will be forgiven, and they will inherit the world to come (*1 En.* 5:6–7).[14]

The same idea of a group of elect who claim for themselves the title "the righteous and the chosen" (or "the righteous and the holy," or variations thereof) and who are singled out for their preferential treatment at the end of days is picked up and developed further in the *Book of Parables*.[15] The text seems to suggest that the group has suffered from persecution and that some of them have died (*1 En.* 47:1, 48:7, 53:7, 62:11–12). Now they are comforted and promised protection from their oppressors, "the kings and the mighty" (*1 En.* 46:4, 62:1, 63:1). The *Parables* say of the resurrection of the dead (*1 En.* 51:1; see in particular 62:1), "the righteous and the chosen will have arisen from the earth," at which there will be a judgment scene (*1 En.* 46:4–8; 48:8–10; 60:2, 10), and "the righteous and the chosen" will be granted life eternal and a restored earth (*1 En.* 45:4–6, 58:3, 61:4, 62:13–15). Enoch mentions repeatedly that on his otherworldly journeys he has seen the place where the chosen will dwell. "There I saw the dwelling places of the chosen" (*1 En.* 41:2); and "east of the garden where the chosen and righteous dwell" (*1 En.* 60:8).[16]

The central individual in the judgment scenes of the *Parables* is a transcendent figure who sits on the throne for judgment. This figure has many titles, among them "the Son of Man" (*1 En.* 46:2–4, 48:2, etc.) and "the Messiah" (*1 En.* 48:10, 52:4). His titles "the Chosen One" (*1 En.* 39:6; 40:5; 48:10; 45:3–4; 49:2–4; 51:3, 5, etc.) and "the Righteous and the Chosen One" (*1 En.* 53:6) correspond closely to the group of "the righteous and the chosen." Their close relationship is further reinforced by the composition of the *Parables:* the epithet "the

Chosen One" (Eth. *xeruy*) is used particularly in connection with "the chosen ones." In the Hebrew Bible, the title "Chosen One" is used in the Servant Songs in Second Isaiah (Isa 41:8, 9, 42:1, 43:10, 20, 44:1, 2, 45:4, 47, 49:7) to designate God's Servant.[17] In the *Parables*, this individual has been elevated to become a transcendent and preexistent figure, who judges the world but spares "the chosen ones."

To summarize, in the Apocalypse of Weeks God chooses twice, first Abraham and through him all of Israel, and then again a group of the elect, "the chosen of the chosen," who lived at the time of the author. Similarly, the *Parables* take the perspective of a group called "the chosen." Here the term may well have some "sectarian" connotations. One of the epithets of the messianic figure who will spare them on the day of reckoning is "the Chosen One." Finally, it is noteworthy that in a reasonably unified corpus like *1 Enoch* the term "chosenness" is largely confined to the first five chapters of the *Book of the Watchers,* the Apocalypse of Weeks, and the *Parables*. Elsewhere in *1 Enoch*, the term "the righteous" is preferred.

PSALMS OF SOLOMON

Israel and Jerusalem play a prominent role in the eighteen psalms that make up the *Psalms of Solomon*. The writers of the *Psalms* identify themselves with "Israel" (*Pss. Sol.* 7:8–10, 8:23–34, 9:1–11, 10:4–8, 14:1–5, 18:1–5).[18] They also call themselves "the devout" (*Pss. Sol.* 10:5–8, 13:10, 14:3–5) and "the righteous" (*Pss. Sol.* 3:5–8, 9:7, 10:1–4, 13:9, 14:1–5, 15:6–9, 16:15), who reach out to their God and long for salvation (*Pss. Sol.* 12:6, 14:5, 18:1–5). A teleological focal point in the collection as a whole is the eschatological vindication of Israel, as colorfully expressed in the last two poems (*Pss. Sol.* 17:26–29, 18:1–9).[19]

"The righteous" define themselves in relation to their God but also vis-à-vis other groups in Israel. These are merely called "the sinners" (*Pss. Sol.* 3:9–12, 4:3–5, 13:6, 14:6–9, 15:10–12) and "the wicked" (*Pss. Sol.* 12:1–6), and no further identification about them is given.[20] In addition, some of the psalms express great hostility toward the nations (*Pss. Sol.* 1:2–4, 7:1–3, 6, 8:30). They were written in a situation of considerable distress, when Jerusalem had been attacked, the population killed, their sons and daughters led away into captivity, and the temple desecrated by the enemy (*Pss. Sol.* 2:1–7, 8:14–21; also 17:11–18).[21] It has long been recognized that the attack on Jerusalem described in *Pss. Sol.* 2 and 8 is Pompey's conquest of Judea in 63 B.C.E. Josephus (*Ant.* 14:1–79) provides an account of the events during the reigns of Hyrcanus and Aristobulus, of Pompey's capture of Jerusalem, and of the deportation of Aristobulus and his family to Rome (cf. *War* 1:117–59; also 4QpNah 3–4).[22] *Psalms of Solomon* 2:26–27 relate the death of Pompey in 48 B.C.E., and the collection of the *Psalms of Solomon* as a whole may have been compiled in the decades thereafter, probably in or around Jerusalem.

Pompey's arrogant behavior in Jerusalem is described in *Pss. Sol.* 2 and 8.[23] The author makes no secret of his loathing for the Roman general. According to *Ps. Sol.* 2, Pompey breached the temple walls, trampled on the altar, and took many Jews captive to Rome (*Ps. Sol.* 2:1–2, 6). The events described in *Ps. Sol.* 8 are similar: Pompey captured fortified Jerusalem, killed the Jewish leaders, and exiled their families (*Ps. Sol.* 8:18–21). But the story is remembered not simply for its historical value. More than simply telling the story of Pompey, the author(s) of the *Psalms of Solomon* emphasizes that the Roman general was only acting on God's behalf and that his actions, though deplorable, were merely a response to the sins of the people of Jerusalem.[24] Indeed, the bulk of the poems is devoted to a description of these sins. They include various moral and ethical violations such as sexual improprieties, but the main charge is that the temple officials have polluted the temple (*Pss. Sol.* 2:3–4, 8:11–13).[25] It would be difficult to miss the paraenetic purpose of the poems.

It is in this context that we must understand the language of chosenness in the *Psalms of Solomon*. Right at the outset in *Ps. Sol.* 1, the poem that serves as an introduction to the entire collection, Mother Jerusalem laments over her arrogant children that their lawless acts exceeded those of their Gentile conquerors (*Ps. Sol.* 1:8; that Israel's sin surpassed that of the nations is repeated emphatically in *Ps. Sol.* 8:13). The poet compares Israel's lawlessness to that of the nations and finds that the attacks on Jerusalem, instigated by God, are fully justified. On the opposite end of the collection, in *Ps. Sol.* 17, the acknowledgment of Israel's sins is repeated (*Ps. Sol.* 17:5–20).[26] But there we find also the reminder that God *chose* David and his human descendants *forever* (*Ps. Sol.* 17:4).[27] The poet therefore calls on God to restore the Davidic dynasty: "See, O Lord, and raise up for them their king, the son of David, at the time which you chose, O God, to rule over Israel your servant" (*Ps. Sol.* 17:21). This is followed by a description of the advent of the Messiah, a royal Davidic figure who will rule as king in Jerusalem and drive out the nations (*Ps. Sol.* 17:22–46).[28] Finally, in the last poem (*Ps. Sol.* 18), the poet recalls God's love for Abraham and his descendants. The attributes that describe Israel recall the similar titles in Gen 22:2 of Isaac—a potent allusion to Israel's progenitor now bound but soon released to new life.[29] "Your judgments are over the whole earth with pity, and your love is upon the offspring of Abraham, the sons of Israel. Your discipline is upon us as on a firstborn, an only son, to turn back the obedient soul from ignorant stupidity" (*Ps. Sol.* 18:3–4).[30]

The chosenness of Israel is also the subject of *Ps. Sol.* 9. The poet first recalls that God is a righteous judge who forgives those who repent and confess their sins (*Ps. Sol.* 9:1–7), and then he turns his attention to Israel.

> [8]And now, you are our God, and we are the people whom you have loved.
> Look, and be compassionate, O God of Israel, for we are yours,
> And remove not your pity from us, lest they attack us.
> [9]And you chose the offspring of Abraham above all the nations,
> and you placed your name upon us, O Lord,
> and you will not reject us forever.
> [10]You made a covenant with our fathers concerning us,
> and we shall hope in you when we turn our souls toward you.
> [11]The mercy of the Lord is upon the house of Israel forever and ever.
> (*Pss. Sol.* 9:8–11)

The poet appeals to God to have mercy on Israel, as Israel fears an imminent attack from the nations. The plea to be compassionate is based on Israel's chosenness: Israel is the people loved by God, a people who belong to God (v. 8); God has chosen Abraham and his descendants from among the nations, he has called them by his name, and he has promised not to reject them forever (v. 9); and the covenant with Israel remains the foundation for Israel's hope (v. 10).[31]

THE TESTAMENT OF MOSES

The *Testament of Moses* as we have it today, a work otherwise known as the *Assumption of Moses*, dates from the turn of the C.E.[32] Its beginning and ending are lost, but the general contours of the text are clear. The narrative frame of the book (*T. Mos.* 1:1–9 and 11:1–12:13) tells of an encounter between Moses and his successor, Joshua (the scene is modeled after Deut 31:23–30, 34:9). Moses is about to die and summons Joshua to give him his last instructions. The book thus presents itself as the written record of Moses's oral testament.

Framed by the narrative are Moses's instructions to Joshua (*T. Mos.* 1:10–10:15). They consist largely of an *ex eventu* prophecy of the history of Israel (the historical review proper begins in *T. Mos.* 2:1). The historical overview begins with the taking of the land and ends in the eschaton. The Mosaic "prophecy" of Israel's past is selective, however. Rather than aiming for completeness or historical accuracy, a principal motivation behind the recasting of Israel's past in the *Testament of Moses* is to retell the events in light of the Deuteronomic scheme of history. Specifically, history is divided into two cycles (chs. 2–4 and 5–10), each following the same sequence of sin (2; 5:1–6:1), punishment (3:1–4; 6:2–8:5), a turning point/repentance (3:5–4:4, 9), and salvation (4:5–9, 10).[33]

The idea of chosenness is attested in the narrative frame of the book, that is, in the first cycle, and again (though less so) in the eschatological hymn of the second cycle, in chapter 10. Specifically, there are four aspects of chosenness that are emphasized in the *Testament of Moses:* the notion that God created the world for Israel; Jerusalem as the chosen place; Israel as the chosen people; and the eschatological elevation of Israel above all nations.

First, we begin with creation. Moses begins by calling on Joshua to be strong. Then he goes on to reveal to him a mystery. "He [God] created the world on behalf of his people" (*T. Mos.* 1:12). In pseudepigraphic literature this is the first attestation of the idea that God created the world for his people, an idea that will be repeated in *4 Ezra* and *2 Baruch*, two works of the late first century C.E.[34] The idea may well derive from the Song of Moses in Deut 32, a text that stands in the background of the *Testament of Moses*.[35] Johannes Tromp puts it well: "This concept should not be taken as some kind of metaphysical conviction about the reasons and motifs for creation, but rather as a strong expression of the idea of Israel's election."[36] Moses does not leave it with that, however. He adds that God kept the purpose of his creation a secret so that the nations "might abjectly declare themselves guilty" (*T. Mos.* 1:13) by their ill-informed deliberations—we are not told what the deliberations are about, but probably they concern the meaning of creation. God created the world for Israel, though this has not yet been revealed publicly. The implied scope of the Mosaic statement is remarkable: the election of Israel effectively *precedes* creation.[37] This will finally be made manifest at the end of time, which is imminent.

Moses returns to the topic of creation at the end of the book in chapter 12. There he assures Joshua that history, including the history of Israel's interaction with the nations, will unfold according to God's predetermined plan, which was put into place at the beginning of time. Once again, the overtones of Deut 32 are unmistakable. "God has created all nations on earth, and he foresaw us, them as well as us, from the beginning of the creation of the earth until the end of the world. And nothing has been overlooked by Him, not even the smallest detail" (*T. Mos.* 12:4).

Second, we turn to Jerusalem. After Moses revealed to Joshua the secret of creation, he appoints him chief archivist of the written tradition (*T. Mos.* 1:16–17). He gives Joshua "this writing," presumably a copy of the core of the *Testament* (now *T. Mos.* 2:3–10:10), so that later Joshua will know "how to preserve the books which I shall entrust to you" (*T. Mos.* 1:16; cf. 10:11 and 11:1), presumably a reference to the Torah. More significant than the mode of preservation for our purposes is the place where Joshua is to put the book. Moses tells him to deposit it "in earthenware jars in the place which he [God] has chosen from the beginning of the creation of the world" (*T. Mos.* 1:17). The formulaic language implies that the locus where Joshua shall deposit the precious jars is none other than Jerusalem—and, more specifically, the place where the temple in Jerusalem will be, even though Joshua could hardly have been aware of the true significance of the place. The same language of God's choosing a place is used in Deuteronomy in the context of the centralization of the worship (Deut 12:5, 11, 14; 14:23; 15.20, etc.; see also Neh 1:9 and 2 Chr 7:12).[38] Moses then continues to explain to Joshua that in this place "his [God's] name may be called upon until the day of recompense when the LORD will surely have regard for His people" (*T. Mos.* 1:18). The place will retain its significance until the end-time. In other words, the Mosaic designation of the locus as the place chosen by God where the *Testament* is to be stored not only anticipates the building of the Jerusalem temple centuries after Joshua but even looks to the eschaton.[39]

Third, let us examine the chosen people. Toward the end of his first cycle of historical "prophecies," Moses refers to an anonymous intercessor who will arise at the time of the exile and pray on behalf of the exiles (*T. Mos.* 4:2–4). The intercessor will appeal to God for Israel's release from captivity on two grounds: first, because God himself has chosen Israel; and second, because God entered into a covenant with the Israelites.

> LORD, King of All on the throne on high, who rulest the world, who wanted this people to be your chosen people. Then you wanted to be called their God, according to the covenant which you made with their fathers. (*T. Mos.* 4:2)

The doxology lays the ground for the plea for mercy that follows. It was God who wanted to choose Israel, and it was God who wanted to be called their God. The election of Israel was then sealed by the covenant, the guarantor for Israel's salvation ("Heilsgarantie").[40] It is on these grounds that the anonymous intercessor pleads with God to have regard for the Israelites and to bring the exile to an end. A little later Moses assures Joshua that God will hear the prayer "because of the covenant which he had made with their fathers" (*T. Mos.* 4:5).[41]

Fourth, Israel will be exalted in eschatological time. The second cycle in the *Testament of Moses* culminates in an eschatological hymn

(*T. Mos.* 10:1–10). The introduction to the poem declares that God will establish his kingdom and avenge the Israelites against their enemies (*T. Mos.* 10:1–2). There follows a description of a theophany: God leaves his heavenly throne, the earth trembles, and the natural order is thrown into disarray (*T. Mos.* 3–7).[42] The purpose of the theophany, finally, is revealed in the last part of the hymn. God will raise Israel to the heavens, so that they will see their enemies from on high and praise God (*T. Mos.* 10:8–10). There is no explicit language of chosenness in this hymn, but the idea is related: at the end of time, God will work vengeance on the enemies of Israel, destroy their idols, and exalt Israel to the stars.[43] The eschatological vindication of Israel and the punishment of her enemies is a recurring motif in pseudepigraphic writings, including our next two works.

FOURTH EZRA

The last two books to be discussed are two apocalypses of the historical type, *4 Ezra* and *2 Baruch*. Both were composed a couple of generations after the Roman destruction of the Jerusalem temple in the year 70 C.E. It has long been observed that *4 Ezra* and *2 Baruch* are linked to each other by a number of features: both texts are set fictitiously at the time of the fall of Jerusalem in 587 B.C.E., a historical moment of paradigmatic, even revelatory significance; both apocalypses are attributed to a biblical scribe of renown from the exilic and early postexilic periods; and both compositions share a number of generic, thematic, and linguistic traits.[44]

4 Ezra opens with a long prayer in which Ezra, who is greatly distressed over the desolation of Jerusalem, first recounts Israel's history from Adam to the Babylonian Exile (*4 Ezra* 3:4–27) and then compares the current fate of Babylon—standing in for Rome—with that of Israel (*4 Ezra* 3:28–36). The historical review that occupies the first part of the prayer sets the stage for Ezra to make his point in the second: even though Israel has hardly been blameless in the past, Babylon has not been any better, and yet God allows Babylon, not Israel, to be prosperous. The idea of chosenness plays a role in both parts of Ezra's prayer. In his historical review, Ezra dwells at some disproportionate length on the time of the patriarchs as it is related in the book of Genesis. Adam and the consequences of his transgression are of great concern to Ezra, and so are Noah and "the many nations" (*4 Ezra* 3:12) that lived after him.[45] After the flood these generations continued to do evil, and so God chose Abraham from among them.

> And when they were committing iniquity before thee, thou didst choose for thyself one of them, whose name was Abraham; and thou didst love him, and to him only didst thou reveal the end of the times, secretly by night. (*4 Ezra* 3:13–14)

Ezra interprets the election of Abraham against the backdrop of the iniquities committed by the postdeluvian nations. They were even more ungodly than their ancestors (here the author may well have in mind the Tower of Babel story in Gen 11:1–9), and so God responded by choosing one of them, Abraham. Not much is said about the act of Abraham's election, but the text does provide a few clues. First, we learn that it was at God's initiative that Abraham was chosen. The short phrase "you chose for yourself one of them (*elegisti tibi ex his unum, cui nomen erat Abraham*)" underscores the inscrutability and arbitrariness of the divine act (cf. Neh 9:7; *1 En*. 93:5). God chose Abraham *for himself*.[46] Second, the subjective nature of the divine choice is further underscored by the affirmation that God had a particular affection for Abraham: "you loved him" (*et dilexisti eum*). The scriptural anchor for this claim is found outside the book of Genesis, in Isa 41:8 and 2 Chr 20:7, where Abraham is the one "who loved Me," or simply "My friend."[47] Third, and more unusual, is Ezra's first remark about Abraham once he was chosen: God revealed to him "the end of times, secretly by night." The latter part of the phrase implies that the revelation took place during the covenant ceremony in Gen 15, which occurred at night (Gen 15:17). Whereas according to the biblical account, the covenant is important mostly because of the promise of descendants to Abraham, Ezra emphasizes an aspect we do not find in Genesis: Abraham was the first human being to whom God revealed the eschatological secrets, the patriarch who was given insight into the end of times.[48]

Following his historical review, Ezra turns to the current fates of Israel and the nations to underscore how they diverge (*4 Ezra* 3:28–36). The seer makes his point emphatically: God has seen the deeds of the Babylonians, and they are no better than Israel. On the contrary, it was Israel who believed in the covenants and kept the commandments. And yet, at present Israel lies subdued, whereas Babylon—that is, Rome— triumphs, or, in Ezra's accusatory words to God, "you have destroyed your people and protected your enemies" (*perdidisti populum tuum et conservasti inimicos tuos* [*4 Ezra* 3:30]). Any idea that Israel's misery can be justified because of Israel's sins, as for example in *Pss. Sol.* 1, is here soundly rejected, if only because the other nations are no less sinful than Israel.

It is this last aspect in particular that continues to trouble Ezra. In the next chapter he bemoans that every day he has to witness Israel's misery. He wants to know from God "why Israel has been given over to the Gentiles in disgrace; why the people whom you loved has been given over to godless tribes, and the law of our ancestors has been brought to destruction and the written covenants no longer exist" (*4 Ezra* 4:23). If in the previous chapter it was Abraham whom God loves, here it is Israel.[49] Ezra is distraught that God would surrender Israel to the Gentiles in an act of disgrace, in spite of the "Torah of our fathers," thereby effectively declaring the covenant to be obsolete. Ultimately it is the reliability of the divine promise that is at stake.

The longest and most explicit meditation in *4 Ezra* on the election of Israel comes in Ezra's second prayer in 5:23–30, a poetic reflection on the nature of chosenness. The prayer readily falls into two parts: the first part (vv. 23–27) consists of eight biblical images that symbolize God's election of Israel; the language is repetitive and formulaic ("from all . . . thou hast chosen for thyself one"), with a recurring contrast between the many (standing in for the nations) and the one (which is Israel).[50] The eighth contrast relates how God chose Israel from among "the multitude of peoples" (*ex omnibus multiplicatis populis* [5:27]). This serves as the transition to the second half of the prayer (vv. 28–30), in which Ezra wonders why God has scattered Israel among the nations and handed Israel over to her enemies. It remains incomprehensible to the seer why Israel's enemies are given the upper hand, even though

Israel remained faithful to the covenants. And why does God punish Israel by means of the sinful nations?[51]

Ezra's accusations become noticeably more poignant in 6:55–59. There Ezra returns once again to the contrasting comparison of the nations and Israel, but now the point of comparison is no longer loyalty versus disloyalty to the covenant but rather the complex, if enigmatic, interrelationship of creation, election, and, ultimately, redemption.

> [55] All this I have spoken before thee. O LORD, because thou hast said that it was for us that thou didst create this world. [56] But as for the other nations which have descended from Adam, thou hast said that they are nothing, and that they are like spittle, and thou hast compared their abundance to a drop from a bucket. [57] And now, O LORD, these nations, which are reputed as nothing, domineer over us and trample upon us. [58] But we thy people, whom thou hast called thy firstborn, only-begotten, kin, and dear one, have been given into their hands. [59] If the world has indeed been created for us, why do we not possess our world as an inheritance? How long will this be so? (*4 Ezra* 6:55–59)

This brief pericope is framed by a reference to creation (vv. 55 and 59): Ezra claims that God created the world for Israel but that Israel does not possess the world.[52] Worse still, the nations rule over and "trample on" Israel. What distinguishes this from previous passages in *4 Ezra* is the harsh, ontological language in which Ezra pitches the nations against Israel. God has proclaimed that the nations are "nothing," "like spittle" (*dixisti eas nihil esse, et quoniam salivae adsimilatae sunt*),[53] and that they should be compared to "a drop from a bucket" (Isa 40:15, 17). Israel, on the other hand, is God's "firstborn," the "only begotten," who is "zealous" for God and "most dear"—epithets that describe Isaac in the Akedah in Gen 22:2.[54]

In a recent article on the idea of election in *4 Ezra*, John Collins has made much of this passage.[55] Collins takes offense at *4 Ezra*'s belief in election because of its disparaging treatment of non-Israelites. He grants that the book presumes a situation in which Israel has just been defeated and hence is in no position to mistreat anyone. "Nonetheless, Gentiles can scarcely fail to find Ezra's language of election offensive."[56] Ezra's harsh words in *4 Ezra* 6:56 in particular reflect what Bruce Longenecker has dubbed "ethnocentric covenantalism."⁵⁷ Collins agrees. "The 'ethnocentric covenantalism' of Ezra regards the nations as spittle; the eschatological wisdom of Uriel seems to care only whether they keep the law; the apocalyptic visions consign them to destruction."⁵⁸

Collins's critique of the concept of election as ethnocentric is hardly new.⁵⁹ But is it an appropriate characterization of *4 Ezra*'s theology? Taken out of context, Ezra's derogatory statement that the nations are like "spittle" would indeed be damning. But there is a specific context here that cannot be ignored: the book responds to the recent demolition of Jerusalem. *4 Ezra* is not a theological treatise that ruminates in general terms about of the eschatological fate of all nations, and Ezra does not speak about "Gentiles" vs. Jews in general. The seer is concerned about Babylon—a cipher for Rome—and he expresses his hope for the eschatological turning of the tables, as it were, when the defeated will be set free. What is more, even the Jews will find little comfort in *4 Ezra*'s apocalyptic program. To brand *4 Ezra*'s theology "ethnocentric covenantalism" suggests, erroneously, that according to *4 Ezra* those who are part of the covenant will be saved at the end of time whereas those who stand outside the covenant will be condemned to eternal damnation. This notion has already been dismantled in the Enochic Apocalypse of Weeks, as we saw, where it is made clear that belonging to "the whole race of the chosen root" (*1 En.* 93:8) did *not* save "the chosen" from divine punishment, nor is it what we find in *4 Ezra* either. Uriel stresses over again that only a few of the righteous will be saved in the end: "Let many perish who are now living, rather than that the law of God which is set before them be disregarded!" (*4 Ezra* 7:20). Ezra is forced to concede: "And now I see that the world to come will bring delight to a few, but torments to many" (*4 Ezra* 7:47).⁶⁰ The covenant is no longer the operative principle, let alone a guarantee for salvation, as many in Israel are doomed to perish. We can discuss what the purpose of such an admittedly pessimistic outlook might be—one possible explanation would be that these passages are essentially paraenetic, i.e., that they call on the faithful to return to the covenant *now* so that they will be counted among the righteous *then*— but to find in *4 Ezra* a simple division between Israel, for whom salvation is guaranteed, and the Gentiles, who are destined to perish, is missing the point.

Once Ezra has taken Uriel's message to heart, his tone changes noticeably, and he moves from accusation to plea. In a short but strongly worded appeal toward the end of the third vision, the seer turns to his angelic interlocutor and says: "But spare your people and have mercy on your inheritance, for you have mercy on your own creation" (*4 Ezra* 8:45).

SECOND BARUCH

Like *4 Ezra*, *2 Baruch* is set at the time of the Babylonian destruction of Jerusalem, even though it was composed at the end of the first century C.E. Baruch, erstwhile the secretary and close confidant of the prophet Jeremiah, now has become a prophet in his own right who has effectively succeeded Jeremiah. As *2 Baruch* continues to tell the story that began in the Hebrew Bible, it remains firmly anchored in the tradition of Jeremiah: in form it closely follows its biblical predecessor, and in content it relates the events that surround the sacking of Jerusalem.[61]

Much of what we find in *2 Baruch* regarding the concept of chosenness resembles *4 Ezra*, though the author of *2 Baruch* likes to give the familiar ideas his own interpretive twist. Above we observed, for example, that early on in *4 Ezra* the seer challenges God and wonders "why the people whom you loved has been given over to godless tribes" (*4 Ezra* 4:23). *2 Baruch* begins with a narrative frame that sets the scene for the book: it relates how on the eve of the Babylonian destruction of Jerusalem God calls on Baruch to leave the city (*2 Bar.* 1:1–9:1). Visibly distraught, Baruch seeks to dissuade God from delivering Jerusalem up for destruction and, like Ezra, begins to argue with God. His argumentative strategy, too, revolves around a contrasting view of Israel and her enemies: the Babylonians are those who hate God, whereas God loves Israel. Says Baruch: "So then I am responsible for Zion, for they who hate You will come to this place and pollute Your sanctuary, and lead Your inheritance into captivity, and make themselves masters of those whom You have loved" (*2 Bar.* 5:1; cf. 3:5, 8:2). The motif of Israel as the people whom God loves reappears a few times throughout the book. In chapter 21, in a prayer which Baruch says while sitting in the

Kidron Valley, Baruch reminds God: "On account of Your name You have called us a 'Beloved people'" (Syr. ʿamāʾ ḥabībāʾ [*2 Bar.* 21:21]). And in chapter 48, another lengthy prayer, Baruch pleads with God in moving language not to reject His people: "And do not cut off the hope of our people, and do not abridge the times of our aid. For this is the people whom You have chosen, and these are the people to whom You have found no equal" (*2 Bar.* 48:19b–20).[62]

The idea of chosenness appears in *2 Baruch* in three larger contexts: one is the integrity and preservation of the land of Israel at the end of time as the place chosen by God; the second is the righteousness of the sages and the merit of their deeds for later generations; and the third is the eschatological orientation of *2 Baruch* in general that dominates the book and defines its conceptualization of the relationship between Israel and the nations.

We have seen the first aspect, the significance of space as the chosen locale for God's activities, already in the *Testament of Moses*. In *T. Mos.* 1:17 Moses orders Joshua to hide certain books "in the place which He [God] has chosen from the beginning of the creation of the world," an obvious reference to the privileged status of Jerusalem, singled out by God already at the moment of creation. The same motif of Jerusalem as the chosen city is also attested in *2 Baruch*, in the context of the advent of the Messiah. In *2 Bar.* 40:1–3, a scene highly reminiscent of Dan 7, the Messiah appears in Jerusalem, summons the last wicked ruler to Mount Zion, indicts him and his entourage for their wicked deeds, pronounces judgment, and puts him to death.[63] Then the Messiah protects the rest of the people, as God explains to Baruch, "those found in the place that I have chosen" (Syr. haw dmeštkaḥ bʾatrāʾ dagbit [*2 Bar.* 40:2]). In other words, the Messiah protects the prophetic remnant in Israel in the age of the eschaton (see also *2 Bar.* 77:4). In an important study, Liv Ingeborg Lied has underscored the abiding importance of space in the eschatology of *2 Baruch* and of early Jewish apocalyptic literature in general.[64] Far from becoming obsolete at the end of time, the Land of Israel maintains its chosen status. Lied's insistence to broaden our understanding of Jewish eschatology to find in it a combined conceptualization of space *and* time receives additional support from the other messianic pericopes in *2 Baruch*. According to the first messianic passage in *2 Bar.* 29:2–30:5, the Messiah will appear in Israel, protect its inhabitants and provide them with an abundance of food. Indeed, the messianic presence will initially be felt *only* in Israel. And according to the third and longest description of the Messiah, it is the Land of Israel itself that will guard those who live in it. At the visitation of the Messiah, "the Holy Land will have mercy on its own and protect its inhabitants at that time" (71:1).[65]

The second aspect of chosenness in *2 Baruch* concerns the righteousness of the sages. Like Ezra, Baruch is quick to admit that Israel has not been blameless before God and that many in Israel have sinned. But he also points out that those who were righteous in the past were able to live their lives in confidence. They even interceded before God on behalf of others because they trusted in their deeds (*2 Bar.* 85:2), and they were saved by their deeds (*2 Bar.* 52:7), the very deeds that are now preserved in the heavenly reservoirs (*2 Bar.* 14:12). And so, Baruch reasons, their righteousness should have outweighed Israel's sins and prevented the destruction of Jerusalem. "And lo, they strove, and not even for them did You have mercy on Zion. And if others did evil, Zion should have been forgiven on account of the deeds of those who did good deeds and should not have been destroyed on account of the deeds of those who committed iniquity" (*2 Bar.* 14:6–7; cf. 21:11).[66]

In addition to the righteous, Baruch also remembers the patriarchs and God's promises to them, which, our author is adamant, persist, even though the recent violent events in Jerusalem may call their power into question. After reminding God that he has called Israel his "Beloved People" (*2 Bar.* 21:21), Baruch goes on to evoke the memory of Abraham, Isaac, and Jacob specifically.[67] "It is for them, You said, that You created the world" (*2 Bar.* 21:24). The claim that God created the world for Israel is already familiar from the *Testament of Moses* and *4 Ezra.*[68] The same claim is also made in *2 Baruch*, albeit with some variation. According to *2 Bar.* 14:18–19, God made the world for *all* human beings, not just for Israel;[69] according to *2 Bar.* 15:7 the world was created specifically for the righteous;[70] and according to *2 Bar.* 21:24–25, as we just saw, God made the world for the three patriarchs in Genesis and those who were like them. Such a juxtaposition of divergent concepts may irritate the modern reader in search of a single point of view, but it is hardly at odds with the nature of early apocalyptic writings in general, which are by nature composites—intellectual amalgams of diverse traditions. In spite of this diversity of viewpoints, the divine interlocutor is able to answer all of Baruch's concerns—that God should have saved Zion because of the righteousness of the sages, and that the world was created for the righteous—with a single promise of the new world. "And with respect to the righteous about whom you said that because of them the world has come [into existence], so also that [world] which is to come will come [into existence] because of them. For this world is to them a struggle and a labor with much trouble, but that which is coming is a crown with great glory" (*2 Bar.* 15:7–8).[71]

The divine insistence on the ephemeral nature of this world and the repeated promise of the world to come leads us finally to the third aspect of chosenness in *2 Baruch,* the eschatological outlook that pervades the book. *2 Baruch*'s perception of Israel's status vis-à-vis the nations is inextricably bound up with the hope for Godly intervention and the expectation that the divine defeat of Israel's enemies is imminent.[72] Whereas Ezra dwells at some length on the fact that at present the nations are prospering whereas Israel lies in ruins, Baruch soon comes to realize that God is about to overthrow Israel's opponents. And so the seer abandons his complaint about the nations and turns to his fellow mourners and asks them, "Why are you looking for the decline of those who hate you?" (*2 Bar.* 52:6; cf. 83:5)—there is no need to hope for the downfall of the enemy since the eschaton will soon make right what is wrong now. This should not be interpreted as yet another proof of the vengeful nature of apocalyptic writings, a class of texts which modern readers love to think of as the enfant terrible of early Jewish literature, if only because apocalypses allegedly incite violence against the nations. Quite to the contrary, Baruch calls on his audience *not* to look for the demise of Israel's foes and to leave the matter to God, who is sure to intervene soon. This hardly means that the wrong that Israel's enemies have done will be forgotten. In the last of *2 Baruch*'s three messianic pericopes, the Messiah is said to assume the role of an eschatological warrior king: he summons all nations to Jerusalem and annihilates many of them. Then he sits down to pass judgment on those who remain. It is telling that the nations will be judged not based on their behavior in general but specifically on how they have treated Israel in the historical past (*2 Bar.* 72:2–6).[73]

Perhaps the most poignant passage in this respect comes in the epistle toward the end of the apocalypse. The seer comforts his addressees, telling them that God will avenge Israel on her enemies "according to all that they have done to us" (*2 Bar.* 82:2) and that the divine judgment is not far off. There follows in *2 Bar.* 82:3–9 a poem on the eschatological fate of the nations. The poem is made up of seven verses, each devoted to a false impression Israel currently has of the nations. Each verse in the poem consists of three lines: first what Israel beholds, then an accusation of the nation's wrongdoing, and finally a damning prediction of their demise.

> [3]Lo, for now we see the multitude of the prosperity of the nations,
> while they act wickedly.
> But they resemble a breath.
>
> [4]We behold the multitude of their power,
> while they act unjustly.
> But they resemble a drop.
>
> [5]We behold the firmness of their strength,
> while they resist the Mighty One every hour.
> But they shall be accounted like spittle.
>
> [6]We ponder the glory of their greatness,
> while they do not keep the commands of the Most High.
> But like smoke they will pass away.
>
> [7]We meditate on the fairness of their beauty,
> while they are led by the pollutions.
> But like grass that withers they will dry up.
>
> [8]We consider the force of their cruelty,
> while they do not remember the end.
> But like a wave that passes they will be broken.

⁹We remark the pomp of their strength,
while they deny the beneficence of God, who gave [it] to them.
But like a cloud that passes they will pass. (2 Bar. 82:3–9)

— The texts we have discussed present only a slim excerpt of a significant library of Jewish books written toward the end of the biblical period and beyond. More books could be added but the main picture would not change: the apocryphal and pseudepigraphic writings testify to a dynamic and intellectually engaging debate—rooted in the Hebrew Bible and among diverse Jewish circles—at a crucially important moment in the history of early Jewish thought. Throughout the debate the chosenness of Israel recurs frequently, and in various mutations, as a topic of concern. We should be wary of any overly facile understanding that can only think of this ancient biblical idea as an expression of Israel's superiority and a condemnation of the "Gentiles." The picture is considerably more complex, and the Apocrypha and Pseudepigrapha contribute immeasurably to our understanding of this complexity.

NOTES

1. Jon D. Levenson, *The Death and Resurrection of the Beloved Son: The Transformation of Child Sacrifice in Judaism and Christianity* (New Haven: Yale University Press, 1993), esp. 55–169.

2. Jon D. Levenson, "The Universal Horizon of Biblical Particularism," *Ethnicity and the Bible* (ed. Mark G. Brett; *BibInt* 19; Leiden: Brill, 1996), 143–69.

3. Jon D. Levenson, "Chosenness and Its Enemies," *Commentary* 126.5 (2008): 25–31.

4. For a masterly discussion of the literature see Loren T. Stuckenbruck, "Apocrypha and Pseudepigrapha," in *The Eerdmans Dictionary of Early Judaism* (ed. John J. Collins and Daniel C. Harlow; Grand Rapids: Eerdmans, 2010), 143–62; and Michael E. Stone, *Ancient Judaism: New Visions and Views* (Grand Rapids: Eerdmans, 2011). For a concise overview, see Simon J. Gathercole, "Election," in *Dictionary of Early Judaism*, 571–73.

5. There is some debate whether the Apocalypse of Weeks was originally an independent composition or whether it was always part of the *Epistle*. Here we note that the notion of chosenness does not seem to appear elsewhere in the *Epistle*, where the author refers to "the righteous" and "the devout," but not to "the chosen."

The secondary literature on *1 Enoch* has grown exponentially in recent years. A useful overview is Gabriele Boccaccini, ed., *New Light on a Forgotten Connection* (Grand Rapids: Eerdmans, 2005); on *1 Enoch*'s composition, see Michael A. Knibb, "The Book of Enoch or Books of Enoch? The Textual Evidence for 1 Enoch," in *The Early Enoch Literature* (ed. Gabriele Boccaccini and John J. Collins; JSJSup 121; Leiden: Brill, 2007), 21–40.

6. The translation is from George W. E. Nickelsburg and James C. VanderKam, *1 Enoch: A New Translation* (Minneapolis: Fortress Press, 2004).

7. "The chosen" already appear in *1 En.* 1:1–5:9, the introduction to the *Book of the Watchers*, which may well have inspired the Apocalypse of Weeks. References to "the chosen" in the Dead Sea Scrolls include *Musar le-Mevin* at 4Q418 69 ii 10 ("chosen ones of truth"), and the following self-designations of the Qumran community: "his [God's] chosen ones" (1QpHab 5:4); "his [God's] chosen" (1QpHab 9:12, i.e., the Teacher of Rigteousness); "the chosen by the will [of God]" (1QS 8:6); "the chosen ones" (1QS 9:14); and "the congregation of his chosen ones" (4QpPs^a 1–2 ii 5). Loren T. Stuckenbruck, *1 Enoch 91–108* (CEJL; Berlin: De Gruyter, 2007), 74–76.

8. George W. E. Nickelsburg, *1 Enoch 1: A Commentary on the book of 1 Enoch, Chapters 1–36; 81–108* (Hermeneia; Minneapolis: Fortress Press, 2001), 442.

9. Nickelsburg, *1 Enoch 1*, 445. Cf. Isa 41:8, 51:1–2; 2 Chr 20:7. See also *Apoc. Ab.* 14:2, where the angel says to Abraham: "Know from this that the Eternal One whom you have loved has chosen you"; *Jub.* 2:20.

10. Stuckenbruck, *1 Enoch 91–108*, 118.

11. The Aramaic text from 4QEn^g 1 iv 12–13 reads as follows: "And with its end] there shall be chosen e[lect one]s as witnesses of righteousness from the eternal plant of righteousness, to whom shall be given sevenf[old] wisdom and knowledge." Stuckenbruck, *1 Enoch 91–108*, 123.

12. Nickelsburg, *1 Enoch 1*, 448; Stuckenbruck, *1 Enoch 91–108*, 124. *1 En.* 100:6 mentions that "the sons of the earth will contemplate these words of the this epistle," thus leaving the door open for outsiders to be brought in, as long as they comply with the Enochic teachings.

13. Gabriele Boccaccini, ed., *Enoch and the Messiah Son of Man: Revisiting the Book of Parables* (Grand Rapids: Eerdmans, 2007); Michael A. Knibb, "Enoch, Similitudes of (1 Enoch 37–71)," in *Dictionary of Early Judaism*, 585–87.

14. Nickelsburg, *1 Enoch 1*, 162.

15. On the multiple connections between the *Book of the Watchers* and the *Parables*, see James C. VanderKam, "The Book of Parables within the Enoch Tradition," in *Enoch and the Messiah Son*, 81–99.

16. Cf. *1 En.* 45:4, 48:1, 51:5, and 70:3.

17. James C. VanderKam, "Righteous One, Messiah, Chosen One, and Son of Man in 1 Enoch 37–71," in *The Messiah: Developments in Earliest Judaism and Christianity*, (ed. James H. Charlesworth; Minneapolis: Fortress, 1992), 169–91, here 189. With regard to David, see *Pss* 78:70, 89:20–22.

18. I follow the translation by Kenneth Atkinson, "Psalms of Solomon," *NETS*: 763–76.

19. George W. E. Nickelsburg, *Jewish Literature between the Bible and the Mishnah* (2nd ed.; Minneapolis: Fortress, 2005), 238–47; James R. Davila, *The Provenance of the Pseudepigrapha: Jewish, Christian, or Other?* (JSJSup 105; Leiden: Brill, 2005), 161.

20. "Righteousness" is also the key term in the Apocalypse of Weeks discussed above. See Nickelsburg, *1 Enoch 1*, 441; Stuckenbruck, *1 Enoch 91–108*, 72. The opposition between "the righteous" and "the sinners" is a commonplace in texts with an eschatological focus. This is true for the Enochic *Book of Parables* and the *Epistle of Enoch*. See Stuckenbruck, *1 Enoch 91–108* on *1 En.* 92:3–5; 97:1–2; 98:4–8; 99:6–9; 100:5, 9; 102:4–103:8; 104:5–9.

21. Michael A. Knibb, "Temple and Cult in the Apocrypha and Pseudepigrapha: Future Perspectives," in *Essays on the Book of Enoch and Other Early Jewish Texts and Traditions* (SVTP 22; Leiden: Brill, 2009), 388–406, here 389.

22. Shani Berrin, "Pesher Nahum, Psalms of Solomon and Pompey," in *Reworking the Bible: Apocryphal and Related Texts at Qumran* (ed. Esther G. Chazon, Devorah Dimant, and Ruth A. Clements; STDJ 58; Leiden: Brill, 2005), 65–84; James C. VanderKam, *From Joshua to Caiaphas: High Priests after the Exile* (Minneapolis: Fortress/Assen: Van Gorcum, 2004), 350.

23. The other two poems with historical allusions are *Pss. Sol.* 1 and 17. Kenneth Atkinson, "Herod the Great, Sosius, and the Siege of Jeruslem (37 B.C.E.) in Psalms of Solomon 17," *NovT* 38 (1996): 313–22, has shown persuasively that *Pss. Sol.* 17 alludes to the siege of Jerusalem by Herod the Great in 37 B.C.E. See also Kenneth Atkinson, *I Cried to the Lord: A Study of the Psalms of Solomon's Historical Background and Social Setting* (JSJSup 84; Leiden: Brill, 2004), 211–22; Nickelsburg, *Jewish Literature*, 247.

24. Michael E. Stone, "Reactions to Destructions of the Second Temple: Theology, Perception, and Conversion," *JSJ* 12 (1981): 195–204, here 197, has shown how in response to previous destructions and desecrations of the Jerusalem temple (Nebuchadnezzar in 587 B.C.E. and Antiochus IV Epiphanes in 169 B.C.E.), authors similarly explained the events as a divinely sanctioned punishment.

25. Knibb, "Temple and Cult," 388–92.

26. Note in particular the formulation in *Pss. Sol.* 17:5: "And, because of our sins, sinners rose up against us."

27. On David's chosenness, see 2 Sam 6:21; 1 Kgs 8:16, 11:34; Ps 78:70; 1 Chr 28:4; and Acts 13:34.

28. Atkinson, *I Cried to the Lord,* 139–44; John J. Collins, "A Shoot from the Stump of Jesse," in *The Scepter and the Star: Messianism in Light of the Dead Sea Scrolls* (2nd ed.; Grand Rapids, Mich.: Eerdmans, 2010), 52–78, here 52–60.

29. Levenson, *Death and Resurrection,* 125–69.

30. Note the close parallel in *4 Ezra* 6:58: "But we, your people, whom you have called your firstborn, only-begotten, kin, and dear one, have been given into their hands." See the discussion by Michael E. Stone, *Fourth Ezra* (Hermeneia; Minneapolis: Fortress, 1990), 189.

31. Cf. *Ps. Sol.* 7:8, 10:4. Like the Apocalypse of Weeks (*1 En.* 93:5, 8), the *Psalms of Solomon* use the plant metaphor for Israel's chosenness: "Their planting is rooted forever; they shall not be pulled up all the days of heaven; for the portion and the inheritance of God is Israel" (*Pss. Sol.* 14:4–5). On the historical background of Ps 9, see Atkinson, *I Cried to the Lord,* 190–93.

32. That the *Testament* stems from the early first century C.E. is clear from the references to Herod and his sons in *T. Mos.* 6:1–9. However, some have argued, with George W. E. Nickelsburg leading the charge, that chs. 6–7 are a secondary addition to a work which was originally composed in the second century B.C.E. during the time of Antiochus Epiphanes. See his "An Antiochan Date for the Testament of Moses," *Studies on the Testament of Moses* (ed. George W. E. Nickelsburg; SBLSCS 4; Cambridge, Mass.: Society of Biblical Literature, 1973), 33–37; and now in his *Jewish Literature,* 74–77, 247–48. It is not clear, however, that chs. 6–7 really are an interpolation. The case for the unity of the *Testament* has most recently been made by Norbert J. Hofmann, *Die Assumptio Mosis: Studien zur Rezeption massgültiger Überlieferung* (JSJSup 67; Leiden: Brill, 2000), 329. The translation of the *Testament* is by Johannes Tromp, *The Assumption of Moses: A Critical Edition with Commentary* (SVTP 10; Leiden: Brill, 1993).

33. Nickelsburg, *Jewish Literature,* 75. Both cycles employ the Deuteronomic scheme, albeit to different ends. Hofmann, *Die Assumptio Mosis,* 45–80, offers a careful reading of the two blocks and their divergent theological emphases and concludes that the latter is intended to interpret the former: "So wäre es sogar durchaus denkbar, dass der zweite Block als Korrektiv zum deuteronomistischen Geschichtsbild im ersten geformt ist" (78).

34. Cf. *4 Ezra* 6:55, 59; 7:11; and *2 Bar.* 14:19. John J. Collins, "The Date and Provenance of the Testament of Moses," in Nickelsburg, *Studies on the Testament of Moses,* 15–32, here 27. On the relationship between the *Testament of Moses, 4 Ezra,* and *2 Baruch,* see Hofmann, *Die Assumptio Mosis,* 273–88. Rabbinic texts that express the idea that creation was for the sake of Israel are listed by Stone, *Fourth Ezra,* 188–89.

35. Joel Kaminsky (oral conversation, May 2011) suggests that the idea is also implicit in Second Isaiah, especially in ch. 40 where the nations are viewed as insignificant, and in ch. 43, where God is trading other nations to redeem Israel.

36. Tromp, *Assumption of Moses*, 141.

37. Cf. Eph 1:4: "Just as he chose us in him [Christ] before the foundation of the world (καθὼς ἐξελέξατο ἡμας ἐν αὐτῷ πρὸ καταβολῆς κόσμου) to be holy and blameless before him in love." Cf. also 1QS 3:15–16.

38. On Jerusalem as the chosen city in Pseudepigraphic writings, see *4 Bar.* 1:5 ("your chosen city" [τὴν πόλιν τὴν ἐκλεκτὴν]); *T. Lev.* 10:5; *T. Zeb.* 9:8; 3 Macc 2:9. Note also our discussion above on *Pss. Sol.* 9:9.

39. Curiously, J. Priest, "Testament of Moses," *OTP* 1:928, translates *T. Mos.* 2:6, "(The two tribes will) offer sacrifices in the chosen place for twenty years," whereas the underlying Latin simply reads, "Et adferent victimas per annos XX," with no reference to a "chosen place."

40. Hofmann, *Die Assumptio Mosis*, 75.

41. The entire scene that combines the prayer for mercy, the attribute of Israel as the people loved by God, and the appeal to the covenant, is highly reminiscent of the pericope discussed above in *Pss. Sol.* 9:8–9.

42. Tromp, *Assumption of Moses*, 232–37.

43. The promise that God will exalt Israel on the back of an eagle (*T. Mos.* 10:8) stands in stark contrast to the self-glorification of the inhabitants of Jerusalem, who, according to *Pss. Sol.* 1:5, "exalted themselves to the stars, they said they would never fall." Cf. *L.A.B.* 23:2.

44. On the consanguinity of *4 Ezra* and *2 Baruch*, see George W. E. Nickelsburg, *Jewish Literature*, 283–85; Klaus Berger, *Synopse des vierten Buches Esra und der syrischen Baruch–Apokalypse* (Tübingen: A. Francke, 1992), 1–3. The literary histories of *4 Ezra* and *2 Baruch* and the multiple affinities that exist between them can be explained most plausibly if we assume that oral performance and literary composition contributed to the shaping of the books. See Matthias Henze, "*Fourth Ezra* and *Second Baruch:* Literary Composition and Oral Performance in First Century Apocalyptic Literature," *JBL* 131 (2012): 181–200. All translations of *4 Ezra* are taken from Stone, *Fourth Ezra*.

45. The reference to Jacob is surprisingly terse and kept to a single verse: "You set apart Jacob for yourself, but Esau you rejected; and Jacob became a great multitude" (*4 Ezra* 3:16; cf. Mal 1:2–3).

46. Philo, *De Gigantibus*, 1:64; *Mutatione Nominum*, 1:66, 69, 71, 82. On rabbinic portraits of Abraham's piety, see Jon D. Levenson, "The Conversion of Abraham to Judaism, Christianity, and Islam," *The Idea of Biblical Interpretation: Essays in Honor of James L. Kugel* (ed. Hindy Najman and Judith H. Newman; JSJSup 83; Leiden: Brill 2004), 3–40. Cf. *Jub.* 2:19 on the election of Israel,

"Behold I shall separate for myself a people from among all the nations. . . . And I will sanctify them for myself." See also *Jub.* 19:18.

47. "Friend of God" then became Abraham's "unofficial title" among early interpreters. It is widely attested in the literature of the Second Temple period and beyond. James L. Kugel, *Traditions of the Bible: A Guide to the Bible As It Was at the Start of the Common Era* (Cambridge, Mass.: Harvard University Press, 1998), 258, lists numerous texts.

48. A number of targumic and rabbinic texts describe how God showed Abraham the future course of history; see Stone, *Fourth Ezra*, 71. In addition, see *2 Bar.* 57:2 about the time of Abraham: "It was then that the belief in a future judgment was conceived, the hope for a renewed world was then built, and the promise of the life that is coming after this was taking root." On *2 Bar* 57:1–3, see Matthias Henze, *Jewish Apocalypticism in Late First Century Israel: Reading Second Baruch in Context* (Tübingen: Mohr Siebeck, 2011), 275–78.

49. Cf. Jer 31:3 and Hos 11:1.

50. The images are: the forests of the earth/the vine; all the lands/one region; the flowers of the earth/one lily; the depths of the sea/one river; the cities/Zion; the birds/one dove; the flocks/one sheep; the multitude of peoples/one people. Stone, *Fourth Ezra*, 126–27.

51. Ezra's language is harsh and uncompromising: "If thou didst really hate thy people, they should be punished at thy own hands" (*4 Ezra* 5:30; cf. Mal 1:2–3).

52. Cf. *T. Mos.* 1:12, "He [God] created the world on behalf of his people." See also *4 Ezra* 6:59, 7:11; and *2 Bar.* 14:19.

53. The closest parallel, once again, comes from *2 Baruch:* "But they shall be accounted as spittle" (82:5).

54. Cf. *Ps. Sol.* 18:3–4; Stone, *Fourth Ezra*, 184.

55. John J. Collins, "The Idea of Election in 4 Ezra," *JSQ* 16 (2009): 83–96.

56. Ibid., 94.

57. Bruce W. Longenecker, *Eschatology and the Covenant: A Comparison of 4 Ezra and Romans 1–11* (Sheffield, UK: JSOT Press, 1991), 34.

58. Collins, "The Idea of Election," 95.

59. Joel S. Kaminsky, "Did Election Imply the Mistreatment of Non-Israelites?" *HTR* 96 (2003): 397–425; and his *Yet I Loved Jacob: Reclaiming the Biblical Concept of Election* (Nashville: Abingdon Press, 2007), 107–19.

60. This pessimism is expressed repeatedly throughout the book. See, for example, *4 Ezra* 8:3: "Many have been created, but few shall be saved." Cf. 8:1, 8:55, and 9:15–16. Note also the poignant passage in 9:21–22: "So let the multitude perish that has been born in vain, but let my grape and my plant be saved."

It is not clear whom the images of the grape and the plant represent, though presumably the angel is here thinking of the few eschatological survivors of Israel (Stone, *Fourth Ezra*, 300).

61. Pierre-Maurice Bogaert, "Le personage de Baruch et l'histoire du livre de Jérémie: Aux origines du livre de Baruch," *BIOSCS* 7 (1974): 19–21; idem, *L'Apocalypse syriaque de Baruch: Introduction, traduction du syriaque et commentaire* (2 vols., SC 144–45; Paris: Cerf, 1969); and more recently J. Edward Wright, "Baruch: His Evolution from Scribe to Apocalyptic Seer," in *Biblical Figures outside the Bible* (ed. Michael E. Stone and Theodore A. Bergren; Harrisburg, Pa.: Trinity Press International, 1998), 264–89.

62. Similarly, Baruch begins his epistle to the exiles with the words: "I remember, my brothers, the love of Him who created us, who loved us from of old, and never hated us" (*2 Bar.* 78:3).

63. For a discussion of this important scene, see David Edward Aune, with Eric Stewart, "From the Idealized Past to the Imaginary Future: Eschatological Restoration in Jewish Apocalyptic Literature," *Restoration: Old Testament, Jewish, and Christian Perspectives* (ed. James M. Scott; JSJSup 72; Leiden: Brill, 2001), 147–77, here 153; Loren T. Stuckenbruck, "Messianic Ideas in the Apocalyptic and Related Literature of Early Judaism," in *The Messiah in the Old and New Testaments* (ed. Stanley E. Porter; Grand Rapids: Eerdmans, 2007), 90–113, here 110–11.

64. Liv Ingebord Lied, *The Other Lands of Israel: Imaginations of the Land in 2 Baruch* (JSJSup 129; Leiden: Brill, 2008), esp. 185–241.

65. In *2 Bar.* 29:2, God protects the inhabitants of Israel, in 40:2 it is the Messiah who protects them, and in 71:1 the Land itself. Robert Henry Charles, "II Baruch: I. The Syriac Apocalypse of Baruch," in *The Apocrypha and Pseudepigrapha of the Old Testament* (ed. Robert Henry Charles; 2 vols.; 1913; repr., Oxford: Clarendon, 1998), 497, has found here three different sources, but this is forced. On the term "Holy Land" (*2 Bar.* 63:10, 71:1, 84:8), see Daniel J. Harrington, "The 'Holy Land' in Pseudo–Philo, 4 Ezra, and 2 Baruch," in *Emanuel: Studies in the Hebrew Bible, Septuagint, and the Dead Sea Scrolls in Honor of Emanuel Tov* (ed. Shalom M. Paul, Robert A. Kraft, Lawrence H. Schiffman, and Weston W. Fields; VTSup 94; Leiden: Brill, 2003), 661–72; and Lied, *Other Lands of Israel*, 198–210.

66. The idea that in the end God will have mercy on Israel because of Israel's righteous who have since fallen asleep is also attested in Pseudo-Philo, L.A.B. 35:3: "But he [God] will have mercy, as no one else has mercy, on the people of Israel, though not on account of you but on account of those who have fallen asleep." Cf. Rom 11:28–29. Friedrich Avemarie, "Erwählung und Vergeltung: Zur optionalen Struktur rabbinischer Soteriologie," *NTS* 45 (1999): 108–26.

67. According to *T. Levi* 15:4, the merit of the three patriarchs saved Israel from total annihilation by the Babylonians: "And unless you had received mercy through Abraham, Isaac, and Jacob, our fathers, not a single one of your descendants would be left on the earth" (cf. *T. Asher* 7:7).

68. Cf. *T. Mos.* 1:12; *4 Ezra* 6:59 and 7:11.

69. Cf. *4 Ezra* 8:44.

70. Cf. *4 Ezra* 8:1 and 9:13.

71. Frederick James Murphy, *The Structure and Meaning of Second Baruch* (SBLDS 78; Atlanta: Scholars Press, 1985), 31–67.

72. We should take note of another crucially important piece in *2 Baruch*'s rendering of Israel's relationship with the nations, the Torah. In his final public address to the people, Baruch reminds his hearers solemnly that God has singled out Israel from among the nations by giving them the Torah. "To you and to your fathers the LORD gave the Torah above all nations" (*2 Bar.* 77:3). Ever since, the Torah has been a source of trust for Israel (see *2 Bar.* 48:22). But there is another side to the coin. Since with the Torah Israel has had full knowledge of the divine intent, Israel can no longer plead ignorance. In harsh language God speaks to Baruch about the impending judgment: "But My judgment exacts its own, and My Torah exacts its right" (*2 Bar.* 48:27).

73. Cf. *4 Ezra* 13:25–52. Michael E. Stone, "The Concept of the Messiah in IV Ezra," in *Religions in Antiquity: Essays in Memory of Erwin Ramsdell Goodenough* (ed. Jacob Neusner; SHR 14; Leiden: Brill, 1968), 295–312, here 302; and John J. Collins, "A Shoot from the Stump of Jesse," 52–78, here 77–78. The Syriac of *2 Bar.* 72:2–6 is difficult; see Bogaert, *L'Apocalypse syriaque*, 2:126–28.

CHAPTER 9

"A House of Prayer for All Peoples" (Isaiah 56:7) in Rabbinic Thought

MARC HIRSHMAN

In Isa 56:6–7 we hear the prophet calling out to the foreigner and saying: "As for the foreigners who attach themselves to the LORD . . . I will bring them to My sacred mount and let them rejoice in My house of prayer. Their burnt offerings and sacrifices shall be welcome on My altar; for My house shall be called a house of prayer for all peoples" (56:6–7).[1] This is an ingathering of peoples who served God and loved God from afar. God will bring them to Jerusalem, gladly accept their sacrifices, and bestow on them happiness in God's prayer house, since, after all, God's house is a house of prayer for all peoples. Isaiah's notion of a "house of prayer for all peoples" remains also, if not primarily, a place of sacrifice as indicated in the end of the verse quoted above: "their burnt offerings and sacrifices shall be welcome on My altar, for My house shall be called a house of prayer for all peoples." It seems that this view (born in the exile, as we will see further on) envisaged a two-pronged temple, where sacrifice and prayer would thrive side by side. This model harkens back to earlier instances such as Hannah's prayer in 1 Sam, where the pilgrimage sacrifice is accompanied by her spontaneous prayer. Moreover, even though God declares in Isaiah that the temple is a house of prayer for all people, the prophecy is addressed specifically to those foreigners or Gentiles who "attach themselves to the Lord . . . who keep the Sabbath . . . and hold fast to My covenant" (Isa 56:6). These foreign adherents to God are rewarded by a pilgrimage to Jerusalem and willing acceptance of their sacrifices. These ritual acts of prayer and sacrifice are normative, ongoing rituals. This vision stands in contrast to the earlier vision in Isa 2, which saw the Temple Mount as the site for instruction to and judgment of the nations at end of days. The portrayal in chapter fifty-six emphasizes service to God rather than instruction or judgment.

In Jon Levenson's early and important essay "From Temple to Synagogue: 1 Kings 8," he proved the affinity between 1 Kgs 8:23–53 and our passage from Isaiah, emphasizing "that the reinterpretation of the Temple as a place of prayer is known from other sixth-century literature, most prominently from Third Isaiah . . . ."[2] The relevant passage, 1 Kgs 8:41–43, reads:

> If a foreigner who is not of Your people Israel comes from a distant land for the sake of Your name—for they shall hear about Your great name and Your mighty hand and Your outstretched arm—when he comes to pray to(ward) this house, oh hear in Your heavenly abode and grant all that the foreigner asks You for. Thus all the peoples of the earth will know Your name and revere You.

In this essay, I will explore the impact of this exilic broadening of the temple's role on post–Second Temple rabbinic thought regarding the temple as both a venue of prayer and sacrifice for the Gentiles. Levenson indicated at the end of his essay: "The liturgical order that the rabbis made normative is only a temporary institution while we await the final consummation of the divine plan."[3] The rabbinic comments on these passages in Isaiah and Kings will shed light on how they construed the Gentile's relationship in the past to prayer and sacrifice[4] in God's temple, which would surely serve as a road map for the eventual restoration which was, in their eyes, only a matter of time.

Let me begin with a curious but instructive adaptation of 1 Kgs 8 found in *t. Ber.* 3:14–16, where the *Tosefta* discusses the physical orientation of one who prays, both when one is unable to find one's bearings and more pertinently when one can. Verses from this chapter (and its parallel in 2 Chr 6) are cited to depict the geographic locations and orientations of all persons who pray, including those living abroad (2 Chr 6:38), in the Land of Israel (6:34), in Jerusalem (6:32), within the temple itself (1 Kgs 8:30), and in a case not covered in the biblical text, those unable to find their bearings.[5] As Saul Lieberman points out, 2 Chr 6:32 refers to the Gentile, who according to Lieberman, following R. Shmuel Eideles, "cannot enter the Temple and therefore prays to the house."[6] This being the case, the denouement of the *Tosefta* (3:16) is most curious: "It turns out that all of *Israel* are praying to one place." The *Tosefta* has taken Solomon's universalistic prayer and reassigned a proof text which speaks specifically of the Gentile to Jews, thus giving the entire passage a particularistic twist. "All of Israel," and only Israel, are praying to one spot![7] This transformation is less shocking than it might seem at first glance, since the *Tosefta* limits its view to Jews, but it still remains curious.

The next source that treats our topic is an amoraic midrash from the opening homilies of *Lev. Rab.* that also offers a surprising view of the historical function of the tabernacle, the temple's predecessor, and its palliative effect on the nations. As we will see, this midrash, attributed to an early-third-century amora, is reworked in later midrashic collections in a direction quite opposite to the particularistic adaptation we noted above in the *Tosefta*. We read in *Lev. Rab.* 1:11:

> Said R. Yehoshua b. Levi: Had the Nations of the World known how beneficial (*yafe*) the Tent of Meeting was for them, they would have surrounded it with encampments and fortresses. You find that until the Tabernacle was erected, the Nations of the World would hear the sound of the *dibbur* (*logos* [word]) and they would defecate in their palaces.[8]

The thrust of R. Yehoshua's idea is that the nations were unable to receive the power of God's word and that the tabernacle served to shield them from the terror of God's voice. R. Yehoshua's point of departure is probably an earlier midrash found in the *Mekhilta*, a tannaitic compilation. There we read:

> When the Holy One ... stood up and said: "I am the LORD thy God, the earth trembled ... At that time all the kings of the nations of the world assembled and came to Balaam the son of Beor. They said to him: Perhaps God is about to destroy his world." (*Bahodesh* 5)[9]

The enormous power of God's voice, depicted in the biblical accounts of Sinai, reaches its crescendo in Ps 29, where the psalmist exclaims: "The voice of the LORD is power ... (it) breaks cedars!" This same awesome voice speaks to Moses in the tabernacle, but now, according to our source, the Gentiles are mercifully sheltered from its power.

That being the case, there is a change of tone between the *Mekhilta*'s depiction of Sinai and *Leviticus Rabbah*'s view of the tabernacle. One can hardly miss the derisive tone in the *Leviticus Rabbah* passage, portraying the Gentile princes as cowering in their places and this in the most graphic terms. This inflection has displaced the lighter, almost comic tone of the earlier *Mekhilta* passage. The mocking tone of the later midrash accords well with the genre of mocking idolatry and idolaters which began in Isaiah and continued through rabbinic times.[10] It is clear, however, that Yehoshua b. Levi's notion of the tabernacle as protecting the nations from God's word stands in ironic counterpoint to Solomon's dedication of the temple, which was to be a source of salvation for the Gentiles who addressed their prayers to the Temple and to God who listened in heaven.

Later rabbinic thought takes this very anti-Gentile notion in *Leviticus Rabbah* and turns it on its head, restoring it to the universalistic motif in Solomon's prayer. A later midrash, *Tanhuma* (Buber) *Teruma* 8 cites the *Leviticus Rabbah* passage that treats the Tabernacle and continues the discussion to the temple, but with a strikingly new message.

> R. Yehoshua b. Levi said: Were the nations of the world to know how beneficial the Tabernacle was for them they would have surrounded it

with encampments to protect it.... Don't say (only) the Tabernacle, but also the temple was good for them. Whence? For thus did Solomon arrange in his prayer "Or if a foreigner who is not of Your people Israel [...] oh, hear in your heavenly abode." (1 Kgs 8:41–43)

But an Israelite who comes to pray, what does he say? "Render to each person according to his ways as you know his heart to be" (1 Kgs 8:39). But the Gentile whether they do or not, give him all he demands, "Thus all the peoples of the world will know Your name." (1 Kgs 8:43)[11]

We have then a duplicate statement of R. Yehoshua, in an almost identical formulation, but augmented by a passage that takes the temple rather than the tabernacle as its subject. The *Tanh.* passage takes the universalism of Solomon's prayer one step further, insisting that the language of the prayer in 1 Kgs 8:41–43 actually accords the Gentile preferential treatment. The individual Jew's prayer is answered according to the worthiness of the one praying. But according to this later *Tanh.* source, the Gentile's request of the God of Israel is automatically answered, disregarding entirely the issue of the worthiness of the Gentile offering the prayer. This dispensation is offered in order to teach the Gentile to revere the God of the Jews. In Solomon's prayer, the Gentile turns to the God of Israel after hearing of God's mighty deeds. In our source, God converts the Gentiles by immediately fulfilling their requests. In the parallel version of the standard edition of the *Tanh.*, this passage culminates in a future world where all the nations of the world will recognize God's special relationship with Israel and themselves adhere to Israel. Zech 8:23 is cited as the ultimate formulation of the nations joining Israel in worshiping God.

How can we explain the shift in attitude from R. Yehoshua Ben Levi's mocking statement of the role of the tabernacle in *Leviticus Rabbah* to the universalistic vision that accompanies his statement in the context of the temple in the *Tanh.* (Buber) text? This expansive and inclusive vision of the *Tanh.* runs counter to what Israel Knohl has shown to be an opposite trend concerning Gentile sacrifices, where the *Tanh.* is less accepting than earlier sources.[12] Research of the *Tanh.* has progressed significantly over the last decades, but we are still a long way from a comprehensive view of the range and evolution of rabbinic thought and theology presented there.[13]

Let us turn to what I take to be another Second Temple vision[14] of the Jerusalem temple as a locus for all peoples' prayers. Psalm 65:2–5 reads:

> Praise befits you in Zion, O God; vows are paid to You;
> All mankind comes to You, You who hear prayer.
> When all manner of sins overwhelm me, it is You who
> forgive our iniquities.
> Happy is the person You choose and bring near to dwell in Your
> courts; may we be sated with the blessings of Your house, Your holy
> Temple.

The NJPS renders *kol basar* as "mankind" and relegates the more literal "all flesh" to a footnote. This passage and the psalms that immediately surround it look toward the eventual recognition of Israel's God by all people. As in Solomon's prayer, this prayer envisages all flesh, all humans, approaching God, who hears prayer. Those who are fortunate will be chosen by God to be brought near and reside in God's courtyards, basking in God's goodness. Does this also include, *kol basar*, all human beings? Will they be brought near[15] and reside in God's courtyards? It is important to note that here also the temple courtyards are a venue of prayer. How was this verse understood by the Jewish sages of late antiquity?

The verse is cited five times in Tannaitic literature, twice in parallel sources in the two *Mekhiltot* (with minor but interesting differences) and once more in *Sifre Num.* 42 with a partial parallel in *Sifre Zuta*. Let us begin with the *Mekhilta d'Rabbi Yishmael* in the Lauterbach translation, adopted by Judah Goldin in his important work *The Song at the Sea*:[16]

> How comely Thou art, how majestic in holiness! For unlike the rule with flesh and blood is the rule of the Holy One, Blessed be He. The rule with flesh and blood is that one cannot say two things simultaneously. But He Who Spake and the World Came to Be proclaimed the

> Ten Commandments in one utterance, something impossible for flesh and blood to do, as it said, "And God spoke all these words saying...."[17] (Exod 20:1)
>
> The rule of flesh and blood is that one cannot hear clearly when two people cry out simultaneously. But that is not the case with Him Who Spake and the World Came to Be. On the contrary, even when all the inhabitants of the World come and cry out before Him, He hears their cries clearly, as it is said, "O Thou that hearest prayer, unto Thee doth all flesh come." (Ps 65:3)

God's uniqueness is measured here in God's ability to both speak many words simultaneously and, no less, to hear many voices simultaneously. Noteworthy is the fact that the almost verbatim parallel in *Mekhilta d' Rashbi* omits the phrase containing "all the inhabitants of the World come and cry before him," but this may be no more than an omission due to homoioteleuton. The import of both sources is that God listens to the cries/prayers of all flesh. God's speaking and listening capacities are wholly other than those of a human being.

The other passage which sheds light on our verse is found in *Sifre Num.* 42, where we read:

> One verse says, "You hear prayer" (Ps 65:3) and the other verse says, "You have screened yourself off with a cloud [that no prayer may pass through] (Lam 3:44). How can these two verses be upheld? Until the decree is sealed, "You hear prayer," after the decree is sealed . . . [no prayer may pass through].

The theological conundrum posed by the verse in Lamentations, a God who no longer hears prayer, is dissolved through positing a point of no return. Once God's decree is final, even prayer won't help. This difficult theological issue is interesting in its own right, but it follows hard on the heels of a similar exegesis which concerns Israel only—God will "lift up his countenance" (Num 6:26) only until their decree or fate is sealed, since God must be impartial (Deut 10:17: "shows no favor" lit. "lift up his countenance"). Did the *Sifre* intend this verse, Num 6:26, to speak of God's special relationship with Israel by linking it to the previous exegesis, which spoke of Israel's doing God's will? Or are we to take the passage quoted above from the *Sifre* as describing God, the hearer of prayer, in relation to all who pray to God and not just Israel? The *Sifre* context would seem to indicate that the verse was being applied solely to Israel, but recently M. Kahana, in his extensive commentary on the *Sifre,* posits a possible affinity between our text and Rom 2:9–11.[18] If his suggestion is correct, this *Sifre* passage is to be taken as another universalist position and describes God's behavior when listening to the prayer of all humankind.[19]

I return to our opening passages of 1 Kgs 8 and Isa 56 to suggest the following reading of these passages as interpreted by the rabbinic sages. All of Israel prays to one place wherever they may be. The exilic Deuteronomist held that God's name was in the temple, though God resided above, since even the heavens cannot accommodate the Divine. The *Tanh.* passage went as far as to accord to the Gentile prayer in Jerusalem immediate and unconditional acceptance, a patronizing concession to the Gentile's recognition of the God of Israel.[20] Ironically, in late Second Temple times the Gentile was met in Jerusalem by a warning not to enter the temple of Jerusalem on pain of death. This is attested both in Josephus and in the Soreg inscription.[21]

As Yochanan Muffs taught many years ago, Second Temple Judaism sees a shift from a temple-centered religion to a Bible-centered one, a shift from the Ps 23 vision of luxuriating in God's house and sweetness to Ps 119's paean to the Law. The most fortunate Jews in late Second Temple times combined both visions. They studied and preached in the temple's courtyards. This is attested in *t. Sanhedrin* 6, which claims that there was a *beit midrash* (a house of study) where the Sanhedrin retired on Shabbat to study, rather than adjudicate. This is no less clear in the synoptic Gospels' view of Jesus teaching and preaching in the temple, and Peter and Paul are reported to have gone to the temple to pray at the time of the Tamid offering.

But when the temple was destroyed for the second time in 70 C.E., Torah became the ultimate locus of God's presence; God's words were, in some way, part and parcel of God's being. A bitter debate ensued in rabbinic literature as to whether the Gentiles should be allowed the same access to God's word, God's Torah, as they were to God's Temple.[22]

It was Leopold Zunz, in his magnificent 1832 history of midrash, who wrote that the synagogue and the Torah therein had become the national homeland of the Jew.[23] The Torah became the ultimate source and location of Jewish nationalism, but it was a mobile home! Was it really necessary any longer to study God's Torah in God's temple in Jerusalem, Sinai in Zion?[24] Or was it not always the case since antiquity that there was no one center, but at least two foci, as the great twentieth-century thinker Simon Rawidowicz asserted?[25]

Our short study, focusing on Isa 56 and 1 Kgs 8 and their interpretation in rabbinic literature, has shown that the twin issues of the universal appeal of Judaism, on the one hand, and its geographical locus, on the other, have allowed for quite differing views over the last three millennia.

NOTES

1. All biblical translations are from the NJPS.

2. Jon D. Levenson, "From Temple to Synagogue: 1 Kings 8," in *Traditions in Transformation: Turning Points in Biblical Faith* (ed. Baruch Halpern and Jon D. Levenson; Winona Lake, Ind.: Eisenbrauns, 1981), 158–59.

3. Ibid., 165.

4. Concerning Gentile sacrifice see I. Knohl's article "Accepting Sacrifices from the Gentiles," [Hebrew] *Tarbiz* 48 (1979): 341–45.

5. See Lieberman's lengthy discussion and correction of the verse 1 Kgs 8:44: "They pray (*we-hitpallělû*) to the Lord in the direction (*derek* = via) of the city which you have chosen and the house which you have built," emphasizing the end of the verse. But all the versions of the *Tosefta* read *we-yitpallělû* and continue in a version unknown in the Masoretic Text. If the verb form is correct, it is to be found in Scripture only at 2 Chr 7:14 in God's answer to Solomon's prayer: "and they will pray and *seek my face,*" which would be a lovely proof text. More likely is that the good manuscripts of both the *Tosefta* and the parallel at *Sifre Deut.* 29 use a non-masoritic formulation of Kings and Chronicles, which needn't (or possibly shouldn't) be corrected and still point to the verses Lieberman has noted. See his notes in *Tosefta Ki-fshuta* (3rd ed. [augmented]; New York: Jewish Theological Seminary, 2001), 1:43–45, and Finkelstein's comments on the *Sifre* passage (*Sifre: Deuteronomy* [New York: Jewish Theological Seminary, 1966–69]) ad locum.

6. *Tosefta Ki-fshuta,* 44 on line 69.

7. This is even more so the case if we don't follow Eideles/Lieberman's interpretation and read the *Tosefta* not as applying to the Chronicles verse, which originally spoke of the Gentile, but as applying instead to the Jew who was in Jerusalem, but not near the temple.

8. "*Nitrazin be-tôk panniktêhen.*" The first word, *nitrazin*, has been studied extensively. See M. Moreshet, *Lexicon Hapoal* (Ramat Gan: Bar Ilan Press, 1980), 392–93, who defines it as "torn or split" and cites its appearance in *Tosefta*. Lieberman devotes a long and erudite philological treatment of the passage at *t. Sot.* 8:7 (*Tosefta Ki–fshuta*, 704–5) and follows Rashi in interpreting the word *nitraz* to mean, "soiled themselves." It might be that we have a midrashic play on Ps 29:7: "The voice of the Lord convulses the wilderness (*midbar*)." The word *panniktêhen* is evidently a Greek loanword whose identification and meaning remain elusive. Krauss suggested πινακοθηκή=*Bildersaal* in his *Griechische und lateinische Lehnwörter im Talmud, Midrasch, und Targum* (Berlin: S. Calvary, 1899), 465, but in his additions to this work Löw points to other suggestions and evidently remains unconvinced by any of them. I have followed a suggestion by Brüll, referred to by Löw in his glosses on Krauss, mainly because of the usage of the word in the *Targum* to Ps 68:30.

9. J. Z. Lauterbach, ed. and trans., *Mekilta de–Rabbi Ishmael*, vol. 2 (Philadelphia: Jewish Publication Society, 1933), 2:233.

10. See S. Lieberman, *Hellenism in Jewish Palestine* (New York: Jewish Theological Seminary, 1962), 115–38.

11. *Sefer Vehizhir* (parasha *Teruma*) adds simply "and not only was the Temple beneficial for the Peoples of the world but even the Tabernacle" (ed. Israel Freiman; [Leipzig: 1873, repr. Israel]), 156. On the provenance of *Sefer Vehizhir*, see N. Danzig, *Introduction to Halakhot Pesuqot* (New York: Jewish Theological Seminary, 1993), 64–65n128.

12. Knohl, "Accepting Sacrifices."

13. In the meantime see Marc Bregman, *The Tanhuma-Yelammedenu Literature: Studies in the Evolution of the Versions* (Piscataway, N.J.: Gorgias Press, 2003).

14. In his commentary, Briggs sees v. 3 as the hand of "a later glossator influenced by Isa 56:7 and 66:23" who "gives this worship a universal reference by insertion of *unto Thee all flesh*" (*Psalms* [Edinburgh: T and T Clark, 1907]), 81.

15. In rabbinic literature *qrb* is a technical term "for admission of a candidate into the *Haburah*" (S. Lieberman, *Texts and Studies* [New York: Ktav, 1974], 200–201, especially n. 8).

16. Judah Goldin, *The Song at the Sea* (Philadelphia: Jewish Publication Society, 1990), 197–99.

17. I have used the NJPS rather than Lauterbach's quote of "in one utterance" in the context of the verse, too. Those words do not exist in the Hebrew of the midrashic text as part of the verse.

18. See Menahem I. Kahana, *Sifre on Numbers: An Annotated Edition* (Jerusalem: Hebrew University Magnes Press, 2011), 2:324–25.

19. Kahana contrasts the *Sifre* text with versions in later rabbinic texts, *Tanh. Tzav* 5, which explicitly restrict this verse in Numbers, describing God's graciousness to Israel and not to the Gentiles.

20. Unless I am being overly literal in my own reading of the verse, God is extraordinarily attentive to the Gentile who comes to pray, but only when the Gentile physically approaches the temple either on a personal pilgrimage or as part of an international acclamation of the God of Israel as in Isa 66.

21. See E. Bickerman's wonderful essay, "The Warning Inscriptions of Herod's Temple," *JQR* n.s. 37 (1947): 387–45.

22. See, e.g., M. Goodman, *Mission and Conversion* (Oxford: Oxford University Press, 1994), 132–33, who relies on later sources. The relevant talmudic passages are brought and discussed by Robert Goldenberg, *The Nations That Know Thee Not* (New York: New York University Press, 1998), 87–88 and especially 160n38.

23. L. Zunz, *Die gottesdienstlichen Vorträge der Juden historisch entwickelt* (Berlin, 1832), 1–2.

24. J. Levenson, *Sinai and Zion: An Entry into the Jewish Bible* (Minneapolis: Winston Press, 1985).

25. S. Rawidowicz, *Studies in Jewish Thought* (Philadelphia: Jewish Publication Society, 1974) is a translation of some of his more extensive Hebrew works. In ch. 3, he develops his idea of "the two houses," which are not the temporal houses but modes of religiosity. In the next chapter, "Israel the Ever-dying People," he continues to stress the importance of a unified Israel (223). Most interesting is his comment on our topic: "The first house is of Israel and for the Gentiles, 'a house of prayer for all the peoples'. . . . But the second house is a house of Torah, and only for Israel" (159). Compare M. Hirshman, "Rabbinic Universalism in the Second and Third Centuries," *HTR* 93 (2000): 101–15.

CHAPTER 10

The Descent of the Wicked Angels and the Persistence of Evil

JAMES KUGEL

I am pleased to offer the following brief study of ancient biblical interpretation in honor of my longtime friend Jon Levenson. From the time of our first meeting—by my count, some forty-two years ago—I have regularly, and gratefully, benefited from his wit and insight. His scholarship has always been a model of integrity and intellectual honesty (qualities hardly to be taken for granted, even in the university) as he has pursued some of the most important topics in biblical studies. It is indeed a privilege to be among those acknowledging his great contribution to the field and wishing him continued success in the years to come.

— Despite this volume's overall theme of Israel's election, I have decided to devote my essay to another favorite Levenson topic, the persistence of evil. In the following I would like to consider the development of a particular bit of ancient biblical interpretation elaborating on this theme, one that originated in contemplation of the first four verses of chapter 6 in Genesis. But before getting down to specifics, I wish to evoke briefly an aspect of ancient biblical interpretation that is sometimes overlooked.

Of course, speaking about ancient *biblical* interpretation is in itself a much-acknowledged anachronism:[1] no one disputes that there was a great deal of interpretation before there was a fixed canon of texts that constituted Israel's sacred library, that is to say, before there was anything resembling a "Bible." Indeed, what might therefore be called, with only a touch of Levensonian irony, prebiblical biblical interpretation—that is, explications and interpretations of different parts of the Pentateuch and various other books even before these came to be included in one or another official canon—such interpretation abounds in the second and first centuries B.C.E, in the Dead Sea Scrolls as well as in the biblical Apocrypha and Pseudepigrapha.

But it was not just the inventory of writings that was not yet fixed; the texts themselves were still somewhat in flux. This has been demonstrated clearly by the Qumran manuscripts: ancient texts continued to be modified in ways great and small,[2] and different "editions" of the various books that were later included in the biblical canon(s) seem to have circulated freely in the first and second centuries B.C.E. Sometimes the differences between these editions are slight, but at other times they are considerable. One well-known example of the latter (but it is hardly the only one) is the book of Jeremiah. One form of the book is preserved in the Septuagint and two Qumran fragments, 4Q71 (4QJer^b) and 4Q72a (4QJer^d), whereas another form is represented by the Masoretic text as well as by the Qumran texts denoted 4Q70 (4QJer^a), 4Q72 (4QJer^c), and 4Q72b (4QJer^e). The latter version presents a considerably longer book of Jeremiah and arranges the material in different order; apparently (though perhaps not irrefutably),[3] it bears witness to a process of supplementation and reordering carried out on a massive scale.

None of this process is surprising to someone schooled in the ways of modern biblical scholarship, since earlier periods in the history of

Israel had witnessed even more dramatic changes in the texts that were destined for the Hebrew Bible. Indeed, there is scarcely a book in the Hebrew canon that is not acknowledged today to have been the product of ongoing supplementation and rearrangement, sometimes on a massive scale. To cite but one example, the last third of the book of Isaiah is indisputably not the work of the eighth-century prophet named Isaiah; it came, rather, from an anonymous writer (or writers) who lived a century and a half after Isaiah, during the time of the Babylonian exile and the return to Judea. But even the thirty-nine chapters that precede this anonymous prophet's words are not all one piece. For example, the oracles against foreign nations (chapters 13–23) are now generally thought to have come from different hands during or following the period of Assyrian ascendancy in the ancient Near East. Likewise, the "Isaiah Apocalypse" (chapters 24–27) is widely recognized to be an independent unit which may have been composed during the Babylonian exile or after the return to Zion. The focus of chapters 28–33 belongs, in the opinion of many scholars, back in the eighth century, but then the text turns to the condemnation of Edom (chapter 34–35), which many people believe again belongs to the time of the Babylonian exile or that immediately following it.

A question rarely asked is relevant here: What is the conception of Scripture that underlies such changes? Or, a bit more polemically: how *sacred* was sacred Scripture if people in those days felt free to rearrange it and add to it, inserting their own ideas or opinions and often distorting or changing entirely the original sense of the text? To this question I wish to return at the end of this study; for now, however, I think it sufficient to point out the obvious and say that a gradual process of narrowing is clearly evident in the evolution of the texts concerned. Back in an earlier day, texts were apparently quite malleable. Then, with time, the options became more limited: an explicative gloss or two, or minor additions, subtractions or rewordings, were still possible, but the heavy lifting of earlier centuries was no longer thinkable. Soon, the Sacred Writ would be altogether immutable.

Or would it? Even before the petrifaction of sacred texts was a fait accompli, a parallel strategy for preserving their fundamental malleability was in the works, namely, ancient biblical interpretation. "The text may say X," ancient interpreters endlessly assert, "but what it really means is Y."[4] This assertion underlies the whole phenomenon of the so-called Rewritten Bible[5]—texts like the book of *Jubilees* or the *Genesis Apocryphon* from Qumran, which retell and explain biblical narratives in their own words—as well as commentaries proper, such as are found in the writings of Philo of Alexandria, or 4Q252 and other *pesher* texts from Qumran. And this same approach continued to be endorsed and elaborated by still later Jewish and Christian interpreters, in rabbinic midrash and in the exegetical writings of the Church Fathers. These two forms of malleability are not usually presented as part of a single continuum,[6] but viewed from a distance, their basic affinity is unmistakable.

Particularly relevant in this connection are the so-called "Reworked Pentateuch" texts from Qumran (4Q158, 4Q364, 4Q365, 4Q366, and 4Q367), which have dramatically raised the question of where the border lies between the text itself and the interpretation thereof.[7] Long before these Qumran texts were published, scholars were familiar with the textual variants in the Samaritan Pentateuch, to which these Qumran texts bear some resemblance.[8] One striking feature of the Samaritan Pentateuch that differentiates it from both the Masoretic text and the Old Greek (Septuagint) version is its quite conscious effort to harmonize different parts of the Torah—sometimes by smoothing out rather trivial matters such as the spelling of names, but at other times harmonizing on a larger scale.[9] An example of the latter is the Samaritan Pentateuch's insertion of material from Deut 5:26 (some Bibles: 5:29) and Deut 18:18–22 into its version of Exod 20:19–22. The resultant Exodus text includes God's promise to Moses that he will have a prophetic successor—a promise that is found in the Masoretic and Septuagint texts only in Deuteronomy. (The arrangement of Samaritan Pentateuch seems altogether appropriate since, according to the Deuteronomy texts, God's promise to Moses was originally made at the time of the great revelation at Mount Sinai, which is first recounted in Exod 20.)

There can be little doubt that the Samaritan Pentateuch was and is considered by the Samaritans as the correct, canonical text of the Torah. Even if they were aware of other text traditions, this would hardly affect the canonical status of their Pentateuch in their own eyes. Theirs must have been simply, at least for them, the correct Torah (or else they surely would have adopted some other version). But then, where does one draw the line between text and commentary? Was the so-called Reworked Pentateuch likewise considered simply another version of the Pentateuch? Although it bears a clear relationship to the Samaritan Pentateuch, it differs in one important respect. While the Samaritan Pentateuch for the most part[10] harmonizes, combining texts from one part of the Pentateuch with another in order to create a more consistent whole, the Reworked Pentateuch also adds new material here and there (whether of its own devising or imported from some other Second Temple period text is difficult to say). Thus, for example, chapter 15 of the book of Exodus recounts that Moses and the Israelites had sung a song of thanksgiving after their successful crossing of the Red Sea. The biblical text then states that Miriam, Aaron's sister, also led the women in song (Exod 15:20–21). According to the Masoretic text and the Septuagint, the words of that song altogether parallel the opening words of the song that Moses and the Israelites had just sung: "Sing to the Lord for He has gloriously triumphed, horse and rider He has cast into the sea." Not so the Reworked Pentateuch. There (4Q365 frgs. 6a col ii and 6c), Miriam clearly sings a song of her own. This part of the scroll is quite fragmentary, but there is no doubt that Miriam has been given a set of lyrics quite different from that of Moses and unknown from any other source.[11]

Such bits of evidence have caused scholars to ponder the very rubric "Reworked Pentateuch." Were not these texts simply someone else's version of the Pentateuch? This certainly seems a possibility, especially in view of their close cousin, the Samaritan Pentateuch.[12] Or do its little additions and changes put the work into a different category, not a formal text of the Pentateuch exactly, but a modestly explicative reworking thereof, one whose author was basically content to leave most of the Pentateuch as he had received it, but who felt here and there that some explanatory gloss or other insertion was just what the text needed to be perfect, or perfectly understood?[13] Or—more fundamentally—is our whole notion of Scripture as a fixed text simply out of keeping with the views current in the late Second Temple period?[14] Any of these alternatives seems possible, but all of them raise a further question: how many changes—and of what sort—were needed before a text of Scripture became an explicative paraphrase, or a wholly different (and largely interpretive) retelling such as the book of *Jubilees*? As various scholars have suggested,[15] it may be indeed possible to compile a set of criteria enabling us at some point to draw a line between an actual scriptural text (albeit one different from other extant textual witnesses) and a rewriting of, or running commentary on, a scriptural text. But the very attempt to do so may obscure the point being raised here: from the Qumran evidence it seems rather clear that an altogether smooth path leads from altering the text itself through editorial or scribal insertions to altering the text through external works of commentary. In fact, long before the biblical text had become quite immutable, there already existed a highly developed tradition of interpretation whose basic message was: "I know the text doesn't say this, but what it really means is such-and-such."

The dramatic changes introduced by ancient interpreters—far outstripping the minor modifications introduced by Scripture's last text-revisers—extend the question mentioned above well beyond the second or first centuries B.C.E. What indeed *is* the conception of Scripture underlying such major and long-term changes? Indeed, despite the fact that it was stuck with a virtually fixed text, ancient biblical interpretation nevertheless ended up changing the sense or significance of an overwhelming number of biblical laws, stories, prophecies, and other writings. (My own study of ancient biblical interpretation suggests to me that, far from merely preserving the status quo of malleability that had preceded it, the early stages of ancient biblical interpretation were characterized by even greater freedom, allowing interpreters to "deduce" from innocent-looking details in scriptural narratives facts not in evidence, indeed, conversations or whole incidents unreported in Scripture, as well as motives and means left unspecified by the narrative, and to exercise a similar freedom in interpreting scriptural laws and scriptural prophecy.)[16] This went on for centuries and centuries after canonization. At what point, then, did Scripture really begin to be more fixed and immutable? I do not intend to try to offer even the most general answer to this question, other than to say that such an answer would probably bring us up to uncomfortably recent times and reiterate what

I have already implied—that the two kinds of freedom mentioned, textual and interpretive, are really all part of a single mentality, one that seems particularly strange to us today precisely because our own way of thinking about the Bible has become (albeit relatively recently) very different from what prevailed in ancient times.

In order to bring this process into somewhat clearer focus, I would like here to examine a specific series of changes that came about in connection with Gen 6:1–4. These verses, cited below in italics, ought first to be considered in their overall scriptural setting.

> [28] When Lamech had lived one hundred eighty-two years, he became the father of a son; [29] he named him Noah, saying, "Out of the ground that the LORD has cursed this one shall bring us relief from our work and from the toil of our hands." [30] Lamech lived after the birth of Noah five hundred ninety-five years, and had other sons and daughters. [31] Thus all the days of Lamech were seven hundred seventy-seven years; and he died. [32] After Noah was five hundred years old, Noah became the father of Shem, Ham, and Japheth.
>
> *6:1 When people began to multiply on the face of the ground, and daughters were born to them, [2] the sons of God saw that they were fair; and they took wives for themselves of all that they chose. [3] Then the LORD said, "My spirit shall not abide in mortals forever, for they are flesh; their days shall be one hundred twenty years." [4] The Nephilim were on the earth in those days—and also afterward—when the sons of God went in to the daughters of humans, who bore children to them. These were the heroes of old, warriors of renown.*
>
> [5] The LORD saw that the wickedness of humankind was great in the earth, and that every inclination of the thoughts of their hearts was only evil continually. [6] And the LORD was sorry that he had made humankind on the earth, and it grieved him to his heart. [7] So the LORD said, "I will blot out from the earth the human beings I have created—people together with animals and creeping things and birds of the air, for I am sorry that I have made them." [8] But Noah found favor in the sight of the LORD.
>
> [9] These are the descendants of Noah. Noah was a righteous man, blameless in his generation; Noah walked with God. [10] And Noah had

three sons, Shem, Ham, and Japheth. ¹¹ Now the earth was corrupt in God's sight, and the earth was filled with violence. And God saw that the earth was corrupt; for all flesh had corrupted its ways upon the earth. (Gen 5:28–6:11)

Many biblical scholars and ordinary readers—from the anonymous author of one of the earliest parts of *1 Enoch* to commentators in our own time[17]—have seen in those four verses an instance of the rampant sinfulness that caused God to bring about the great flood: the "sons of God" (presumably, angelic beings) mated with the daughters of men, and this led directly to the disaster that followed. But a closer examination of those verses will reveal that they really have nothing to do with the flood or God's wholesale destruction of humanity; in fact, there is nothing negative said in them about humanity at all. Neither do those verses make any mention of sin or divine disapproval thereof, nor of any coming cataclysm. Not one word! On the contrary, they are all about something rather positive, the origins of those people whom the end of the passage calls "the heroes that were of old, warriors of renown."

What, then, was the intended role of these four verses? Originally, they were meant to be a continuation of the genealogy that immediately precedes them, that is, the last verses of Gen. 5. Having ended its list of the first generations of humanity stopping at Noah, the text then went on to include a brief note about those who are not covered in this genealogy, namely, those "heroes of old, warriors of renown"—legendary, semi-divine figures of the sort familiar from ancient folklore, some of whom were apparently known in ancient Canaan as the Nephilim.[18] The fame of these ancient heroes was no doubt celebrated in song and story, even if, for one reason or another, most of their legends never made it into the final version of the Bible's history.[19]

So the question that these four verses sought to answer was: Where did those "heroes of old, warriors of renown"—still well known when this passage was written—where did they come from? If they lived way back in ancient times, why are they not mentioned in the preceding genealogy? And the answer given in those four verses is that these "heroes of old" did not have human fathers: rather, their superhuman strength or courage—as well as, apparently, their great longevity—derived precisely from the fact that they were descended from the "sons of God," who at a certain point mated with those lovely daughters of mankind.

"And why," one might ask, "don't people today live as long, and perform the same sort of amazing deeds, as those *heroes of old* once did?" The answer given by this passage is that, at some point, God decided that He would not continue to permit the mixing of divine creatures with humans: "Then the Lord said, 'My spirit shall not abide in mortals forever, for they are flesh; their days shall be one hundred and twenty years.'" In other words, this divine-human mating will cease—not because it is bad (the text does not say that)—but just because, at a certain point, God decided not to allow any more of these superheroes to be born. From now on, humans will be entirely human, and they will live only a normal human lifespan of 120 years maximum; that is why there are no more superheroes walking the earth. This is where the genealogy of chapter 5 really ended, and it was followed immediately by the flood narrative proper.

In fact, my guess is that Gen 6:1–4 actually represents an early insertion into an existing, written account of humanity's early ancestors. The reason is that, in their present location, these verses definitely interrupt the narrative flow. Having reached the time of Noah and his sons in Gen 5:32, the text ought naturally to have continued into the story of the flood itself—and it probably did so, originally. But then someone thought of the problem of the superheroes' absence from this list of early ancestors and set out to remedy the omission. If so, the intrusion of Gen 6:1–4 into this narrative takes us back to the time when the text was still a rather malleable thing. The disappearance of those "heroes of old" in later times required some explanation, and so a whole paragraph was inserted here, in its most logical place.

As for the reason for God's bringing the flood and destroying almost all of humanity along with birds and beasts, the narrative gave its answer only in the next paragraph, and it is the Bible's frequent answer for acts of divine wrath: human sinfulness. People often become lawless, violent, or simply *bad* in the Bible, and this usually leads to divine punishment. What their crimes actually were is often left unstated; they simply *were* sinful, just as, long after the flood, the people of Sodom were "very wicked sinners against the Lord" (Gen. 13:13), without any further details. Still later, with the rise of various oppressors of Israel's tribes during the period of the Judges, the Bible's default reason for punishment comes down once again to human sinfulness—the ancient Israelite equivalent of "round up the usual suspects."

So, sinfulness caused the flood. Such an explanation no doubt sufficed for a while. Eventually, however, people must have wanted to know precisely what the generation of the flood had done that was so bad—if for no other reason than to avoid being destroyed for doing the same thing. It was then that the old appendix to chapter 5's genealogy took on a new aspect, and we pass from the Age of Text Alteration to the Age of Text Interpretation. Suddenly (or perhaps gradually), the paragraph originally intended to explain the disappearance of the superheroes was enlisted for a new purpose, explaining God's reason for bringing the flood. This was hardly a natural or self-evident move: as we have seen, there is nothing in our passage that asserts that the "sons of God" or their offspring had done anything wrong, nor is there any reference in the rest of the flood story to their supposed role in bringing the cataclysm about. Nevertheless, some ancient interpreter or school of interpreters sought to explain the flood by making that connection, and the very fact that it was not made *within the text*—the fact that no further hint was inserted into Gen 6:1–4, nor any back-reference introduced into the rest of the story—bears eloquent witness to the now nearly immutable nature of the text. Yet such was the power of authoritative interpretation that once ancient sages came to espouse the idea that Gen 6:1–4 set out the cause of the flood, people simply accepted that explanation as fact. There must have been something wrong, something horribly wrong, with the act that gave birth to those superheroes—an act that one writer has recently described as "crossing heavenly lines for immoral purposes."[20]

Thus, the very first midrashic act in the story I am tracing consisted of reinterpreting those four verses not as the conclusion of a genealogy but as the start of the flood narrative. I have no doubt that this midrashic act goes back a long way, perhaps to even before the third century B.C.E., when it first appeared in print. In any event, what seems to be the most ancient Jewish account suggesting a causal connection between the flood and this act of divine-human mating is found in *1 Enoch:*

> And when the sons of men had multiplied, in those days, beautiful and comely daughters were born to them. And the Watchers, the sons of heaven, saw them and desired them. And they said to one another, "Come let us choose for ourselves wives from the daughters of men, and let us beget for ourselves children." And Shemihazah, their chief, said to them, "I fear you will not want to do this deed, and I alone shall be guilty of a great sin." And they all answered him and said, "Let us all swear an oath, and let us all bind one another with a curse, that none of us turn back from this counsel until we fulfill it and do this deed." (*1 En.* 6:1–4)[21]

This text, it is plain to see, starts off by restating the first two of our four verses in Genesis. The only significant difference is that the "sons of God" in Genesis are here identified as the Watchers, the *'irin*, a class of angels, who are described as the "sons of heaven." (The latter is certainly a euphemism for "sons of God," but not a difference in kind.) The leader of the Watchers, Shemihazah, is worried that his colleagues may back out, and it is for this reason that they all swear an oath and a binding curse that they will all participate. This is presented later on as a name etymology for their place of landing, Mount Hermon: "And they called the mountain 'Hermon' because they swore and bound one another with a curse on it" (*1 En.* 6:6). But it is certainly remarkable here that the mating of the Watchers with the daughters of men is now defined as a "great sin," as it was not in the biblical text.

In truth, there was no small amount of confusion as to what the sin actually consisted of. Perhaps because the human part of these divine-human unions was rather passive (after all, Genesis had said that the sons of God simply *took wives for themselves of all that they chose*, so that the women apparently had little say in the matter) or perhaps because, even if the women were actively guilty in this sin, this still left the human males in the clear—for either or both of these reasons, various other traditions developed that attributed to humans of both sexes a more active, and hence a more damning, role.

These traditions have been studied extensively, so there is little reason to review them in detail here.[22] In brief: the angels passed on forbidden knowledge to the women, and this pillow talk eventually reached the males. As a result, both men and women began to sin. The men learned metallurgy and the makings of instruments of war, which they soon turned on one another; or else the knowledge of metallurgy led the men to manufacture jewelry for their women, and/or the women themselves became expert in the cosmetic arts, either of which inevitably leads to lewdness. The Watchers were also said to have taught the people spells and sorcery, as well as the cutting of roots (perhaps for the purpose of provoking abortions). According to *1 Enoch* and other sources, any or all of these things may have led God to bring about the flood. It also seemed likely that people had begun to sin with animals and birds, since God destroyed animal life as well as humans in the flood.

Then, of course, there was also the matter of the offspring of the sons of God, the Nephilim mentioned in Gen 6:4. Creatures by the same name are mentioned later on in the Pentateuch in the book of Numbers, where they are portrayed as being of giant stature[23] (which is why the Septuagint and other sources refer to them in Genesis as "the giants").[24] Thus, if the actual union of angels and humans did not seem sinful enough to justify God's bringing the flood, then perhaps it was these resultant giant hybrids, the Nephilim, who pushed things over the edge. After all, God had said in Gen. 6:3, "My spirit shall not abide in mortals forever, for they are flesh." This certainly sounded like a reference to these half-human half-angelic creatures; if God said that they were no longer to exist, was it not because they themselves were evil? So it was that the *1 Enoch, Jubilees,* and other Second Temple works presented these offspring as cannibals: first they ate each other, and when that supply of meat ran out, they began to eat human beings—hence the violence and blood-sopped impurity that corrupted the earth. In the words of *1 En.* 7:3: "The giants began to kill men and devour them . . . and they drank the blood."

When, in *1 Enoch,* the four great angels, Michael, Sariel, Raphael, and Gabriel, report to God on all these happenings, God immediately resolves to send a purifying flood to wipe the earth clean of its iniquity. This is likewise stated outright in *1 Enoch:*

> Then the Most High said, and the Great Holy One spoke. And He sent Sariel to the son of Lamech, saying: "Go to Noah and say to him in My name: 'Hide yourself.' And reveal to him that the end is coming,

that the whole earth will perish; and tell him that a deluge is about to come on the whole earth and destroy everything on the earth." (*1 En.* 10:1–2)

With this, the exegetical problem that started things off was now solved. The cause of the great flood was clear: some wicked angels began to mate with the daughters of men, which was itself an act of impurity unprecedented and unrepeated in history. If that were not enough, those angels then passed on to the females forbidden knowledge which they soon shared with the human males. Both sexes then took an active role, committing all manner of sins—though perhaps it was the violence of their offspring, the Nephilim, that brought things to such a wicked pass, or possibly it was a combination of all these things. In any case, all these various motifs were aimed at answering the main question arising out of the flood narrative in Genesis: Why did it happen at all?

There was, however, a related exegetical question, one less often recognized as such. It concerns the end of the flood narrative in Genesis, when God vows never again to inundate the earth:

> Then Noah built an altar to the LORD, and took of every clean animal and of every clean bird, and offered burnt offerings on the altar. And when the LORD smelled the pleasing odor, the LORD said in his heart, "I will never again curse the ground because of humankind, for the inclination of the human heart is evil from youth; nor will I ever again destroy every living creature as I have done. As long as the earth endures, seedtime and harvest, cold and heat, summer and winter, day and night, shall not cease." (Gen. 8:20–22)

The exegetical problem posed by this passage is clearly stated by Philo of Alexandria in his *Quaestiones et Solutiones in Genesis:*[25]

> What is the meaning of the words, "And the Lord God said . . . 'Never again will I curse the earth because of the deeds of men, for the thought of man is resolutely turned toward evils from his youth. Therefore, never again will I smite all living flesh as I did on another occasion.'" . . . How then (did it happen) that, with the same cause present and with

His knowing from the start that the thought of man is resolutely turned toward evils from his youth, He [God] first destroyed the human race through the flood, but after this said that He would not again destroy (them), even though the same evils remained in their souls? (*QG* 2:54)

A good question! To ancient interpreters, it seemed most unlikely that God had somehow decided to lower His standards and not be so picky any more. Rather, something must have happened to guarantee that humanity would never go astray again. But what? It could not be that He had made sure to kill off those wicked hybrids, the Nephilim, since that passage from the book of Numbers made it clear that at least some of them had survived. (Perhaps, as giants, they could simply have kept their heads above water while everyone else perished.) Besides, the Watchers themselves seem to have been the first and principal cause of God's decision to wipe out humanity. The logical way to make sure that humans would never again fall into such sin was to kill off all the Watchers, so that they could never again repeat their sin with the women or in some other way lead humanity astray.

But there was a problem with that solution as well. Angels, according to the common understanding, cannot be killed. And so they were not killed off in this account either. Instead, the exegetical motif of the Watchers' sinful behavior ended with their being imprisoned, tied up, and held in the depths of the earth. Again, here is part of the narrative of *1 En.* 6–11, the most ancient form of this motif:[26]

And to Michael, He [God] said: "Go, Michael, bind Shemihazah and the others with him, who have united themselves with the daughters of men, so that they were defiled by them in their uncleanness. And . . . bind them for seventy generations in the valleys of the earth, until the day of their judgment and consummation, until the eternal judgment is consummated. Then they will be led away to the fiery abyss, and to the torture, and to the prison where they will be confined forever." (*1 En.* 10:11–13)

Although it is sometimes assigned a very early date (late fourth or early third century B.C.E.), this passage actually seems to combine two different exegetical motifs. For what would be the point of binding the angels now if in any case they are to be sentenced on "the day of their judgment" to be "led away to the fiery abyss ... and to the prison where they will be confined forever." Why not send them to that prison right away? There may be no irrefutable proof of this, but it seems that the original idea was simply to tie up the unkillable Watchers and render them powerless so as to prevent any further corruption of human beings; later, this understanding was harmonized with the Second Temple picture of hell, that fiery abyss which was to become their final resting place.[27]

As a side note, something else about this passage should be noted. The descent of the Watchers and their subsequent imprisonment in the depths of the earth ought in no way to be construed, as it sometimes is,[28] as a primordial "myth" designed to explain the origin of evil. What kind of explanation of the origin of evil is it to say that a group of wicked angels came down to earth, caused some trouble, and then ended up being tied up to await final sentencing? Where is heaven-generated evil going to come from if its only perpetrators are all in handcuffs?[29] No, the story of the wicked angels is not about the origin of evil, nor is any such claim found in the story itself. Rather, as we have seen, it started off as an attempt to portray the originally independent first four verses of Gen 6 as the proximate cause of the flood. That primal act of impurity, wedding the human with the divine, was what brought about disaster, and if God subsequently promised that there would be no more cataclysms of that sort, it was because those who had led humanity astray were now safely tucked away in a subterranean prison.

A strikingly common phenomenon in ancient biblical interpretation is that the creation of an exegetical motif often solves one problem only to create another, and this is precisely what happened with this motif as well. Binding up the Watchers did indeed explain how God could promise never to bring another flood. But if those bad angels were now subdued, why was there still evil in the world?

To this question a number of answers were presented. One is found in *1 En.* 15, which is certainly a later modification of the original story in *1 En.* 6–11.[30] At the start of *1 En.* 15, Enoch is told to "reprove the Watchers," which he proceeds to do: "Why have you forsaken the high

The Descent of the Wicked Angels and the Persistence of Evil 225

heaven," he asks, "and lain with women, and defiled yourselves with the daughters of men?" (*1 En.* 15:3). But he then turns to the subject of their offspring, the Nephilim/giants:

> But now the giants who were begotten by the spirits and flesh—they will call them [i.e. they will henceforth be considered] evil spirits on the earth, for their dwelling will [indeed] be on the earth. The spirits that have gone forth from the body of their flesh are evil spirits, for from humans they came into being, and [yet also] from the holy Watchers was the origin of their creation. Evil spirits will they will be on the earth, and evil spirits they will be called. . . . And the evil spirits of the giants <lead astray>, do violence, make desolate, and attack and wrestle and hurl upon the earth and <cause illnesses>. . . . These spirits rise up against the sons of men and against the women, for they have come forth from them. (*1 En.* 15:8–12)

Here, the existence of evil on earth derives specifically from the hybrid nature of the Nephilim/giants. Born of women, they are earthly creatures; but the "spirit" part of them has now become detached from their bodies (which, presumably, were wiped out in the slaughter that preceded the flood), leaving these malign spirits free to roam the earth. It is they who are responsible for any wickedness that continues to exist after the flood: "These spirits rise up against the sons of men and against the women" and cause evil.

A somewhat different answer is presented in the book of *Jubilees*. Following the flood, Noah's grandsons find themselves afflicted by wicked demons, who lead them into folly and sin such as existed before the flood. Noah prays to God not to allow the wicked spirits to rule over his descendants:

> "You know how Your Watchers, the fathers of these spirits, have acted during my lifetime. As for these spirits who have remained alive, imprison them and hold them captive in the place of judgment. May they not cause destruction among your servant's sons, my God, for they are savage and were created for the purpose of destroying. May they not rule the spirits of the living, for You alone know their punishment; and

may they not have power over the sons of the righteous from now and forevermore." Then our God told us [the angels of the presence] to tie up each one. (*Jub.* 10:5–7)[31]

So far, this is a restatement of the basic story of *1 En.* 6–11: the Watchers are to be tied up and restrained forever. But then the satanic figure of *Jubilees*, the angel Mastema, objects (this is the continuation of the above passage):

> When Mastema, the leader of the spirits, came, he said: "Lord creator, leave some of them before me; let them listen to me and do everything that I tell them, because if none of them is left for me I shall not be able to exercise the authority of my will among mankind. For they are meant for (the purposes of) destroying and misleading before <my punishment> {Me}, because the evil of mankind is great." Then He said that a tenth of them should be left before him [Mastema], while He would make nine parts descend to the place of judgment. He told one of us [angels] that we should teach Noah all their medicines because He knew that they would neither conduct themselves properly nor fight fairly. We acted in accord with His entire command. All of the evil ones who were savage we tied up in the place of judgment, while we left a tenth of them to exercise power on the earth before the satan. (*Jub.* 10:8–11)

So this is *Jubilees*' "Ten Percent Solution" to the problem of evil. Most of the wicked angels were indeed tied up, in keeping with the narrative of *1 En.* 6–11. There would never need to be another flood. But the ten percent that were allowed to roam free, although they were not numerous enough to once again push humanity over the brink, were nonetheless responsible for such evil as still persists on the earth.

Sometimes two motifs designed to answer the same exegetical question exist side by side. This phenomenon is sometimes called "overkill": a text will give two reasons for why something happened, or explain that it came about in two different ways.[32] In the case of the exegetical problem created by God's promise never to bring another flood, a second solution was proposed, and it came to coexist with both

Jubilees' Ten Percent Solution and the detached evil spirits of *1 En.* 15. This motif proposed a complete overhaul of humanity after the flood, a retooling of human nature: God resolved to make a better brand of human being so that there would no longer be any necessity to destroy humanity. Here is the motif in *1 Enoch:*

> [God instructs Michael:] Cleanse the earth from all impurity and from all wrong and from all lawlessness and from all sin, and [remove] godlessness and all impurities that have come upon the earth. And *all the sons of men will become righteous,* and all the peoples will worship (Me), and all will bless Me and prostrate themselves. [Then] all the earth will be cleansed from all defilement and from all uncleanness, and I shall not again send upon them any wrath or scourge for all the generations of eternity. (*1 En.* 10:20–22)

The same motif is found in *Jubilees:*

> He [God] obliterated all from their places; there remained no one of them whom he did not judge [i.e., punish] for all their wickedness. *He made a new and righteous nature* for all his creatures so that they would not sin with their whole nature until eternity. Everyone will be righteous—each according to his kind—for all time. (*Jub.* 5:11–12)

An echo of this same motif is found much later, in the writings of Josephus:

> God loved Noah for his righteousness, but, as for those men, He condemned not them alone for their wickedness, but resolved to destroy all mankind then existing and to create *another race pure of vice.* (J.A. 175)

But this solution raised the same problem that the "Binding of the Angels" motif had raised before. If human nature was retooled after the flood, so that now everyone is perfect, why are there still so many mean and nasty human beings around, in fact, so many outright sinners? God Himself must be aware of their existence, since He ends up having to punish them. Was the retooling a total failure?

Apparently this problem did not bother the author of *1 Enoch*, nor did it seem to trouble the author of *Jubilees* (or Josephus). It did, however, occur to that person I have come to call the *Jubilees* Interpolator, an anonymous redactor who introduced some twenty-nine insertions into that book, most of them only a verse or two long, but reflecting views very different from those of the original author on certain matters of biblical law.[33]

Immediately following the passage just cited, the Interpolator proposed his own solution to the problem that the "retooling" motif had created. Yes, humanity was now better than before; there would be no need for a new flood. But if human beings are still being conspicuously punished for misdeeds—in a way that actually did not occur before the flood—it is because the retooling of humanity had been accompanied by another, complementary reform: Henceforth, human beings would be held to the strictest standards of justice, so that they would be punished automatically and promptly for every infraction:

> He made a new and righteous nature for all his creatures so that they would not sin with their whole nature until eternity. Everyone will be righteous—each according to his kind—for all time. (*Jub.* 5:12)

To these words, written by the original author of *Jubilees*, the Interpolator added:

> The judgment of them all has been ordained and written on the heavenly tablets; there is [to be] no injustice. (As for) all who transgress from their way in which it was ordained for them to go—if they do not go in it, judgment [i.e., punishment] has been written down for each creature and for each kind. There is nothing which is in heaven or on the earth, in the light, the darkness, Sheol, the deep, or in the dark place—all their judgments [punishments] have been ordained, written, and inscribed. He will exercise judgment [punishment] regarding each person—the great one in accord with his greatness and the small one in accord with his smallness—each one in accord with his way. He is not one who shows favoritism nor one who takes a bribe, if He says He will execute judgment against each person. If a person gave everything on

earth He would not show favoritism nor would He accept (it) from him because He is the righteous judge. (*Jub.* 5:13–16)

This strict, immutable standard of justice sounded altogether fearsome. Where did divine mercy come in? Frankly, the *Jubilees* Interpolator didn't care much about divine mercy for other peoples, but he did care about the Jews, and so was quick to explain that for the sons of Jacob, a certain escape clause existed:

> Regarding the Israelites it has been written and ordained: "If they turn to Him in the right way, He will forgive all their wickedness and will pardon all their sins." It has been written and ordained that He will have mercy on all who turn from all their errors once each year. (*Jub.* 5:17–18)

The Interpolator is speaking, of course, about the Day of Atonement. However harsh the new regime of strict justice may prove for other peoples, for Israel God has created a possible way out. So long as they repent of their sins sincerely (that is, "If they turn to him in the right way"), and so long as those sins were not intentional but merely inadvertent slip-ups (what the Interpolator calls "their errors," unintentional sins), Israelites will be fully forgiven in the annual observance of the Day of Atonement.

With this, then, we have reached the end of a long series of changes in the meaning of the biblical text within the Second Temple period. That series started with the insertion of Gen 6:1–4 at the end of the long genealogy of chapter 5. The original purpose of this insertion was to account for the birth of ancient superheroes, "warriors of renown," as well as to explain why such creatures are no longer in existence. But that insertion eventually came to be used for a new purpose, theodicy. Now it was conceived to explain God's reason for bringing about the flood: those angels who lusted after women were evil, as were their offspring, the Nephilim. In time, this explanation also served to answer another question in Genesis, God's promise never to bring another flood. If the original cause of the flood had been eliminated—that is, if the Nephilim were killed and their angelic progenitors were imprisoned under the earth—then indeed, God's promise made sense. There would never need to be another flood. But that solution only raised another question: had wickedness truly ceased upon the earth? To this problem, two parallel solutions were devised. According to one (found in *1 En.* 15), wickedness had not been entirely wiped out—the spirits of the wicked angels still roamed free, even if they could no longer have wicked progeny. (The *Jubilees* alternative to this motif held that ten percent of the original wicked angels were allowed to exist after the flood.) According to the other, humanity had been retooled so as to eliminate its former wickedness—there might still be some bad apples, but not enough to cause another flood. But was the latter solution really viable? There certainly still seemed to be more than a few bad apples in existence. So the *Jubilees* Interpolator came up with yet a further modification: henceforth God's list of punishable offenses would be all-inclusive (and thus far stricter than they had been in antediluvian times), and their imposition would be virtually automatic. If this new prospect seemed frightening, however, he was quick to add an escape clause for Jews: so long as they were not intentionally wicked, and repented sincerely of their sins, they would be forgiven on the Day of Atonement.

— Here I wish to end my survey, but not before returning briefly to the question left dangling at the beginning of this presentation, namely: What is the conception of Scripture that underlies such changes as the putative insertion of Gen 6:1–4 into the antediluvian genealogy and its subsequent enlistment as an explanation of the flood and all that followed? Certainly these changes had little to do with the text as it had existed in its previous stages, and so the old question recurs: How dare you? How dare someone—an ancient scribe, and sometime later, an authoritative interpreter—so radically reconfigure the words that were part of a sacred text, words presumably of divine origin that therefore ought not to suffer human tampering? To ask the question in these terms, it seems to me, is virtually to offer an answer, namely, that in ancient times such acts were not considered tampering. *In the beginning,* one might say, *God created the malleability.* As it happened with four verses in Gen 6 in late biblical times, so it had happened on a far more massive scale earlier on. Things were apparently inserted or expanded at will. What, for that matter, is the conception of Scripture that underlies such changes as were mentioned in connection with the books of Isaiah or Jeremiah? Clearly, whoever was doing all that rewriting and interpolating and rearranging had a conception of Scripture that admitted such things. It seems to me that in this matter the facts speak for themselves: Scripture was changed again and again—for a long time the texts themselves were altered, and for a long time after that, the meanings attributed to those texts were changed by authoritative interpreters. It is our own way of thinking about Scripture that finds this strange—and for many religious Jews and Christians, theologically unacceptable. The reasons for this would be too long to tell here, and, in fact, I have tried to suggest some of them elsewhere.[34] But for now, suffice it to say that Jews and Christians today seem to be operating on a notion of Scripture that is entirely out of keeping with the one that prevailed at the time their religions were acquiring their salient traits. This is the conclusion to which an examination of Gen 6:1–4 leads, and it is a conclusion with resonance throughout the Bible.

NOTES

1. See on this John C. Reeves, "Problematizing the Bible . . . Then and Now," *JQR* 100 (2010): 139–52.

2. On this subject see most recently the essays collected in H. von Weissenberg et al., *Changes in Scripture: Rewriting and Interpreting Authoritative Traditions in the Second Temple Period* (Berlin: Walter De Gruyter, 2011).

3. Alexander Rofé has argued that the shorter version represents a condensation of the original, longer version: A. Rofé, "The Arrangement of the Book of Jeremiah," *ZAW* 101 (1989): 390–98; idem, "The name Yhwh SEBA'OT and the Shorter Recension of Jeremiah," in *Prophetie und geschictliche Wirklichkeit im alten Israel: FS Siegfried Herrmann* (ed. R. Liwak and S. Wagner; Stuttgart, Kohlhammer, 1991), 307–15. Whichever contention is correct, it is immaterial for my overall point.

4. This was one of the four assumptions shared by ancient biblical interpreters; see J. Kugel, *Traditions of the Bible* (Cambridge, Mass.: Harvard University Press, 1998), 14–19.

5. This term was introduced by G. Vermes, *Scripture and Tradition in Judaism* (Leiden: Brill, 1973), 67–126, and has been much discussed of late: inter

alia, E. Tov, "Rewritten Bible Compositions and Biblical Manuscripts, with Special Attention to the Samaritan Pentateuch," *DSD* 5 (1998): 334–54; Michael Segal, "Between Bible and Rewritten Bible" in *Biblical Interpretation at Qumran* (ed. M. Henze; Grand Rapids: Eerdmans, 2005), 10–28; M. Bernstein, "'Rewritten Bible': A Generic Category Which Has Outlived its Usefulness?" *Textus* 22 (2005): 169–96; D. Falk, *The Parabiblical Texts: Strategies for Extending the Scriptures in the Dead Sea Scrolls* (London: T and T Clark, 2007); and the essays in *Rewritten Bible Reconsidered* (ed. A. Laato and J. van Ruiten; Winona Lake, Ind.: Eisenbrauns, 2008).

6. One important exception is the recent study by S. W. Crawford, *Rewriting Scripture in Second Temple Times* (Grand Rapids, Mich.: Eerdmans, 2008), esp. 39–59. A similar continuum may be observed in the Aramaic targums, which run from the normally rather literal translation of Onqelos to the more freewheeling translations of the Peshitta, Targum Neophyti, etc. and most strikingly, Pseudo-Jonathan. On the growth of this targum: A. Shinan, *The Embroidered Targum: the Aggadah in Targum Pseudo-Jonathan of the Pentateuch* (Jerusalem: Magnes, 1992).

7. On this question see Crawford, *Rewriting Scripture*, and Michael Segal, "4Q Reworked Pentateuch or 4Q Pentateuch?" in *The Dead Sea Scrolls: Fifty Years after Their Discovery* (ed. L. Schiffman et al.; Jerusalem: Israel Exploration Society, 2000), 391–99; A. Petersen, "Rewritten Bible as a Borderline Phenomenon—Genre, Textual Strategy, or Canonical Anachronism," in *Flores Florentino: Dead Sea Scrolls and Other Early Jewish Studies in Honour of Florentino Garcia Martinez* (ed. A. Hilhorst et al.; Leiden: Brill, 2007), 285–306; M. M. Zahn, "The Problem of Characterizing the 4QReworked Pentateuch Manuscripts: Bible, Rewritten Bible, or None of the Above?" *DSD* 15 (2008): 315–39.

8. On this connection: J. Sanderson, *An Exodus Scroll from Qumran: 4QpaleoExod and the Samaritan Tradition* (HSS 30; Atlanta: Scholars, 1986); Ursula Schattner-Rieser, "Der samaritanische Pentateuch im Lichte der präsamaritanischen Qumrantexte," in *Qumran und der biblische Kanon* (ed. M. Becker et al.; Neukirchen-Vluyn: Neukirchener, 2009), 145–68; S. W. Crawford, "The Pentateuch as Found in the Pre-Samaritan Texts and 4QReworked Pentateuch," in *Changes In Scripture* (ed. H. von Weissenberg et al.; Berlin: Walter De Gruyter, 2011), 123–36; also M. Bernstein, "What Has Happened to the Laws? The Treatment of Legal Material in 4QReworked Pentateuch," *DSD* 15 (2008): 24–49. On the Samaritan Pentateuch itself see R. Pummer, "The Samaritans and Their Pentateuch," in *The Pentateuch as Torah* (ed. G. Knoppers and B. M. Levinson; Winona Lake, Ind.: Eisenbrauns, 2007), 237–69; and M. Kartveit, *The Origin of the Samaritans* (SVT 128; Leiden: Brill, 2009), 279–312.

9. One early study: R. Weiss, "Synonymous Variants in Divergences between the Samaritan and Massoretic Texts of the Pentateuch," in *Studies in the Text and Language of the Bible* (Jerusalem: Magnes, 1981), 63–189.

10. The well-known exception to this generalization is the Samaritan Pentateuch's consistent ideological difference from other textual witnesses: where the latter have God speak of "the place where I will choose" and the like, the Samaritan Pentateuch specifically identifies that place as Mount Gerizim, the holy site that God already "has chosen."

11. See E. Tov and S. White, "Reworked Pentateuch," in *Qumran Cave 4. VIII: Parabiblical Texts Part 1* (ed. H. Attridge et al.; DJD XIII; Oxford: Clarendon, 1994), 268–71.

12. This is broadly the current stance adopted (with some nuanced differences) by both E. Tov and S. W. Crawford. The latter writes: "We can say with almost complete certainty that 4Q364 and 4Q365 were intended by the scribes who prepared them to be read as regular pentateuchal texts" (*Rewriting Scripture*, 56). She and Tov have changed their position from their initial assessment; see next note.

13. This was the opinion initially presented by Tov and White in the official publication of these texts, "4QReworked Pentateuch": "This composition contained a running text of the Pentateuch interspersed with exegetical additions and omissions . . . The exegetical character of this composition is especially evident from several exegetical additions comprising half a line, one line, two lines, and even seven or eight lines" (191). See also E. Tov, "Rewritten Biblical Compositions and Biblical Manuscripts," *DSD* 5 (1998): 334–54, and S. W. Crawford, "The 'Rewritten Bible at Qumran: A Look at Three Texts," *Eretz Israel* 26 (1999) (FS F. M. Cross): 1–8.

14. A point raised by many scholars of late. See Crawford, *Rewriting Scripture*, 4–5.

15. See the aforementioned studies by E. Tov, "Rewritten Bible Compositions and Biblical Manuscripts"; M. Segal, "Between Bible and Rewritten Bible"; and White, *Rewriting Scripture;* as well as P. Alexander, "Retelling the Old Testament," in *It Is Written: Scripture Citing Scripture* (ed. D. A. Carson and H. M. Williamson; Cambridge: Cambridge University Press, 1988), 99–121; M. Bernstein, "Rewritten Bible"; and George Brooke, "The Rewritten Law, Prophets, and Psalms: Issues for Understanding the Text of the Bible," in *The Bible as Book: The Hebrew Bible and the Judean Desert Discoveries,* (ed. E. D. Herbert and E. Tov; London: British Library, 2002), 31–40.

16. Again, see Kugel, *Traditions of the Bible.*

17. Among many others, N. K. Gottwald, *The Hebrew Bible: A Socio-Literary Introduction* (Philadelphia: Fortress, 1985), 327; N. Sarna, *Genesis* (Philadelphia: Jewish Publication Society, 1989), 45; Raymond E. Brown et al., *The New Jerome Biblical Commentary* (Upper Saddle River, N.J.: Prentice Hall, 1990) 14; B. W. Anderson, *Understanding the Old Testament* (4th ed.; Upper Saddle River, N.J.: Prentice Hall, 1998) 148; *The Oxford Bible Commentary* (ed. John Barton and John Middiman; New York: Oxford University Press, 2001), 46.

18. The meaning of this name in Gen 6:4 remains elusive. Some scholars have associated it with the "fall" of the Watchers from heaven, but that seems unlikely on two counts: the Genesis text seems to present them as the offspring of the Watchers, created "when the sons of God went in to the daughters of men," and not the Watchers themselves; moreover, the "sons of God"/Watchers, both in Gen 6 and in *1 Enoch*, are not said to have "fallen" at all, but voluntarily went down to earth in order to lust after the human females. It would therefore seem that Nephilim is simply an archaic name for some legendary giants whose existence was not originally tied to any tale of divine-human unions. When Gen 6:1–4 sought to attribute the genealogy of the ancient "heroes of old, warriors of renown" to some lustful angels, it mentioned—but rather as an afterthought—these giant Nephilim as being among those engendered by the angels. They too must be included among the antediluvian creatures who had no human paternity. (Another indication that the existence of these giant Nephilim was well known is their mention in Num 13, without any apparent connection to Gen 6:1–4—there they are simply well-known, proverbial giants.)

19. Hermann Gunkel saw a reference to one such legend in Gen 9:10: "From the legend of the giant Nimrod we have only the proverbial phrase, 'like Nimrod, a mighty hunter before the Lord'" (*The Legends of Genesis* [New York: Schocken, 1964], 101).

20. J. Kugel, *How to Read the Bible: A Guide to Scripture, Then and Now* (New York: Free Press, 2007), 71. The wording is based on that of the White Slave Traffic Act (better known as the Mann Act), signed into law by U.S. President W. H. Taft in 1910, which forbade crossing *state* lines for immoral purposes (more exactly, transporting women "across state lines for the purpose of prostitution or for any other immoral purpose").

21. All translations of *1 Enoch* from G. W. E. Nickelsburg, *1 Enoch 1: A Commentary on the Book of 1 Enoch, chapters 1–36; 81–108* (Hermeneia; Minneapolis: Fortress, 2001).

22. Some of these were summarized in D. Dimant, *The Fallen Angels in the Dead Sea Scrolls, Apocrypha and Pseudepigrapha, and Related Writings* (PhD diss., Hebrew University, 1974). A detailed study of the traditions in *1 Enoch*, the writings of Philo of Alexandria, and selected Dead Sea Scrolls is found in Archie T. Wright, *The Origin of Evil Spirits* (Tübingen: Mohr-Siebeck, 2005). See also Kugel, *Traditions of the Bible*, 194–212.

23. "There we saw the Nephilim (the Anakites come from the Nephilim); and to ourselves we seemed like grasshoppers, and so we seemed to them" (Num 13:33).

24. Note that the Septuagint uses *gigantes* to translate both *nĕpîlîm* and *gibbôrîm* in our passage.

25. Translation from R. Marcus, *Philo Supplement I: Questions and Answers on Genesis* (LCL; Cambridge, Mass.: Harvard University Press, 1953), 134.

26. See also *1 En* 10:4–6 and Nickelsburg, *1 Enoch 1*, 224.

27. A crucial text for the picture of hell as a place of burning fire was Isa 30:33, as well as 33:12–14. See also *1 En* 18:15, 21:7, 90:24, etc.; also 4 Ezra 7:36; 4 Macc 12:12; Rev 19:20, 21:8. On the date of *1 En* 10:11, see Nickelsburg *1 Enoch 1*, 165–66.

28. In particular, George W. E. Nickelsburg and Michael Stone have done much to promote the notion that the account of the fallen angels began as a mythic explanation of the origin of evil. See, for example, Nickelsburg, "The Bible Rewritten and Expanded," in M. E. Stone, *Jewish Writings of the Second Temple Period: Apocrypha, Pseudepigrapha, Qumran Sectarian Writings, Philo, Josephus* (CRINT 2; Assen: Van Gorcum, 1984) 90–91; idem, *1 Enoch 1*, 46–47; idem, *Jewish Literature between the Bible and the Mishnah* (2nd. ed; Minneapolis: Augsburg Fortress, 2005), 48–50; Stone, *Scriptures, Sects, and Visions: A Profile of Judaism from Ezra to the Jewish Revolts* (Philadelphia: Fortress, 1980), 32; idem, "The Axis of History at Qumran," in his *Apocrypha, Pseudepigrapha, and Armenian Studies* (Louvain: Peeters, 2006), 61–78.

29. As we shall see, it was precisely the implication of this scenario—that evil had thus been eliminated once and for all—that created two later modifications of this original "myth" in both *1 Enoch* and *Jubilees*.

30. See Nickelsburg, *1 Enoch 1*, 229–30.

31. All translations from *Jubilees* are taken from: J. C. VanderKam, *The Book of Jubilees* (CSCO 533; Scriptores Aethiopici 88; Louvain: Peeters, 1989).

32. J. Kugel, *In Potiphar's House: The Interpretive Life of Biblical Texts* (San Francisco: HarperCollins, 1990), 38, 134, 146, 256–57.

33. See J. Kugel, "On the Interpolations in the *Book of Jubilees*," *RevQ* 24 (2009): 215–272.

34. Kugel, *How to Read the Bible*, esp. 662–89.

CHAPTER 11

The Election of Israel Imperilled
Early Christian Views of the "Sacrifice of Isaac"

KEVIN MADIGAN

As Jon Levenson has perceived, the figure of Isaac and the narrative of the Akedah echo repeatedly and profoundly through what is now the canonical literature of Christianity. Already in Mark 1:11, where a heavenly voice declares, "You are my beloved son; with you I am well pleased," we begin to encounter echoes of the Akedah, as Levenson has observed. Such linguistic, theological, and narrative reverberations are also heard in all four gospels and in various of the letters of Paul as well.[1] Levenson has masterfully, and it seems, sufficiently treated this issue. Even if further examination of the influence of the Akedah on the literature of the New Testament were desirable or necessary, the present author's linguistic and historical background sadly precludes him from undertaking such a task.

In this paper, therefore, I would instead like to treat certain pivotal moments in the earliest postcanonical uses of the Akedah including: brief references to it in second-century literature; its fuller treatment in the homilies and exegesis of early Christian interpreters such as Origen (ca. 185–ca. 251); its depiction in early Christian catacomb art; and its appropriation in key texts from the early Christian monastic movement. I shall suggest[2] that the narrative of the Sacrifice of Isaac as it was interpreted outside the context of the canonical scriptures, profoundly shaped early Christian self-understanding, theology, and practice. Needless to say, it did so even as it reshaped, adapted, and modified aspects of the story in Genesis in accordance with its own emerging corporate and ecclesiastical identity.

EARLY CHRISTIAN NON-EXEGETICAL REFERENCES

1 Clement

1 Clement[3] is perhaps the earliest noncanonical text (it would be wrong, chronologically, to say *post*canonical, as *1 Clement* was almost certainly written before many of the canonical texts of Christianity). The author of this text was long taken to be Clement (not helpfully, as there is no other letter from the author: *2 Clement* is neither a letter nor written by the author).

Modern scholarship no longer accepts the attribution. To start with, the letter is sent in the name of the church of Rome as such and not in the *name* of any single individual, even though, on philological grounds, it seems certain that a single author composed it; it is the *identity* of that author that is in question. Clement is not mentioned anywhere in the letter. It may well be true that Clement was some sort of leader in the church of Rome. Ehrman suggests that Clement had some sort of "official role in the church, at least in Hermas's time [early second century] as some kind of secretary in charge of foreign correspondence."[4] Later church fathers, however, declared Clement to be the second or third "bishop of Rome" (Irenaeus, *Haer.* 3.3.1; Eusebius, *Hist. Eccl.*, 3.1.5.34), who was ordained by Peter (Tertullian, *Praescr.* 32). The association of Clement with Rome and with this letter thus seems to be an attempt to retroject a second- or third-century ecclesiological situation (especially the monarchical episcopate), ideal or realized, back into the first century. For proto-Catholic Christians, this could have been a way of establishing their own authority by employing the celebrated notion of "apostolic succession."

In dating the texts, we are on firmer grounds than in identifying the author, even though the traditional grounds for its dating have been largely repudiated.[5] That the document refers to the deaths of Peter and Paul having occurred "within our own generation" (chapter 5) is suggestive. So, too, is the assertion that leaders of Christian churches appointed by apostles of Jesus are still alive (chapters 42 and 44). Again, there is no indication that the hierarchical ecclesiological structures so important to later second-century, early-Catholic figures such as Irenaeus—that is, a single bishop supported by presbyters and deacons—had yet been established. Indeed, the letter uses terms such as "bishops" and "presbyters" promiscuously. All of this suggests a date in in mid nineties of the first century under Domitian.

The occasion of the letter is even more clear. It explicitly addresses itself to the church at Corinth. Apparently, that church had experienced an internal revolt in which some younger group of members had deposed the established older leaders and thus factionalized the church. Intriguingly, the church at Rome assumes its right to assert its authority over this situation of (in its view) disorder. It rebukes the younger members for presumption in subverting the established order of ministry, according to which elders and their successors should only be appointed by apostles.

The crucial texts for our purposes are as follows:

Abraham, who was called "The Friend," was found to be faithful, when he became obedient to the words of God. (*1 Clem.* 10.1)

Isaac gladly allowed himself to be brought forward as a sacrifice, confident in the knowledge of what was about to happen. (*1 Clem.* 31:3)

Characteristically relying on the LXX rather than canonical New Testament writings (some of which he may not have known and some of which, as we have noted, did not yet exist), Clement writes to a schismatic group of the Corinthian church stressing Abraham's *obedience*, in the presumed hope that the splinter group would follow the great patriarch's example of submissiveness to a higher divine authority. It was Rome's emphatic wish that the schismatic group quit its divisive activities and reassociate itself with the church governed by duly appointed bishops and priests—that is, those appointed by successors to the apostles. Here Abraham is identified with the virtue and obedience with which he will be yoked in much early Christian literature.

Again, the crucial language of Clement's second remark, on Isaac, is that Abraham's son *willingly* obeyed his father. Like his father, then, Isaac embodies the qualities that Clement wishes the revolutionary faction within the Corinthian church to imitate. Tantalizingly, Clement also observes that Isaac knew the future, though *1 Clement* does not tell us what part of salvation history he can see. Later Jewish and Christian writers would argue that he confidently imagined his own resurrection.

Epistle to Barnabas

Another among the earliest postcanonical references to the sacrifice of Isaac occurs in a Greek work that has come down to us, known as the *Epistle to Barnabas*.[6] This brief text has generated a host of questions related to its dating, provenance, authorship, and intent, not to mention its form or genre, its relationship to later Christian literature (such as the *Didache*), to the traditional Jewish notion of the "two ways"[7] and to the history of Israel and the contemporary Jewish community.[8]

The figure of Barnabas appears in the canonical New Testament as a wealthy Levite from Cyprus who sells his goods and gives the proceeds to "the apostles" (Acts 4:36–37). According to Acts, he became a companion of Paul and participated in the latter's mission to the Gentiles (Acts 9:27, 11:22–26, 13:1–2), though relations between the two were not always harmonious. At Acts 14:4, he is designated an "apostle." In the late second century, Clement of Alexandria asserts (*Strom.* 2:20) that Barnabas was among the seventy commissioned by Jesus. Remarkably, Tertullian identified him as the author of Hebrews (*Pud.* 20).

Like the gospels and so much early Christian literature, *Barnabas* does not itself identify the author, no modern scholar accepts the attribution to Barnabas (among other things, the historical Barnabas must have died before the work was written), and only a few to someone else, perhaps an apostolic father of the same name. The earliest attribution of the *Epistle to Barnabas* was in fact made by Clement of Alexandria in the late second century. Perhaps following Clement, the manuscript tradition designates the work the "*Epistle to Barnabas.*" The genre of *Barnabas* —whether it is a letter or some other literary form such as a homily—has been questioned.[9]

The work is usually dedicated to the period 132–135 C.E. and may thus have been written during the period of the Judean war against the Romans. But again, debate on the dating of the text has flourished. As the author of the text expects the temple to be rebuilt, and as expectations for its reconstruction were fairly widespread before the war, it might be best to place it just slightly earlier, perhaps around 130 during the reign of Hadrian. This is the date preferred by the present author.[10] Some place it much earlier—even as early as the late 70s. Others argue for a time of composition under Domitian (96–98), which would make it roughly contemporaneous with *1 Clement*.

Because the work was first attested by Clement of Alexandria, and because it tends to emphasize the importance of "knowledge" (*gnosis*)—in fact, the author claims to have received special *gnosis* directly from God—most scholars have argued that it was written in Egypt, where various forms of "Gnosticism" thrived. Not all agree, and others have suggested Syria or Asia Minor as likelier places of origin. Very few scholars, however, have contested the broader conclusion that the provenance of the text is the Greek-speaking, eastern provinces of the Roman Empire.

There can be less debate about the text's importance to at least some early Christian communities. An indication of its significance is that it appears in the fourth-century *Codex Sinaiticus* right after a complete version of the New Testament and thus immediately after the Apocalypse. Further testimony to its significance lies in references to it by Clement of Alexandria and by Origen, who regarded it as canonical. Later Christian writers such as Eusebius did not (*Hist. Eccl.* 3.25.4). Indeed, Eusebius dismissed the book as "spurious."

Most scholars believe the text to have been addressed to Gentile Christians, and indeed, a central question of the text is: "To whom does the covenant belong?" Ehrman argues that *Barnabas* is one among those early Christians texts that are "virulently anti-Jewish in [their] message."[11] In answer to the central question, the author argues that the church, not the synagogue, is the heir of the covenantal promises made to Israel. He observes further that the Hebrew Bible is a Christian book that Israel misunderstands, and consequently that Israel has always practiced a false cult.[12] The relevant text for our purposes us reads:

> But also when he was crucified [Jesus] was given vinegar and gall to drink. Listen how the priests in the Temple made a revelation about this. For the Lord gave the written commandment that, "Whosoever does not keep the fast shall surely die" [Lev 23:29], because he himself was about to offer the vessel of the Spirit as a sacrifice for our own sins, that the type [*typos*] might also be fulfilled that was set forth in Isaac, when he was on the altar. (*Barn.* 7:3)[13]

Consistent with the general tenor of the treatise, Barnabas reads Isaac as a type,[14] that is to say, a figural prophecy of a sacrifice that will be offered on Golgotha in Jesus of Nazareth. Implicitly here, Barnabas suggests that Jewish interpreters have misunderstood the meaning of the Akedah, because they do not read it christologically. He also explicitly adds that Jesus's death was a sacrifice offered for human sin. This text is typical of the few very early texts we have in that it alludes to the Akedah only briefly, regards Isaac as a type of Christ's expiatory sacrifice, and refrains from exegetical or theological elaboration.

Melito of Sardis, *Peri Pascha* Fragment 9

Our main sources for the life of Melito, bishop of Sardis,[15] are Eusebius (*Hist. Eccl.* 4.26.1–14) and Jerome (*De vir. Ill.* 24). He was a bishop in the Asian city of Sardis; he died around 180. Like many in the eastern provinces, he was almost certainly a Quartodeciman (that is, one who observed Easter on the same date as the Jewish Passover). Melito had traveled to the Holy Land and seems to have been the first to refer to an "old covenant" (Eusebius, *Hist. Eccl.* 4.26.12–14). Eusebius attributes seventeen works to him, including treatises on baptism, a commentary on the Apocalypse, and an apology addressed to Marcus Aurelius (*Hist. Eccl.* 4.26.2). Fragments of several of these are extant.

Melito's sermon *On the Pascha* was discovered only in 1932 and identified four years later. Though written originally in florid Greek, the sermon survives in Latin, Syriac, Coptic, and Georgian translations. Stewart-Sykes argues that the occasion of the letter was likely a dispute regarding the time of day appropriate for keeping the Pascha.[16]

The relevant text from *On the Pascha* is:

> For as a ram he was bound
> and as a lamb he was shorn
> and as a sheep he was led to slaughter
> and as a lamb he was crucified;
> and he carried the wood on his shoulders . . .
> As he was led up to be slain like Isaac by his Father.
> For it was a strange mystery to behold,
> a son led by his father to a mountain for slaughter.
> But Isaac was silent bound like a ram,
> not opening his mouth nor uttering a sound.
> For not frightened by the sword
> nor alarmed at the fire
> nor sorrowful at the suffering,
> he carried with fortitude the model of the Lord.
>   (*Peri Pascha* Fragment 9)

Melito offers numerous parallels between Isaac and Christ. Both carried wood; Isaac is of course a type of Christ carrying the cross. Both were willing to complete God's will, indicated by their silence. Both were aware of what was to happen to them. Both were led to the sacrifice by their father. But Melito, operating in an environment with large Jewish communities, his work filled with anti-Jewish polemic, seems to introduce more distinctions between type and antitype than his predecessors. For Melito, after all, Isaac, a model of Christ, parallels him but only in order to look forward to him. He is viewed as a type of the redemptive sacrifice of Christ, yet he remains an immature image of what lies ahead. The child was to be fulfilled by the adult (the rabbis maintained that he was an adult). What Melito wants to drive home is that Isaac was not in fact sacrificed and thus remained only the model, waiting to be fulfilled by Christ.

If we were to summarize our remarks on these few first- and second-century texts, it is clear that Isaac, sacrificed or not, was recognized very early on as a type for Christ; that Abraham was understood as a type of obedience; and that Isaac was seen not only as a model of obedience, but also as a type of Christ's willingness to undertake a sacrifice. Some authors, like Melito, introduce multiple differences. What we do not see in this early period is a treatment that could be called exegetical or homiletical. All of that will change with Origen's homily on the Akedah.

ORIGEN'S EXEGESIS OF GENESIS

Origen (ca. 185–251) towers intellectually over the Eastern church of antiquity.[17] Born in Alexandria to parents who were not only Christian but devout (his father was martyred under Septimius Severus in 201), he was charged with the instruction of catechumens, even while continuing his own studies. He was a not uncontroversial figure. Some Christians adulated him; others suspected him for his allegorizing interpretation of the Scriptures and some of his other theological doctrines. For reasons having to do with envy and politics, Origen was exiled by his own bishop from Alexandria. He ended up in Caesarea Maritima, where he spent roughly the last two decades of his life, which were also his most prolific. After being incarcerated and tortured during the Decian persecution he died shortly after June 251.[18]

Origen was probably the most productive and possibly the most influential writer in Christian antiquity. Ancient sources suggest that he produced (by dictation) some two thousand works. He seems to have commented on every book of the Bible and commented on some books (including the collection of Psalms) more than once. Several hundred of his homilies survive. He left an important apology against Celsus, the critic of Christianity. Among his most important and influential works was his theological *On First Principles,* the fourth book of which is a hermeneutical treatise, probably the first in the history of Christianity. Several devotional works survive, such as his treatise *On Prayer* and his *Exhortation to Martyrdom.* Some of his thinking and some of his works—his subordinationism and his emphasis on allegory, as well as his soteriological universalism—were hardened into dogma by his followers, the Origenists, and he was eventually anathematized by the emperor at the fifth ecumenical council at Constantinople in 553.[19] Of the thousands of works that he wrote, only a handful survive complete, together with fragments of other works.

Sixteen of Origen's *Homilies on Genesis* survive, of which all of the eighth and part of the ninth are devoted to the Akedah. Origen imagines the Akedah following the literal sense of the text of Gen 22:1 ("God tested Abraham"), that is, primarily as a test of Abraham. This test, Origen argues, is intended to try and perhaps even to shatter Abraham's faith:

> What say you to these things, Abraham? What kind of thoughts are stirring in your heart? A word has been uttered by God which is such as to shatter and try your faith. What do you say to these things? What are you thinking? What are you reconsidering? Are you thinking, are you turning over in your heart that, if the promise has been given to me in Isaac, but I offer him for a holocaust, it remains that the promise holds no hope? Or rather do you think of those well-known words, and say that it is impossible for him who promised to lie? (*Hom. Gen.* 8.1)

Origen imagines the Akedah as a test with a number of dimensions. Initially, as we see in this text, Abraham is asked to trust in the God who made a promise to him, even though he now asks Abraham to offer as a holocaust the young boy through whom the promise is to be realized. The founding father of Israel is asked to repose his faith in the One who commands him to kill the seed through whom descendants numberless as the stars will spring. In other words, one dimension of the test is to measure Abraham's fidelity to the promise in circumstances when it seems all but obvious that the promise, along with Abraham's faith, will be shattered.

Origen wonders explicitly what Abraham is thinking when given the command. Does he imagine, Origen wonders, that the promise given to him in Isaac, who is about to be offered for a holocaust, actually holds no hope? Or, instead, does Abraham imagine that it is impossible for God to lie and thus that the promise should remain indefectible? Origen's response to this question may surprise. It rides upon his reading of Paul's understanding of Abraham, "the faithful man":

> The Apostle, therefore, has reported to us the thoughts of the faithful man, that the faith in the resurrection began to be held already at that time in Isaac. Abraham, therefore, hoped for the resurrection of Isaac and believed in a future which had not yet happened. (*Hom. Gen.* 8.1)

Given how Origen interprets the remainder of the homily, it is surprising that he begins by emphasizing Abraham's faith in the resurrection of Isaac. Surely, that faithful expectation would deprive the story, and Origen's reading of it, of the suspense and strong feeling which now fill it and make it so interesting and moving. But in Origen's reading, this faith in the future resurrection is quickly eclipsed both by Abraham's paternal terror for his son, and the great patriarch's fear that the promises of God, which were to be fulfilled through Isaac, would not be fulfilled. Abraham, Origen says, hoped for, or even had foreknowledge of, the resurrection of Isaac and thus believed in a future for which there had not yet been any precedent or suggestion in history. No matter what Isaac's fate then, even had he actually been sacrificed by his father, God would have caused him to be raised up again.

Origen observes later in the sermon that when Abraham informs the servants that he and the child will go and will return to them, he is not deceiving them. He truly intended to offer the child as a burnt offering, which is of course why he carries wood, and to return with Isaac—presumably dead—because he was certain that God was able to raise him from the his lifeless state. Most ancient exegetes believed that this was not a reference to the general, eschatological resurrection. Instead, God would, they believed, raise Isaac immediately after his death and, as Abraham promised, he would return with his father down the mountain. One might think that, for Origen, such faith would alleviate the intensity of Abraham's anxiety and grief. But Origen actually understands Abraham to be experiencing radically contrary affections, many of them caused by the careful, intentionally affecting diction of the Deity. Reminding us that Abraham was being *tested*, Origen observes that God need not have piled affecting adjective upon adjective, but he does.

> But all these things happened because God was testing Abraham. But now meanwhile the text says, "God was testing Abraham and says to him: 'Take your dearest one whom you love.'" For to have said "son" would not have been enough, but "dearest" also is added. Let this too be considered. Why is there still added also, "Whom you love"? But behold the importance of the test. The affections of a father are roused by the dear and sweet appellations repeated frequently, that by awaking memories of love, the paternal right hand might be slowed in slaying his son and the total warfare of the flesh might fight against the faith of the soul. (*Hom. Gen.* 8.2)

God reminds Abraham that Isaac is Abraham's dearest son, the one whom he loves. These modifiers and even the naming of his son intensify the torment that Abraham experiences and compound the internal psychic trauma that Abraham endures. What would in any case presumably have been a tug of war between the command of the flesh and that of God becomes, by the language carefully chosen by God, an intense battle; indeed, according to Origen, a "total warfare [between] flesh of soul" (8.2). God also explicitly names his son so that Abraham might recall the promise made by God to him, namely that in Isaac the promises of God would be fulfilled. The narrative gives no hint that Abraham felt sorrow or any similar affect at the prospect of having to slay his own son and observes that he moves through the story as if in a trance. But the memory of the promise, Origen says, actually produces momentary "hopelessness" (8.2) in Abraham when he thinks of the promises that were made to whom by God. In short, Origen imagines an emotionally charged narrative in which Abraham staggers internally between hope and hopelessness while never hesitating externally from fulfilling the sovereign command of God.

Indeed, even the command to "go into the high land" is intended to augment Abraham's anxiety and dread. Origen observes that the lengthening of this long journey serves mainly to "tear Abraham to pieces with his thoughts" (8.3), and was commanded by God in order that

Abraham might be tormented by the oppressive command and the great affection he had for his only son. But the command is also ordered so that the period of struggle between affection and faith, the love of God and the love of flesh, the charm of things present and the expectation of things future—that all these opposites might be sharpened and Abraham's struggle made more arduous. We learn that there was no mountain nearby, and that Abraham's internal and external journey, and therefore his utter agony, was prolonged for three days. In other words, God emphasizes in every word and every command the value Abraham attaches to his son.

Again, Origen argues that this was done knowingly and intentionally, so that the father's heart might consider his son during the entire lengthy journey and so anxieties might multiply in his heart. "Behold," Origen says, "behold to what an extent the test is heaped up" (8.5). The test is indeed so intensified that Origen does not hesitate at one point in his commentary to call God Abraham's tempter.

Yet, Origen observes at length, Abraham takes Isaac immediately, without hesitation or murmuring, to Moriah (Gen 22:3). Indeed, Abraham's instant obedience is a major leitmotif or theme of his sermon. Origen emphasizes that Abraham does not deliberate, does not reconsider, does not take counsel with any man, but "immediately sets out on the journey" (8.4). Noteworthy here is that, to this point, Origen almost entirely ignores Isaac's affections and thoughts.

Although Origen does not read the text christologically to this point, observing only that the three-day journey is "filled with mysteries" (8.4), he does so interpret Isaac's potential for becoming a sacrificial victim:

> That Isaac himself carries on himself "the wood for the holocaust" is a figure, because Christ also "himself carried his own cross," and yet to carry "the wood for the holocaust" is the duty of a priest. He himself, therefore, becomes both victim and priest. But what is added also is related to this: "And they both went off together." For when Abraham carries the fire and knife as if to sacrifice, Isaac does not go behind him, but with him, that he might be shown to contribute equally with the priesthood itself. (*Hom Gen.* 8.6)

The third day, on which the two conclude their journey and on which the sacrifice is offered to God, is unsurprisingly interpreted as a type of Christ's resurrection, and the wood that Isaac carries for the holocaust a figure for the wood carried by Christ at his crucifixion according to the Gospel of John (19:17). Origen emphasizes the typological dimensions of the preparation for the sacrifice and dwells on the detail of Isaac himself carrying the wood for the burnt offering—an obvious figure, in Origen's mind, of Christ carrying his own cross. Furthermore, to carry wood for the burnt offering is the duty of a priest, so Isaac thus becomes victim and priest. When Genesis adds, "and they both went off together," this is to show that Isaac does not go *behind* but *with* Abraham, so that he might be shown to contribute equally with the priesthood itself (*Hom. Gen.* 8.6).

When Origen comes to consider Isaac's question, "Where is the lamb?" he again observes that Isaac begins his question by saying, "My father!" and Abraham responds by saying, "Here I am, my son" and "God will provide, my son," twice emphasizing the filial relation that binds father and son so tightly. Again, the test becomes almost unbearable here; Origen goes so far as to say that Abraham's heart was "pierced." And though he was utterly firm in his faith, nonetheless he responds with moving paternal affection, responding, "What is it, son?" (*Hom. Gen.* 8.6).

It is not impossible that Origen's reading of this text here was influenced by his ideas on martyrdom, on which he wrote a famous treatise, *An Exhortation to Martyrdom*. There he speaks of martyrdom as a test which requires steadfastness and endurance, and he explicitly compares martyrs to Abraham, who like the great patriarch, leave children behind and place love of God before affection of the flesh.[20]

Early Christian Art

As is widely known, the Christian catacombs are filled with images, mostly taken from the Hebrew Scriptures, of captivity and death and miraculous recovery from danger by the intervention of God. Think, for example, of Jonah and the whale, Daniel and the lion's den, the three men bound on the gridiron of fire by Nebuchadnezzar in Dan 3, and so forth.

Either two or three depictions of the Akedah exist in the catacombs from the pre-Constantinian period. Here we observe three depictions of the Akedah in the Via Latina catacomb. The question is, how to interpret them? Understood in this Christian context, one might see these images as representing a promise that God would deliver his saints from death and bring them back to life. Like the other stories just mentioned, this one was presumably painted as a representation of God's desire to deliver his faithful from what appears to be a final captivity.

Robin Jensen, however, has given us good reason to rethink these conclusions. Among other things, as she observes, "rejecting this image's function as a symbolic textual reference to Christ's passion requires that scholars discount the mass of textual evidence that makes this precise typological connection," including *Barnabas, Peri Pascha,* and some of the other texts we have considered. Jensen goes on to point out that among other early Christian writers, Irenaeus, Tertullian, Clement, and Origen "also elaborated the Christ-Isaac parallels," a connection that continued to be made through the fourth and fifth centuries.[21] Perhaps it is best to conclude that both meanings are possible (chronology could be a factor in determining meaning), that the theme of deliverance from death is certainly imaginable in the context of the catacombs, especially in the pre-Constantinian period, but that it was gradually superseded by the typological connection between the Akedah and Christ's sacrifice on the cross.

Monastic Use

I want to suggest one final way in which the Akedah was used in Christian thought and practice. Here I would like to move to the fourth century and to the emergence of monasticism in the deserts of Egypt. As is well known, monastic life was governed to some extent by the memory of the martyrs and the extent to which martyrs were understood to have undergone and passed a challenging test of faith, contempt for this world, and obedience. It is in connection with that last virtue that some monastically important and influential ascetic literature appropriates the Akedah.

Figure 1. Sacrifice of Isaac, Catacomb of Via Latina. Photo: Estelle Brettman, The International Catacomb Society.

Figure 2. Sacrifice of Isaac, Catacomb of Via Latina. Photo: Estelle Brettman, The International Catacomb Society.

I am thinking especially of a text called the *Apophthegmata Patrum,* or "The Sayings of the Desert Fathers."[22] The *Apophthegmata Patrum* belongs to a literary genre that began to emerge from the late fourth century, namely, collections of sayings from the hermits of the Egyptian desert. Such collections were organized around brief, oracular pronouncements that were alphabetically ordered or, as in the case of the *Apophthegmata,* ordered by subjects important to monastic life. Many of these collections contain the same or similar sayings, which suggests a complicated network of literary dependence. Among the most famous Latin collections are those contained in the work of Cassian, whose influence was incalculably multiplied by Benedict of Nursia recommending them in his widely observed *Rule.*

The *Apophthegmata* contains sayings on self-control, poverty and possessions, patience, prayer, humility, and so on. Here I want to concentrate on the saying about the central monastic virtue of obedience. In this saying, we are told of a man who comes to a famous abba (father, something akin to an ascetic guru) of the Thebaid, hoping to become a monk. He is asked by the abba if he has any ties, to which he responds, "Yes, I have a son." The abba immediately commands him, "Then go and throw him in the river, and then you can become a monk." The man immediately departs to throw his son into the river. Meanwhile, the abba sends some monks to prevent him from doing so. As the father holds his son and is about to throw him into the river, he is stopped by the monks. In the end, the son is saved by the command of the ancient abba, while the father of the saved son, according to the text, "became a monk of high worth, tested through obedience."[23]

This little story is evidently modeled on the Akedah. The father's instant willingness to obey a command understood to be a word from God, the last-second intervention of agents sent by higher divine authority and a reward granted to the father, understood as a gift for having passed a test of obedience—all of this suggests a retelling of the Akedah. For the author of this text, as well as for Origen, the story stands as an illustration of the necessity of obedience and the inevitability of a gracious reward for having passed this most difficult of texts, the willingness to suppress strong filial affection in the face of a sovereign command from high authority.

— This brief survey of uses of the Akedah only begins to suggest the profundity of its influence on early Christian use, thought, and life. Much more can and hopefully will be said about the Akedah in early Christian and medieval exegesis, thought, and practice as a response to changing ecclesiastical, political, and social conditions. What is clear so far is that certain themes dominate its use in early Christian wrtings and art. Early Christian artistic depictions of the Akedah may have been intended to symbolize God's willingness to deliver his faithful from vicissitude, captivity, and (again) even the ultimate danger of death. Both major protagonists in the Genesis narrative are seen by early Christians as paradigms or types, Abraham as a model of fidelity, Isaac as a sign of a sacrificial victim *in potentia* and of the resurrection promised to God's faithful. Many Christian authors regard the entire narrative as a sort of trial or test of Abraham, especially of the great patriarch's fidelity and even of the Deity's willingness to give up his beloved son and thus to imperil the election of Israel. But that is perhaps to put it too flatly. Jon Levenson has put it, characteristically, with more insight and elegance: "In Christianity, Abraham's refusal to spare his beloved son becomes a paradigm for another father's incomparable act—the heavenly father's refusal to spare his own beloved son, and this, in turn, becomes the basis of the hope for forgiveness, reconciliation and atonement."[24]

NOTES

This previously unpublished paper, now significantly revised, was first delivered at the 16th annual Nostra Aetate Lecture at Fordam University in October 2008. The topic was the significance of the "Sacrifice of Isaac" in Jewish and Christian religious traditions of commentary and interpretation. On that occasion, Jon Levenson delivered a paper on aspects of Jewish literature on the Akedah. I have used quotation marks in the title of this paper for obvious reasons. For the sake of convenience, I will not use them for the remainder of the paper, confident that readers are aware that Isaac is not in fact sacrificed in the narrative whose Christian use and theological and literary connection to the death of Jesus of Nazareth's sacrificial death seems to suggest he was.

1. Jon D. Levenson, *The Death and Resurrection of the Beloved Son: The Transformation of Child Sacrifice in Judaism and Christianity* (New Haven: Yale University Press, 1993), 200–219.

2. I underline that my study is merely suggestive and does not aspire, fruitlessly, to be comprehensive.

3. Critical edition, *The Apostolic Fathers* (2 vols.; ed. and trans. Bart D. Ehrman; Cambridge, Mass.: Harvard University Press, 2003).

4. Ehrman, *Apostolic Fathers*, 1:21. Ehrman goes on acutely to observe that "if the bishop of Rome himself had written the letter, one might expect him to assert his authority by mentioning his position" (1:22).

5. The letter begins by referring to calamities suffered by the Roman church, which scholars have sometimes (relying on Eusebius) taken to be a persecution undertaken by Domitian. Unfortunately, there is no very good evidence that such a persecution was launched by that emperor at the end of the first century.

6. Critical edition (with French translation) found in P. Prigent and R. A. Kraft, *Epitre de Barnabé, SC* (1971); English translation may be found in R. A. Kraft, *Barnabas and the Didache*, vol. 3 (ed. R. M. Grant; The Apostolic Fathers; New York: Nelson, 1965).

7. In this sense, it shares an important theme and perhaps even literary form and content with the *Didache*, which shared its apocalyptic perspective. The "two ways," the way of light and the way of darkness, is a theme deeply rooted in the Hebrew Bible (see, e.g., Deut 30:15–19) and the theme with which *Barnabas* concludes (chs. 18–20). Intriguingly, there are analogous themes and forms in non-Jewish Greek literature and in the literature of Greek-speaking Judaism. How the discourse on the two themes made it into *Barnabas* and even the question of its potential literary interdependence have been much debated.

8. Recent discussions include J. C. Paget, *The Epistle of Barnabas: Outlook and Background* (Tübingen: Mohr, 1993) and R. Hvalvik, *The Struggle for Scripture and Covenant: The Purpose of the Epistle of Barnabas and Jewish-Christian Competition in the Second Century* (Tübingen: Mohr, 1996).

9. See L. W. Barnard, "Is the Epistle to Barnabas a Pastoral Homily?" in *Studies in the Apostolic Fathers and Their Background* (New York: Schocken, 1966), 73–85.

10. Following Ehrman, *Apostolic Fathers*, 7.

11. Ehrman, *Apostolic Fathers*, 3.

12. See S. Lowy, "The Confutation of Judaism in the Epistle of Barnabas," *JJS* 11 (1960): 1–37.

13. English translation from Ehrman, *Apostolic Fathers*, 37.

14. The category *typos* is used throughout the text. See, e.g., *Barn.* 7.10, 11.

15. Critical edition and French translation of *Peri Pascha:* ed. O. Perler, *Sur la Pâque et fragments* (*SC* 123; Paris: Éditions du Cerf, 1966); English translation, *Melito of Sardis: On Pascha and Fragments* (trans. S. G. Hall; Oxford: Clarendon, 1979).

16. Melito of Sardis, *On Pascha* (ed. Alistair Stewart-Sykes; Crestwood, N.Y.: St. Vladimir's Press, 2001), 18–19.

17. Origen, *Homélies sur la Genèse,* ed. Henri de Lubac, S.J., et Louis Doutreleau, S.J. (*SC* 7; Paris: Éditions du Cerf, 1976); English translation, *Homilies on Genesis and Exodus* (trans. Ronald E. Heine; *Fathers of the Church* 71; Washington, D.C.: Catholic University of America Press, 1982).

18. See Joseph Wilson Trigg, *Origen* (New York: Routledge, 1998).

19. See Elizabeth Clark, *The Origenist Controversy: The Cultural Construction of an Early Christian Debate* (Princeton, N.J.: Princeton University Press, 1992).

20. Rowan Greer, ed., *Origen* (New York: Paulist Press, 1979), 69.

21. Robin M. Jensen, *Understanding Early Christian Art* (New York: Routledge, 2000), 143–46.

22. English translation in Owen Chadwick, ed., *Western Asceticism: Selected Translations with Introductions and Notes* (Philadelphia: Westminster Press, 1958).

23. Chadwick, ed., *Western Asceticsim,* 151–52.

24. Jon D. Levenson, "Abusing Abraham: Traditions, Religious Histories, and Modern Misinterpretations," *Judaism* 47/3 (Summer 1988): 259–77, 260.

CHAPTER 12

The Salvation of Israel in Romans 9–11

MARK REASONER

In 1985 Jon Levenson published two works that have been of great benefit to me. His *Sinai and Zion: An Entry into the Jewish Bible* has been very useful as a text for an undergraduate course on the covenants of the Bible. From this book, my students and I learned that the scope of the Mosaic covenant is this-worldly, concerned with justice and the flourishing of life in the land.[1] The second work, the essay "The Universal Horizon of Biblical Particularism," has helped me see the complementarity of the universal horizon and particular focus found so often in the Scriptures, including the point that Paul is far from a universalist since he looks to baptism and faith in Christ as entry points into the "sons of God" in Galatians.[2] With my appreciation and debt to these works acknowledged, I would like to reexamine what Paul writes about the salvation of Israel in his letter to the Romans. While the reading of "all Israel will be saved" as a spiritual salvation—whether for the Church or for ethnic Israel—has long been dominant among Romans interpreters, the political and scriptural contexts of Romans 9–11 require us to recognize that the literal sense of Paul's expression "all Israel will be saved" includes the idea that corporeal, ethnic Israel will be restored in its land.

ISRAEL'S PLIGHT ACCORDING TO PAUL

In Rom 8:19, 21, Paul refers to a future revelation and glory for the "sons of God" and "children of God." Both these phrases evoke the strong affirmation of the Hebrew Bible that the Israelites are the son or sons of Yhwh.[3] In Rom 8:35, Paul lists the threats to the corporate existence of the elect. The elect in view are usually understood to be Christ-followers because Paul has mentioned election in verse 30 and asked the question at the beginning of verse 35: "What will separate us from the love of Christ?" The question in Rom 8:33, however—"Who will bring a charge against God's elect?"—seems to be an allusion to Isa 50:8–9.[4] And the sevenfold list: "anguish, distress, persecution, famine, nakedness, peril, sword," functions as a summary of the curses described in Lev 26:14–39. These curses resonate also with the threat of exile, for famine is closely associated with exile in descriptions of the exiles experienced by the elect in Paul's scriptures (Amos 4:2, 6; 5:5; 2 Kgs 25:3–12). The list ends with the "sword," a reality of Paul's world that he returns to in Rom 13:4. In the scriptural context of the woes that may come upon God's people, the sword is linked to exile in Lev 26:33, 36 and in Jer 9:15. Paul pauses after "the sword" to quote in Rom 8:36 from a national lament psalm (LXX Ps 43:23/MT Ps 44:23), presumably to bring to a conclusion this section of his letter. The quotation raises more questions than it answers, since those suffering are righteous ones suffering with God's full knowledge. There is first of all the theological question of why God allows the righteous to suffer, which is raised in some strands of Wisdom literature and the prophets.[5] There is also the question of why Paul quotes from this psalm in which the righteous are suffering when he has already taken pains to show that his people are sinful (Rom 2:17–24; 3:1–9) and will return again to the idea that his people somehow are not righteous (Rom 9:30—10:4), but are instead a subset of humanity whom God has shut up to disobedience (Rom 11:32).

Perhaps Paul quotes from Ps 44 because this psalm is more concerned about how God's people have been scattered and disgraced among the nations (MT Ps 44:12–16) than any of the other psalms that ask for God's help for a sinful people. The psalm ends with a request for redemption based on God's steadfast love, but no answer is given from God.

The preceding survey of the political resonances in Rom 8:33–36 is not exhaustive, but it is enough to show that the question of Israel's political status in the world does not begin at Romans 9. It comes into full view by Rom 8:18, after having been signaled already at 3:3–6 as a topos demanding attention. Even if Paul, as most commentators conclude, is writing about Christ-followers from among Gentiles and Jews as the "elect" here in Rom 8:30, 33, his allusion to Isa 50:8–9, his list of hardships that seems to come out of Lev 26, and his quotation from a national lament psalm (LXX Ps 43/MT Ps 44) raise the question of Israel's political status in the world. In short, Paul's way of describing future glory for a people whose very existence is threatened raises a question about the political future of God's first love, ethnic Israel.

The quotation in Rom 8:36 from a national lament psalm (LXX Ps 43) thus provides the introduction to Paul's own lament over his people. Indeed, the genre of Rom 9–11 is best identified as a lament psalm, for in it Paul laments and explores the dissonance between his perception of God's promises and the condition of his people. And like many of the canonical lament psalms, Rom 9–11 ends with a stanza of praise to God, celebrating in suprahistorical fashion that God will bring about salvation for his people in the end.[6]

But what exactly is Paul lamenting? He does not define Israel's problem in the opening of this section; it is simply assumed that the readers understand why Paul would have unceasing grief for his "brothers, [his] kin according to the flesh, who are Israelites, whose is the adoption and the glory and the covenants and the law and the worship and the promises, whose are the fathers and from whom is the Messiah according to the flesh" (9:3–5).[7]

In Rom 9–11 Paul's concern is with "Israelites" (9:4, 11:1) or "Israel" (9:6, 31; 11:2, 25, 26). In these three chapters, the Israel/Israelite terms predominate over *Ioudaios*, which is Paul's default term elsewhere in Romans.[8] If Paul is following the distinction between "Israel" and "the Jews" that Josephus followed, it means that here in Rom 9–11 he is concerned not simply with Jews of the southern kingdom who returned from the Babylonian exile, but with all who can be connected to the twelve tribes.[9]

While I accept Jason Staples's suggestion that the predominance of "Israel" and "Israelites" in this section of Romans fits with Paul's focus on the return of the northern tribes, a possible objection to this position is that in Rom 11:1 Paul identifies himself as an "Israelite" from the tribe of Benjamin. To this objection a clarification is in order: With Staples, I see significance in the concentration of "Israel" and "Israelite" in Rom 9–11, but these terms do not mean that Paul is referring specifically to the ten northern tribes. They mean that he is referring to the whole nation of those who inherited the Abrahamic and Mosaic covenants conceived as the twelve tribes. In this sense Paul, from the tribe of Benjamin, can be an Israelite. The example that follows Paul's insistence that he is an Israelite is clearly set in the northern kingdom (Rom 11:2–4, quoting 1 Kgs 19:10, 14), also indicating that Paul is thinking of all twelve tribes here. We will see below how Paul's scriptural quotations in Rom 9:20–33 also confirm the possibility that he regards the exile of the northern tribes as an integral part of the scriptural background from which he prays that his kinfolk, Israel, will be saved.

Within chapters 9–11, the contexts of the scriptural quotations and the images that Paul uses (Esau, Pharaoh, potter and vessels, stumbling stone, olive tree) include the political dimension of Israel's plight in the world. These quotations and images are earth-focused or politically oriented. Even the question of faith that was first broached in Rom 3:3 and explicitly raised again at Rom 9:31, "In what or whom does Israel trust?"—which Christian exegetes often place outside the category of Israel's political situation—is inextricably linked to the section of Isaiah that Paul uses to process the question of Israel's faith (Rom 9:30–33; LXX Isa 28:16, 8:14). Paul's combined use of LXX Isa 28:16 and 8:14 in Rom 9:33 comes from the context of Isaiah's challenge to King Ahaz of Judah to trust God even when Israel and Aram are threatening to replace him with a ruler who will join their league against Assyria.[10] If the scriptures Paul quotes are any indication of why he is grieving over

Israel, one would have to conclude that his grief is prompted at least in part by the disconnect he perceives between the political realities of first-century Israel and the patrimony he so wistfully describes in this letter (Rom 3:1–2, 9:4–5, 11:28). By means of the scriptures he is quoting, Paul is signaling that the "salvation" of Israel for which he prays includes political autonomy and restoration from exile.

Most of the scriptures that form the skeletal, weight-bearing structure of Rom 9–11 are pointedly political. After the references to the Abraham and Sarah narratives in Rom 9:7, 9, Paul includes a reference to the older serving the younger (Gen 25:23), a text that fits with a number of politically charged comparisons of Jacob and Esau. Lest there be any mistake and we miss the national dimensions of the Jacob and Esau comparison, Paul follows up with a quotation of Mal 1:2–3, which comes from the introduction to a prophetic text that is clearly concerned with the homeland of the Jews and its place among the nations of the earth.[11]

The potter-and-clay analogy, which continues through the "vessels of wrath fit for destruction" phrase of 9:22, evokes imagery of God working with foreign rulers in pursuit of the mysterious fulfillment of his plans for Israel. Jeremiah glosses his potter's vessels with "a nation or a kingdom" (Jer 18:7–9). Or if we go to the actual site of Paul's potter quotation, Isa 45:9, we can see that it is immediately followed by a defense of God's raising up of Cyrus (Isa 45:13) with the ultimate goal of the salvation of Israel, who will never be put to shame (Isa 45:17). The analogy also evokes God's promise to the anointed in Ps 2:9 that he will "shatter [the nations] like potter's ware."

The famous use of Deut 30:12–14 in Rom 10:6–8 is definitely a christological gloss. But does it point to life in heaven? The context of the text in Deut 30 is clearly about a this-worldly political flourishing of Israel. The following quotations from Isaiah, Joel, and the Song of Moses in Rom 10 all deal with the political deliverance of Israel.

In Rom 11:1, Paul insists that God has not rejected his people, offering himself as an example of an Israelite who is still among the remnant. At this point, alert readers will register an objection: if the salvation Paul envisions includes the restoration of corporeal Israel in the land, how could Paul, who was not living in the land and who was actually afraid of returning to Jerusalem (Rom 15:30–32), call himself one of the remnant? A response to this question hinges on the meanings of *tsedaqah* and *dikaiosunē*. The first time that Paul offers the argument regarding the remnant, in Rom 9:27–29, it is followed immediately by his explanation that the nations received a righteousness on the basis of faith (*katelaben dikaiosunē . . . ek pisteōs*). The scriptures Paul uses to ground this explanation are LXX Isa 28:16 and 8:14. LXX Isa 28:16 adds a preposition and pronoun to the Masoretic phrasing, so that the prophet advocates trusting "in it/him," in the stone that God has laid in Zion. For Paul, it is this faith that constitutes one's membership in the remnant. Unlike the Targum, which reads the stone as a fierce king—probably the Roman emperor—Paul understands the stone to be Christ. Thus for Paul, the remnant who trusts in the stone laid in Zion—which he reads as Christ—are the ones who will live in the land. As in LXX Isa 28:15, 17–18, such faith engenders hope in future deliverance and safety in the land.[12] Security in the land is not a present possession for those pictured as the remnant, either in Isa 28 or in Paul's description of the remnant in his day.

In Rom 11:12, the "wealth of the nations" has a very material connotation when it comes in Paul's scriptures.[13] Yes, Paul is reworking it to include the idea that Israel's unbelief has prompted the wealth of the nations, but he does so based on the blessing Paul assumes will come back to Israel, as seen at the end of Rom 11:12 and in verses 14–16 as well. It is clear that Paul has retained his scriptures' idea that the wealth of the nations will flow into Israel. The "wealth of nations" Paul has in mind in Rom 11:12 includes not simply a spiritual conversion but also a hope for material bounty, and could perhaps have motivated his dogged execution of a Gentile collection for Jews in Jerusalem (Rom 15:25–32).

THE SPECTER OF ROME IN ROMANS

Paul's quotation of Mal 1:3–4 in Rom 9:13 contains his only use of the name "Esau." Who is Esau or Edom in first-century Jewish consciousness? In the rabbinic literature of the Tannaitic period, Esau is Rome. G. Cohen has dated the earliest rabbinic connection between Edom/Esau and Rome to Rabbi Akiba ben Joseph in the second century C.E., and Carol Bakhos concurs.[14] Still, we may note that the first-century c.e. book of *4 Ezra* is very concerned with Israel's humiliation before the nations (4:22–25) and emphasizes that the Messiah will judge Rome (11:1–12:39). Significantly for those who are reading Rom 9:7–13, it also contains a paraphrase of Mal 1:2–3 that follows a description of the covenant with Abraham (*4 Ezra* 3:15–16). While no specific equivocation is made between Edom and Rome in this first-century text, the foundational concerns and the political reference to Jacob and Esau found in Mal 1, which Paul also uses, seem to be initial steps toward the known designation of Rome as Edom.

A further suggestion that Paul's letter identifies Edom with Rome is Paul's mention of "the sword." Edom is famous in the Scriptures for living by the sword (Gen 27:40), and the sword is definitely a concern of Paul in this letter (Rom 8:35, 13:4). Rome, as Edom, lived by the sword.[15] But of course this parallel is not conclusive in itself; "Edom" and "Esau" might only evoke the Herod family in first-century hearers' minds. We shall return to the description of a power that does not use the sword in vain (Rom 13:4) later in this section. It is also noteworthy that Paul follows the reference to Esau with a reference to Pharaoh. Though Paul's letter antedates the following rabbinic quotation, the latter does illustrate how an exegetical mind nearer to the political realities of Paul's day might work. Our source is a Passover homily from the *Pesikta de Rab Kahana*, in which both Pharaoh's nation, Egypt, and Edom are associated with Rome: "As with Egypt He took each of the chiefest among them and slew them, so, too, with Edom: *A great slaughter in the land of Edom, among them to come down shall be the Remim* (Isa 34:6–7), that is, as R. Meir expounded it—among those to come down shall be the Romans [preeminent among all the peoples of Edom]."[16]

Why the reference in Rom 9:17 to Pharaoh as someone God raised up, quoting Exod 9:16? Perhaps this is partially because the connection between the Roman emperor and the ancient Pharaohs of Egypt was closer than we typically assume. The Ptolemies were granted pharaonic titles by Egypt's priestly caste and her bureaucracy, and Roman emperors also were depicted with pharaonic traditions.[17] Did Paul know that the Roman emperor was equated with Pharaoh? I cannot prove this. Suffice it to say that today, the link between the *princeps* and Pharaoh in

Egypt is conclusive in the material evidence. On the walls of the temple of Dendur (Tuzis), now reassembled in the Sackler Wing of the Metropolitan Museum of Art in New York, Augustus is depicted as a pious pharaoh offering sacrifices to Egyptian gods.[18] The large statue from Karnak on the right at the end of corridor G49 in the Egyptian Museum in Cairo is of a pharaoh who is identified either as Ptolemy V or Augustus. Another Egyptian, if not pharaonic, connection to the imperial cult is also amply evidenced by Claudius's request to have the golden statue known as the *Klaudiakē Eirēnē Sebastē* brought to Rome from Alexandria.[19] Deir el-Shelwit, a temple from the second half of the first century, depicts Galba, Otho, Vespasian, and Domitian as pharaohs.[20]

In light of the Roman imperial emphasis on the emperor as God's specially chosen or elect, Paul's language of election in Rom 9 seems well crafted (as we also see in 8:29–30). In Rom 9, Paul continues his consideration of the election of the Roman emperor. While I cannot prove that the equation between the Egyptian pharaoh and the Roman emperor would be transparent to the first hearers of this letter, anyone celebrating the Passover in Rome would make that connection.[21] In chapter 8 Paul insisted that Jesus is the one who is elected as son of God, and that others are elected to be conformed to the image of the son. Here in chapter 9 Paul examines more closely the idea of God's election of the pagan ruler. This is surely Paul's answer to the common first-century theme of the Roman emperor being predestined by the gods to rule the world.[22] Paul's answer is that God has raised up the Roman emperor as he raised up Pharaoh, in order to show God's power and magnify God's name. Paul's concern tracks with the prophets who also wrestle with how God can raise up foreign rulers and accomplish divine purposes for his chosen people through them.[23] This reading of the Pharaoh as indicative of foreign rule over the Jews fits with the context that follows in the "vessels of wrath" section (Rom 9:17–22), which I will consider in the next main section of this paper. We could now read Paul's christological reference to the stone laid in Zion—which in Isa 28:16 is a chosen stone (MT—*pinnat yiqrat;* LXX—*eklekton*)—as an assertion of the divine election of Jesus (already hinted at in Rom 8:29) and distinct from the divine election of the emperor that was voiced in the propaganda contemporary to Paul.

The concluding bracket of this section, Rom 12–15, also contains signals of concern over Roman dominance. In chapter 12, Paul writes that people are not to work vengeance (Rom 12:17, 19). In the context that follows he explains why a human government that works vengeance can still be obeyed (Rom 13:1–7). Readers have long noted the abrupt topic change at 13:1. Why does Paul introduce government here? The most adequate explanation is that government has been in view since the middle of Rom 8. In that chapter, Augustan eschatology and the doctrine of imperial predestination are reversed. Paul's scriptures and the imagery he uses in chapters 9–11 also evoke to first-century ears an assertion from below that the Roman dominance over God's chosen people, the Jews, cannot stand forever. Rom 13:1–7 might then serve as a pro forma endorsement of the status quo for the safety of Paul and his audience, while simultaneously reconfiguring imperial theology to insist that the earthly government is established by God.[24]

Paul quotes from a national lament psalm after ending his first list of threats in Rom 8 with the word "sword." Then in his explicit discussion of the governing powers, Paul warns that Rome does not bear the sword in vain (Rom 13:4). In the context of propaganda from Nero's reign, this is a direct subversion of the peace language evoked by the poet Calpurnius Siculus, who emphasizes the end of sword-wielding by Rome:

> Amid a secure peace, the Golden Age springs to a second birth, at last kindly Themis, throwing off the gathered dust of her mourning, returns to the earth; blissful ages attend the youthful prince ... He, a very God, shall rule the nations, the unholy War-Goddess shall yield and have her vanquished hands bound behind her back, and, stripped of weapons, turn her furious teeth into her own entrails ... All wars shall be quelled in Tartarean durance ... Fair peace shall come ... Clemency has commanded every vice that wears the disguise of peace to go far away; *she has broken every maddened sword-blade ... Peace in her fullness shall come; knowing not the drawn sword,* she shall renew once more the reign of Saturn in Latium, once more the reign of Numa who first taught the tasks of peace to armies that rejoiced in slaughter ... Numa who first hushed the clash of arms and bade the trumpet sound 'mid holy rites instead of war.[25]

In contrast to the poet's insistence that Rome under Nero is not using a drawn sword, Paul asserts that the sword is a real danger that the Roman government still wields (8:35; 13:4). If Paul is insistent that the Roman sword still threatens Israel, then in light of texts such as Lev 26:33, 36, and Jer 9:15 it is probable that Paul sees Israel's first-century condition as a sort of exile.

At the end of the letter's argument, the scriptural quotations found in Rom 15:9–12 from the Song of Moses, the Psalms, and Isaiah also challenge Roman dominance over Israel, since they envision the Messiah, his people, and the nations praising the God of Israel, who has reinstated "the root of Jesse" to rule over the nations who hope in this Davidic king.

Rom 15:10 quotes the first part of Deut 32:43. The verse as found in Deuteronomy concludes with a political edge: "Rejoice O nations, with His people; for he will avenge the blood of his servants, and will render vengeance on his adversaries, and will atone for his land and his people." The context of this part of the scriptural catena thus is fully engaged with a view toward the redemption of Israel from the nations and restoration to its land.

The final quotation in the catena, from Isa 11:10, immediately precedes the prediction that the Lord will recover the remnant of his people "from Assyria, Egypt, Pathros, Cush, Elam, Shinar, Hamath, and from the islands of the sea. And he will raise a banner for the nations, and will gather the exiled ones of Israel, and will gather the dispersed of Judah from the four ends of the earth" (Isa 11:11–12). Thus for those who know Isaiah, the conclusion of this scriptural catena evokes the hope for a return from exile, a hope raised in Rom 11:25–27, as I will argue in the next section. The God of hope is invoked in blessing after the scriptural catena as an alternative to the deified hope *(spes)* celebrated on Claudius's coins and worshiped in Rome.[26]

THE SALVATION OF ISRAEL AS RESTORATION IN THE LAND

So far, I will not have been persuasive to some of my fellow Christian readers. The very canonization and rearrangement of the Jewish Scriptures by the church is built on the assumption that the earthly experiences of Abraham's people depicted in these scriptures' narrative, poetic, and legal genres are intended to point to the spiritual experiences of those in Christ. Alert readers will sharpen this objection further by noting how Paul in 1 Cor 10:1–13 claims that the Israelites' wilderness experiences "happened as examples (*typoi*) for us" (10:6), Christ-followers "upon whom the end of the ages has come" (1 Cor 10:13). But the context on either side of Rom 11:26 makes it clear that Paul must be discussing corporeal Israel, as I argue below when considering N. T. Wright's position that a redefined, nonethnic "Israel" is in view in Rom 11:26. The Augustinian idea that Jerusalem can signify a heavenly city, so eloquently expressed in his *City of God*, does have a basis in the New Testament.[27] A later interpreter of Paul offers this signification in Heb 12:22–24. But in the text of Romans, it is clear that Paul cannot see past the center of his spiritual universe, Jerusalem on earth, where an uncertain fate awaits him (15:30–32). Furthermore, if Augustine is right that the earth and heavenly cities are always intermingled on this earth, then readers of Rom 9–11 must be open to the literal sense of Israel as ethnic Israel and her plight and salvation as that plight and salvation which Israel's prophets addressed in their writings.[28] My argument in this paper is not an attempt to dismiss the centuries of Christian exegesis that reads "Israel" in Scripture as a figure of the church. I am simply asking that when we as Christians read Rom 9–11 in our Scriptures, we consider that Paul's literal sense of "Israel" is the ethnic or corporeal Israel. And as we can see from the scriptures that Paul quotes, this Israel's salvation must include the idea of a political salvation on earth.

My identification of ethnic Israel finds some common ground with Paul Griffiths's commentary on the Song of Songs. He alludes to the way in which Christian interpreters can find signification in the lover and the beloved to such an extent that "the human beloved and the eroticism of the text vanishes." He concludes that "[b]etter, certainly more Christian, is to read in such a way as to preserve both the text's figures and what they figure."[29] Indeed, in light of Paul's warning in Rom 11:20–23, Christian readers of Romans should take pains to make exegetical space for corporeal, ethnic Israel. In that sense, my argument for ethnic Israel and her political salvation as included in the text's literal sense is, in Griffiths's phrase, "certainly more Christian."

John A. Battle, Jr., has helpfully pointed out that Paul's quotations from the prophets in Rom 9:20–33—with the single exception of Isa 45:9 in part of verse 20—all depict the time of Assyria's looming conquest of Israel.[30] In Isa 10, from which Paul quotes in Rom 9:27–28, Assyria is God's rod, and their own club is God's fury. It is significant that in Isa 10 not only rod (vv. 5, 15, 24) and club (v. 5) are used, but also ax (vv. 15, 34), saw (v. 15), staff (v. 24), whip (v. 26, belonging to God), and yoke (v. 27). Assyria as a foreign power is linked to Egypt in Isa 10:24, just as Paul has quotations regarding Pharaoh and Assyria in this chapter. While there is not an exact verbal quotation of Paul's phrase *skeuē orgēs* ("vessels of wrath") in Isa 10, it is significant that in LXX Isa 10:28, the Assyrian enemy places his *skeuē* in Michmash, on his way to Jerusalem. The Assyrian enemy will receive God's wrath to the point of destruction, according to LXX Isa 10:24–34.[31] The "vessels" that this enemy leaves in Michmash will thus come under the divine wrath directed against their owners. The enemy is showing wrath, but will ultimately experience God's wrath when God works salvation—political deliverance—for God's people. If Paul's phrase "vessels of wrath" in Rom 9:22 refers in its scriptural context to "the heathen nations God uses to judge Israel," and if Paul is using the phrase in the same sense, we can see that his focus remains on the political vulnerability of his people.[32] Paul uses Hosea in Rom 9:25–26 to explore the identity of Israel, but we would be remiss if we overlooked the fact that Hosea includes the threat of Israel's defeat at the hands of Assyria and its later restoration with the house of Judah (Hos 1:5; 2:2). We have already seen in the section on "Israel's Plight" that the Isaiah texts Paul combines in Rom 9:33 belong in the context of Judah's national instability due to the repercussions of Assyria's threat to the north. These quotations point ahead to Rom 11:27, where his quotation of a text from Jeremiah directly concerns the restoration of the houses of Israel and Judah. Thus, from the quotation of Mal 1:2–3 in Rom 9:13 on to the end of the chapter, all Paul's scriptural quotations relate to the political situation of the physical heirs of Abraham, Isaac, and Jacob.

Romans 10 is Paul's christological interpretation of how Israel should have believed, which he concludes with a catena of scriptural texts from the writings, the law, and the prophets in Rom 10:18–21. We have already noted that some of the quotations in this chapter come from contexts that deal with the political stability of the people who are God's first love. We have also seen how Paul's identification of himself as an Israelite from the southern kingdom of Judah is followed by his exemplary story from the kingdom of Israel, of Elijah, and of the remnant (Rom 11:1–5).

In Rom 11:15 we read, "For if their rejection means the reconciliation of the world, what will their return/reception mean except life from the dead." As Jon Levenson has shown so well, "life from the dead" in Ezekiel has a political, this-worldly connotation and is associated with the restoration of Israel in the land after God's judgment on Israel and her foreign enemies. "The Jewish expectation of a resurrection of the dead is always and inextricably associated with the restoration of the people Israel; it is not, in the first instance, focused on individual destiny. The question it answers is not, 'Will I have life after death?' but rather, 'Has God given up on his promises to his people?'"[33] Paul's reference to "life from the dead" in Rom 11:15 is thus an answer to his question earlier in that chapter, "Has God abandoned his people?" (Rom 11:1), which should be glossed as "Has God decided to leave Israel scattered among the nations and subjugated under Rome?" The phrase "life from the dead" also evokes Hosea's prediction (an echo of Hos 2:2, from Rom 9:25–26): "The people of Judah and the people of Israel shall assemble together and appoint one head over them; and *they shall rise from the ground*—for marvelous shall be the day of Jezreel!" (Hos 2:2, my emphasis). As in the Jeremiah passage from which Paul quotes in Rom 11:27, the restoration of the houses of Israel and Judah is in clear view.

With this survey of Paul's scriptures in mind, his assertion in 11:26 that all Israel shall be saved must speak primarily of the restoration of exiled tribes and of the political health of Israel here on earth: "Israel according to the flesh," as Paul might say, whom he considers to be in an unbroken connection to his churches (1 Cor 10:1–4, 18). Paul's brief quotation from Jeremiah's new covenant prediction (LXX Jer 38:34 in Rom 11:27a) primarily refers to the return of the exiled and assimilated northern tribes to live back in the land, since the prediction in Jeremiah relates to the houses of Israel and Judah, not to the Gentiles.[34] In light of the preceding chapters with their preponderance of material relating politically to Israel, Paul's climactic "all Israel shall be saved" (Rom

11:26) thus serves as a prediction that all Israel, including the northern tribes, shall be restored.

We can grasp now how intimately concerned Paul's choice of scriptures is with Israel's political plight. This is especially so for the new covenant text that Paul quotes in Rom 11:27, which in its context (MT Jer 31/LXX Jer 38) predicts the return of both houses of Israel from exile. Thus Paul's mention of "partial hardening" at 11:25, which leads right into the Jer 31:33 quotation, may include the matter-of-fact idea that *some* of Israel are still in exile. This is consistent with the way that Paul's scriptures link hardening and the similar expression of being stiff-necked with exile.[35] Another advantage of including exile as part of the semantic field for "partial hardening" in Rom 11 is that it allows us to bring more nuance into the debate over whether Paul thought his nation was in exile, à la N. T. Wright's instincts that the ongoing exile of Israel is a concern for New Testament authors.[36] The question for students of Paul's letter to the Romans is: how does Paul map the preoccupation of his scriptures with exile onto the gospel his letter seeks to define? Wright helpfully reminds us that "salvation" in first-century Jewish perspective was not about "the end of the space-time universe, and/or of Israel's future enjoyment of a non-physical, 'spiritual' bliss," but that it was rather about "rescue from the national enemies, restoration of the national symbols, . . . inauguration of the age to come, liberation from Rome, the restoration of the Temple, and the free enjoyment of their own Land."[37]

But Wright does not carry this insight through to his exegesis of Rom 9–11. Regarding the "all Israel will be saved" of Rom 11:26, Wright says: "The phrase 'all Israel,' then, is best taken as a polemical redefinition, in line with Paul's redefinitions of 'Jew' in 2:29, of circumcision in 2:29 and Phil 3:3, and of 'seed of Abraham' in Rom 4, Galatians 3, and Rom 9:6–9. It belongs with what seems indubitably the correct reading of 'the Israel of God' in Gal 6:16."[38] The problem with Wright's interpretation is that he seeks to read Paul as a thinker as consistent as Wright himself. But Paul's letters give clear evidence of holding ideas in tension. Yes, Paul is willing to redefine Israel at certain places in his letters. Indeed, he tries out different approaches to his question regarding Israel's plight, including a redefinition of Israel (Rom 9:6–9) or a limitation of her salvation only to a remnant (Rom

9:27–29; 11:1–5).[39] But he ends by affirming "this mystery": "all Israel will be saved." And in the immediate context of Rom 11:25–27, where ethnic Israel is played off against the Gentiles in Rom 11:11–15, 17–24, and in the clear references to ethnic Israel in Rom 11:28–31, it is difficult to say that Paul has redefined Israel so that its literal sense here is the church. Since Paul is referring to the corporeal, ethnic nation at the climax of his musings over Israel, the texts he has used to drive his argument from Rom 9:13 on to 11:27 indicate that his concern for Israel includes her exile and that his hope for Israel's salvation includes the restoration of Israel and Judah. Since Jeremiah's new covenant includes the picture of a restoration of Israel and Judah and since Paul quotes from Jer 31:33, which specifically mentions a covenant with "the house of Israel," we have to affirm that the literal sense of Paul's mystery includes the restoration of all Israel.[40] Paul's conclusion reminds us of the book of Job, which brings resolution to the mystery of suffering only by recalling readers to the inscrutable mind of God. Indeed, after declaring the mystery of Israel's salvation, Paul's hymn in Rom 11:33–36 includes two quotations from Job.[41]

Paul is not unique in viewing a return from exile as salvation for Israel. As Brant Pitre has argued, the descriptions Jesus gave in Mark 13 of the tribulation and the coming of the Son of Man also view the "ingathering of the exiles" as integral to Israel's salvation.

> The suggestion that Jesus of Nazareth as an eschatological prophet could have spoken to his disciples of proclaiming the "good news" in synagogues and sanhedrins as well as "to the nations," is historically quite plausible. Indeed, if one of Jesus' central hopes was for the coming of the End of the Exile, as I am suggesting, it would actually be almost impossible to believe that he was not aware of the fact that in the final chapter of one of the greatest prophets in the Old Testament, the ingathering of the scattered tribes of Israel apparently takes place only after those sent by God had proclaimed his glory "among the Gentiles." (Isa 66:19–20)[42]

Jason Staples's argument that the "fullness of the nations" in 11:25 (*plērōma tōn ethnōn*) is an allusion to Gen 48:19 (LXX *plēthos ethnōn*;

MT *ml'-hgwym*), indicating that Ephraim's descendants become the fullness of the nations, specifies how the salvation of Israel includes the return from the exile. If Staples is right, Paul's statement in Rom 11:25 could be paraphrased: "A hardening has happened to part of Israel" until the descendants of Ephraim enter in, and then all Israel will be saved.[43] Staples's argument introduces a new explanation for why the full number of Gentiles coming in precedes "all Israel will be saved" in Paul's logic (Rom 11:25–26). Past readers of Romans have been content to conceive of the interface between the early Christian movement and surrounding cultures only according to the strongly binary model of Acts. In that routine depiction, Paul offers his gospel first to diaspora Jews in a synagogue; once the Jews have officially rejected his message, he offers it to the Gentiles of the area.[44] This has led scholars to consider that the salvation Paul writes of in Rom 11 is spiritual, marked only by a baptism of the Holy Spirit, without any sense of the political dimensions of salvation for Israel on this earth. It has also led scholars to view the sequence in Rom 11:25–26 as simply the chiastic resolution to what is seen in Acts. When Staples offers a reasonable argument from Gen 48:29 that the fullness of the nations in Rom 11:25 is a reference to Ephraim, he shows a different and tighter logic behind Paul's assertion that when the full number of Gentiles comes in, all Israel will be saved. He is saying that since the northern tribes have been absorbed by the nations, a return of all the nations to the land inherently implies the salvation of all Israel.

One weakness of Staples's suggestion is that the aspect of assimilation is not explicitly listed in curse lists that describe the horrors of exile. The language of Lev 26:38, "the land of your enemies shall consume you," surely must be read in light of the first line of the verse and of the usual connotation of *'kl* in judgment contexts: it signifies destruction rather than assimilation. But assimilation is the reality behind the command in Exod 34:15–16; an interpolation like Deut 7:3; the ambiguity in descriptions of the occupation as in Josh 23:9–13; perhaps the narrative in 2 Kgs 17:24–41; and the specter behind the difficulty that Nehemiah and Ezra have with intermarriage.[45]

Staples's idea is consistent with the context of the phrase from Jer 31:34 (LXX Jer 38:34), and one value of this interpretive approach is that it lets us rethink the "partial hardening" Paul uses as a description for Israel in Rom 11:25. New Testament scholars would generally take this phrase to be only equivalent to Paul's description of how "the rest were hardened" in Rom 11:7, meaning that those who did not believe in Jesus have hardened hearts. In the first part of chapter 11 this seems to be what Paul primarily has in view. If we begin reading from Paul's christological glosses of Deut 30 in Rom 10:5–8 and continue through Rom 11:10, the "hardening" scenario in Rom 11:7–10 seems to mean that some Israelites, including Paul (Rom 11:1) and "the elect" (Rom 11:7), have confessed that Jesus is Lord and believe that God raised him from the dead (Rom 10:9). Those who have not have been hardened. But if we allow Paul's scriptures to speak in their original contexts, including the connection between the term "hardened" and synonyms of exile as documented below in note 35, there must be a concern for the hardening of Israel that leads to exile or has allowed an exile to continue.

A second value of this interpretive approach to the salvation of Israel in Rom 11 is that it lets us take a second look at Paul's phrase, "full number of the Gentiles comes in" (11:25). Why does Paul say "comes in"?[46] He has already mentioned the "wealth of the world" and the "wealth of nations" in Rom 11:12, an idea with a thick scriptural basis. Instead of simply taking this generic verb to mean "believe in Jesus" or "be saved" in the otherworldly sense, it is more responsible to read it in light of the "wealth of nations" motif of Paul's scriptures and in the context of the "restoration from exile" scriptures Paul quotes in Rom 11:26–27. This interpretation fits with the possibility that the collection from Paul's Gentile churches for the poor in Jerusalem is in some sense Paul's contribution to bringing the Gentiles and their wealth to Zion, in fulfillment of such texts as Isa 66 and Zech 8.[47] Whether one accepts Staples's thesis that the Gentiles coming in includes the northern tribes, or whether the northern tribes' return is pictured as part of Israel's salvation that will occur after non-Jewish Gentiles "come in," it is exegetically more responsible to consider that Paul means what Isa 66 means, especially since canonical Isaiah is the prophet whom he most quotes in this section. When a full number of Gentiles return to the land, the exile will be over and the houses of Israel and Judah will be restored.

I have been assembling pieces of a mosaic to determine what constitutes the basis for Paul's grief over Israel and what Paul means by "all Israel shall be saved." No single piece of the mosaic is conclusive, but taken together the mosaic depicts the probable portrait of Paul, a Jew who is concerned and hopeful for the political situation of his people. The argument so far in this paper, drawing from a consideration of how Rom 9–11 is framed in the letter and from contextual readings of Paul's scripture quotations in Rom 9–11, is that the literal sense of Paul's grief for Israel includes his nation's political subjugation at the hands of Rome. When he predicts the salvation of all Israel in Rom 11:26, the literal sense of his prediction is that the houses of Israel and Judah will be restored in the land.

PAUL THE PARTICULARIST

It remains for us to consider how this reading of Israel's salvation in Rom 9–11 affects our understanding of Paul. Christian scholars traditionally view Paul as a universalist, in the sense that he wants to extend the blessings of Israel's messiah to all the nations so that Jew and Gentile become an indistinguishable one or a "new Israel."

Jon Levenson has ably shown that the universal scope of God's mercy on the world must have a beginning point of God's election of a particular people.[48] While Christian scholars might agree, and state that the particular starting point for Paul's universal vision of salvation is the election of ethnic Israel and her messiah, I am arguing that Paul retains his particular focus on Israel even when he can state that the full number of Gentiles come in and that God shuts up all to disobedience in order to have mercy on all (Rom 11:25, 32). Since the literal sense of "all Israel will be saved" in Rom 11:26 includes a salvation described by Paul's scriptures as a restoration of both Israel's houses in their land, we Christian readers need to note the strong particularism that remains in Paul.

The results of our look at Israel's scriptures in Paul's argument also should draw our attention to the phenomenon of ideological tensions between universalism and particularism in the context of Israel's exile. Weinfeld's model of a universalistic mindset and a particularistic reaction that arise out of the Babylonian exile needs to be considered by New Testament scholars.[49] His model of course can be broadened to include the first-century Judaisms reflected within the New Testament. Weinfeld's idea that the universalistic and particularistic approaches were resolved by the rabbis' decision to accept Gentiles who kept Torah reminds us of Paul's opponents in Galatia, or "the Jews" of Acts 15:1. Paul's idea that the Gentiles to whom he brings his gospel—could these include some "Gentiles" who were assimilated Jews as Staples suggests?—need not keep Torah, now begins to appear radical enough to evoke the opposition Paul seems to be facing in Galatians and 2 Corinthians. What is Paul's resolution of the problem? It is not the one-sided universalism that Enlightenment-based scholarship has found in Paul through the last centuries to the present.[50]

Yes, Paul keeps a window open to a universal view. Especially in Romans, we see Paul seeking to give an account of how the God of Israel deals with all people, from before the time that the Torah was given onward. But as Levenson has ably shown, a universal horizon can only be meaningful if it is grounded in some form of particularism. Paul, who is especially concerned for his fellow heirs of the Abrahamic and Mosaic covenants, definitely grounds this concern in a vibrant, ethnic particularism that is too often ignored by New Testament readers. New Testament scholars might try to play along with Weinfeld and state that Paul has transmuted the "holy seed" idea of the rigorous particularism arising out of the exile onto Christ, whom he identifies as the seed of Abraham in Gal 3:16 and the seed of David in Rom 1:3. These texts definitely show one way in which Paul takes the particularism he has inherited. But we must also remember that one of Paul's goals for asking Gentiles to identify with Christ is their holiness. This shows itself not only in the list of what God has accomplished in Christ in Rom 8:30–31, but also in Paul's intense reaction in Romans against any suggestion that he is recommending that his followers may live in sin (Rom 3:8, 6:1–23) and in his summaries of the results of his gospel in bringing the Gentiles as a holy offering to God (Rom 15:16, 1 Cor 6:9–11). Then those who follow Christ can claim to share—as contingent beneficiaries—in the divine favor first offered to the corporeal nation of Israel.

Levenson's exegetical conclusion from Gal 3:26–29 that Paul is not a universalist is also borne out by a look at the final scriptural catena in Romans, the grand quotation of Rom 15:9–12 that seems to bring the argument of the letter to a close.[51] Here we see that the nations praise God along with God's people (Rom 15:10 quoting LXX Deut 32:43). In none of the texts do we find the single people created by the destruction of the Law as it is envisioned by a later author in the Pauline school (Eph 2:14–16), nor the "third race" of later Christian interpreters.[52] The appeal to Paul's having said that in Christ there is no longer Jew or Greek (Gal 3:28) fails to recognize the context of this and other statements by Paul about ethnic identity. While Paul sees that in God's dealings with humanity, baptism and faith mark the final initiation rites for Jew and Greek, slave and free, male and female (Gal 3:28), he makes it clear that in the business of living their lives on the earth, real distinctions remain between Jew and Greek (1 Cor 9:20–21). We know that his followers continued to uphold ethical distinctions in how slave, free, male and female should live (Eph 5:21–28, 6:5–9, Col 3:18–25).

The literal sense of Paul's grief and hope for his "brothers, kinfolk according to the flesh, Israelites" includes the political subjugation and eventual restoration of Israel and Judah. Since he argues in this way, Paul's particularism must be kept in full view, for even while writing that God works in order to have mercy on all, the "all" he pictures is always Israel and the nations, not an undifferentiated and new body politic (Rom 11:32, 15:9–12).

— I first met Jon Levenson while a graduate student. In 1987, I went to his office to meet him and ask for information about a required Hebrew proficiency test. In our conversation, he learned that I was an alumnus of an evangelical college and seminary. He then began to look for a sheet of paper that described the proficiency test. It took him a while to find this paper and when he finally found it, he apologized for the delay as he was handing it to me. I replied, "That's all right, Mr. Levenson, I had confidence that you would find it." His rejoinder has stayed with me until today: "You're from [such-and-such] College. You should have said, '*I had faith* that you would find it!" Here's to Jon

Levenson and his winsome ways of helping Jews and Christians talk about their foundational convictions.

NOTES

An earlier version of this paper, entitled "On Earth, Not in Heaven: The Political Salvation of Israel in Romans 9–11," was read in the Pauline Epistles section of the SBL annual meeting on November 18, 2006, in Washington, D.C. It was then posted on the Paul Page, http://www.thepaulpage.com/. This paper is a thorough expansion and revision of that paper. It is a privilege to be able to contribute an essay in honor of Jon D. Levenson here, and I wish to register my appreciation and thanks for his friendship.

1. Jon D. Levenson, *Sinai and Zion: An Entry into the Jewish Bible* (Minneapolis: Winston, 1985), 50–56.

2. Jon D. Levenson, "The Universal Horizon of Biblical Particularism," in *The Universal Horizon of Biblical Particularism* (New York: American Jewish Committee, 1985), 3–14, 18–19, 21–22. The essay is reprinted with minor revisions in *Ethnicity and the Bible,* (ed. Mark G. Brett; Leiden: Brill, 1996), 143–69, and in *Commitment and Commemoration: Jews, Christians, Muslims in Dialogue* (ed. André LaCocque; Chicago: Exploration Press, 1994), 53–72.

3. Exod 4:22; Deut 14:1; 32:5–6, 18–19; Isa 43:6, 45:11; Jer 3:19, 31:9, 20; Hos 2:1, 11:1.

4. Joseph A. Fitzmyer, S. J. *Romans: A New Translation with Introduction and Commentary* (AB 33; New York: Doubleday, 1993), 532.

5. Job 31:1–40; Eccl 3:16–21, 9:2–3; Jer 20:7–18; Hab 1:2–4, 13. But cf. *Ps. Sol.* 15:6–7, which says that famine and sword will not threaten the righteous.

6. On quotation of LXX Ps 43 in Rom 8:36, see Tyler Stewart, "The Cry of Victory: A Cruciform Reading of Psalm 44:22 in Romans 8:36," *Journal for the Study of Paul and His Letters* 3/1 (2013): 25–46. A. Katherine Grieb has identified Romans 9–11 as a lament psalm; see *The Story of Romans: A Narrative Defense of God's Righteousness* (Louisville: Westminster John Knox, 2002), 90: "One could almost say that Paul, in writing his own lament psalm in Romans 9–11, writes representatively on behalf of Israel, appealing to God from the language of Israel's own Scriptures, the same 'oracles of God' (3:2) entrusted to Israel by God."

7. All translations from the New Testament are mine unless otherwise noted.

8. *Ioudaios* in Romans occurs in 1:16; 2:9–10, 17, 28–29; 3:9; 9:24, 10:12.

9. Jason A. Staples, "What Do the Gentiles Have to Do with 'All Israel'? A Fresh Look at Romans 11:25–27," *JBL* 130 (2011): 374–76.

10. J. Ross Wagner, *Heralds of the Good News: Isaiah and Paul "In Concert" in the Letter to the Romans* (NovTSup 101; Leiden: Brill, 2002), 136–45.

11. See Mal 1:5 ("Great is the LORD beyond the borders of Israel!"), 1:11 ("My name is honored among the nations, . . . My name is honored among the nations—said the LORD of Hosts"); 3:24 (". . . so that, when I come, I do not strike the whole land with utter destruction"). All quotations from the Hebrew Bible are from NJPS.

12. I am indebted here to Wagner, *Heralds of the Good News*, 143–45.

13. Gen 12:16, 20:14–16; Exod 12:35–36; Isa 60:5–18; Zech 14:14; Ezra 7:14–23.

14. Gershon Cohen, "Esau as Symbol in Early Medieval Thought," in *Studies in the Variety of Rabbinic Cultures* (Philadelphia: Jewish Publication Society, 1991), 245, as found in Carol Bakhos, *Ishamel on the Border: Rabbinic Portrayals of the First Arab* (Albany: SUNY), 63–64.

15. See Virgil, *Aen*. 10.372–73: *ferro rumpenda per hostis est via*, "'Tis the sword must hew a way through the foe" (trans. H. Rushton Fairclough; LCL; Cambridge, Mass.: Harvard University Press, 1954).

16. *Pesikta de-Rab Kahana: Rab Kahana's Compilation of Discourses for Sabbaths and Festal Days* (trans. William G. Braude and Israel J. Kapstein; Philadelphia: Jewish Publication Society of America, 1975), Piska 7.11 (p. 152).

17. J. Rufus Fears, *Princeps a Diis Electus: The Divine Election of the Emperor as a Political Concept at Rome* (Rome: American Academy in Rome, 1977), 20, 70–71.

18. *Egypt from Alexander to the Early Christians* (ed. Roger S. Bagnall and Dominic W. Rathbone; Los Angeles: J. Paul Getty Museum, 2004), 247–48.

19. Stefan Weinstock, "Pax and the Ara Pacis," *JRS* 50 (1960): 50, citing Letter of Claudius to the Alexandrians, Pap. Lond. 1912, lines 34 ff.

20. Bagnall and Rathbone, *Egypt* 197.

21. On the Egypt–Rome connection, note also the interpretation of Rev 11:8 as designating Rome. The first corrector of Sinaiticus added *kai eggus ho potamos* ("and near the river") right after Sodom, connecting Egypt to the city of Babylon and hence to Rome. Oecoumenius and Andrew of Caesarea take it as Jerusalem, but Hoskier lists other manuscripts that add Babylon after Egypt. These would thus also link "Egypt" to Rome.

22. Fears, *Princeps a Diis Electus*.

23. Isa 44:24—45:6; Hab 1:6–11; 2:9–12, 15–16.

24. Arland J. Hultgren, *Paul's Letter to the Romans: A Commentary* (Grand Rapids, Mich.: Eerdmans, 2011), 469.

25. Calpurnius Siculus, *Eclogue* 1.42–68 in *Minor Latin Poets* (trans. J. Wight Duff and Arnold M. Duff; LCL; Cambridge, MA: Harvard University Press, 1961). My emphasis; Themis is the Greek goddess of justice/righteousness.

26. Cf. the sestertius minted during Claudius's reign, indexed as RIC 99, Cohen 85cf, BMC 124, Sear (RCV 2000), no. 1853. See also Mark Edward

Clark, "*Spes* in the Early Imperial Cult: The "Hope of Augustus," *Numen* 30/1 (1983): 80–105.

27. Augustine, *Civ. Dei* 18.29.

28. Augustine, *Civ. Dei* 18.54.

29. Paul J. Griffiths, *Song of Songs* (Brazos Theological Commentary on the Bible; Grand Rapids, Mich.: Brazos, 2011), xxxix. See, e.g., how Griffiths keeps ethnic Israel and the church simultaneously in view in his exegesis of this text (106).

30. John A. Battle, Jr., "Paul's Use of the Old Testament in Romans 9:25–26," *Grace Theological Journal* 2/1 (1981): 124.

31. Battle, "Paul's Use," 127: "In Paul's context the thought predominates that these vessels will *receive* God's wrath" (his emphasis). He goes on to cite the "son of destruction" in 2 Thess 2:3 as a parallel use of the genitive.

32. Ibid., 125.

33. Jon D. Levenson, *Resurrection and the Restoration of Israel: The Ultimate Victory of the God of Life* (New Haven: Yale University Press, 2006), 162–63 (restoration after judgment), 165 (quotation).

34. Staples, "What Do the Gentiles Have To Do with 'All Israel'?," 380.

35. Especially 2 Chr 36:13 in context; see also *T. Levi* 13:7. The related expression of being stiff-necked is usually linked to destruction, as in Exod 32:9–10, 33:3, 5; Deut 9:13–14. But in Ezek 2:3–4 there is a connection made between exile and the stiff-necked condition, and this is implied in Deut 31:27–29 as well.

36. N. T. Wright, *The New Testament and the People of God* (Minneapolis: Fortress, 1992), 268–71 (note quotations of Tob 14:5–7; Bar 3:6–8; and 2 Macc 1:27–29 on 270); 299–301; idem, *Jesus and the Victory of God* (London: SPCK, 1996), 126–27, 209.

37. Wright, *New Testament and the People of God*, 300.

38. N. T. Wright, "The Letter to the Romans: Introduction, Commentary, and Reflections," in *The New Interpreter's Bible*, vol. 10 (ed. Leander E. Keck; Nashville, Ky.: Abingdon, 2002), 690.

39. See my discussion under the heading "The Argumentative Pattern of Rom 9–11" in "Romans 9–11 Moves from Margin to Center, from Rejection to Salvation: Four Grids for Recent English-Language Exegesis" in *Between Gospel and Election: Explorations in the Interpretation of Romans 9–11*, eds. Florian Wilk and J. Ross Wagner (Tübingen: Mohr Siebeck, 2010), 82–86.

40. Jer 31:31 (LXX 38:31) mentions both Israel and Judah. Paul's Jeremiah quotation in Rom 11:27a is a paraphrase of LXX Jer 38:31.

41. Rom 11:33–36; v. 34a quotes LXX Job 40:13; v. 35 quotes Job 41:3. See also Jon D. Levenson, *The Book of Job in Its Time and in the Twentieth Century* (Cambridge, MA: Harvard University Press, 1972), 19, 28–29.

42. Brant Pitre, *Jesus, the Tribulation, and the End of the Exile: Restoration Eschatology and the Origin of the Atonement* (Tübingen: Mohr Siebeck, 2005), 291.

43. Staples, "What Do the Gentiles Have To Do with 'All Israel'?" 385–88, at 387.

44. Acts 13:44–49, 18:1–8, 19:8–10, 28:17–28.

45. I follow the lead of Bernard M. Levinson in *The Jewish Study Bible* annotations of Deuteronomy, who notes how Deut 7:3 seems out of sync with the preceding verse. See also Josh 23:6–13; Ezra 9:1–10:44; Neh 13:23–28. On the evidence for possible variations of assimilation in biblical Israel, see Joel S. Kaminsky, *Yet I Loved Jacob: Rethinking the Biblical Concept of Election* (Nashville, Ky.: Abingdon, 2007), 126–28.

46. Paul uses this verb, *eiserchomai*, only at Rom 5:12, 11:25; 1 Cor 14:23, 24.

47. Rom 15:30–32. See the discussion at the end of "Israel's Plight" section, above.

48. Levenson, *Universal Horizon*, 21–22.

49. Moshe Weinfeld, "Universalism and Particularism in the Period of Exile and Restoration" [Hebrew], *Tarbiz* 33 (1964): 228–42.

50. Alain Badiou, *Saint Paul: The Foundation of Universalism* (trans. Ray Brassier; Stanford: Stanford University Press, 2003). Giorgio Agamben argues against Badiou's universalistic reading of Paul in *The Time that Remains: A Commentary on the Letter to the Romans* (trans. Patricia Dailey; Stanford: Stanford University Press, 2005), 52.

51. Levenson, *Universal Horizon*, 18–19.

52. *Ep. Diog.* 1.1. See Denise Kimber Buell, *Why This New Race: Ethnic Reasoning in Early Christianity* (New York: Columbia University Press, 2005).

CHAPTER 13

Populus Dei
Luther on Jacob and the Election of Israel (Genesis 25)

BROOKS SCHRAMM

In a trenchant discussion of the significance of the Jacob cycle in Genesis for a theological understanding of the Hebrew Bible, Jon Levenson has stated:

> It cannot be underscored enough that the man of whom this story is told is the eponymous ancestor of the nation, Jacob/Israel. At its deepest level the Jacob narrative is more than biography: it is the national history and speaks, therefore, of the self-conception of the people Israel and not merely of the pranks of the trickster from whom they are descended. In its most important features, the pattern of Jacob's life will be reproduced in the story of his son Joseph—another younger son beloved of his parent, exalted above his brothers, and condemned to exile and slavery because of their fratricidal jealousy. The immediate

link between the two successive stories of exaltation and humiliation is Jacob's doing what the Deuteronomic law of the birthright would come to forbid, "treat[ing] as first-born the son of the loved [wife] in disregard of the son of the unloved one who is older" (Deut [21]:16), that is, favoring Rachel's son Joseph. But, as we shall see . . . this favoritism, no less than Rebekah's, reflects God's own preference and testifies anew to the inegalitarian character of the God of the chosen people.

The striking parallels between the stories of Jacob and Joseph are thus, at the profound level, owing to their common refraction of the foundational story of the people Israel. Like much in Genesis, these two narrative cycles adumbrate the great national epic in which the people of God, "Israel . . . My first-born son" (Exod 4:22), leaves the promised land in extremis, endures enslavement and attempted genocide in Egypt, and yet, because of the mysterious grace of God, marches out triumphantly. The story of the humiliation and exaltation of the beloved son reverberates throughout the Bible because it is the story of the people about whom and to whom it is told. It is the story of Israel the beloved son, the first-born of God.[1]

As the life of the eponymous ancestor of the people Israel is described as one of seemingly constant struggle, so the reception history of his story is also marked by struggle, much of it quite bitter. Both Jewish and Christian interpreters have seen in the story of Jacob clues to the deepest questions of human and religious identity and of the nature of God. One such interpreter was the great Christian reformer, Martin Luther (1483–1546), and it is to Luther's interpretation of the theological significance of God's choice of Jacob over Esau in Gen 25—"the elder will serve the younger"—that this essay is devoted.[2]

LUTHER ON ELECTION

In the realm of theology there is likely nothing that Martin Luther despised more than the Jewish claim to be the children of Abraham and the chosen people of God. His polemic against this Jewish claim is articulated countless times in his written corpus: the Jews lay exclusive claim to the title of God's chosen, look down on all other people, and, ultimately, look forward to the messianic annihilation of all Gentiles.³ He would contend against Jewish chosenness literally until the day of his death.

On the other hand, the doctrine of election itself is at the very center of Luther's own theology. It is not chosenness as such against which he contends but rather Jewish chosenness based on natural descent. That God chooses, and rejects, is theologically axiomatic for Luther. Why God does so is beyond human knowing. According to Luther, when speaking of God one must distinguish strictly between *Deus absconditus* (also called *Deus non revelatus*, *Deus nudus*) and *Deus revelatus*. Why God chooses, and rejects, is the ultimate *mysterium tremens*, for it resides in the inscrutable—impenetrable—inner life of God.⁴ Human attempts to inquire into this *mysterium* constitute original sin itself.⁵ In harmony with Exod 33:23 ("I will remove my hand, and you will see my backside, but my face will not be seen"), a favorite text of Luther's, the human being has access only to God's backside not to God's face.⁶ That God elects Israel is never contested by Luther. But who or what is Israel? That is the driving question for him. Luther understands Judaism's doctrine of election as utterly exclusive, and thus a denial of his own as well as all other believing Gentiles' status as elect. This, as much as anything else, accounts for why the stakes are so high for him.

ENARRATIONES IN GENESIN

Luther's career as a professor of Bible at the University of Wittenberg began with lectures on the Psalter (*Dictata super Psalterium*) which he delivered over the years 1513–1515.⁷ These first lectures by the young professor are saturated with anti-Jewish references and allusions.⁸ At the opposite end of his career stand the lectures on Genesis (1535–1545), a work rightly called his magnum opus.⁹ The chronology of these lectures is not precise, and in addition it is known that they were interrupted on numerous occasions, not the least of which was the plague. The best estimate regarding Luther's treatment of Gen 25:19–34 is that it took place in the fall of 1540.[10] Since we know that the Genesis lectures were concluded in November 1545, it is noteworthy that Luther's rigorous exegetical engagement with the figures of Jacob and Joseph (Gen 25–50) coincides with the period of time when the majority of his most infamous anti-Jewish treatises were written and published.[11] Demonstrating the manifold connections between the Genesis lectures and these late anti-Jewish polemical treatises would far exceed the scope of this study. Nevertheless one can say with some confidence that there is more going on here than mere chronological overlap, for there is a high degree of coherence in terms of what Luther says about the Jews in general and about rabbinic interpretation in particular.[12]

The crucial problem in the study of Luther's Genesis lectures is that of transmission history. The published version of the lectures does not derive from Luther's pen, and Luther's lecture notes (with a few small exceptions) have not survived, thus raising the question of authenticity and integrity.[13] In Luther's broader corpus where both lecture notes and printed version have survived, we know that the editors took liberties. In the case of the Genesis lectures, it is apparent that the two primary editors, Veit Dietrich and Hieronymous Besold, labored to give the lectures the form of an academic commentary. Their editorial work likely included the insertion of explicit citations to Christian and classical writers that Luther would have mentioned only in passing in the classroom.[14] More problematic is the question of the degree to which the editors have altered certain of Luther's theological positions in the direction of his closest colleague, Philip Melanchthon. Erich Seeberg and his student Peter Meinhold in particular argued for a relatively high degree of theological alteration by the editors.[15] More recent work has argued for significantly less, and the winsome phrase of Jaroslav Pelikan is noteworthy in capturing the current state of the question: "The hands are sometimes the hands of the editors, but the voice is nevertheless the voice of Luther."[16] In addition, Peter von der Osten-Sacken has now argued for the important further nuance that the editorial work on the lectures is not uniform.[17] Clear indications of editorial tampering are much less in evidence from Gen 22:3b onward, that is, in the long section edited by Besold. Thus we are in the fortunate position of having a text that is much more reliable precisely in those sections chronologically closest to the 1543 polemical treatises.[18]

In terms of Luther's approach to Genesis itself, we are confronted with a massive amount of material, and find Luther ruminating at one time or another on virtually everything under the sun.[19] But there are consistent currents of thought running throughout the lectures, providing a window into the theological questions that continued to occupy him in his final years, including not least that of the significance of God's choice of Jacob over Esau.

Messiah/Son of God

A persuasive case can be made to the effect that Gen 3:15 ("I will put enmity between you and the woman, and between your seed and her seed; he will strike your head, and you will strike his heel") was regarded by Luther as the single most important text in the Bible. All editions of the Luther Bible include this marginal note for the reader of Gen 3:15: "This is the first gospel and promise of Christ on earth, to the effect that he will overcome sin, death, and hell and save us from the power of the Serpent. In this Adam believed together with all of his descendants, (and) by which he became a Christian and was saved from his Fall."[20] His interpretation of this one passage runs like a red thread throughout the Genesis lectures and functions as the lynchpin in his overall reading of the Christian Bible as a theological unity. For Luther, the seed of the woman is the Messiah/Son of God, and this text proclaims the promise of his coming. Those who belong to the Messiah/Son of God are those who trust in this promise. The serpent is Satan, and his seed represents those who belong to him. The Messiah/Son of God and Satan and those who belong to them are thus locked in perpetual struggle until the last day.

In Gen 3:15 Luther is cognizant that "seed of the woman" in its plain sense refers to humanity in general. But he argues that the very indefiniteness of the plain sense is an intentional diversion introduced into the text by God in order to make Satan suspicious and fearful of all women, such that any woman might potentially give birth to the "Crusher."[21] Eve for her part does not fully comprehend the promise either. She, like Satan, recognizes the messianic import of the words, but when Cain is born she thinks that she is The Woman and that Cain is The One promised.[22] Thus Luther calls the passage "very very clear yet at the same time very very obscure."[23] It awaits its illumination from subsequent passages such as Gen 22:18; 49:10; Isa 7:14; and finally Luke 1:35. As the line of descent of The Seed becomes ever more evident to God's faithful people, it also becomes clearer to Satan, who will more and more pour out his wrath on the line of Judah.

Taking off from Paul's interpretation of the "seed of Abraham" in Gal 3:16, 19, Luther interprets every instance of "the seed of Abraham/Isaac/Jacob" from Gen 3:15 to the end of the book as a reference primarily to "The Seed" and secondarily to "those who belong to The Seed." But Gen 3:15 itself is a clear yet obscure clue to even more. "The seed of the woman" is a loaded phrase implying two things. That the one to be born is "the seed of a woman" means that he will not be "the seed of a man," thus implying the virgin birth and simultaneously the two natures of Christ, the Son of God. Thus the one to be born is "The Seed of The Woman."[24] The two natures of The Seed of The Woman are crucial to Luther's overall understanding of Gen 3:15 because the drama of salvation and damnation announced there is premised on the desperate demise of the human beings who are the addressees—Adam and Eve certainly, but also all those who would read this text. Luther was true to traditional Christian reading of Gen 3 as the story of the fall of humanity into sin, but few if any before Luther emphasized so radically the depth of the fall, particularly in terms of the systematic theological implications and interconnections that he derived from it. He issues repeated warnings against minimizing the gravity and the depravity of the human condition, because doing so inevitably minimizes the work of God. His extreme anthropological position is thus mirrored in his unrelenting emphasis on human salvation as being exclusively a divine action. In Luther's view, the only remedy for *malum peccati originalis* is a God-human, and thus his anchoring of the two natures in this text is not to be underestimated. It pervades his thought on the entire Bible. Not only is Gen 3:15 "the first gospel," it is the entire thing *in nuce*.

Exempla fidei ad nostram doctrinam

Over and over again in Luther's *Genesis* he focuses on the characters in the stories as real, historical human beings. His treatment of these stories is in harmony with an admonition he himself issued in his *Preface to the Old Testament:* "I beg and really caution every pious Christian not to be offended by the simplicity of the language and stories frequently encountered there, but fully realize that, however simple they may seem, these are the very words, works, judgments, and deeds of the majesty, power, and wisdom of the most high God."[25] Contrary to so much of the tradition before him, Luther argued that the stories of Genesis have no need for elaborate allegories; rather, the substance of the matter is to be sought in what the characters actually experienced, thought, and felt.[26] He himself was fascinated by the lives of the patriarchs and matriarchs (most especially in regard to procreation), and he never misses an opportunity to emphasize that they are far greater examples for Christians than the traditional saints of the church venerated by the monks.

But examples of what? Of faith/trust in the promises of God, promises that most often seem to have run aground. He was deeply affected by the alternations in the lives of the saints of Genesis and saw them as engaged in a constant struggle against doubting God's promises. What God promised and what the saints felt or experienced were invariably in contradiction. A cynical critic might say that what Luther found when he looked at the mothers and fathers of Genesis was himself.[27] To a large extent, he would agree with that.[28] And he likely would fail to see the problem. He was convinced that the human being has remained essentially the same in character throughout all history.[29] In terms of the dynamics of religious life, the gap between the Bible and the sixteenth century was not large at all to Luther's mind.

The gap for him was rather in terms of clarity of revelation. The faith of the saints of Genesis was harder and more admirable, because their faith was in a sheer promise, as opposed to those Christian saints who lived and live on the other side of the Christ event. Thus, the saints of Genesis become for Luther the examples of faith in its purest form.

He spares no praise for them and clearly delights in their stories. Beyond that, the faith of the leading characters in Genesis has the intended function of serving as exemplary "for our instruction," or "for our consolation" (Rom 15:4). Indeed, Luther would say this is the primary function of the book of Genesis itself. And just as the faith of the Genesis saints was harder, so the *tentationes* that they experienced were deeper and more haunting. He often emphasized this point, especially in his treatment of Gen 1–11; e.g., "our temptations, crosses, and vexations . . . are nothing in comparison with those of the holy fathers." Why? Because they lived so long![30]

Luther's overall attraction to Genesis is summed up nicely in his *Preface to the Old Testament:* "The first book of Moses therefore is made up almost completely of examples of faith and unfaith, and of the fruits that faith and unfaith produce. It is virtually an evangelical book."[31]

The Rabbis

Luther's *Genesis,* like the overwhelming majority of his writings, is polemical. The usual suspects, Jews—heretics—pope—Turk—*Schwärmer,*[32] are attacked with regularity. A prominent characteristic of his anti-Jewish invectives (which appear throughout the lectures) is the overt hostility he expresses toward rabbinic interpretation of the Bible in general and of Genesis in particular. What he actually knew of rabbinic interpretation, and how he knew it, has still not been resolved satisfactorily.[33] There can be no question of Luther himself using rabbinic sources directly, for even by his own admission his Hebrew (much less his Aramaic) was inadequate for that. His primary conduits into rabbinic learning were Nicholas of Lyra, whose biblical commentaries Luther utilized throughout his career, as well as the *Additiones* to Lyra by Paul of Burgos and Sebastian Münster's *Hebraica biblia latina.* He also expressly acknowledges dependence on two anti-Jewish treatises in particular, *Victoria adversus impios Hebreos* by Salvagus Porchetus, and *Der gantz Jüdisch Glaub* by Anthonius Margaritha.[34]

Be all this as it may, over the course of his career Luther developed a visceral antipathy toward the rabbis, and in the Genesis lectures in particular we encounter denigration after denigration. At best the rabbis are arbitrary, at worst nonsensical. At best they know grammar, at worst they are devoid of theological understanding.[35] He reacted vehemently against rabbinic ambiguity/plurality of meaning, and he called their readings "gemachte Grammatica" (artificial grammar). By way of example I quote here an extended diatribe, which captures in one place the level of antagonism that one encounters throughout the Genesis lectures, and illustrates as well the overall attitude with which Luther pursues his interpretation of Genesis over against Judaism. It occurs in his treatment of Gen 25:21:

> For the sake of those who at some time or other will read the commentaries of the rabbis let us next add something of the Jewish nonsense. At this point they raise the question why Isaac did not marry another wife after he had discovered in the course of almost 20 years that his wife was barren, while in the example of Sarah they conclude that 10 years should be allowed for discovering barrenness or fecundity. Their answer is that in Isaac's case the situation is different from what it is in the case of Abraham. They say that because Isaac was sacrificed to God and became a burnt offering by the direction of God, he was not permitted to marry another wife. Thus Paul wants a bishop to be the husband of one wife (1 Tim 3[:2]). Everybody sees how absurd and worthless these ideas are. Nevertheless, they must be touched on at times, in order to advise those who are students of the Hebrew language to read the sayings and writings of the Jews with discretion. We acknowledge, of course, that it is a great benefit that we have received the language from them; but we must beware of the dung of the rabbis [*rabbinorum stercoribus*], who have made of Holy Scripture a sort of privy in which they deposited their foulness and their exceedingly foolish opinions. I am advising this because even among our own theologians many give too much credit to the rabbis in explaining the meaning of Scripture. In the matter of grammar I readily bear with them; but they lack the true sense and understanding [*vero sensu et intellectu*], in accordance with the well-known words in Isa 29[:14]: "The wisdom of their wise men shall perish, and the discernment of their discerning men shall be hid." This statement declares that there will be no understanding of Scripture among the Jews. No, this book of Holy Scripture has been

closed for them and sealed. "With an alien tongue the LORD will speak to this people" (Isa 28[:11]). And they know nothing else than sheer blasphemies against the Christian religion.³⁶

Ecclesia

The term "ecclesia" is omnipresent in Luther's *Genesis,* and he uses it in many different ways. Thus he can speak of the ecclesia of Cain, of Nimrod, of Ishmael, of Esau, of the pope, of the Turk, and especially of Satan. These different uses are all a function of what he regards as the equivocal character of the term, and while he freely throws it around, he also concedes that these uses are actually improper.³⁷ Properly speaking, the term should only connote *ecclesia vera Dei,* and any ecclesia other than this is properly *falsa ecclesia.*

It is to the church in precisely this sense that the book of Genesis bears witness, according to Luther. Jaroslav Pelikan has argued that Luther conceived of Genesis as "the history of the church as the people of God."³⁸ For Luther, and this is of crucial importance, the church as *ecclesia vera Dei* is not merely, or even exclusively, a New Testament phenomenon. Quite the contrary, the church has been present from the beginning, and Luther anchors its formal establishment to Gen 2:16–17 (the prohibition against eating from the tree of knowledge of good and evil).³⁹ Luther's view of Genesis as literally the book of the church is made possible by his conviction that the New Testament is actually older than the Old, and thus he can refer without hesitation to characters in Genesis as Christians.⁴⁰ A poignant example is his description of the death of Jacob:

> Finally the fact that Jacob draws up his feet into the bed indicates a special custom of that people, and Moses points out that Jacob sat on his bed when he spoke to his sons. But when he had finished speaking, he laid his head on the bed and drew up his feet into it. By doing so he now showed that he had willingly and knowingly given up his spirit in faith and hope in the Christ who was to come. He raised his feet from the ground, laid them on the bed, and said: "I depart in the name of Christ."⁴¹

This understanding on Luther's part should make clear that he is as far removed from Marcionism as it is possible to be. He elevated the significance of the Old Testament for Christian theology to a degree seldom seen before him, and yet it is this very move that placed him on an unavoidable collision course with Judaism.[42] Heinrich Bornkamm has stated this tension concisely: "No one who has even superficially looked into [Luther's] writings can doubt his passionate opposition to the Jews as blasphemers of Christ on the one hand, and his deep love for the Old Testament on the other. He had no difficulty maintaining both, as paradoxical as this may appear to some people today."[43] Over the course of his career, he wrote and spoke, by any estimation, a remarkable number of despicable things about Jews and Judaism.[44] In all of his anti-Jewish fulminations, one thread is invariably there, and that is the exegetical thread.[45] When one considers how few Jews there were in all of sixteenth-century Germany, and fewer still in Luther's Saxony, his focus seems completely out of proportion.[46] But for him, clearly, it was not. The Jew, more than anything, was an exegetical threat. The sense of this threat is palpable throughout Luther's *Genesis,* and the question that is driving him is that of who can rightfully lay claim to the title *populus Dei.*

POPULUS DEI: "THE ELDER SHALL SERVE THE YOUNGER" (GEN 25)

For Luther, the stories of Cain and Abel, Ishmael and Isaac, and Esau and Jacob all answer the same question: Who are the people of God? Though utterly offensive to human reason, Luther was convinced that God's promise to, or choice of, one character and the rejection of the other, and the subsequent strife to which this choice gives rise, was intended to teach *the* fundamental theological truth. And the gravitas of this truth is what always and everywhere gives rise to conflict:

> This is not an unimportant disagreement and struggle. And it is not without cause that our adversaries are angry with us in such a hostile manner, for we are debating about the most important matters in the entire world—not about the empire and not about wealth, prestige, or

power but about eternal damnation and eternal life. This is the reason why the hatreds are so bitter. And nowhere are they bitterer than in disagreements in the matter of religion, for it is a most important and most serious cause. Are we children of God or children of the devil?[47]

Luther regarded Gen 25:19–34 as the text that presents the question at hand in its most tensive form. God's in utero choice of Jacob over Esau is the definitive statement regarding the nature of God and the way in which God works in the world.

Paul's treatment of this very passage in Rom 9:1–13 provides Luther a way in to the text, especially:

Not everyone who is from Israel is Israel. (9:6b)

It is not the children of the flesh who are the children of God, but rather the children of the promise are counted as seed. (9:8)

For not yet having been born nor having done anything good or bad, in order that the purpose of God which is according to election might continue, not based on works but on the one who calls,[48] it was said to her, "the elder will serve the younger." As it is written, "Jacob I loved, but Esau I hated." (9:11–12)

Luther is explicit in claiming that only Paul has been able to treat the passage as it deserves and that he therefore is merely drawing out at greater length what Paul has already said.[49]

Duplex nativitas

Gen 25:21b reads: "And Rebecca, his wife, conceived." This half-verse sets off the heart of Luther's interpretation. "Consequently this passage teaches the same thing that Paul teaches in his Epistle to the Romans, where he distinguishes birth as a result of the flesh, that is, as the result of creation, from spiritual birth."[50] This twofold birth corresponds precisely to the dichotomy between flesh and spirit, the fundamental dichotomy in all of Luther's thought. The flesh is that which is natural, normal, temporal, and corrupt. The spiritual is that which is eternal. Natural birth is shared by all, whereas spiritual birth or rebirth happens only via God's promise // God's call // God's election.[51] Jacob, like Isaac before him, signifies that natural birth is not sufficient (*non satis est*) but that rebirth is required in order to claim the title of *filius // populus Dei*, and thus attain salvation. This distinction between the two births, the first and the second, "is the source of perpetual war from the beginning of the world to the end, not about trivialities but about that glorious title 'church,' the people of God, the kingdom of heaven, and eternal life."[52] The struggle of the infants *in utero* teaches that this conflict is primal and illustrates that the struggle between flesh and spirit is perpetual. Thus, Luther is able to describe two parallel but antithetical trajectories:

1st Birth → Serpent's Seed → Cain → Ishmael → Esau → Church of the Devil
2nd Birth → Woman's Seed → Abel → Isaac → Jacob → Church of God

When he states that the flesh, or natural birth, is insufficient, he means that flesh on its own is dead and profits nothing before God: "Where there is [natural] birth alone, there is condemnation."[53] His proof texts for this claim here and everywhere are John 3:6 ("That which is born of the flesh is flesh") and Isa 40:6 ("All flesh is grass, and all its glory[54] is like the flower of the field"). The essential characteristic of those who are the people of God is that they "hear not the God who creates but the God who calls."[55] Thus, and most importantly, one is not born into the status of *populus Dei*, one is promised // called // elected into that status over and above one's natural status.

It is this teaching or distinction that, from Luther's perspective, causes the Jews to "howl and almost go mad; for with respect to the first birth they are insane, and they do not ascend to the cognition of the other birth, and thus they perish."[56] That the Jews do not ascend to the cognition of the second birth can be stated even more bluntly: "The Jews ... do not have the call."[57]

How does Luther know this? Though his argument smacks of circularity (or at least begs the question), it goes essentially like this: The call and the promise of God are synonymous. The promise is the promise of the Messiah/Son of God. The promise and faith in the promise are indivisible.[58] Because the Jews do not believe the promise, they do not have it. Thus they do not have the call either. And where the call is absent, there is no true church, no people of God, no salvation.

The chief function of the story of the conception and birth of Jacob and Esau is, therefore, to prove the claim that apart from the call the first birth is utterly useless (*prorsus inutilis*) before God—even for Abraham, Isaac, and Jacob.[59] Isaac and Jacob are the sons of the promise not because they were born of Abraham and Sarah, Isaac and Rebecca, but because the Word/call was spoken to them and not to their respective brothers who were born of the same parents.[60] To my mind, this is the crucial move that Luther makes, and it is a significant one. For in order to make the point that he wants to make, he has subtly moved from the language of addition to that of displacement, as if Jacob's natural descent from Abraham and Sarah, Isaac and Rebecca, is actually irrelevant.[61]

The prime illustration of this proof and of its ongoing validity is the story of the twelve patriarchs themselves. Contra Genesis itself, where the promise of God and the identity of the people of God are channeled directly into the fleshly descendants of Jacob, Luther reads the stories of the twelve patriarchs as merely illustrative of the first birth, which is "the source and origin of all evils."[62] The sons of Jacob/Israel are murderers, committers of incest, and even patricides. Their stories are designed to show what the fallen human is by nature: "completely like Cain and inclined to murder near relatives."[63] Furthermore, "[t]he historical accounts of the kings and of the judges and finally that frightful crime when they crucified the Son of God and their Messiah bear witness to the same thing."[64] The story of the two infants conceived and struggling in the womb of Rebecca is the story of two churches, the true and the false. Jacob himself, just like Abraham and Isaac before him, gives birth to a twofold progeny. The one part, the largest part, is purely carnal, and it continues in the Jews of today, who are really not "Jacobites" at all but rather "Esauites" and "Ishmaelites." The other part represents the true descendants of Jacob, who are both born of his flesh and who also believe in the promise. These are, or will be, the Jewish Christians, "the remnants of Jacob." The true Jew, the true descendant of Jacob, is therefore a Jewish Christian—the others are not really Jews at all.[65]

Key to Luther's argument in all of this is his conviction that Israel, like all other people, is subject to the flesh/spirit dichotomy, and the influence of Rom 9:6b is unmistakable. Like Paul, Luther will not equate Israel *secundum spiritum* with Israel *secundum carnem*. But he sharpens the dichotomy in a way that Paul apparently does not. In his early lectures on Romans, he glosses Paul's "not all who are from Israel are Israel" with "not all, *but a few,* who are from Israel are Israel, *truly Israel*.[66] Only a few of fleshly Israel were ever spiritual Israel. God made a covenant with and promises to fleshly Israel, but the true content of this covenant and of these promises is spiritual, and only that small part of fleshly Israel which was also spiritual Israel perceived this and participated in it.

The Oracle

Gen 25:23 reads: "And the Lord said to her, 'Two nations are in your womb, and two peoples born of you shall be divided, and the one shall be stronger than the other, and the elder shall serve the younger.'" Luther regards the oracle spoken to Rebecca (by Shem) as the cornerstone in the entire argument. Again, with the aid of Paul in Rom 9:10ff., he proposes that the oracle bears two levels of meaning, a legal sense (*legaliter; carnaliter; secundum litteram*) and a spiritual and true sense (*spiritualis et verus*). The first level of meaning corresponds to the fleshly and temporal realm, and in it both boys receive fleshly and temporal promises. The four-part prophecy describes in advance the history of Edom and Israel, with Edom corresponding to the stronger and the elder, and Israel to the weaker and the younger. In this first level of meaning, all four aspects of the oracle have been fulfilled historically. But because the fourth element, Israel's subjugation of Edom, lasted only from David to Ahab, the overall sense of the prophecy is that Esau will rule, *secundum carnem,* although Jacob nevertheless remains heir and lord.

For Luther, the key to the full and proper interpretation of this passage resides in Paul's bringing of Mal 1:2–3 into the equation: "I loved

Jacob, but Esau I hated" (Rom 9:12). This move on Paul's part demonstrates that in his interpretation of Gen 25:19ff. he is dealing not with temporal promises but rather with "true," i.e., spiritual, promises.[67] This is the level of meaning that the Jews do not understand because they read the words of the oracle only *secundum carnem*. They overplay the promise of carnal rule in the fourth part of the oracle and dream that they are being promised worldly dominion; in so doing they miss the sense of the whole passage, which is that the temporal/carnal promise contains within it the spiritual promise, and this promise is for Jacob alone.[68] "The one shall be stronger than the other, and the elder shall serve the younger" means that "from that weak part the Son of God had to be born, in order that salvation might not be from the Gentiles and from the Edomites but might be from the Jews [John 4:22]. Everything has been written on account of Christ, who came from that line of the smaller people."[69] This then is the true meaning of the birth of these two boys: the one, the stronger, has the promise *secundum corpus;* the other, the weaker, has the promise *secundum spiritum*. And those who adhere to the spiritual promise becomes heirs to that promise as well, i.e., the people of God.

In all of this Luther is doing nothing less than defining the term "people of God" in a completely spiritual manner, precisely what he understands Paul to be saying in Rom 9:8—"It is not the children of the flesh who are the children of God, but rather the children of the promise are counted as seed." In so doing, he is simultaneously establishing the theological principle that what makes the people of God the people of God has always been the same: "those who believe God [i.e., in God's promise of the Seed] become children of Abraham and children of God,"[70] regardless of birth or natural descent. The people of God are, and always have been, those who believe/trust in the promise of God contra all appearances. We have already noted how far removed Luther is from Marcionism (viz., the Jews never were the people of God). But this theological principle demonstrates that he is not simply a traditional Christian supersessionist either (viz., the Jews were the people of God but are no longer). He can certainly use traditional supersessionist language, and he does so often, but his understanding of "people of God" as a thoroughgoing spiritual reality complicates the issue significantly. If one can even say such a thing, Luther is a suprasessionist, in the sense that for him the true Jew has always been a de facto Christian. But if this is so, then an obvious question emerges.

WHY ISRAEL *SECUNDUM CARNEM?*

Luther never denies the distinctive role of Israel *secundum carnem* in the Old Testament. Fleshly Israel, and no other people or nation, was the vessel designated to carry the promises of God. Luther never tires of pointing out to his students, readers, and hearers that Israel was utterly unique among the nations of the ancient world, and that this uniqueness consisted in the specific linkage between God's promises and the flesh of Israel, which made Israel both a corporal/fleshly and a spiritual phenomenon. Israel shared this both/and with no other people of antiquity. "But this people had this prerogative above all the other peoples and kingdoms of the world: God had revealed Himself in His word, manifested Himself by many and sundry miracles and signs, and declared Himself to be the God of this people."[71] Israel was the people to whom God drew near and in whose midst God dwelt. The Gentiles, though they too were ruled by God, were not aware of this because God dealt with them only by hidden counsel rather than via revelation.[72] All of these considerations pale, however, in light of the significance Luther attributes to the Seed. Israel *secundum carnem* was the chosen bearer of the Seed, and God's special attachment to and special dealings with Israel were for this primary reason: "Das Heil kommt von den Juden" (John 4:22).[73] This is the reason as well for God's protection and preservation of Israel in the biblical period.

In spite of these positive things that Luther is able to say elsewhere about Israel's flesh, in his treatment of Jacob and Esau in Gen 25 something utterly negative is in view having to do with how the promise to Israel's flesh jibes with *duplex nativitas.* The relationship is not without tension. What Luther wants to argue is that the election of fleshly Israel was intended precisely to teach Israel (i.e., "the exceedingly arrogant nation destined to be the descendants of Abraham"),[74] and via Israel the world, the negative lesson that the flesh profits nothing before God. In other words, that God elected Israel's flesh precisely to teach that the flesh profits nothing:

> Therefore this doctrine, which distinguishes between the true and the false church, is necessary. God presented it to the Jews first, in order to destroy the pride they had in the glory of their blood by means of these outstanding examples in both houses, namely, that of Abraham and that of Isaac. For both Ishmael and Isaac were born of the same blood of Abraham. Nevertheless, Ishmael is not the heir; for he wants to be saved through the first birth, and through it alone. But Isaac is the heir because he has the Word and the promise. Thus Esau and Jacob were descendants not only of one father but also of the same mother, and this is a stronger argument than the preceding one. For the father is the same, the mother is the same, and the blood is the same. But why is Jacob preferred to Esau? I answer that the call came to Jacob. On the basis of the first birth Esau presumes that the inheritance of the kingdom falls to him. God is displeased with that presumption and wants the renewal of his nature, apart from which no right to the kingdom or inheritance is left to be added. And on the basis of these passages we can powerfully and most effectively refute even our Jews, who still dream of that glory of the blood today. For two are begotten from the same blood, the one being the heir, the other not; and they are distinguished by the call. They are equals in regard to all glory of the flesh; but the one has the Word and hears it, the other despises it.[75]

For Luther, there is flesh in general, which is condemned. Then there is Israel's flesh, i.e., the flesh from which the Son of God would be born. This is the flesh that God protected, *propter electos*, until Shiloh came (Gen 49:10). Israel's flesh, however, is still flesh, and Israel must not glory in it. But to Luther's mind, that is precisely what Israel does, definitively and finally, by not acknowledging the Son of God. The failure of this acknowledgement is simultaneously the failure to reckon with the spiritual nature of true Israel. The result is an Israel that can do nothing but entrust itself to the flesh, i.e., to natural descent. And an Israel that glories in its flesh is, finally, a Cain, an Ishmael, an Esau, a Turk, a pope. But fleshly Israel is not simply identical with these other classes of people. For Luther, from the beginning of his career until the end, the Jew is prototypical and represents the absolute antithesis of what he considered fundamental to being a Christian.[76]

The post–70 C.E. continuing existence of Israel *secundum carnem* was a lifelong problem for Luther. He saw "a deep rupture"[77] in the history of fleshly Israel, marked by the crucifixion of Jesus and the Roman destruction of Jerusalem, and as a result he saw no continuity between biblical and postbiblical Israel. Though he could attempt to account for it in different ways, his most consistent answer was that the Jews continue to exist as an example of what it means to live under the wrath of God—a grace-less existence. For the Jew as Jew there was, and could be, no hope. And certainly no claim to the title of people of God. Yet in the midst of such attitudes, together with all their many tendrils, Luther's explications of the travails of the lives of the saints (*tentationes sancti*) of Genesis and of God's hidden and inscrutable manner of working in the world are often stunningly masterful and deeply moving, as when in reflecting on Rebecca's deep distress over the commotion in her womb in Gen 25:22 he can say things like: For the people of God, "nothing in the world appears to be more deceitful than the word of God and faith, nothing more empty than the hope of the promise. Finally, nothing seems to be more nothing than God himself."[78] But the applicability of such a theological insight to Israel *secundum carnem* is something that does not come to his mind.

NOTES

1. Jon D. Levenson, *The Death and Resurrection of the Beloved Son: The Transformation of Child Sacrifice in Judaism and Christianity* (New Haven: Yale University Press, 1993) 66–67.

2. To Jon Levenson, in acknowledgement of an educational debt that cannot be repaid. And *todah rabbah* as well to the coeditor of this volume, Joel Kaminsky, without whose patience, help, and encouragement I never would have passed my first Levenson course ("Numbers and its Jewish Exegesis," Winter Quarter 1985).

3. Luther's description of the New Testament letter of James as an "epistle of straw" is well known. Less well known is his visceral hatred for the book of Esther, which for him encapsulates everything that is wrong with Judaism, e.g.:

"Their heart's most ardent sighing and yearning and hoping is set on the day on which they can deal with us Gentiles as they did with the Gentiles in Persia at the time of Esther. Oh, how fond they are of the book of Esther, which is so beautifully attuned to their bloodthirsty, vengeful, murderous yearning and hope. The sun has never shone on a more bloodthirsty and vengeful people than they are who imagine that they are God's people who have been commissioned and commanded to murder and to slay the Gentiles. In fact, the most important thing that they expect of their Messiah is that he will murder and kill the entire world with their sword. They treated us Christians in this manner at the very beginning throughout all the world. They would still like to do this if they had the power, and often enough have made the attempt, for which they have got their snouts boxed lustily." *Luther's Works* (American Edition; Saint Louis: Concordia Publishing House; Philadelphia: Fortress Press, 1961– [hereinafter cited as LW]), 47:156–57. See also, e.g., LW 2:264, and Hans Bardtke, *Luther und das Buch Esther* (Tübingen: Mohr [Siebeck], 1964).

4. Luther's most sustained treatment of this subject matter is *De servo arbitrio*, in *D. Martin Luthers Werke. Kritische Gesamtausgabe* (Weimar: Hermann Böhlau, 1883– [hereinafter cited as WA]), 18:600–787; LW 33:15–295, which was a response to Erasmus's *De libero arbitrio diatribe sive collatio*. For a more concise treatment, see Luther's lectures on Gen 26, WA 43:457–463; LW 5:42–50.

5. "Est enim curiositas ista ipsum peccatum originis" (WA 43:459; LW 5:44).

6. Translations from the Bible and from WA are those of the writer.

7. WA 3, 4, 55/1, 55/2; LW 10, 11. The lectures, as in the case of all of his academic lectures, were delivered in Latin.

8. Tightly summarized by Peter von der Osten-Sacken, *Martin Luther und die Juden: neu untersucht anhand von Anton Margarithas "Der gantz Jüdisch glaub" (1530/31)* (Stuttgart: Kohlhammer, 2002), 47–74. Though it is still common to hear (especially in American Lutheran circles) the opinion that Luther's anti-Jewish stance was primarily confined to the later stages of his career, twentieth-century Luther scholarship has demonstrated that his theological evaluation of Judaism was essentially consistent from beginning to end. The harshness of what he thought should be done to/with/about the Jews certainly escalated over time, but he never wavered in what he thought about Judaism as such. See Reinhold Lewin, *Luthers Stellung zu den Juden: ein Beitrag zur Geschichte der Juden in Deutschland während des Reformationszeitalters* (Neue Studien zur Geschichte der Theologie und der Kirche 10; Berlin: Trowitzsch & Sohn, 1911; repr., Aalen: Scientia Verlag, 1973); Wilhelm Maurer, *Kirche und Synagoge: Motive und Formen der Auseinandersetzung der Kirche mit dem Judentum im Laufe der Geschichte* (Stuttgart: Kohlhammer, 1953); idem, "Die Zeit der Reformation," in *Kirche und Synagoge: Handbuch zur Geschichte von Christen und Juden: Darstellung mit Quellen* (2 vols.;

ed. Karl Heinrich Rengstorf and Siegfried von Kortzfleisch; Stuttgart: Klett, 1968, 1970), 1:375–429; Johannes Brosseder, *Luthers Stellung zu den Juden im Spiegel seiner Interpreten: Interpretation und Rezeption von Luthers Schriften und Äusserungen zum Judentum im 19. und 20. Jahrhundert vor allem im deutschsprachigen Raum* (Beiträge zur ökumenischen Theologie 8; Munich: Max Hueber Verlag, 1972); C. Bernd Sucher, *Luthers Stellung zu den Juden: Eine Interpretation aus germanistischer Sicht* (Nieuwkoop: B. de Graaf, 1977); Walther Bienert, *Martin Luther und die Juden: Ein Quellenbuch mit zeitgenössischen Illustrationen, mit Einführungen und Erläuterungen* (Frankfurt am Main: Evangelisches Verlagswerk, 1982); Mark U. Edwards, Jr., *Luther's Last Battles: Politics and Polemics, 1531–46* (Leiden: E. J. Brill, 1983); Olaf Roynesdal, *Martin Luther and the Jews* (PhD diss., Marquette University, 1986); Heinz Kremers et al., eds., *Die Juden und Martin Luther—Martin Luther und die Juden: Geschichte, Wirkungsgeschichte, Herausforderung* (2nd ed.; Neukirchen-Vluyn: Neukirchener Verlag, 1987); Thomas Kaufmann, "Luther and the Jews," in *Jews, Judaism, and the Reformation in Sixteenth-Century Germany* (ed. Dean Phillip Bell and Stephen G. Burnett; Leiden: Brill, 2006) 69–104.

9. WA 42–44; LW 1–8. For a fine recent treatment of this great work, see John A. Maxfield, *Luther's Lectures on Genesis and the Formation of Evangelical Identity* (Kirksville, Mo.: Truman State University Press, 2008).

10. See Peter Meinhold, *Die Genesisvorlesung Luthers und ihre Herausgeber* (Forschungen zur Kirchen- und Geistesgeschichte 8; Stuttgart: W. Kohlhammer, 1936) 123–41; also the remarks of the general editor of Luther's exegetical writings in the American Edition, Jaroslav Pelikan, in LW 4:vii–viii.

11. [1] *Against the Sabbatarians* (1538), WA 50:312–37; LW 47:57–98. [2] *On the Jews and Their Lies* (1543), WA 53:417–552; LW 47:121–306. [3] *On the Ineffable Name and On the Lineage of Christ* (1543), WA 53:579–648; English trans. in Gerhard Falk, *The Jew in Christian Theology* (Jefferson, N.C.: McFarland and Company, 1992), 163–224. [4] *The Last Words of David* (1543), WA 54:28–100; LW 15:265–352. Also germane are the lectures on Isa 9 and 53: *Enarratio capitis noni Esaiae* (1543/44), WA 40/3:595–682; *Enarratio 53. capitis Esaiae* (1544), WA 40/3:683–746. These late Isaiah lectures will be translated in the new LW edition from Concordia Publishing House, *Luther's Works: American Edition, New Series* (ed. Christopher B. Brown).

12. One important difference that should be noted is that we do not find in the Genesis lectures any reference to the medieval *Gräuelmärchen* about the Jews that are commonplace in the 1543 treatises. See Osten-Sacken, *Martin Luther und die Juden*, 153.

13. The lectures were originally published as four volumes: 1544 (Gen 1–11), 1550 (Gen 12–24), 1552 (Gen 25–36), 1554 (Gen 37–50).

14. "A remarkable circumstance is the accuracy with which most classical citations are quoted. Luther had an astonishing memory, as his Biblical quota-

tions show. He had also read around in the classics and knew some classical works almost by heart. But the citations here in Genesis are almost uniformly accurate; and where a comparison of lecture notes with printed version is possible, it becomes evident that the editors took a chance phrase or allusion from Luther's lectures and amplified it into a full-blown and accurate citation" (J. Pelikan, LW 1:x).

15. Erich Seeberg, *Studien zu Luthers Genesisvorlesung: Zugleich ein Beitrag zur Frage nach dem alten Luther* (Gütersloh: "Der Rufer" Evangelischer Verlag, 1932); Meinhold, *Die Genesisvorlesung Luthers und ihre Herausgeber*.

16. Pelikan, LW 1:xii. See also Ulrich Asendorf, *Lectura in Biblia: Luthers Genesisvorlesung (1535–1545)* (Göttingen: Vandenhoeck & Ruprecht, 1998), esp. 370–428; Maxfield, *Luther's Lectures on Genesis*, 1–9.

17. Osten-Sacken, *Martin Luther und die Juden*, 145–47.

18. A general rule of thumb when dealing with Luther's Genesis lectures is to beware of statements that cannot be corroborated from elsewhere in Luther's corpus.

19. It takes three tall, thick volumes in the Weimar edition to contain the Genesis lectures: WA 42–44 (LW 1–8).

20. "Dis ist das erst Evangelium und Verheissung von Christo geschehen auff Erden, Das er solt, Sünd, Tod und Helle uberwinden und uns von der Schlangen gewalt selig machen. Dar an Adam gleubet mit allen seinen Nachkomen, Davon er Christen und selig worden ist von seinem Fall" (LW DB 8:45).

21. "Thus this promise and this threat are very clear, and yet they are also very indefinite" (LW 1:193).

22. After several earlier attempts, in 1545 Luther finally settled on this translation of Eve's words in Gen 4:1: "Jch habe den Man des HERRN." The marginal gloss makes clear what he intends by this translation: "Ey Gott sey gelobt, Da hab ich den HERRN den Man, den Samen, der dem Satan oder Schlangen den Kopff zutretten sol, Der wirds thun" (WA DB 8:47).

23. "Promissio haec clarissima simul etiam obscurissima est" (WA 42:146,6–7; cf LW 1:195).

24. Luther had inherited the tradition from the Vulgate that Mary was the Crusher—"ipsa conteret caput tuum"—but he rejects it, changing *ipsa* to *ipsum*.

25. LW 35:236.

26. Although Luther never abandoned allegory and continued to use it throughout his career, he did sharply constrain the parameters of how it could be used, viz., only as a demonstrable explication of what he regarded as the *unus, literalis, legitimus, proprius, germanus, purus, simplex, constans sensus*. See Siegfried Raeder, "The Exegetical and Hermeneutical Work of Martin Luther," in *From the Renaissance to the Enlightenment* (vol. 2 of *Hebrew Bible / Old Testament: The History of its Interpretation* (ed. Magne Sæbø; Göttingen: Vandenhoeck & Ruprecht,

2008) 363–406 (esp. 375!). The still unsurpassed work on Luther and allegory remains Gerhard Ebeling, *Evangelische Evangelienauslegung: eine Untersuchung zu Luthers Hermeneutik* (Darmstadt: Wissenschaftliche Buchgesellschaft, 1962 [1942]), esp. 48–90.

27. E.g., when Luther lectures on Gen 25:19ff., the mention of Isaac's marital age as forty sets off a sizeable excursus on Isaac's "chastity," viz., Isaac waited to marry until the lust of young manhood had passed. Luther was forty-one when he married.

28. Luther would never dare to equate himself with these characters; he did, however, identify with them. His closest identification was likely with Noah, or at least the time of Noah. See John M. Headley, *Luther's View of Church History* (New Haven: Yale University Press, 1963), 263–64.

29. See Heinrich Bornkamm, *Luther and the Old Testament* (ed.Victor I. Gruhn; trans. Eric W. and Ruth C. Gritsch; Mifflintown, Pa.: Sigler Press, 1997 [1969]), 18.

30. LW 2:216–17. In 1541 Luther wrote his *Supputatio annorum mundi* [Computation of the Years of the World] (WA 53:22–184), which included careful analysis of the ages of the patriarchs in Genesis with an eye toward establishing which patriarchs were comtemporaries.

31. WA DB 8:12,31–33. Cf. LW 35:237.

32. This term, literally "swarmers," and the Latin *fanatici*, are the terms Luther used to refer to left-wing reformers.

33. See Hans-Ulrich Delius, *Die Quellen von Martin Luthers Genesisvorlesung* (Munich: Chr. Kaiser Verlag, 1992); Maxfield, *Luther's Lectures on Genesis*, 48–59.

34. Margaritha, son of a learned Jewish family, was a convert to Christianity and a contemporary of Luther. His work, which included a translation into German of many of the daily morning prayers (apparently the first ever), was published in 1530. It was the primary source informing Luther's *On the Jews and their Lies* (Jan. 1543). See Maria Diemling, "Anthonius Margaritha on the 'Whole Jewish Faith': A Sixteenth-Century Convert from Judaism and His Depiction of the Jewish Religion," in *Jews, Judaism, and the Reformation in Sixteenth-Century Germany* (ed. Dean Phillip Bell and Stephen G. Burnett; Leiden: Brill, 2006), 303–33; Osten-Sacken, *Martin Luther und die Juden*, 162–208. Porchetus, a Carthusian monk, wrote his treatise in the early fourteenth century (printed 1520), and it formed the basis of Luther's most scatological anti-Jewish writing, *On the Ineffable Name and On the Lineage of Christ* (Mar. 1543).

35. Luther's preferred way to describe rabbinic tone deafness to theology was to say that they do not comprehend the "subject matter" (*res; die Sache*) of the text. The subject matter is the sense of the whole (i.e., the Christian Bible), and the whole must constrain the meaning of the parts. See, e.g., LW 3:72–73.

36. LW 4:351–52. A more explicit example from *On the Ineffable Name:* "It is prohibited for us Christians to believe or view as right the interpretation and commentaries of the rabbis concerning the scriptures on pain of losing the grace of God and eternal life. We may read it in order to see what kind of devil's work they promote among themselves and protect ourselves from it. For thus says Moses [Deut 28]: 'God will strike you with madness, blindness, and a delirious heart.' This Moses did not say of the damned Goyim, but about his circumcised saints, the noble blood, nobility of heaven and earth, who call themselves Israel. Hereby however, God damns their understanding, explanations, and interpretations through their own action as utter madness, blindness, delirium, all that which they belabored in scripture these fifteen hundred years God not only calls and judges false and lies but also deliberate blindness, delirious, mad thing" (Falk, *The Jew in Christian Theology*, 221).

37. See LW 4:34–35.

38. LW *Companion Volume: Introduction to the Exegetical Writings*, 89.

39. LW 1:103–15.

40. See e.g., *Lectures on Deuteronomy*, LW 9:63.

41. LW 8:319.

42. Luther's most beloved claim about the Old Testament is a double-edged sword: "Here [i.e., in the Old Testament] you will find the swaddling cloths and the manger in which Christ lies, and to which the angel points the shepherds. Simple and lowly are these swaddling cloths, but dear is the treasure, Christ, who lies in them" (LW 35:236).

43. Bornkamm, *Luther and the Old Testament*, 1.

44. Osten-Sacken, *Martin Luther und die Juden*, 15, states bluntly: "Die antijüdischen Schriften Luthers gehören entsprechend in die vorderste Reihe judenfeindlicher Abhandlungen, Reden und Predigten in der gesamten Kirchengeschichte."

45. It is often overlooked, or at least devalued, that the largest section of Luther's most infamous treatise, *On the Jews and their Lies*, is devoted to exegesis of specific Old Testament texts.

46. "It is characteristic of Luther's relationship to the Jews, to the extent that it found literary expression and had a public impact, that as a rule he spoke *about* the Jews, not however *with* or *to* them ... For Luther the Jews were never at any point in his lifetime 'conversation-partners' in the sense that they had something to say that might have influenced either Christian theologians in their conversations with Jews or their theological judgments about them. There is no evidence Luther ever took the initiative to make contact with learned Jews to learn from them as some of his contemporaries did" (Kaufmann, "Luther and the Jews," 73).

47. LW 4:349–50.

48. Luther's German Bible reads, "aus gnade des Beruffers."

49. It is well known that Romans was Luther's primary hermeneutical lens. He was forthright in this regard, even going so far as to say that Romans functions as an "introduction to the entire Old Testament," i.e., Romans teaches Christians how to read the Old Testament (LW 35:380). He followed his own advice with great consistency.

50. LW 4:343. "Idem igitur hic locus docet, quod Paulus in Epistola ad Romanos, ubi distinguit nativitatem ex carne, id est, ex creatione, a nativitate spirituali" (WA 43:384,23–24).

51. Luther uses this language interchangeably in his treatment of Gen 25.

52. LW 4:345. Though Luther did not know Philo, *De Sacrificiis Abelis et Caini* 1–4 is a virtual blueprint for his treatment of this topic.

53. LW 4:345. "Ubi sola nativitas est, ibi est perditio" (WA 43:385,4–5).

54. Reading with LXX and Vul. This passage is the source of Luther's constant polemic against "the glory of the flesh" (*gloria carnis*).

55. LW 4:345.

56. WA 43:385,37–39; cf. LW 4:346.

57. LW 4:347.

58. On this difficult issue, see Luther's discussion of Jacob's death-bed blessings in Gen 49: "Promissio nulla est, si non adsit fides, et econtra nulla est fides sine promissione" (WA 44:728,8–9). See also LW 23:23.

59. "prima nativitas coram Deo nihil est" (WA 43:388,34–35).

60. LW 4:348.

61. What is likely influencing Luther's thought at this point is John 1:12–13, a passage that goes beyond Paul: "But whoever received him, to them he gave authority to become children of God, to those who believe in his name, who are not born of blood, or of the will of the flesh, or of the will of a man, but who are born of God."

62. LW 4:350.

63. "sua natura totum esse Cainicum et parricidialem" (WA 43:388, 29–30). Cf. LW 4:350.

64. LW 4:351.

65. On the logic of this argument regarding Jacob's descendants, see the treatment of Gen 49 in LW 8:199–319. On the true Jew as being a Jewish Christian, see the treatment of Isaac and Ishmael in Gen 21 in LW 4:3–73, esp. 25–35, where he develops the more complex notion of a "triplex semen Abrahae."

66. *Lectures on Romans* (1515–1516), LW 25:80.

67. "Ibi attingit promissiones non temporales, sed veras" (WA 43:400,4; cf LW 4:366).

68. LW 4:366–367. "Sed in istis carnalibus continentur etiam spirituales promissiones" (WA 43:400,6–7).

69. LW 4:367.
70. LW 4:368.
71. LW 2:255.
72. Luther's terms here are *occulto consilio* and *occulto modo*. For further discussion concerning *Iudaici populi res gestae*, see LW 9:33 and LW 2:254–58.
73. This is Luther's translation, and the passage was the inspiration for his early treatise, *That Jesus Christ Was Born a Jew* (LW 45:197–229; WA 11:314–36).
74. LW 4:343.
75. LW 4:349.
76. See Kaufmann, "Luther and the Jews," 72.
77. Bornkamm, *Luther und das Alte Testament*, 1.
78. "Ideoque in mundo apparet nihil esse fallacius verbo Dei et fidei, nihil vanius spe promissionis. Denique nihil magis nihil esse videtur, quam Deus ipse" (WA 43:392,16–18). Cf. LW 4:355.

PART III

Theological Essays

CHAPTER 14

Election and Affection
On God's Sovereignty and Human Action

LEORA BATNITZKY

In his reading of the Apostle Paul, John Calvin accuses Jews and Judaism of putting both too much and too little stock in their status as God's elect:

> In the Epistle to the Romans, where he [Paul] . . . says, "They are not all Israel which are" born "of Israel": because though all were blessed by hereditary right, yet the succession did not pass to all alike. This controversy originated in the pride and vain-glorying of the Jewish people, who claiming for themselves the title of the Church, would make the faith of the gospel to depend on their decision. Just as in the present day, the Papists with this false pretext would substitute themselves in the place of God. Paul, though he admits the posterity of Abraham to be holy in consequence of the covenant, yet contends that

most of them are strangers to it; and that not only because they degenerate, from legitimate children becoming spurious ones; but because the pre-eminence and sovereignty belong to God's special election, which is the sole foundation of the validity of their adoption.[1]

Calvin suggests that the people of Israel's understanding of her election by God is at once too maximalist and too minimalist—too maximalist because Israel is not elect simply by inheritance and too minimalist because works, and the law more generally, does not and cannot affect God's call to his elect: "The very terms election and purpose, certainly exclude from this subject all the causes frequently invented by men, independently of God's secret counsel."[2]

The purpose of this paper is not to make any comprehensive statement about Calvin's view of Jews, Judaism, or even election. Rather, in what follows, I use Calvin's comments about what he contends is a false Jewish view of election as a jumping-off point for considering what might be a Jewish view of the implications of election for affecting God. I would like to suggest that Calvin is right, if not in his evaluation, then certainly in his characterization that important strands of Jewish theology are described by a tension between election and affection. Indeed, a Jewish theological commitment to the election of Israel may heighten the notion that it is possible to affect God, while relinquishing the commitment to election may diminish it. From a philosophical or systematic theological point of view, this position might seem inherently problematic. After all, in an important sense, Calvin is correct that there is a tension between the idea of election and the possibility of affecting God. To take the biblical idea of the election of Israel seriously means to recognize God's sovereignty. God chooses whomever God has decided to choose. If God's choice is absolute, human behavior cannot affect God because then the will of God would stand in some relation to human will. Consequently some may argue that what matters above all else in considering the meaning of divine election is the recognition of God's absolute will, in relation to which there is no human analogy.

But as Calvin himself recognized, any biblical theology must be exactly that: biblical. The God of the Bible (of the Old and New Testaments) is not restricted by the demands of systematic philosophy or theology. Jewish theological reflection may have the advantage here, despite its historical paucity as compared to the Christian tradition. As Jon Levenson has remarked, "because Judaism lacks an overwhelming motivation to deny the pluriform character of the Hebrew Bible in behalf of a uniform reading—such as the christological reading—Jewish exegesis evidences a certain breadth and a certain relaxed posture."[3] Indeed, I will argue in what follows that it is by reason of this posture that Levenson's work offers unique insight into a biblically informed, Jewish conception of election.

A number of twentieth-century Jewish theologians including Martin Buber, Franz Rosenzweig, Abraham Joshua Heschel, and Michael Wyschogrod have returned to the Hebrew Bible in order to articulate what they believe to be more authentic Jewish theologies, that is, theologies unconstrained by the need for systematic dictates external to the biblical text; some of these thinkers, especially Rosenzweig and Wyschogrod, have emphasized the centrality of election to Jewish theology. Among twentieth-century Jewish thinkers committed to these issues, however, Levenson is perhaps unique because of his background as an actual scholar of the Hebrew Bible. Wyschogrod and Rosenzweig have come closest to articulating notions of election and affection similar to Levenson's, but despite their intentions to the contrary, they have remained fixed in the frameworks they have otherwise tried to transcend. Levenson's more biblically informed work may offer a corrective both to Wyschogrod's conception of the election of Israel and to Rosenzweig's notion of God's affectivity. The first and second parts of my paper will address Wyschogrod and Rosenzweig, respectively. After then outlining the contours of Levenson's conceptions of election and affection, I will conclude by considering their ultimate theological implications.

— Let us begin with the issue of Israel's election. Perhaps more than any other twentieth-century Jewish theologian, Michael Wyschogrod has gone against the grain of the dominant trends of modern Jewish thought that emphasize Judaism's rationality and its fundamental confluence with ethical universalism. Wyschogrod maintains that God,

Judaism, and the Jewish people are "not grounded in some alleged eternal verities of reason or on some noble and profound religious sensibility that is shared by men or by a spiritual elite, but on a movement of God toward man as witnessed in scripture."[4] As the title of his now classic *The Body of Faith* suggests, Wyschogrod contends that the Jewish people are literally the body of faith.[5] God, for Wyschogrod, literally dwells within the Jewish people: "It is of course necessary to mumble a formula of philosophic correction. No space can contain God, he is above space, etc., etc. But this mumbled formula, while required, must not be overdone. It must not transform the God of Israel into a spatial and meta-temporal Absolute . . . With all the philosophic difficulties duly noted, the God of Israel is a God who enters space and time . . . God dwells not only in the spirit of Israel . . . he also dwells in their bodies."[6]

The Jewish God, according to Wyschogrod, is a personal God who loves his chosen people passionately and, indeed, erotically. Wyschogrod is at great pains to distinguish between Christian agape and Jewish eros. Agape, argues Wyschogrod, is not ultimately love because "[u]ndifferentiated love, love that is dispensed equally to all, must be love that does not meet the individual in his individuality but sees him as a member of a species, whether that species be the working class, the poor, those created in the image of God, or what not."[7] Wyschogrod acknowledges that a God who loves some people more than others is a difficult concept for modern people to swallow. Yet he asserts that far from limiting God's love or making God's love a scarce resource, God's special love for the people of Israel actually makes it possible for God truly to love all of humanity:

> When we grasp that the election of Israel flows from the fatherhood that extends to all created in God's image, we find ourselves tied to all men in brotherhood, as Joseph, favored by his human father, ultimately found himself tied to his brothers. And when man contemplates this mystery, that the Eternal One, the creator of heaven and earth, chose to become the father of his creatures instead of remaining self-sufficient unto himself, as is the Absolute of the philosophers, there wells up in man that praise that has become so rare yet remains so natural.[8]

Yet despite Wyschogrod's sharp contrast between eros and agape, and thus between Judaism and Christianity respectively, the connection between "the body of faith" and a Christian conception of incarnation is obvious. Wyschogrod acknowledges as much: "[T]he Christian proclamation that God became flesh in the person of Jesus of Nazareth is but a development of the basic thrust of the Hebrew Bible, God's movement toward humankind . . . At least in this respect, the difference between Judaism and Christianity is one of degree rather than kind."[9] Elsewhere, Wyschogrod goes further by maintaining that there is no reason that Jews ought by definition to reject the incarnation of Christ. The reason Jews do not accept Christ is simply because they do "not hear this story, because the Word of God as it [the Jewish people] hears it does not tell it and because Jewish faith does not testify to it."[10]

Wyschogrod explicitly notes that his Jewish theological musings are prompted by his study of the most important Reformed theologian of the twentieth century, Karl Barth. According to Wyschogrod, Barth recognizes that the fundamental basis of Christian life is "obedient listening to the Word of God."[11] *The Body of Faith* is testament to what Wyschogrod has learned from Barth: the basis of Wyschogrod's claims, as he states, is the Bible. Wyschogrod's rejection of the Jewish philosophical tradition is based on his obedient "listening to the Word of God." As a number of critics have rightly noted, "obedient listening to the Word of God" is not a Jewish (or a Catholic) concept. Rather, as Barth emphasizes, "obedient listening to the Word of God" is nothing other than Luther's notion of sola scriptura. The irony of an Orthodox Jewish theologian making use of this hermeneutic should be clear.

My interest, however, is not directly in this hermeneutical issue but in the implications of this issue for what I suggest is the inherent tension in Wyschogrod's Jewish conception of election. For Wyschogrod, the body of faith is not only the combination of divine and human nature, it is also the source of salvation. Here is how Wyschogrod puts it: "Separated from the Jewish people, nothing is Judaism. If anything, it is the Jewish people that is Judaism."[12] Let us note a major difference between Wyschogrod and Barth (and Calvin). For Barth and Calvin, Christ remains separate from the believer. This is the basis of faith: to have faith in Jesus is to believe in something other than oneself. For

Wyschogrod, in contrast, the body of faith believes in itself. Jewish faith is the Jewish people's belief in the very being of the Jewish people. Indeed, Wyschogrod's premise does not admit any other conclusion. This is where Wyschogrod's Protestant hermeneutic, i.e. his implicit affirmation of sola scriptura, converges with his definition of the body of faith. The Bible, on Wyschogrod's reading, allows only one meaning: a personal God with human qualities and human emotions falls in love with Abraham who (literally) fathers the body of faith. On Wyschogrod's reading, there is no room for any other interpretation, rabbinic, mystical, philosophical, or otherwise. Ironically, by making the Jewish people Judaism, Wyschogrod's theology, whose sole purpose is to not shy away from God's scandalous love for the people of Israel, ends up removing God from the conversation.

Why does Wyschogrod's conception of election lead to this self-refuting conclusion? To begin to answer this question, let us return to Levenson's comment, quoted above, that "Judaism lacks the motivation to deny the pluriform character of the Hebrew Bible in behalf of a uniform reading." Wyschogrod's conception of the biblical account of election is strikingly univocal. Indeed, this univocality is definitional for Wyschogrod, whose point is exactly that the Jews, and the Jews alone, are God's elect. But we have seen that this univocality, which Wyschogrod appears to have inherited from Barth, gets in the way of his ability to articulate what is the very theological basis of God's election, which is divine choice. It is here that what has often appeared to be a weakness of Jewishness theology is actually an asset: the pluriform character of the Hebrew Bible, which may well interfere with the kind of uniform reading demanded by christological doctrine, produces a more relaxed posture toward election that is theologically more subtle than Wyschogrod's univocal one, which, as we have seen, ends up denying the centrality of God's ongoing choice in Israel's election.

Levenson's work on election offers a helpful corrective to Wyschogrod's theology. But before turning to the differences between Levenson and Wyschogrod, let us note their affinities. Israel's election is no less fundamental to Levenson's account of the theology of the Hebrew Bible than it is to Wyschogrod's. Especially in his study *The Death and Resurrection of the Beloved Son*,[13] Levenson shows convincingly that Judaism is constituted by a particularistic myth about what it means to be

Election and Affection 315

God's beloved son. But Levenson goes further than Wyschogrod in suggesting not only that Jews do not read scripture as testifying to Christ's truth but also that Judaism by definition rejects this Christian claim and that Christianity, also by definition, rejects the Jews' claim to be God's elect. Against the long-standing caricature that contrasts Judaism's particularism with Christianity's universalism, Levenson contends that Christianity is predicated on Judaism's own myth of being the beloved, younger son who is chosen by God. However, what is required to sustain this myth is precisely the rejection of Christianity's older brother, Judaism. The birth of the Church thus requires the displacement of Israel as God's chosen. Contrary to the universalist reading of Paul, Levenson argues that Paul's

> point is anything but the oneness of the human family or the irrelevance of belonging to Abraham rather than to the nations. He does not argue that Hagar and Sarah, Ishmael and Isaac, are ultimately one, nor that the distinction between Jew and Gentile has, through the Christ, yielded to an affirmation of their common humanity. All to the contrary, it is a point of capital import that it is Abraham, the father of the Jewish people, rather than Adam, the father of the human race, whose blessing Paul seeks to appropriate exegetically for the Church (Gal 3:29).[14]

According to Levenson, the particularistic myth shared by Judaism and Christianity is capable of producing an ethic of love and reconciliation, as the story of Jacob and Esau, for example, demonstrates, but that Judaism and Christianity, precisely because they share this particularistic myth, remain antithetical to one another: "The break," he explains, "is total: contrary to what the biblical archetype might have suggested, the Jews and the Church are not even related, and the discord between them is, by both accounts, something very different from a squabble within the family."[15] By analyzing their respective biblical theologies and the subsequent religious traditions that grow from them, Levenson shows that the self-identities of Judaism and Christianity are intimately bound up with a theological rejection of each other. This rejection does not annul what Levenson calls the "universalistic dimension" of the Jewish and the Christian traditions, but it does mean that if Jews and Christians seek to maintain their respective identities, and hence their universalistic dimensions, then reconciliation between Judaism and Christianity is not, and cannot be, possible: "In light of the universalistic dimension of that legacy (e.g. Gen 9:1–17), it is not surprising that both Judaism and Christianity have proven able to affirm the spiritual dignity of those who stand outside their own communities. But the two traditions lose definition and fade when that universalistic affirmation overwhelms the ancient, protean, and strangely resilient story of the death and resurrection of the beloved son."[16]

At first glance, Levenson's account of Israel's election might appear more rigid than Wyschogrod's. After all, Levenson's theology depicts a situation where, from either a Jewish or a Christian point of view, the other tradition simply has to be wrong. For Wyschogrod, on the other hand, it seems as if it is not a zero sum game; again, he acknowledges that the body of faith and the incarnation are different but on the same spectrum; neither by definition upsets the fundamental anthropology or ontology of the other. If this is the case, then on what basis could Levenson's account of election offer an important corrective to Wyschogrod's?

The question to be asked of Wyschogrod and Levenson is not whose theology makes more room for Christianity or whose theology offers a more rationally coherent account of election. Rather, both are committed to the claim that the test of their respective theologies must be biblical. In other words, which account of election makes more sense on the basis of the biblical text? In attempting to answer this question, we come to a particular irony that is at the heart of not only Wyschogrod's thought, but also that of a number of other twentieth-century Jewish thinkers who sought to leave behind them the rationalist trend of Jewish thought in order to return to the Bible. Modern Jewish thinkers have often remained in the thrall of philosophy even as they attempted to overthrow the philosophical mindset by recognizing that the Bible is not a book written primarily for (or by) philosophers.

While Wyschogrod attempts to return Jewish theology to a biblically informed account of Jewish election, his focus on election actually gets in the way of appreciating the interconnection between election and other biblical themes. Although he acknowledges and in fact emphasizes the importance of law to rabbinic Judaism, he does not connect obedience to the Torah with election. Indeed, Wyschogrod is at pains to state that Israel's election is not conditional on Israel's obedience to God's laws. A nonobservant Jew remains a Jew. Wyschogrod is right that from a biblical point of view, God's covenant with Abraham and by extension with the Jewish people is everlasting, but his account of election ultimately makes Israel's observance of the Torah superfluous. This means that, despite his emphasis on God's erotic love for Israel, and therefore on the erotic quality of God's being in relation to humanity, Wyschogrod's account of election is unable to admit that from a biblical point of view Israel's response to God affects God and therefore, by definition, affects God's continuing love of Israel.[17] In this way, the God described by *The Body of Faith* ends up being but the flip side of the God of the philosophers. While the latter is abstract and unmoved, the former is personal and erotic. But both Gods are alike because for neither one is a relation between human beings and God possible. Instead, the God of *The Body of Faith* is static much like the God of the philosophers is. The difference lies in that one has made a choice (Wyschogrod's God *has* chosen Israel) and the other does not choose. But this difference is less significant than it may appear to be. Once the God of Israel has chosen, according to Wyschogrod's reading of the Bible, nothing changes, save for the reaction of the nations of the world to God's choice.

In contrast to Wyschogrod, Levenson (as the subtitle of his *Creation and the Persistence of Evil* suggests) emphasizes the Jewish *drama* of divine omnipotence. Levenson stresses the dramatic relationship between God and the people of Israel. God and the people of Israel respond to each other, which means that they affect one another. The drama between them challenges not just the partners of the covenant (God and the people of Israel) along with the nations of the world, but also the very facts of creation. As Levenson puts it:

> God's rule will become complete only when the human heart, upon which it partly depends, will be enabled to embrace his commands with wholeness and integrity ... it is in the idea of a multileveled unification in God, in creation, in the human self—that we find the deep root of the profound theology of the *mitsvah* as a theurgic act which flowers a

millennium later in Spanish Qabbalah. It is the *mitsvah* that effects integrity throughout all tiers of reality and enables the life-enhancing divine energy to flow freely and without inhibition.[18]

Let us return to Calvin's commentary on Paul's view of the election of Israel, mentioned at the beginning of this paper. According to Calvin:

> [The] controversy [over election] originated in the pride and vain-glorying of the Jewish people, who . . . make the faith of the gospel to depend on their decision . . . [Yet they] are strangers to it; and that not only because they degenerate, from legitimate children becoming spurious ones; but because the pre-eminence and sovereignty belong to God's special election, which is the sole foundation of the validity of their adoption.

In an important sense, Calvin's description of a Jewish view of election accords with Levenson's. According to both, the Jewish decision to act, i.e. to follow God's laws, is essential to God's special election. Calvin characterizes this Jewish view as pride and vain-glorying because it implies that human goodness is not wholly dependent upon God's grace. Levenson, in contrast, describes this position as an affirmation of human freedom and responsibility, not because Judaism is an optimistic tradition (as some Jewish and Christian caricatures of Judaism would have it), but because it is a redemptive tradition. In Levenson's words:

> If Augustinian theologians would say that the rabbis underestimate the power of innate evil, the rabbis would rejoin that Augustine and other Christian thinkers in the same mold as he have underestimated the realism and doability of the Torah, which was given to creatures of flesh and blood and, through the idea of repentance, takes account of the fragility and transiency of their good intentions . . . Life is a continual war against the Evil Impulse, a war that does not see a definitive victory in present reality, but in which battles can be won. The major weapon in that war is the Torah itself . . . Victories in those battles [are] . . . the fruit of conjoint grace and works, of humanity's inconstant will and God's perdurable revelation and indefeasible benevolence.[19]

In contrast to Levenson's account of election and law (or grace and works), we can see that Wyschogrod's theology of election overemphasizes grace as opposed to works. As Wyschogrod himself acknowledges, Barth, rather than rabbinic or medieval Jewish theology, is his primary influence. I mention this again not to suggest that this influence in and of itself is not authentically Jewish, but instead to point out the contradiction that this influence produces in Wyschogrod's thought: a theology of election premised on God's absolute sovereignty that makes the Jewish people, and not the Torah, into Judaism. While Wyschogrod is at pains to avoid these implications, it is difficult not to conclude that he has cut God out of the conversation either by presenting a kind of humanism in the vein of Mordecai Kaplan or Ahad Ha'am or by divinizing the Jewish people. Wyschogrod's theology of election does away with the Jewish drama of divine omnipotence, in which God not only affects, but is also affected by, his beloved people.

— In the previous section, we saw that Wyschogrod's preoccupation with philosophical issues—and with the rejection of philosophical conceptions of Judaism and the God of the Hebrew Bible in particular—stands in the way of a fuller engagement with multiple biblical themes which may have enhanced, rather than detracted from, his account of election. Wyschogrod is not alone in this regard. As Levenson would after him, Franz Rosenzweig stresses the drama between God and the Jewish people as depicted in the Hebrew Bible. Yet once again, as is the case with Wyschogrod's theology, Rosenzweig remains stuck within the framework that he seeks to oppose. While Rosenzweig rejects the rationalist equation between the God of the Hebrew Bible and the God of the philosophers, he is unable, despite his attempts to the contrary, to take seriously the Bible's conception of creation.

To appreciate the bind in which Rosenzweig ultimately finds himself, it is necessary to consider one important backdrop to his thought, which is the reception of Maimonides's rationalist philosophy. The twentieth-century German-Jewish philosopher Hermann Cohen self-consciously followed Maimonides in attempting to reconcile the Bible with philosophy (Aristotle in the case of Maimonides, Kant in the case of Cohen). Cohen and Maimonides both begin with a philosophical definition of God as wholly other than human. As such, the greatest barrier to reconciliation between the Bible and philosophy is the Bible's tendency to describe God in human terms. The biblical propensity to anthropomorphize may seem to suggest that the Bible is inferior to philosophy (either Kant's or Aristotle's) as a source of knowledge about God. Connected to the general problem of anthropomorphism is the more particular problem of the Bible's account of creation. If God created the world from preexistent matter, as the Hebrew terms *tohu vevohu* might suggest, then the difference not only between God and human beings but also between God and nature might be called into question.

While the meaning of his claim remains subject to highly contested scholarly debate, Maimonides is clear in the *Guide* that the notion of creation ex nihilo is essential to the philosophical defense of the Bible: "the foundation of the whole Law is the view that God brought the world into being out of nothing."[20] More generally, almost the entire first half of Maimonides's magnum opus, *The Guide of the Perplexed*, attempts to explain to the perplexed person the Bible's use of anthropomorphic language to describe God. Maimonides explains that what seem to be biblical anthropomorphisms are actually only metaphors, metaphors that aid the ordinary person in the attempt to grasp God's reality:

> When they [the rabbis] said, "The Torah speaks in the language of people," they meant whatever all people are able to understand at first thought...Therefore they described Him in terms that refer to material being, in order to teach that He exists, since the masses cannot grasp existence at first glance unless it is the existence of a body.[21]

Maimonides argues that the masses need to believe that God has physical attributes in order to believe in God. The only difference between God's attributes and human attributes for the nonphilosophical person is that the former are always bigger and better than the human ones. Thus the masses think that: "God would not exist if He did not have a body with a face ... except that it is larger and brighter."[22] The philosopher recognizes the needs of the masses and understands therefore that anthropomorphic language is *always* metaphorical.

Like Maimonides, Cohen fights the notion that the Bible is inferior to philosophy. Cohen's post-Kantian philosophical context demands that he bracket metaphysical claims about the creation of the world. Yet the idea of God's absolute distinctiveness from both humanity and the created world is as fundamental to Cohen's neo-Kantian philosophy as it is to Maimonides's neo-Aristotelian one. Describing what he calls the contribution to reason of the "sources of Judaism," meaning primarily the Hebrew Bible, Cohen glosses the Bible's account of creation in the following terms: "Throughout the development of religion unity was realized as uniqueness, and this significance of the unity of God as uniqueness brought about the recognition of the uniqueness of God's being, in comparison with which all other being vanishes and becomes nothing. Only God is being."[23] On the issues of anthropomorphism and image making generally, Cohen goes even further than Maimonides had. Whereas Maimonides acknowledges that what appears to be anthropomorphism is the Torah's concession to ordinary human understanding, which is to be corrected by the philosopher, Cohen insists that the Bible outright rejects any concession to the need for images. In Cohen's words: "The shame of the makers as well as the worshipers of the images is set repeatedly as a goal and a test. And the conclusion is important: that they will recognize 'is there not a lie in my right hand?' [Isa 44:20] *To recognize the lie and the self-deception in idol worship* is what matters."[24]

There are at least two reasons that Cohen goes beyond Maimonides on the status of images. First, Cohen's modern, egalitarian sensibility prevents him from simply positing a distinction between the masses and the philosophers. Second, and more relevant to the purposes of this essay, Cohen's rejection of anthropomorphism, or any positive account of image making, is part and parcel of a Jewish polemic against Protestant biblical scholarship. Like his nineteenth-century German-Jewish liberal predecessors, Cohen seeks to reject the claim that Judaism was at best a distortion of the Israelite religion of the "Old Testament." Cohen stresses the continuity between the particularity of Judaism, the prophets, the Law, and what he calls "the pure ideal of monotheism." As he argues in his aptly titled *Religion of Reason out of the Sources of Judaism* (1919), because the Hebrew Bible uniquely preserves the pure ideal of monotheism, nothing less than the future of humanity is at stake in the Bible's rejection of anthropomorphism.

Rosenzweig maintains not only that the Bible, and monotheism more generally, does not reject anthropomorphism but also that monotheism is in an important sense coterminous with anthropomorphism. In a short essay of 1928, "A Note on Anthropomorphism," Rosenzweig contends that the tendency to rationalize away biblical anthropomorphism as epitomized classically by Maimonides and in the twentieth-century by Cohen, is both dishonest and a misunderstanding of the Bible.[25] Indeed, according to Rosenzweig, the very term "anthropomorphism" is laden with rationalist prejudice. Properly speaking, he argues, there is no "anthropomorphism" in the Bible. Rather, "the 'anthropomorphisms' of the Bible are throughout assertions about meetings between God and man."[26] Once we understand that the Bible's descriptions of God are about meetings that take place in time, rather than about essences that are eternal, we can understand that the Bible does not "assert something either about God or about man, but only about an event between the two."[27] Rosenzweig argues that the philosophical problems created by "biblical anthropomorphisms" are a result of a category error. The Bible is not concerned with what God *is*, but rather with how God *acts*, in time, in God's relation to man.[28]

This means that the Bible's many images of God express particular encounters between the human and the divine. The variety of images of God in the Bible is constitutive of monotheism itself. These diverse and different images of God attest to God's infinite freedom to reveal himself and the human's infinite ability to respond to God:

> [T]hey [biblical anthropomorphisms] are the single protection against the backsliding into polytheism, which indeed is nothing but consolidation of a genuine present revelation of the real God to a lasting image of God precisely by this means: resisting the ever-new will of God's revelation.[29]

The images of God in the Bible are not shameful for Rosenzweig, as they are for Cohen and Maimonides. Rather, these images go to the heart of the truth of monotheism itself: "The assumption that they [biblical anthropomorphisms] make is none other than the double one that the Bible commonly makes: namely that God is capable of what he wills ... and that the creature is capable of what he should be."[30]

Rosenzweig's affirmation of biblical anthropomorphism would seem to cohere well with Levenson's account of the drama between God and the people of Israel. So too, Rosenzweig, like Levenson, places the election of Israel at the center of this drama. And like Levenson, Rosenzweig places the tension between Judaism and Christianity, and indeed between Jewish and Christian conceptions of their own election, at the heart of this drama: "Before God, then, Jew and Christian both labor at the same task. He [God] cannot dispense with either. He has set enmity between the two for all time and withal has most intimately bound each to each ... The truth, the whole truth (*die ganze Wahrheit*) thus belongs neither to them nor to us."[31] Yet for all of these striking affinities between Rosenzweig's conception of Israel's election and the human ability to affect God, Rosenzweig can only at best gesture toward a conception of creation.

Strikingly, in his magnum opus, *The Star of Redemption*, Rosenzweig recognizes that the modern theological inability to speak of creation in a meaningful way is at the heart of the crisis of modern theology. As he puts it: "It was creation which theology neglected in the nineteenth century in its obsession with the idea of a vitally present revelation. And precisely creation is now the gate through which philosophy enters into the house of theology ... From theology's point of view, what philosophy is supposed to accomplish for [theology] ... is to ... demonstrate the precondition upon which [theology] rests."[32] The precondition of theology, for Rosenzweig, is not God's creation of the world as a metaphysical fact, however defined, but rather the subjective, individual human experience of mortality.

Rosenzweig himself struggles to move beyond this conclusion. The *Star*'s account of revelation is indeed predicated on an affirmation of creation:

> Here begins that supplement to the divine self-manifestation which merely commenced in the acts of creation ... The "factuality" of God threatened to become lost in his concealment. To regain it, it is not

enough that he become manifest a first time in an infinity full of creative acts [though he does do this, apparently]. There God threatened to lose himself again behind the infinity of creation ... Precisely for the sake of its revelational character, the first revelation in creation thus demands the emergence of a "second revelation."[33]

But because any ontological claim that Rosenzweig makes about creation remains subject to his commitment to the notion that creation becomes a possibility only by way of subjective, individual consciousness of mortality, his ontological description of creation can only be at best metaphorical. Put another way, by dint of his own admission Rosenzweig remains, and must remain, a post-Kantian thinker, which means that he can only speak of creation (or any other metaphysical matter) first and foremost from the perspective of human subjectivity. While the virtues of this theological account of creation may be debated, it has more in common with Cohen's post-Kantian gloss on creation, which must be understood in terms of human subjectivity, than it does with any biblical account that begins with God's decision to create. Once again, the virtues of this position may be debated, but what cannot be debated is the tension between Rosenzweig's explicit attempt to reject the priority of a philosophical framework, on the one hand, and his inability to do so, on the other. To be clear, my point is not to suggest that there is one obvious biblical account of creation that Rosenzweig (or others) may miss. My aim, rather, is to point to the difficulty that a number of modern Jewish thinkers have in considering basic biblical themes (such as creation in Rosenzweig's case or the theurgic dimension of law in Wyschogrod's case), even when their explicit aim is to make the Bible, and not philosophical considerations, the starting point for Jewish theology.

Levenson provides an important corrective to this tension within modern Jewish thought. Levenson begins *Creation and the Persistence of Evil* by situating his analysis of creation in the Hebrew Bible in the context of twentieth-century biblical scholarship and of Yehezkel Kaufmann's now classic *The Religion of Israel, from Its Beginnings to the Babylonian Exile* in particular.[34] Kaufmann's book has a number of important affinities with the rationalist tradition of Jewish thought, including

Cohen's philosophy in particular, that Rosenzweig seeks to reject. As Levenson succinctly puts it, Kaufmann

> deemed ... [mastery] "the basic idea of Israelite religion" and the factor that differentiates absolutely between religion and "paganism," that is, all religions that are not derived from it. Whereas the "pagan" believes "that there exists a realm of being prior to the gods and above them, upon which the gods depend, and whose decrees they must obey," for Israel, "there is no realm above or beside YHWH to limit his absolute sovereignty."[35]

It is not difficult to understand why Kaufmann correlates God's absolute sovereignty with God's mastery of creation. After all, as we saw in our brief discussion of Maimonides and Cohen, if we understand God in philosophical terms, then God cannot be subject to the limitations that define human beings or the created world. If God were subject to such limitations, then God would not be God. Kaufmann, of course, does not begin with philosophical preconceptions, whether Aristotelian or Kantian, as Maimonides and Cohen do. Yet the comparison between Cohen and Kaufmann does allow us to appreciate some of the ways in which the latter's project, like the former's, is fundamentally apologetic in attempting to defend the legitimacy of Judaism in light of anti-Jewish Protestant polemics. Like Cohen before him, Kaufmann must insist against Protestant scholars that the God of the Hebrew Bible is historically, culturally, and theologically unique.

While the Jewish response to Protestant biblical scholarship is far beyond the scope of this essay, I'd like to suggest at a minimum that Kaufmann's insistence on God's mastery and sovereignty is intimately tied to his need to stress the Hebrew Bible's, and hence Judaism's, originality. Despite their very different cultural and political contexts (early twentieth-century Germany and mid-twentieth-century Israel, respectively), Cohen and Kaufmann share this polemical project. Writing in a very different historical, cultural, and political context (late-twentieth-century North America), Levenson is not invested in this polemic. His analysis begins then not by denying the affinities between the Hebrew

Bible and its ancient Near Eastern context but by affirming them. As Levenson summarizes the argument of his book:

> [A]lthough critical scholars are nearly universal in ascribing Genesis 1:1–2:3 to P, the Priestly source in the Pentateuch, the affinities of this crucial text with the Priestly theology of the cultus have not been sufficiently explored. In particular, the connection of this cosmogony with ancient Near Eastern temple building has been missed. This failure . . . has led generally to a neglect of the role of humanity in forming and sustaining the world order therein described. This neglect has helped obscure the fact that this text too deals in large part with the questions of how to neutralize the powerful and ongoing threat of chaos.[36]

Comparing Gen 1:1–2:3 with the Babylonian creation myth *Enuma Elish,* Levenson contends that the primordial chaos out of which God creates (*tohu vavohu*) may continually erupt again. According to Levenson's analysis, it is necessary to recognize the distinction between the hope of God's total mastery of creation (as reflected in Ps 82) and the current reality, which requires human action to affect creation as well as God's own ability to act. It is the human being's task to beseech God to keep his end of his covenant: "The God to whom this theology bears witness is not the one who continually acts in history, but . . . [rather] the God who will reactivate his mighty deeds and close the horrific parenthesis that is ordinary history."[37]

Levenson's focus on creation allows us to appreciate a particular irony about Rosenzweig's claim, quoted above, that "the assumption that they [biblical anthropomorphisms] make is none other than the double one that the Bible commonly makes: namely that God is capable of what he wills . . . and that the creature is capable of what he should be." While Rosenzweig goes a long way in rejecting his rationalist predecessors and what he takes to be their ultimate devaluing of the biblical text, he is unable to move beyond an account of a consciousness of human finitude as the ground for his theology. Rosenzweig recognizes the necessity of divine creation, but he can only do so within a post-Kantian epistemological context. Put another way, creation is central to Rosenzweig's theology yet it testifies first and foremost to the truth of post-Kantian philosophy. The lesson Levenson draws from his study of the Bible's account of creation is particularly apt. He writes:

> The detachment of the physical world from the moral and spiritual worlds (and the casting of the reality of the nonphysical realm into doubt) has been a hallmark of modern Western thought ... One of my goals [is] ... to show that this detachment is not consonant with the theologies of creation in the Hebrew Bible ... The very point that has been seen as a weakness of these biblical conceptions of creation may prove to be an outstanding asset.[38]

— I have tried to show in this essay that in an important sense, a Jewish theology of election does not conflict with Calvin's description of "the Jewish people, who ... make the faith of the gospel to depend on their decision." Calvin is right that from a Jewish theological perspective, redemption does in fact depend upon the decision of the Jewish people. Where Jewish theology would disagree with Calvin of course is in evaluating this as "pride and vain-glorying." Put another way, from a Jewish theological perspective, this "pride and vain-glorying" is the very mark of human freedom and responsibility. We have recognized the distinction between hope and reality, which is also the distinction between creation and redemption, that is depicted in the biblical account of creation. We can now accordingly recognize that pace Maimonides, Cohen, Kaufmann, and indeed Calvin, there need not be a contradiction between a sovereign God who chooses (both to create the world and to have a special relationship with a particular people) and the possibility of human beings affecting God. An electing God and the human possibility of affecting God need not conflict with one another; indeed, God's sovereignty may well require human action.

NOTES

1. John Calvin, *Institutes of the Christian Religion* (3rd ed.; trans. John Allen; Philadelphia: Presbyterian Board of Publication, 1841), 2:430.
2. Ibid, 154.
3. Jon D. Levenson, *Sinai and Zion: An Entry into the Hebrew Bible* (New York: HarperOne, 1985), 4.

4. Michael Wyschogrod, *Abraham's Promise: Judaism and Jewish and Christian Relations* (Grand Rapids, Mich.: Eerdmans, 2004), 214–15.

5. Michael Wyschogrod, *The Body of Faith* (Northvale, N.J.: Jason Aaronson, 1983).

6. Wyschogrod, *Abraham's Promise*, 102.

7. Wyschogrod, *Body of Faith*, 61.

8. Ibid., 65.

9. Ibid., 217.

10. Ibid., 215.

11. Ibid., 216.

12. Ibid., 174.

13. Jon D. Levenson, *The Death and the Resurrection of the Beloved Son* (New Haven: Yale University Press, 1993).

14. Ibid., 216.

15. Ibid., 232.

16. Ibid., 232.

17. For a related criticism of Wyschogrod's theology in the context of a defense of Jewish election, see David Novak, *The Election of Israel: The Idea of the Chosen People* (New York: Cambridge University Press, 1995).

18. Jon D. Levenson, *Creation and the Persistence of Evil: The Jewish Drama of Divine Omnipotence* (2nd ed.; Princeton, N.J.: Princeton University Press, 1984), 46.

19. Ibid., 40.

20. Moses Maimonides, *Guide of the Perplexed* (trans. Shlomo Pines; intro. Leo Strauss; Chicago: University of Chicago Press, 1963), 2:30, 349.

21. Ibid., 1:26, 56.

22. Ibid., 1:1, 21.

23. Hermann Cohen, *Religion of Reason out of the Sources of Judaism* (intro. Leo Strauss; trans. Simon Kaplan; Atlanta: Scholars Press, 1995), 41.

24. Ibid., 56, emphasis in the original.

25. Franz Rosenzweig, *Franz Rosenzweig: Der Mensch und sein Werk. Gesammelte Schriften* (4 vols.; Dordrecht: Martinus Nijholf, 1976–84), 3:735–46.

26. Ibid., 737.

27. Ibid., 737.

28. Ibid., 739.

29. Ibid., 741.

30. Ibid., 741.

31. Franz Rosenzweig, *The Star of Redemption* (trans. William Hallo; Notre Dame, IN: University of Notre Dame Press, 1985), 415–16.

32. Ibid., 107–8.

33. Ibid., 160.

34. Yehezkel Kaufmann, *The Religion of Israel, from Its Beginnings to the Babylonian Exile* (trans. and abridged by Moshe Greenberg; New York: Schocken, 1972).

35. Levenson, *Creation and the Persistence of Evil*, 3. Levenson is quoting pieces from Kaufmann, *Religion of Israel*, 21, 60.

36. Ibid., xxix–xxx.

37. Ibid., 50.

38. Ibid., 27.

CHAPTER 15

Christ and Israel
An Unsolved Problem in Catholic Theology

BRUCE D. MARSHALL

In the first weeks of 2010, Pope Benedict XVI made a public visit to the Great Synagogue of Rome, and was there officially welcomed by the leaders of the synagogue and the Italian Jewish community. It was not the pope's first visit to a synagogue or with Jewish leaders, but on this occasion his presence in midst of the Jewish community drew particular attention. This happened in part because the same Great Synagogue of Rome was the site of John Paul II's historic visit in 1986, purportedly the first by a bishop of Rome since the time of the apostles. But it was also because the pope was criticized, openly if indirectly, by one of the Jewish leaders present. Riccardo Pacifici, president of the Jewish community of Rome and a direct descendant of Italian Holocaust victims, told of the pain still felt by the Jews of Rome over the "silence" of Pius XII, who might have spoken a public word of "comfort" to the Jewish people in their time of deepest need, even if he could not have stopped "the trains of death."[1] The timing of these public comments to the pope seems unlikely to have been accidental. Only a month before, Benedict had declared Pius XII a person of heroic virtue, and so had considerably advanced the cause of his predecessor's sainthood. What does it say about the attitude of Pope Benedict, and of the Church, toward the Jewish people, Mr. Pacifici seemed to ask, that it can regard such a person as heroically virtuous?

My concern here is not with the legacy of Pius XII, but with the deeper conflict that came to the surface, in however cordial and respectful a way, in the Great Synagogue of Rome. Basically this same conflict has been enacted, this drama played out, between Jews and Christians countless times since the Second Vatican Council.

In the Synagogue of Rome, Pope Benedict spoke forcefully of his own love and affection and that of the Catholic Church for the Jewish community of Rome and all Jewish communities throughout the world. He begged forgiveness for any action of the children of the Church "that could in any way have contributed to the scourge of anti-Semitism and anti-Judaism," and he stressed that the dark memory of the Holocaust compels the Church and the Jewish people "to strengthen the bonds that unite us so that our mutual understanding, respect and acceptance may always increase." The pope said much else which expressed his own and the Church's uncompromising commitment to the welfare of the Jewish people, and he was warmly welcomed for it. Yet at the same time it seems clear that the Jewish community of Rome is not convinced that it can trust him, and is not convinced that it can trust his Church. To many Jews the Church evidently sends a painfully mixed message: by some words and deeds, such as the pope's visit to the Synagogue of Rome, the Church seems to make plain its commitment to the well being of the Jewish people, while by others, such as the prospective sainthood of Pius XII, the Church seems to make plain its indifference, and perhaps even hostility, to the well being of the Jewish people.[2]

Particularly among Catholics, it is common to see the mixed message the Jewish community hears from the Church as basically a political problem or a failure of public relations. On this reading the problem can be solved by a more sensitive and adroit handling of

Vatican actions and utterances. But this response is superficial, and is more an obstacle to confronting the underlying difficulty than a way of addressing the problem. The real root of the matter is doctrinal and theological. It is theological, more precisely, in the strict sense of the term: it concerns the coherence of two claims about *God*. One is that the saving mission of Christ and his Church is willed by God to be universal, extending to every human being. The other is that God's covenant with Israel, with the Jewish people according to the flesh, is irrevocable. Both of these claims seem to be essential to Catholic teaching and Catholic faith. But the consistency of the one with the other is less than obvious. Depending on which of these teachings seems to guide the actions of the pope and the Church at the moment, first one message, then its opposite, seems to be heard.

What I hope to undertake here is a modest exercise in *fides quaerens intellectum:* an attempt to understand how these two teachings about God fit together. Since both are evidently nonnegotiable matters of Catholic faith, I assume *that* they fit together in one way or another. What I would like to understand is *how* they fit together—how they are, as a needed minimum, at least consistent with one another.

This attempt at understanding will, I should warn in advance, involve more *quaerens* than *intellectus*. I do not quite know how these two important teachings fit together. No traditional or contemporary way of handling this question really seems to be successful. The main approaches end up playing one of the teachings off against the other, though not usually by design. From this failure of *intellectus* regarding the coherence of Catholic teaching, and not from mishandled publicity or concealed ill will, arises the apparent ambivalence of Catholic witness, the mixed message about the Church's attitude toward the Jewish people and their well being. I will suggest an alternative approach, but only tentatively, since the idea I want to propose itself seems less than fully satisfactory.

It may not be obvious why we should trace the conflict that emerged in the Rome Synagogue to an unresolved theological perplexity about Christ and Israel. That will, I hope, emerge in due course. We need to begin, though, by backing up a few steps. Why should the coherence of these two teachings, of the universal, ecclesially mediated saving mission of Christ and the irrevocable election of Israel—pose any difficulty in the first place? If we can get clear on that we will have attained some valuable understanding of the theological difficulty. By simply *understanding* the problem, we may better see how to address it in such a way as to avoid sending mixed messages to our Jewish brothers and sisters.

II

As Pope Benedict notes in his Synagogue address, *Nostra Aetate* (NA) 4 is the Church's basic charter both for subsequent relations with the Jewish people and for theological understanding of the place of the fleshly descendants of Abraham, Isaac, and Jacob in the saving plan of God. In particular, NA 4 insists with the authority of an ecumenical council—for the first time in the Church's history on this matter—that God's promises to the Jewish people are good forever and that his election of this people from among the nations can never become a thing of the past. "God holds the Jews most dear for the sake of their Fathers; He does not repent of the gifts He makes or of the calls He issues" (NA 4).[3] Here the declaration echoes, naturally, the teaching of St. Paul in Rom 11:28–29, as does the council's earlier teaching on the Church as the people of God in *Lumen Gentium* (LG) 16.[4] Conversely, NA 4 goes on to say, "The Jews should not be presented as rejected or accursed by God, as if this followed from the Holy Scriptures." The Church is "the new people of God," but this cannot be understood in any way that implies the rejection of the Jews or the impermanence of their election.

Nostra Aetate 4 concludes with a reminder that Christ suffered and died "because of the sins of all men and out of infinite love, in order that all may reach salvation." As Christ died for all human beings, so the Church has the responsibility "to proclaim the cross of Christ" for the salvation of every human being, "as the sign of God's all-embracing love and as the fountain from which every grace flows." Precisely because we can exclude no one from the saving reach of the paschal mystery, we can exclude no one from the vocation to union with Christ through faith and baptism. God's call to embrace the public life of the Church is therefore as universal as the saving intention enacted in the paschal mystery, and is included in that mystery. "All human beings are called (*vocantur*) to belong to the new people of God," LG 13 teaches, using the same definite description for the Church that NA 4 would later employ. The Church is therefore "zealous to foster missions" (LG 16).[5]

Just because we human beings can be liberated from sin and attain the end for which God made us only through union with Christ crucified and risen, a share in the paschal mystery must be available to every human being, and not only to those reached by the Church's public proclamation. As *Gaudium et Spes* (GS) 22 puts the point, "Since Christ died for all men (Rom 8:32), and since the ultimate vocation of man is in fact one, and divine, we ought to believe that the Holy Spirit, in a manner known to God, offers to every man the possibility of being associated with this paschal mystery."[6]

For present purposes the salient point in these texts is the universality of God's intention, or will, that human beings belong to the Church. Some, perhaps many, of those who embrace their share in the paschal mystery will be unable—though not unwilling—to fulfill the ecclesial vocation contained within the paschal mystery. But this does not limit that vocation, making it less than universal, nor does it limit the public mission of the Church, which aims at the fulfillment of that vocation. As *Ad Gentes* (AG) 8 points out, God's universal saving will seeks the "full and conscious" acceptance, by way of the Church's mission, of "[God's] work of salvation, which He has accomplished in Christ." Since the Church's mission to preach and baptize fulfills both the saving purposes of God and the most profound desires of the human heart, Christ and his Church "cannot be considered as strangers to anyone, or in any place" (AG 8).[7]

In sum: just as the Church can propose nothing about its own identity and mission which implies that God's election of the Jewish people is no longer in force, so the Church cannot understand the permanence of Jewish election in a way that limits the saving mission of Christ to anything less than the whole of humanity. No human being is outside the sphere of the salvation accomplished by the cross of Christ, and therefore no human being can be excluded—or, as the case may be, exempted—from the mission of the Church, as the universal sacrament (LG 1, 9, 48) and instrument (LG 9) of Christ's saving work.[8]

III

The teaching just summarized makes two claims about what God has irrevocably willed. (1) God has chosen Israel from among all the nations of the earth to be his "treasured possession" forever (in the language of Deut 7:6). (2) God calls all human beings to salvation in Christ by baptismal incorporation into the Church, "the new people of God." One way to see why there might be a problem in the thought that God wills both these things is to recall a common interpretation of NA 4.

Commentators on NA 4 sometimes suggest that what happened at Vatican II with regard to the Church's teaching on the Jewish people is clear and straightforward. By affirming the irrevocability of Israel's election and ruling out any claim that the Jewish people have been rejected or cursed by God, the Church finally corrected a long-standing and tragic error. The error lay precisely in the claim that God had rejected the Jewish people after Christ, and that the Church had superseded Israel as God's elect. The theology of supersessionism was responsible, so the argument goes, for "the teaching of contempt," the anti-Semitism and anti-Judaism forcefully repudiated in NA 4 and in subsequent papal teaching. To maintain that the Jewish people, too, are included in the Church's universal mission to proclaim the gospel and baptize is, on this account, at best a preconciliar outlook and at worst the bitter fruit of an underlying anti-Semitism. Seen in this way, Catholic teaching on Christ and Israel poses not so much a theological perplexity as an educational and moral problem, to be solved by rooting out the deep-going supersessionism still widespread in the Church.

However much ongoing need there is for docility and repentance as Christians confront their abuse of the Jews, there remains something odd, indeed improbable, about the idea that the teaching of NA on the election of Israel simply reverses an error persistent from the very beginning of Christianity. Because this is the teaching of an ecumenical council, we are bound to regard it as an authentic development of doctrine. For just this reason it has to have something in Scripture and tradition to develop *from;* it has to have precedents. The suggestion that on this score the Church simply lived in tragic error until 1965 (probably beginning, indeed, in the New Testament itself), tends not to strengthen but to weaken the authority of NA 4 and hence its place in the hierarchy of truths.

In fact, God's undying fidelity to the fleshly descendants of Abraham, Isaac, and Jacob, including the eschatological salvation of this chosen people, was a widespread teaching in the Catholic tradition before Vatican II. That those who insisted on this also regularly spoke of the Jews and Judaism with contempt, cannot therefore be chalked up to a belief that God had rejected the Jewish people after Christ. Reflecting on why the theology of earlier times often tried to combine a very high view of the irrevocable election of Israel with a very low view of post-biblical Judaism may help us understand the theological problem we now face in light of Vatican II's teaching on Israel and Christ. I will briefly look at Thomas Aquinas as a case in point.

In Aquinas's robust view of Jewish election, God has distinguished Israel permanently and sharply from all other nations and given the Jewish people privileges and responsibilities unique to them. The election of Israel is, to be sure, wholly for the sake of Christ. God chooses this people as his own so that the redeemer of all the nations may one day come forth from them. For Aquinas, however, the christological purpose of Israel's election maximizes the doctrinal and theological importance of the fact that God "elected this people, and no other," rather than marginalizing it.[9] Whatever God is doing in the election of this people is integral to the mystery of Christ, forever inseparable from the person and office of Christ himself.

It is important to observe that Aquinas understands Jewish election in genuinely "carnal" rather than strictly "spiritual" terms. To be a Jew, and so one of God's elect, is first of all simply to be descended (*progenitus*) according to the flesh from Abraham and the other *patres* of Israel. Thomas here explicitly follows the Vulgate rendering of Deut 4:37 ("[Deus] dilexit patres tuos et elegit semen eorum post eos"): God loved the *patres,* and chose (*elegit*) their "seed" or descendants to receive the Law and the benefits that come with it.[10] To Israel belong not simply those who have Jewish faith, but those who have Jewish flesh.[11]

God's promised blessing to the patriarchs and their descendants extends, moreover, not only to the earthly present, but to the eschatological future. God's election of Israel is ultimately, in other words, a promise of salvation. In his love for Abraham, Isaac, and Jacob, God has promised salvation to their carnal descendants until the end of time. For Thomas this follows from passages like Deut 4:37, and is the clear teaching of St. Paul. God showed an abundance of grace and mercy to the fathers of Israel "so that for the sake of the promises made to them [the fathers], their offspring too might be saved."[12]

Moreover, Thomas explicitly rejects the idea that the election of Israel has been made void by Israel's rejection of the gospel and so may be regarded as temporary. He dismisses out of hand the claim that while the Jews were formerly *charissimi* on account of their fathers, they have now, by their refusal of the gospel, been abandoned by God. There is no way to square this idea with St. Paul's teaching that God's gifts and call are "without repentance" (Rom 11:29). As Thomas reads him, Paul regards as wholly false any suggestion that the Jews, by their hostility (*inimicitia*) to the gospel, have lost the future salvation their forefathers were promised by God.[13] This applies, moreover, not only to Jews of the eschatological future, but to those of his own time, the Jews whom Aquinas might see on the streets of Paris. "Let no one despair of the future salvation of the Jews on account of the fact that they do not seem to repent of their sin," that is, of their unbelief.[14] Israel's election cannot be a thing of the past. Thus Thomas openly, indeed emphatically, rejects supersessionism, and warns every gentile Christian to beware of taking the mystery of Israel's unbelief to mean that the Jewish people have been rejected by God. Such a failure of reverence for God's promises and for the mystery of his saving plan may cause those who fall victim to it to forfeit salvation.[15]

To us all this may seem manifestly inconsistent with a number of insupportable things Aquinas says about the Jews, not least his evident assent to the laws of the time that "the Jews, by reason of their guilt, are assigned to perpetual servitude."[16] While we cannot, of course, accept Aquinas's view of the rightful place of the Jews in a just society, he would have reason to be surprised if we suggested to him that his social views contradicted his high claims about Jewish election. As he sees it, the current "servitude" of Abraham's descendants cannot at all be taken as evidence of their rejection, the termination of their election by God. It no more nullifies their election and ultimate restoration than did their scripturally attested exile in Babylon.

There is, I think, a deep problem of consistency here, but it lies in another direction. Aquinas holds, characteristically for traditional Christian reflection on this matter, that the practice of the Mosaic law after Christ (or more precisely, after the public dissemination, the *divulgatio,* of the gospel), is "deadly" (*mortifera*)—it cuts off those who keep it from saving union with God. And this is simply to say that the practice of Judaism has become deadly. For many centuries now, and until the end of time, the person who (for example) has his son circumcised separates himself, and probably his offspring, from God. To be sure, God solemnly commanded this observance to Abraham and his descendants, and Aquinas fully embraces the traditional view that circumcision was, under the "old law," the most efficacious type and anticipation of baptism. But what once gave life—until the coming of Christ—now kills; those who continue to keep any of the ritual laws God gave to Moses "now sin mortally."[17] God wills the election of Abraham's descendants in a wholly irrevocable way, but God does not at all will (or more precisely, no longer wills), the practice of Judaism.

For Aquinas, as for most adherents of this traditional view, such a negative estimate of postbiblical Judaism is not merely arbitrary, the result of simple prejudice against the Jews. It stems, rather, from his commitment to the universality of salvation in Christ. Jesus, and he alone, is the savior of all, and the triune God saves by joining us to him in his passion and resurrection—normally by means of the sacraments of the Church. "Even before the advent of Christ," Aquinas observes, "salvation was never possible for human beings unless they became members of Christ. For, as Acts 4[:12] says, 'There is no other name given to men by which we may be saved.'"[18] Here St. Thomas evidently anticipates the teaching of GS 22. Salvation is possible only as a share in the paschal mystery, realized by way of an appropriate sacramental sign. An "association" with the paschal mystery, as GS 22 calls it, is not simply the *way* to salvation; it *is* salvation. Salvation, as Aquinas puts it, is always union with Christ by faith, while the specific content of that saving faith and of its divinely given sacramental sign varies with human places and times.

For St. Thomas, then, the law of Moses has high and permanent doctrinal import for Christians precisely because it was God's special provision, sacramental in its own right, for God's elect people to be joined to Christ in a saving way before his coming in the flesh. The law was thereby the divinely appointed means by which Israel would bear witness to the savior who was to come. It was a public prefiguration of Jesus Christ, to be fulfilled in its entirety by his incarnation, passion, and glorification (a point clearly retained, we ought to note, in LG 13 and NA 4). The law of Moses, in other words, was given by God precisely as a *pre*figuration of Christ's future advent, and especially of the paschal mystery in which he would bring about the salvation of the world. Since this was the exact purpose for which God gave it, the Old Testament law inherently points forward to a Christ who is yet to come and suffer in the flesh, not backwards to a Christ who has already come and suffered. Pointing to the paschal mystery backwards rather than forwards requires the divine provision of a new sacramental order, given for just this purpose. Baptism, for example, does not compete with circumcision as a sacramental rite by which God joins his people to himself. It *replaces* circumcision as the appropriate sacramental means for union with Christ. It had to replace the sacrament that preceded it, because God's people no longer only hope for his saving presence still to come, but actually have him present in his crucified and risen flesh. In much the same way, circumcision replaced the sacrifices before the law.[19] To continue observing the law of Moses now that Christ has come attests not simply ignorance of his advent and passion in the flesh, but a denial that he has come and suffered. And God, of course, cannot will this denial.

We arrive, then, at what seems to be the basic theological problem about Christ and Israel. Aquinas is a striking witness to this problem, and at times seems to be aware of it (as in *STh* II-II, q. 10, a. 11, to which I will return), though so far as I can see he does not offer any clear solution to it. God wills the election of Israel irrevocably, up to and including the end-time salvation of the descendants of Abraham, Isaac, and Jacob according to the flesh. But God no longer wills the practice of Judaism, indeed he apparently wills that it not be practiced. How, though, are the Jewish people going to make it to the eschaton without Judaism? The practice of Judaism is, it seems, indispensable for the Jewish people to remain, over time, distinct from the gentiles.

Without it they would soon vanish, like the Hittites, into the sea of nations (of *gentilitas*, as the medievals liked to put it, "gentileness," or in traditional Jewish terms, *Goyischkeit*). God, however, evidently does not want humanity to be simply a mass of gentiles. He chooses Israel "out of" the nations, over against the gentiles, and does so forever (Deut 7:6). Visible distinction from the nations is, in other words, necessary for the election of Israel; it is among the constituent or integral parts of the existence of the Jewish people as God's chosen. So it seems that God must will the practice of Judaism for the sake of Jewish election. It also seems that he must not will it, for the sake of the universality of salvation in Christ. Of course God cannot both will and not will one and the same thing, for one and the same time, including the practice of Judaism.

IV

At its core the problem brought to the surface by Aquinas remains our problem. When it comes to thinking theologically about the election of Israel and the primacy of Christ, I am not sure we have advanced much since the thirteenth century. This may seem needlessly, even willfully, pessimistic, since few of us are likely to agree with Aquinas that the practice of Judaism is mortal sin. We are right to disagree with Aquinas about this. One of his merits, though, is to make clear that the underlying issue is what God can coherently be said to will, not the subjective disposition of those who keep, or do not keep, the Mosaic law. The practice of Judaism evidently belongs to God's saving purposes; he wills it. But this does not solve the problem of how the universal vocation of humanity to salvation in Christ and his Church can be squared with the irrevocability of Israel's election. It *is* the problem.

Think, for example, of one approach now often employed in the hope of squaring the vocation of every human being to "full and conscious" life in Christ (AG 8) with the will of God that the children of Abraham keep the full Torah, and so remain visible to the nations as God's elect. According to this suggestion, the Jewish people as a whole will one day embrace life in Christ. God has, as Catholic teaching holds, no saving will for humanity, no covenant with his creatures, except in Christ. However, the Jewish people's union with Christ, and thus the entry of the chosen people into his body, is thoroughly eschatological. God will make the salvation he has accomplished by the cross of Christ plain to all in the end, as Rom 11:25–32 teaches. In the meantime the Church should not seek to make Jews into Christians. To the extent that it is our business at all, the Church should try to help them be faithful Jews. Looked at in this way, neither a witness of the Church to the Jewish people nor the conversion of Jews to Christianity is part of God's historical purpose. A thoroughly eschatological approach to the problem of Christ and Israel thereby achieves the same result as "two covenants" approaches, namely ruling out any mission or witness of the Church to the Jews. It achieves this result, moreover, without recourse to the idea that God has one saving arrangement for Jews (keeping the Torah) and another for gentiles (faith in Christ). From a Catholic point of view this is surely to the good, since the notion of two discreet saving covenants seems openly opposed to the universality of Christ's saving work.

As a practical directive for Christian relations with Jews, where sensitivity and respect are paramount, there is obviously much to be said for this. But as a way of exhibiting the coherence of God's calling of all to salvation in Christ with the election of Israel, it redescribes the difficulty rather than resolving it.

In fact this approach probably works better for other non-Christian religions than it does for Judaism. In the case of religious communities and practices about which the Bible itself tells us nothing, we can be relatively agnostic about the extent to which these communities and their practices are positively willed by God. It is enough to hold that to whatever extent they are, they aim at an embrace of the salvation offered by the cross of Christ, even if "in a way known to God" but perhaps not to us (GS 22). As such they also can be said to aim at "full and conscious" existence in the Church, however obscure the connection between the one and the other may be to us.

In the case of Judaism, however, we know too much. If God wills Israel's observance of the Torah until the end of time, after Christ as well as before, we know both what he wills (the full halakhic life of the

Jewish people), and we know why he wills it: to sanctify his elect people, and so keep them visibly distinct from the nations—from losing themselves in *gentilitas*. This loss is just what seems bound to happen when Jews become Christians, entering the community which embraces all nations and recognizes no national borders. If God wills the practice of Judaism for Abraham's descendants until everything changes at the end, God must, it seems, limit his offer of full and conscious participation in the life of the new people of God. The descendants of Abraham must be excluded from life in the body of Christ, precisely so they can remain God's elect.

If this were right, the Jewish people, unlike the rest of humanity, would have to wait until the eschaton even to be offered the supreme good God intends for them in Christ and his Church. What starts out as a theological effort to honor the election of Israel and the divinely willed integrity of Judaism ends up (inadvertently, to be sure) as a curious inversion of the traditional idea that the Jews must wait until the eschaton for the gift of salvation God promised to their forefathers. For the tradition this exclusion of the Jews from the Church was a punishment, while in the current version it seems to become a kind of gift, given for their own good.

Against this current suggestion, it is surely right to say that no one is excluded from the offer of life in Christ and his Church, as the conciliar texts with which we started insist. But now we are back where we began. It seems impossible that God excludes anyone from this offer of life, yet at the same time it seems that he must do so if Israel is to remain his elect. Surely something is amiss here. These two teachings must both be right, which means they must be harmonious with each other. But our necessary quest for the *intellectus fidei* seems to leave us, at least at present, perplexed rather than satisfied.

Even to have located our perplexity precisely can, I think, be progress. It would help us to avoid sending mixed messages. We are committed—because we believe God is committed—to both the unfailing election and well being of Israel, and to the universal saving mission of Christ and his Church. Even if we do not yet understand how these commitments fit together, we are not willing to regard them as opposites. We are therefore unwilling to settle for any view of the relation between Christ and Israel (whether proposed by Christians or by Jews) which plays these two convictions off against one another, to the detriment of either the Jewish people or the Church.

Yet there remains something deeply unsatisfying about such an intellectual irresolution. Nature and grace alike prompt us to want more, a genuine *intellectus* of the harmony of these two elemental convictions rather than the mere assertion of their coherence. I will conclude with a tentative suggestion on this score, prompted by a passage from the *Catechism of the Catholic Church*.

V

In a passage on the Church and other religions, the *Catechism* makes the following brief observation:

> [W]hen one considers the future, God's People of the Old Covenant and the new People of God tend towards similar goals: expectation of the coming (or the return) of the Messiah. But one awaits the return of the Messiah who died and rose from the dead and is recognized as Lord and Son of God; the other awaits the coming of a Messiah, whose features remain hidden till the end of time; and the latter waiting is accompanied by the drama of not knowing or of misunderstanding Christ Jesus. (§840)

This passage suggests—or at least I take it to suggest—that Jews and Christians alike await the same Messiah. In their anticipation both are, moreover, united to the one Messiah whom they await. That is: Jews and Christians alike look for, and are saved by hope in, the full revealing of the Lord and Son of God, who died and rose for us. The Jewish way of waiting—communal halakhic life—is profoundly different from the Christian way—communal Eucharistic life. Christians are bound to see in the Jewish way of waiting serious misunderstandings of the one for whom both ways look in hope, as Jews are bound to see equally serious, though different, misunderstandings in the Christian way. Nonetheless, Christians cannot regard the messianic hope of the Jewish people as empty, as aimed at nothing real. Christians must see Jewish anticipation of the one to whom the Law and the prophets bear witness as aimed, in reality, at no one other than Christ Jesus. As such, the messianic expectation of the Jewish people mysteriously joins them to Jesus Christ, in his full revealing yet to come. The practice of the levitical cult, so Catholic tradition has long maintained, embodied the hope of ancient Israel for Jesus Christ still to come in the flesh. That expectation united Israel with saving effect to Christ yet unborn. In a way not wholly unlike this, so the passage from the *Catechism* seems to indicate, the hope of the Jewish people now unites them to Christ yet to come in glory.

Since the return of Christ in glory is itself included in the paschal mystery, Christians can and should see in the Jewish expectation of the Messiah still to come a divinely willed share in that saving mystery, a way of being joined to Christ. Because it joins to Christ, a Torah-observant life, given by God to set his elect people forever apart from the nations, cannot be opposed to a certain kind of membership in the new people of God. It must *be* Israel's divinely willed way of belonging, however unexpectedly, to the new people of God. According to Catholic teaching, after all, no human being can be joined to Christ without also entering into a positive relationship with his Church, however difficult it may be to specify the precise character of that relationship.[20]

Thus the *Catechism* suggests what we could call a chastened or tempered eschatological account of the way Israel's election coheres with the universal primacy of Christ, in contrast to the thoroughly eschatological account described in the previous section. The Jewish people and the Church do not simply take separate paths to the eschaton. Rather Catholics can and should think of faithful Jewish life as, by God's design, already involving a share in the paschal mystery, and aiming at a "full and conscious" participation in the ecclesial embodiment of that mystery. At the same time, the realization of that aim will for the most part come only at the end of history, since the practice of Judaism, also by God's design, secures within history the permanent distinction of Jew from Gentile. In this way the Jewish people too are included in the vocation to ecclesial life in Christ which Catholic teaching sees as extending to every human being, while their distinctive existence and mission as the people elected by God from among the nations remains secure.

Should Catholic theology be able to understand the practice of Judaism in this way, that practice might be the middle term needed to join two doctrines whose coherence is otherwise obscure. The divinely given means by which the election of the Jewish people endures over time—their halakhic life, in expectation of the Messiah yet to come—would also be the means by which the Jewish people have their own unique place in the universal vocation of humanity to ecclesial life in Christ.

It is important to observe, though we can only touch on the matter here, that the view of Christ and Israel suggested by the *Catechism* is not entirely novel. Here too we have a development of Catholic teaching, which as such must have precedents. At one point, for example, Thomas Aquinas unexpectedly extends the figurative significance inherent in Jewish worship from the time before Christ into the Christian present. St. Thomas vigorously embraces, as we have seen, the patristic commonplace that the "ceremonial law" prefigured the future advent of Christ, and thereby united Israel by faith to Christ still to come. When he considers whether the Christian society in which he lived ought to be open to the presence of Jewish worship, however, Thomas sets aside his usual insistence that the divinely mandated worship of Abraham's descendants can only be a veridical figure of Christ before he has come in the flesh, not after. On the contrary, even now, in medieval Paris, Jewish worship "represents to us what we ourselves believe, in a kind of figure"—*quasi in figura*.[21] Christians therefore ought to accept the presence of Jewish worship.

Thomas nowhere develops the striking suggestion he makes in this one passage. Were one to do so, it would obviously require dropping Thomas's usual view that worship according to the provisions of the "old law" can no longer bear figurative witness to Jesus Christ now that he has come in the flesh. Here Thomas clearly says they do just that. As a result it would also be necessary to take leave of the idea that continued observance of Jewish law (ritual circumcision, for example) is inherently sinful—*mortifera*. Practices that attest Jesus Christ surely cannot be sinful, so if Jewish worship attests Christ "in a kind of figure," it can neither deny him nor point to some other Messiah besides him. Developing this particular idea in St. Thomas might, in other words, lead to a view of the election of Israel and the universal saving significance of Christ like that now suggested by the *Catechism*.

Is this suggestion a genuine solution to the problem with which we have been concerned, or merely another way of redescribing it? A number of difficulties would surely have to be resolved in order to see it as a real solution. For the moment we will note only one.

It might be objected that the approach just outlined reconciles the election of Israel with the call of every human being to life in Christ by severing, at least for some human beings, the connection between union with Christ and the sacraments of the Church. For this approach a real union with Jesus Christ is the effect—though not, of course, the explicit intention—of the faithful Jewish life that will sustain the elect people until the end of time. Of course many human beings do participate in the paschal mystery without the sacraments of the Church, as GS 22 teaches. But the approach I have suggested for a Catholic understanding of Jewish election evidently makes a different, and much stronger, claim. God *intends* that some human beings receive a share of the life in Christ, and thereby also a share in the life of the Church, precisely by being faithful Jews. Baptism and the entire sacramental economy into which we enter by baptism is not simply unavailable to them through no fault of their own. God does not intend it for them.

For Catholic theology, this is surely an unhappy conclusion. It seems to require an unacceptably extrinsic and juridical, if not simply arbitrary, connection between the sacramental life of the Church and life in Christ, to which every human being is called. But participation in this sacramental economy is not merely a legal requirement for life in Christ. The world is reconciled to God, and the Church is born, from Christ's total act of self-giving on the cross. This very gift of self pours forth in the baptismal water and the eucharistic blood that flow from the open side of the slain redeemer (cf. John 19:34).[22] The sacraments of the Church are thus integral to the paschal mystery in which every human being is called to share. They are the precise way in which Jesus Christ gives his own life to his body, and to us as members of his body. How God could coherently be thought to call every human being to *this* life, yet not call every human being to these sacraments, is at best unclear. This helps explain why Catholic reflection on the sacramental mediation of Christ's grace and salvation (Thomas Aquinas has served as our example) typically exhibits both a very high view of the efficacy of the "ceremonial law" before the passion of Christ, and a very low view of it after Christ. The paschal mystery, its actual unfolding in time, changes everything.

At this point we might reasonably be tempted to give up thinking about the matter and to proclaim with St. Paul that God's ways are past finding out (cf. Rom 11:33–36). All reflection on Christ and Israel ought to be such that we can rightly end with that doxology. But when it comes, it ought to be an offering of praise and glory for what we have seen, if in a mirror dimly, rather than a lament over our inability to see.

Perhaps the suggestion for understanding the mystery of Christ and Israel we have sketched out here will come to nothing and difficulties of the sort I have just raised will prove insurmountable. In that case we will nonetheless have obtained, I hope, at least some of the understanding we seek: a clearer grasp of the theological problem we face, and of why it is so difficult to resolve. That alone would help us send fewer mixed messages to our Jewish sisters and brothers. If we can make progress with this or another suggestion by coping with serious objections, then the needed effort promises something more. It holds out the hope of a genuine, if partial, *intellectus* of Catholic faith in both the universal saving mission of Christ and his Church and God's undying love for the Jewish people.

NOTES

Earlier versions of this paper were given at the University of Notre Dame and as the annual Aquinas Lecture at the Dominican School of Philosophy and Theology in Berkeley. I am grateful for the many helpful comments I received in both places.

1. Pacifici's remarks were widely reported; my account follows that of the Catholic journalist John Allen at http://ncronline.org/blogs/all-things-catholic/theologian-pope-sidelines-theology.

2. For Pope Benedict's address see *Acta Apostolicae Sedis* 102 (2010): 100–106; for an informal account, see John Allen's column in the previous note.

3. Unless otherwise noted, the translations of Vatican II texts are those on the Vatican website: http://www.vatican.va/archive/hist_councils/ii_vatican_council/index.htm.

4. "In the first place [among 'those who have not yet received the Gospel [but] are related in various ways to the people of God'] we must recall the people

to whom the testament and the promises were given and from whom Christ was born according to the flesh (Rom 9:4–5). On account of their fathers this people remains most dear to God, for God does not repent of the gifts He makes nor of the calls He issues." Thus LG 16 might more precisely be regarded as the place where the permanence of Jewish election becomes ecumenical teaching for Catholics.

5. Similarly *Ad Gentes:* "[M]issionary activity derives its reason from the will of God, 'who wishes all men to be saved and to come to the knowledge of the truth. For there is one God, and one mediator between God and men, Himself a man, Jesus Christ, who gave Himself as a ransom for all' (1 Tim 2:4–5), 'neither is there salvation in any other' (Acts 4:12). Therefore, all must be converted to Him, made known by the Church's preaching, and all must be incorporated into Him by baptism and into the Church which is His body" (AG 7). Thus "[t]he members of the Church are impelled to carry on such missionary activity by reason of the love with which they love God and by which they desire to share with all men the spiritual goods of both its life and the life to come" (AG 7).

On the universality of the Church's mission, compare the very first paragraph of the *Catechism of the Catholic Church:* "[A]t every time and in every place, God draws close to man. He calls man to seek him, to know him, to love him with all his strength. He calls together all men, scattered and divided by sin, into the unity of his family, the Church" (§1). This thought recurs in the *Catechism.* "The Church is catholic because she has been sent out by Christ on a mission to the whole of the human race" (§831, citing LG 13). "[A]ll salvation comes from Christ the Head through the Church which is his Body" (§846, citing LG 14), therefore "'the Church . . . has the obligation and also the sacred right to evangelize' all men" (§848; the internal quotation is from AG 7). *Catechism of the Catholic Church* (2nd English ed.; Vatican City: Libreria Editrice Vaticana, 1997). I have modified the rendering of §848—specifically the conclusion of the internal quotation—in light of the Latin typica of the *Catechism* at http://www.vatican.va/archive/catechism_lt/index_lt.htm).

6. This text is, to be sure, of great importance for understanding the relationship of Christ and the Church to all non-Christian religions, and not only to the Jewish people and their religion. Each case is different, however; that of the Jews and Judaism not least because Christian scripture speaks explicitly of God's purposes for this particular people. I have slightly modified the translation.

7. As a note in the conciliar text itself points out, John XXIII had already insisted (*Mater et magistra,* 180) that "by divine right the Church extends to all peoples . . . it is not, therefore, nor does it consider itself as, just an institution which is imposed on [any] people from without."

8. Esp. LG 9: The Church is "taken up (*adsumitur*) by [Christ] as an instrument for the redemption of all" (translation slightly altered), and at the same time "for each and all it [is] the visible sacrament of this saving unity."

9. "God gave the law and other special benefits to this people for the sake of the promise he made to their fathers that Christ would be born from them ... he elected this people so that from it, and not from any other, Christ would be born." (*STh* I-II, q. 98, a. 4, c; cf. I-II, q. 104 a. 2 ad 2. The translations of Aquinas are my own.)

10. Cf. *STh* I-II, q. 98, a. 4, c. The special dignity of the Jews, Aquinas observes in comment on Rom 9:4–5, belongs to them in the first place simply on account of their origin (*ex origine*). They are the nation or people (*gens*) descended from Jacob, and precisely as such they enjoy a unique dignity among all the nations: "that is, because they are descended according to the flesh from these fathers, who were most highly acceptable to God" (*In Rom* 9, 1 [no. 745]); here too Aquinas cites Deut 4:37. *S. Thomae Aquinatis Super Epistolas S. Pauli Lectura* (vol. 1; 8th ed.; ed. Raphael Cai, O.P.; Turin: Marietti, 1953), 135b.

11. Similarly, Jesus's original "sheepfold" (John 10:16) is the Jews, namely all those "who belong to the *flesh* of Israel" (*de genere carnis Israel*). *In Ioannem* 10, 4 (no. 1417), my emphasis (*S. Thomae Aquinatis Super Evangelium S. Ioannis Lectura* [5th ed.; ed. Raphael Cai; Turin/Rome: Marietti, 1952], 264b).

12. *In Rom* 11, 4 (no. 923; note the reference to Deut 4:37 at the outset of this passage).

13. "Someone might object [to the future salvation of the Jews on account of God's love for the patriarchs] by saying that the Jews, even if they used to be most beloved [to God] because of their fathers, are nevertheless barred from future salvation by the hostility they have against the gospel. But the apostle says this is false ... [H]e says, as it were, that when God gives a gift to people, or calls them, this is 'without repentance,' because God does not change his mind about this." *In Rom* 11, 4 (no. 924).

14. *In Rom* 11, 4 (no. 927); cf. 11, 2 (no. 889); 11, 3 (no. 909). Similarly, when St. Paul says that human unbelief fails to nullify the faithfulness of God (Rom 3:3), this means that God's faithfulness to the Jews—the prerogatives he gave them, rooted in the promise to Abraham that he would "multiply and magnify this people" (cf. Gen 22:17) cannot be undone by the infidelity of the chosen people. See *In Rom* 3, 1 (no. 253).

15. Thus Paul's warning to the gentile Christians in Rome (cf. Rom 11:25): "Ignorance of this mystery would condemn you" (*esset vobis damnosa*, citing I Cor 14:38). *In Rom* 11, 4 (no. 913).

16. *Epistola ad ducissam Brabantiae*, ed. Leonine, vol. 42, 375.23–25.

17. *STh* I-II, q. 103, a. 4, c: "Just as a person sins mortally who now, in confessing his faith, says that Christ is yet to be born, so also a person sins mortally who now observes the ceremonial law, which the patriarchs observed with reverence and faith." Cf. q. 104, a. 3, c: "The ceremonial laws have been voided, so that they are not only 'dead,' but even 'deadly,' for those who observe them after Christ ... [T]herefore the observance of them is contrary to true faith" (while it

remains possible, by contrast, to follow the "judicial" precepts without sin, even though they too can be used in a deadly way). Thomas takes the same position in his commentary on Romans, despite the high view of Jewish election articulated there: "The requirements of the law are not only dead, but deadly, so that anyone (*quisquis*) who observes them sins mortally" (*In Rom* 14, 1 [no. 1087]).

To be sure, the precise meaning of this dictum depends on Aquinas's complex view of what it takes for human acts to count as mortal sins. In this case, however, he seems to leave little room for mitigation. After the coming of Christ has radically altered the situation of all human acts, the good intentions of those who practice circumcision and the other ancient ceremonies cannot alter the evil character of these acts: "[T]empore autem non suo observata, [legalia] sunt facta mala. Et ideo bona intentione fieri non possunt bene." *In IV Sent*. d. 1, q. 2, a. 5, qla. 3, ad 3 (no. 317) (=*S. Thomae Aquinatis Scriptum super Sententiis* [ed. M. F. Moos; vol. 4; Paris: Lethielleux, 1947], 67).

18. *STh* III, q. 68, a. 1, ad 1.

19. "Before the coming of Christ, human beings became Christ's members by faith in his future advent, with circumcision as the sign of this faith . . . Before circumcision itself was instituted, human beings became Christ's members by faith alone, with the offering of sacrifices, by which the patriarchs professed their faith . . . After the coming of Christ, human beings [still] become members of Christ by faith . . . But faith in a reality now present is manifested by a different sign [viz., baptism] than that by which it was exhibited when the reality was still to come" (*STh* III, q. 68, a. 1, ad 1).

20. Thus the *Catechism* introduces its discussion of the unique relationship of the Jewish people to the Church by quoting LG 16: "Those who have not yet received the Gospel are related to the People of God in various ways" (§839).

21. "Ex hoc autem quod Iudaei ritus suos observant, in quibus olim praefigurabatur veritas fidei quam tenemus, hoc bonum provenit quod testimonium fidei nostrae habemus ab hostibus, et quasi in figura nobis repraesentatur quod credimus." *STh* II-II, q. 10, a. 11, c [on the *testimonium*—though not the *figura*—cf. *In Rom* 11, 2 (no. 881)]. I discuss this text in more detail in "*Quasi in Figura*: A Brief Reflection on Jewish Election, after Thomas Aquinas" and "Postscript and Prospect," *Nova et Vetera* (English ed.) 7/2 (2009): 477–84, 523–28.

22. On this see the eloquent *Catechism* §766.

Publications by Jon D. Levenson

BOOKS AND MONOGRAPHS

Inheriting Abraham: The Legacy of the Patriarch in Judaism, Christianity, and Islam. Princeton, N.J.: Princeton University Press, 2012.

Abraham between Torah and Gospel. The Père Marquette Lecture in Theology 2011. Milwaukee: Marquette University Press, 2011.

Resurrection: The Power of God for Christians and Jews. With Kevin J. Madigan. New Haven: Yale University Press, 2008.

Resurrection and the Restoration of Israel: The Ultimate Victory of the God of Life. New Haven: Yale University Press, 2006.

Esther. Old Testament Library. Louisville: Westminster/John Knox Press, 1997.

Creation and the Persistence of Evil: The Jewish Drama of Divine Omnipotence. San Francisco: Harper and Row, 1988. 2nd edition with new preface, Princeton, N.J.: Princeton University Press, 1994.

The Death and Resurrection of the Beloved Son: The Transformation of Child Sacrifice in Judaism and Christianity. New Haven: Yale University Press, 1993.

The Hebrew Bible, the Old Testament, and Historical Criticism: Jews and Christians in Biblical Studies. Louisville: Westminster/John Knox, 1993.

Sinai and Zion: An Entry into the Jewish Bible. Minneapolis: Winston Seabury, 1985.

Traditions in Transformation: Turning Points in Biblical Faith. Edited with Baruch Halpern. Winona Lake, Ind.: Eisenbrauns, 1981.

Theology of the Program of Restoration of Ezekiel 40-48. Harvard Semitic Monograph Series 10. Missoula, Mont.: Scholars Press, 1976.

The Book of Job in its Time and in the Twentieth Century. LeBaron Russell Briggs Prize Essay in English. Cambridge, Mass.: Harvard University Press, 1972.

ESSAYS

"The Meaning of Hanukkah." *Wall Street Journal,* December 16, 2011, A17.

"The Idea of Abrahamic Religions: A Qualified Dissent." *Jewish Review of Books* 1:1 (Spring 2010): 40–42, 44.

"Monotheism and Chosenness: The Abrahamic Foundation of Judaism and Roman Catholicism." Joseph Cardinal Bernardin Jerusalem Lecture, March 26, 2009. (Lecture delivered at DePaul University.) Booklet issued by the American Jewish Committee (Chicago office), the Archdiocese of Chicago, and the Jewish United Fund of Metropolitan Chicago, 2010.

"Chosenness and Its Enemies." *Commentary* 126:5 (December 2008): 25–31, with a reply to correspondents in *Commentary* 127:3 (March 2009): 7–8.

"The Logic of Lament." *The Jerusalem Report* 19:9 (August 18, 2008 / 17 Av, 5768): 44.

"Reasons for Redemption." *The Jerusalem Report* 17:26 (April 16, 2007 / 28 Nisan, 5767): 43.

"Response: The Theology of Pain and Suffering in the Jewish Tradition." Pages 126–32 in *Pain and its Transformations: The Interface of Biology and Culture.* Edited by Sarah Coakley and Kay Kaufman Shelemay. Cambridge, Mass.: Harvard University Press, 2007.

"Teaching the Texts in Contexts." *Harvard Divinity Bulletin* 35:4 (Autumn 2007): 19–21.

"The Birthday of the New Adam." *The Jerusalem Report* 17:12 (October 3, 2006 / 11 Tishrei, 5767): 39.

"Judaism Addresses Christianity." Pages 581–608 in *Religious Foundations of Western Civilization: Judaism, Christianity, and Islam.* Edited by Jacob Neusner. Nashville: Abingdon, 2006.

"Can Roman Catholicism Validate Jewish Biblical Interpretation?" *Studies in Christian-Jewish Relations* 1:1/19 (2005–6): 170–85. Online: http://escholarship.bc.edu/scjr/vol1/iss1/19. "The Agenda of *Dabru Emet.*" *Review of Rabbinic Judaism* 7 (2004): 1–26.

"The Conversion of Abraham to Judaism, Christianity, and Islam." Pages 3–40 in *The Idea of Biblical Interpretation: Essays in Honor of James L. Kugel.* Edited by Hindy Najman and Judith H. Newman. Leiden and Boston: Brill, 2004.

"Do Christians and Muslims Worship the Same God?" *The Christian Century.* 121:8 (April 20, 2004): 32–33.

Introduction to and annotations of "Genesis." Pages 8–101 in the *Oxford Jewish Study Bible.* Edited by Adele Berlin and Marc Z. Brettler. New York: Oxford University Press, 2004.

"Did God Forgive Adam? An Exercise in Comparative Midrash." Pages 148–70 in *Jews and Christians: People of God.* Edited by Carl E. Braaten and Robert Jenson. Grand Rapids: Eerdmans, 2003.

"The Fact of Death and the Promise of Life in Israelite Religion." Pages 139–54 in *The Papers of the Henry Luce III Fellows in Theology,* vol. 6. Edited by Christopher I. Wilkins. Pittsburgh: Association of Theological Schools, 2003.

"Controversy: Jewish-Christian Dialogue, Jon D. Levenson and Critics." *Commentary* 113:4 (April 2002): 17–21.

"Response: Natural and Supernatural Justice." Pages 177–85 in *Judaism and Ecology: Created World and Revealed Word.* Edited by Hava Tirosh-Samuelson. Cambridge, Mass.: Center for the Study of World Religions, Harvard Divinity School, 2002.

"Resurrection in the Torah? A Reconsideration." *CTI* [Center of Theological Inquiry] *Reflections* 6 (2002): 2–29.

"The Resurrection of the Dead and the Construction of Personal Identity in Ancient Israel." Pages 305–22 in *Congress Volume Basel 2001.* Edited by A. Lemaire. Supplements to *Vetus Testamentum.* Leiden: Brill, 2002.

"How Not to Conduct Jewish-Christian Dialogue." *Commentary* 112:5 (December 2001): 31–37.

"Religious Affirmation and Historical Criticism in Heschel's Biblical Interpretation." *Association for Jewish Studies Review* 25 (2000/2001): 25–44.

"Is Brueggemann Really a Pluralist?" *Harvard Theological Review* 93:3 (2000): 265–94.

"The New Enemies of Circumcision." *Commentary* 109:3 (March 2000): 29–36.

"The Perils of Engaged Scholarship: A Rejoinder to Jorge Pixley." Pages 239–46 in *Jews, Christians, and the Theology of the Hebrew Scriptures.* Edited by Alice Ogden Bellis and Joel S. Kaminsky. Atlanta: Society of Biblical Literature, 2000.

"The Seekers," *Commentary* 107:6 (June 1999): 38–45.

"Abraham Among Jews, Christians, and Muslims: Monotheism, Exegesis, and Religious Diversity." *ARC* [The Journal of the Faculty of Religious Studies, McGill University] 26 (1998): 5–29.

"Abusing Abraham: Traditions, Religious Histories, and Modern Misinterpretations." *Judaism* 47:3 (1998): 259–77.

"The Contradictions of A. J. Heschel." *Commentary* 106:1 (July 1998): 34–38.

"Heschel's *The Sabbath* at Century's End." *Harvard Divinity Bulletin* 28:1 (1998): 613–15.

"The Problem with Salad Bowl Religion." *First Things* 78 (December 1997): 10–12.

"The Exodus and Biblical Theology: A Rejoinder to John J. Collins." *Biblical Theology Bulletin* 26:1 (Spring 1996): 4–10.

"Response to the Five Reviews of *The Death and Resurrection of the Beloved Son*." *Dialog* 34:1 (Winter 1995): 63–66.

"Interpreting the Bible: Three Views." *First Things* 45 (August/September 1994): 42–44.

"The Bible: Unexamined Commitments of Criticism." *First Things* 30 (1992): 24–33.

Statement. Pages 69–72 in *American Jews and the Separationist Faith: The New Debate on Religion in Public Life*. Edited by David G. Dalin. Washington: Ethics and Public Policy Center, 1992.

"Theological Liberalism Aborting Itself." *The Christian Century* 109:5 (February 5–12, 1992): 139, 141, 143, 145–47, 149.

"Zion Traditions." Pages 1098–1102 in vol. 6 of *The Anchor Bible Dictionary*. Edited by David N. Freedman. 6 vols. New York: Doubleday, 1992.

"Cataclysm, Survival, and Regeneration in the Hebrew Bible." Pages 39–68 in *Confronting Omnicide: Jewish Reflections on Weapons of Mass Destruction*. Edited by Daniel Landes. Northvale, N.J.: Jason Aronson, 1991.

"Exodus and Liberation." *Horizons in Biblical Theology* 13 (1991): 134–74.

"The God of Abraham and the Enemies of 'Eurocentrism.'" *First Things* 16 (October 1991): 15–21.

"The Good Friday–Passover Connection." Op-ed piece in the *New York Times*, March 29, 1991, A23.

"The Hermeneutical Defense of Buber's Hasidism: A Critique and Counterstatement." *Modern Judaism* 11 (1991): 297–320.

"Must We Accept the Other's Self-Understanding?" *Journal of Religion* 71 (1991): 558–67.

"Indoctrination is Not Education." A brief statement in "Opening Academia Without Closing It Down: A Campus Forum on Multiculturalism." *New York Times*, December 9, 1990.

"A Response to Professor Greenstein." Pages 47–54 in *The State of Jewish Studies*. Edited by Shaye Cohen and Edward Greenstein. Detroit: Wayne State University, 1990.

"Theological Consensus or Historicist Evasion? Jews and Christians in Biblical Studies." Pages 109–45 in *Hebrew Bible or Old Testament? Studying the Bible in Judaism and Christianity*. Edited by John J. Collins and Roger Brooks. Notre Dame, Ind.: University of Notre Dame, 1990.

"Covenant and Consent: Biblical Reflections on the Occasion of the 200th Anniversary of the United States Constitution." Pages 71–82 in *The Judeo-Christian Tradition and the U.S. Constitution: Proceedings of a Conference at Annenberg Research Institute, November 16–17, 1987*. Edited by David M. Goldenberg. Philadelphia: Annenberg Research Institute, 1989.

"Liberation Theology and the Exodus." *Midstream* 35:7 (October 1989): 30–36.

"The Eighth Principle of Judaism and the Literary Simultaneity of Scripture." *Journal of Religion* 68 (1988): 205–25.

"The Hebrew Bible, the Old Testament, and Historical Criticism." Pages 19–59 in *The Future of Biblical Studies: The Hebrew Scriptures*. Edited by R. E. Friedman and H. G. M. Williamson. Semeia Studies. Decatur, Ga.: Scholars, 1987.

"The Sources of Torah: Psalm 119 and the Modes of Revelation in Second Temple Judaism." Pages 559–74 in *Ancient Israelite Religion*. Edited by Patrick D. Miller, et al. Philadelphia: Fortress, 1987.

"Why Jews Are Not Interested in Biblical Theology." Pages 281–307 in *Judaic Perspectives on Ancient Israel*. Edited by J. Neusner et al. Philadelphia: Fortress, 1987.

"Hebrew Bible in Colleges and Universities." *Religious Education* 81 (1986): 37–44.

"The Jerusalem Temple in Devotional and Visionary Experience." Pages 32–61 in *Jewish Spirituality from the Bible through the Middle Ages*. Edited by A. Green. New York: Crossroad, 1986.

"A Jewish Studies Location for Biblical Studies: Does It Make a Difference?" *Association for Jewish Studies Newsletter* 36 (Fall 1986): 16–19.

"Is There a Counterpart in the Hebrew Bible to New Testament Anti-Semitism?" *Journal of Ecumenical Studies* 22 (1985): 242–60.

"A Technical Meeting for $N'M$ in the Hebrew Bible." *Vetus Testamentum* 25 (1985): 61–67.

"The Universal Horizon of Biblical Particularism." Pamphlet for the American Jewish Committee, New York. American Jewish Committee, 1985. Reprinted with small revisions as pages 143–69 in *The Bible and Ethnicity*. Edited by Mark G. Brett. Leiden: Brill, 1996.

"Ezekiel in the Perspective of Two Commentators." *Interpretation* 38 (1984): 210–17.

"The Last Four Verses in Kings." *Journal of Biblical Literature* 103 (1984): 353–61.

"Some Unnoticed Connotations in Jer 20:9." *Catholic Biblical Quarterly* 46 (1984): 223–25.

"The Temple and the World." *Journal of Religion* 64 (1984): 275–98.

"Covenant and Commandment." *Tradition: A Journal of Orthodox Jewish Thought* 21 (1983): 42–51.

"The Paronomasia of Solomon's Seventh Petition." *Hebrew Annual Review* 6 (1982): 131–35.

"Yehezkel Kaufmann and Mythology." *Conservative Judaism* 36:2 (1982): 36–43.

"From Temple to Synagogue: 1 Kings 8." Pages 142–66 in *Traditions in Transformation*. Edited by B. Halpern and J. D. Levenson. Winona Lake, Ind.: Eisenbrauns, 1981.

"The Political Import of David's Marriages." Coauthored with Baruch Halpern. *Journal of Biblical Literature* 99 (1980): 507–18.

"The Theologies of Commandment in Biblical Israel." *Harvard Theological Review* 77 (1980): 17–33.

"The Davidic Covenant and Its Modern Interpreters." *Catholic Biblical Quarterly* 41 (1979): 205–19.

"1 Samuel 25 as Literature and as History." *Catholic Biblical Quarterly* 40 (1978): 11–28; revised version published as "1 Samuel 25 as Literature and History." Pages 220–42 in *Literary Interpretation of Biblical Narratives*, vol. 2. Edited by Kenneth R. R. Gros Louis. Nashville: Abingdon, 1982.

"On the Promise to the Rechabites." *Catholic Biblical Quarterly* 38 (1976): 508–14.

"Poverty and the State in Biblical Thought." *Judaism* 25 (1976): 230–41.

"The Scroll of Esther in Ecumenical Perspective." *Journal of Ecumenical Studies* 13 (1976): 440–52.

"Textual and Semantic Notes on Nah. 1:7–8." *Vetus Testamentum* 25 (1975): 792–94.

"Who Inserted the Book of the Torah?" *Harvard Theological Review* 68:3–4 (1975): 203–33.

"Life with Jews is Not Yet Jewish Life," *Sh'ma* 3 (1973): 110–12.

"The Spindle-Whorl Inscription from Chatal Hüyük: A Forgery." *Bulletin of the American Schools of Oriental Research* 209 (1973): 37–40.

"The Grundworte of Pier delle Vigne." *Forum Italicum* 5 (1971): 499–513.

Doctoral Dissertations Supervised by Jon D. Levenson

Noble, John T. "'Let Ishmael Live Before You': Finding a Place for Hagar's Son in the Priestly Tradition." Department of Near Eastern Languages and Civilizations, Harvard University, 2013.

Nussberger, Mark A. "'Is the Lord in Our Midst or Not?': Conceptions of Divine Presence in Ancient Jewish and Christian Interpretations of the Calf Incident." Harvard Divinity School, 2012.

Hancock, Rebecca. "Esther and the Politics of Negotiation: An Investigation of Public and Private Spaces in Relationship to Possibilities for Women's Role as Royal Counselor." Department of Near Eastern Languages and Civilizations, Harvard University, 2012.

Rainbow, Jesse. "Textual Loss and Recovery in the Hebrew Bible." Department of Near Eastern Languages and Civilizations, Harvard University, 2012.

Windham, Mary Ruth. "An Examination of the Relationship Between Humans and Animals in the Hebrew Bible." Department of Near Eastern Languages and Civilizations, Harvard University, 2012.

Held, Shai A. "Reciprocity and Responsiveness: Self-Transcendence and the Dynamics of Covenant in the Theology and Spirituality of Abraham Joshua Heschel." Committee on the Study of Religion, Harvard University, 2011.

Billings, Rachel. "'Israel Served the Lord': The Book of Joshua as Paradoxical Portrait of Faithful Israel." Department of Near Eastern Languages and Civilizations, Harvard University, 2010.

Kaplan, Jonathan. "A Divine Love Song: The Emergence of the Theo-erotic Interpretation of the Song of Songs in Ancient Judaism and Early Chistianity." Department of Near Eastern Languages and Civilizations, Harvard University, 2010.

Crawford, Cory. "Architecture and Cultural Memory: Iconography and the Visual Program of the Solomonic Temple in Historical, Political, and Social Context." Department of Near Eastern Languages and Civilizations, Harvard University, 2009.

Goering, Gregory Schmidt. "'To Whom Has Wisdom's Root Been Revealed?': Ben Sira and the Election of Israel." Harvard Divinity School, 2006.

Halverson-Taylor, Martien. "The Development of Exile as Metaphor in the Hebrew Bible." Department of Near Eastern Languages and Civilizations, Harvard University, 2006.

Short, John Randall. "The Story of David's Rise as Political Apology: A Reconsideration." Harvard Divinity School, 2006.

Schifferdecker, Kathryn. "Out of the Whirlwind: Creation Theology in the Book of Job." Harvard Divinity School, 2005.

Frechette, Christopher. "The Name of the Ritual: Investigating Ancient Mesopotamian 'Hand-lifting' Rituals with Implications for the Interpretation of Genre in the Psalms." Harvard Divinity School, 2005.

Wong, Fook-Kong. "Manna Revisited: A Study of the Mythological and Interpretive Contexts of Manna." Harvard Divinity School, 1998.

Laniak, Timothy. "From the Margin to the Middle: The Pattern of Shame and Honor in the Book of Esther." Harvard Divinity School, 1997.

Lyke, Larry. "'And the two of them struggled in the field': Intertextuality and the Interpretation of the Mashal of the Wise Woman of Tekoa in 2 Samuel 14:1–20." Harvard Divinity School, 1996.

Kaminsky, Joel S. "Punishment Displacement in the Hebrew Bible." University of Chicago, 1993.

Schramm, Brooks. "The Opponents of Third Isaiah: A Contribution to the Social History of the Restoration." University of Chicago, 1993.

Contributors

Gary A. Anderson, Hesburgh Professor of Catholic Theology, University of Notre Dame

Leora Batnitzky, Professor of Religion, Princeton University

Richard J. Clifford, S.J., Professor of Old Testament, Boston College School of Theology and Ministry

W. Randall Garr, Professor of Religious Studies, University of California, Santa Barbara

Greg Schmidt Goering, Assistant Professor of Religious Studies, University of Virginia

Matthias Henze, Watt J. and Lilly G. Jackson Professor in Biblical Studies, Rice University

Marc Hirshman, Mandel Professor of Jewish Education, The Melton Centre for Jewish Education, The Hebrew University of Jerusalem

Joel S. Kaminsky, Professor, Department of Religion, Smith College

James Kugel, Chair of the Institute for the History of Jewish Bible, Bar Ilan University

Kevin Madigan, Winn Professor of Ecclesiastical History, Harvard Divinity School

Bruce D. Marshall, Lehman Professor of Christian Doctrine, Perkins School of Theology, Southern Methodist University

R. W. L. Moberly, Professor of Theology and Biblical Interpretation, Durham University

Mark Reasoner, Associate Professor of Biblical Theology, Marian University

Kathryn Schifferdecker, Associate Professor of Old Testament, Luther Seminary

Brooks Schramm, Professor of Biblical Studies, Lutheran Theological Seminary, Gettysburg, Pennsylvania

Index of Sources

BIBLE, APOCRYPHA, AND OTHER ANCIENT TEXTS

Genesis	16, 45–46,	1:13–31	9
	59, 65, 67,	1:14–19	9, 149
	91–95, 115,	1:20–23	9
	125, 131–32,	1:24–25	9
	139, 170, 182,	1:24–31	9
	188, 220–22,	1:26	10
	229, 234, 237,	1:26–31	9
	243, 253, 281,	1:27	84
	283–93, 298,	1:28	18–20
	300–302, 326	1:29	20
1	1–22	1:31	14
1–11	164, 287, 300	2–9	19
1:1–2	9, 148	2–11	18
1:1–2:3	326	2:1–3	9
1:1–2:4	1–22	2:1	10
1:1–2:4a	148, 154, 169	2:1–3	11
1:2	154	2:2	11
1:3–5	9	2:3	11
1:3–13	9	2:16–17	289
1:6–8	9	3	285
1:9–10	9	3:15	284, 285
1:9–13	9	4:1	301
1:10–11	9	4:15	87
1:11–13	9	5	217

Index of Sources

Genesis (*cont.*)		13:17	39
5:28–6:11	217	13:18	95
5:32	218	14:12	36
6	224, 230, 234	14:12b	36
6–9	57	14:13	36
6:1–4	211, 216–34	14:14–16	36
6:3	221	14:19	38
6:4	234	14:19bβ	38
7:1–2a	75	14:21–24	36
7:2	75	14:22bα	38
7:2b	75	14:22bβ	38
7:2ba	75	15	36
8:1	104	15:1a	38
8:13	15	15:1b	36
8:14–17	37	15:1bαα	38
8:20–22	222	15:1bαb	38
9:1–17	316	15:1bβ	38
9:10	234	15:1–6	24
9:25	162	15:2a	36
10–11	19–20	15:2aαb	39
10:10	20	15:2aβ	38
11	127	15:3	37
11:1–9	182	15:4	37
12	90–91, 136	15:4–5	37
12–24	300	15:5	74, 127
12–50	8	15:5a	37
12:1–3	159, 164	15:5b	37
12:2	37	15:6	24, 36–40
12:3a	162	15:6a	24, 37
12:3b	90	15:6b	23, 24
12:7	95	15:7bα	23
12:8	38	15:7bβ	23
12:16	277	15:8	148
12:17	45	15:8bα	39
13:4	38	15:8bβ	39
13:12	36	15:9–11	23
13:13	218	15:17	182
13:15–16	37	15:18a	23
13:16	127	15:18–21	39

15:18b–21	23	25:19ff.	295, 302
15:20–21	74	25:19–34	282, 291
17:1	108–9	25:21	288
17:5	23	25:21b	291
17:14	65	25:22	298
18:17–19	107	25:23	260, 294
20:7	95	25:27	95
20:14–16	277	26	299
20:17	95	26:4	74
20:18	45	26:13–14	95
21	304	26:24	109
21:17–21	128	26:25	95
22	24, 95, 99, 109, 131	27:29	162
		27:33	45
22:1	244	27:40	262
22:1–2	128	28:3	109
22:2	117, 184	28:13–14	159
22:3	249	28:14	109
22:4	110	30:27	45
22:5–6a	130	30:29–30	95
22:6b–7	130	30:30	109
22:7	140	30:43	109
22:10	110	31:54	95
22:11	128	33:3b	282
22:12	95, 99, 109–10	33:19	95
22:13	95	34:8	78
22:15–18	126	35:11	109
22:17	74, 128, 349	35:14	95
22:17–18	159	35:22	46
22:18	285	35:29	95
22:20–23	128	36:28	108
22:20–24	127	36:33–34	93
22:21	110	37–50	300
24:60	127	37:33	28
25	281, 290–96, 304	37:35	129
25–36	300	38	142
25–50	283	39:19	93
25:8	95, 109	42:38	129
		43:14	109

Genesis (cont.)		14:28	34
44:29	129	14:30	34
45:26	28	14:31	31
45:27–28a	30	14:31aα	34
48:3	109	14:31aβ–b	34
48:19	270	15	214
48:29	271	15:7–10	169
49	304	15:8	148, 152
49:4	46	15:13	15
49:10	285, 297	15:20–21	214
		16	11
Exodus	15, 93, 214	16:17–20	12
3:8	74	16:23	11
3:17	35, 74	16:29–30	12
3:31bβ	35	19:1a	164
4	30	19:3–6	108
4:1	30–31	19:3b–8	164
4:5	30	19:5–6	107
4:8a	31	19:9	31, 34
4:8b	31	19:16	262
4:8–9	30	20	213
4:9	31	20:1	205
4:22	92, 276, 281	20:8–11	12
4:22–23	108	20:12	25
4:31	35	20:19–22	213
6:3	95	22:28b	67
9:16	262	23:23–33	72
12:35–36	277	25–31	14
13:5	74	25:1–30:10	14
14	34	25:1–31:17	12
14:10	34	25:37	15
14:13	34–35	28:1–39	15
14:14	25	30:11–16	14
14:14a	34	30:17–21	14
14:19–20	34	30:22–33	14
14:21	34	30:34–38	14
14:24b	34	31:1–11	14
14:25b	34	31:12–17	12
14:27	34	31:16	12

31:17	12, 14	21:8	16
32	47	23:19	241
32–34	47	25:42	109
32:9–10	278	26	258
32:10	46	26:14–39	257
32:13	159	26:33	257, 265
32:25–29	55, 65	26:36	257, 265
33:3	278	26:38	271
33:5	278	26:42–45	108
33:23	282	27	85
34:8	78	27:20–21	85
34:11–16	72	27:28	85
34:15–16	271		
39:32	15	Numbers	48, 209, 221, 223
39:43	15	1–25	48
40:2	15	3:13	169
40:9–11:9	15	6:26	205
40:33b–34	15	8:17	169
		12:7–8	109
Leviticus	16, 65, 84	13	93, 234
11	16–17	13–14	33, 47
11:2–8	16	13:2	30
11:3	17	13:33	234
11:9–12	16	14:11	31
11:20–23	16–17	14:20–38	47
11:20–26	17	15:19–20	169
11:27	16–17	16:5	159
11:29	16	16:7	159
11:41–42	16	18:1–7	161
11:44	16	18:19	169
11:45	16	18:24	169
17:4	65	18:26	169
17:9	65	20:7–12	32
18:29	65	20:12	31
19:2	16	22–24	48
20:7	16	23:19–21a	48
20:18	65	26	48
20:26	16	26–36	48
21:6–8	159	26:63–65	47

Numbers (cont.)

31:28	169
31:52	169
32:20–22	19
32:22	19
32:29	19

Deuteronomy

	47, 70–79, 87–88, 97, 116, 133, 137, 213, 265, 278
1	33
1:8	33
1:10	74, 159
1:25b	33
1:26	33
1:30–31	33
1:32	31, 33
2:12	75
2:21	75
3:2	36
4:29–31	54
4:37	336, 337, 349
5:12–15	13
5:16	25
5:22–31	77
5:26	213
6:4–9	79
6:20–25	79
6:23	83
6:25	83
7	77–83
7:1	80, 81, 83
7:1–2a	75
7:1–5	71–73, 75–78, 88
7:1–26	83
7:2	75–76, 83
7:2b	75
7:2bα	75
7:3	80, 271, 279
7:3–4	75, 87
7:4	75
7:5	76
7:6	79, 88, 335, 340
7:6–7	109
7:6–8	78, 88, 164
7:7–8	107, 108
7:10	75
7:17	74
7:17–19	74
7:24	75
8:20	75
9	47
9:1–3	74
9:3	75
9:3–5	30
9:4–9	164
9:8	75
9:13–14	278
9:14	75
9:23	31
9:24	25
10:15	164
10:17	205
10:22	74
12:5	180
12:11	180
12:14	180
13:16 (Eng. 13:15)	70
14:1	276
14:1–21	17
14:21	161
14:23	180
15:20	180
16:18–19	18
18:13	109
18:18–22	213
20	81

20:3	36	2:11	83
20:3–4	35	2:12	83
20:16	76, 87	5:13–15	82
20:16–18	71–72, 76, 88	10:28	87
20:17	75	10:30	87
21:10–14	87	10:33	87
21:11	78	10:37	87
21:16	281	10:39–40	87
22:7–34	83	11:11	87
25:5–10	142	11:14	87
28	303	18:1	19
28:7	74	23:6–13	279
28:8	109	23:9–13	271
28:12	109	24:2–13	108
28:66	31, 33	24:32	95
30	260, 272		
30:12–14	260	Judges	54, 116, 219
30:15–19	254	1:21–33	71
31:23–30	178	5:4–5	151, 169
31:27–29	277	11:20	41
32	179		
32:1–43	260, 265	Ruth	136, 142
32:5–6	276	1:8–9	135
32:7–9	169	1:12–13	135
32:9–10	98	2:11–12	136
32:13	98	3:12	142
32:14	110		
32:18–19	276	1 Samuel	49
32:33	265	2:27–31	49
32:43	267, 275	2:27–36	61
33:2–3	169	2:30	49–50
33:3	152	2:35	51
33:26	151	2:35–36	50
33:29	36	9:1–2	51
34:9	178	10:1	51
		10:10	51
Joshua	49, 65, 69, 81–83, 87, 116, 178–80	10:20–21	51
		11	51
		13:13–14	52

1 Samuel (*cont.*)

15	52, 85
15:3	69
15:9	69
15:28	52
15:31–32	52
15:32–33	69
16	52
16:14	52
24:7 (Eng. 24:6)	52
27:8–11	34
27:12	31, 33
28:2	34
28:6	52
31:4	52

2 Samuel

1:14	52
3:18	109
6:21	194
7	50, 53
7:11b–16	65
7:16	35
11	86
22:3	35
22:8	151
22:8–16	169
22:10–13	151
22:14	152
22:15	152
22:16	152

1 Kings

2:27	65
5:10	108
8	200–201, 206–7
8:16	194
8:23–53	200
8:30	201
8:39	203
8:41–43	66, 200, 203
8:43	203
8:44	207
9:3	169
9:4–5	35
9:7	169
9:20–21	71
10:6	28
10:7	28
10:7aα	28
11:32–38	109
11:34	109, 194
19:10	259
19:14	259
19:18	57
22:19	10
25:3–12	257

2 Kings

5	66
9:7	109
16:5	35
16:7–9	35
17:7–14	32
17:14	31
17:24–41	271
19:11	86
23:27	65

1 Chronicles	207
1:42	108
7:14	207
23:1	109

2 Chronicles	207
6	201

6:32	201	9:14	13
6:34	201	10:31 (Heb 10:32)	13
6:38	201	13:15–22	13
7:12	180	13:23–28	279
7:14	207		
7:16	169	Job	92–97, 102, 107, 109–11, 116, 119, 121, 125, 131, 133, 141–42, 270
7:20	169		
9:5	28		
9:6	28		
9:6aα	28		
20:7	182, 192	1:1	95–96, 99, 109
20:20	28, 31, 35	1:2	95
23:6	159	1:3	93, 95
28:4	194	1:5	95
30:8	169	1:6–11	120
31:18	159	1:8	96, 99, 109–10
32:7	28–29	1:9	119
32:8a	29	1:9–10	97, 121
32:15	28, 31	1:10	95
32:17	28	1:11	110
35:3	159	1:20–21	120
36:13	278	1:21	103
36:14	169	1:22	120
		2:3	96, 99, 109, 120
Ezra	81, 83, 271	2:4–5	120
7:14–23	277	2:5	110
8:28	159	2:9 (LXX)	141
9–10	80	2:9–10	121
9:1–2	80	2:12	110
9:1–10:44	279	3	105
10:8	81	3:17	103
		3:19	103
Nehemiah	24, 271	4:18	31, 35
1:9	180	5:17	109
9	23	6:4	109
9:7	172	6:14	109
9:7–8a	23	7	101
9:7b	23	7:5–6	103

Job (cont.)
7:12 101
7:17–19 101
9:13 154
9:16 27
9:17–18 27
10:11–12 98
10:18–19 104
12 110
12:9 109
13:15 101
13:20–22 101
14:13–15 104
14:15 99
14:19 104
15:5 35
15:15 31
15:22 26
15:23b 26
15:31 31, 35
17:1 104
19:25–27 104
19:26 104
19:26–27a 105
19:26a 110
20:12 25–26
22:29 25
23:11–12 99
24:22 31, 33
26:12 154
29 26, 98
29:2–5 98
29:6 98, 110
29:24 26, 35
31 98–99
31:1–40 276
31:13–15 99
31:16–19 99
31:26–28 99
31:32 99
38:1 101
38:8–11 154
39:9a 33
39:11a 33
39:12 31, 33
39:24 40
40:13 (LXX) 278
40:25–32
(Eng. 41:1–8) 154
41:3 278
42:3 101
42:5 105
42:7 101
42:7–8 96, 101
42:8 96
42:8–9 95
42:11 95
42:14–15 105
42:17 95
42:17b–17c (LXX) 108

Psalms 243, 265
2:9 260
3:4 36
18:8 151
18:8–16 169
18:10–13 151
18:13 152
18:14 152
18:16 152
23 206
27:2–3 27
27:4–5 27
27:9 27
27:12 27
27:13 27
27:14 27

29:3	14	89:6–38	14
29:10	14	89:10–15 (Eng.	
33:6–9	148	89:9–14)	53
35:5	163	89:11 (Eng. 89:10)	154
36:13 (Eng. 36:12)	163	89:20 (Eng. 89:19)	169
37:25–26	134	89:20–22	193
39:10–13	110	89:29	35
44 (LXX 43)	257, 258, 276	92:3–5	193
44:12–16	258	93	14
46	14	93:1–4	154
48	14	97:1–2	193
48:13–15	14	98:4–8	193
65:2–5	204	99:6–9	193
65:3	205	100:5	193
65:7–8 (Eng.		100:9	193
65:6–7)	154	102:4–103:8	193
68:5 (Eng. 68:4)	151	103:21	10
68:7–8 (Eng.		104:5–9	193
68:7–9)	169	104:6–9	154
68:9	151	104:24	148
68:30	208	105	108
68:31–34 (Eng.		105:26	109
68:32–35)	169	106:12	35
74	154	106:16	159
74:12–17	154	106:24	24
76	14	106:43	25
78	51	115:16	10
78:17–22a	33	116:9–10a	33
78:22	14, 31, 35	119	206
78:56–67	51	119:66	31, 35
78:67	65	139	98
78:67–68	51	139:12	25
78:68–72	51	139:13	98
78:70	108, 194	148:2	10
78:80	109		
79:12	87	Proverbs	133, 160
82	326	1:4	160
89	53	1:32	160
89:4–5	35	3:19	148

Proverbs (*cont.*)

6:31	87
7:7	160
8:5	160
8:29	154
8:30	148
10:2	123, 133
11:27	160
13:21	160
14:15	31
14:15a	28
14:18	160
14:19	160
14:32	163
17:13	160
17:20	160
19:17	142
22:3	160
24:16	87
26:25	31, 35
27:12	160

Ecclesiastes

3:16–21	276
7:14	160
9:2–3	276

Song of Songs	266

Isaiah

	29, 35, 54, 56, 58, 96, 175, 199–209, 260, 265
1:18	25
2:2–4	107
6:13	57
7:1	35
7:4	35
7:4–9	39
7:9b	35
7:11–12	39
7:14	285
8:14 (LXX)	259, 261
9	175, 300
10	267
10:5	267
10:15	267
10:24	267
10:24–34 (LXX)	267
10:26	267
10:27	267
10:28 (LXX)	267
10:34	267
11:10	265
11:11–12	265
13–23	212
20:3	109
24–27	212
28	261
28–33	212
28:11	289
28:15 (LXX)	261
28:16 (LXX)	259, 261, 263
28:17-18 (LXX)	261
29:14	288
30:33	235
33:12–14	235
34:6–7	262
34–35	212
37:11	86
40:1	103
40:2	55
40:6	292
40:15	184
40:17	184
41:8	175, 192
41:8–9	97
41:8–10	108

41:20	109	60:3	107
42	109	65	58, 61
42:1	109, 175	65:9	109
43:6	276	65:13–15	57
43:10	29, 31, 107, 109, 175	66	209, 272
		66:19–20	270
43:11–13	29	66:23	208
43:14–21	107		
43:20	175	Jeremiah	56, 96, 102, 186, 211, 231, 260, 267–68, 270, 278
44:1	175		
44:1–2	109		
44:1–3	108		
44:2	175	1:5	169
44:20	321	3:19	276
44:21–28	108	7	51
44:24–45:6	277	7:12–15	51
45:1–7	108	9:15	257, 265
45:4	175	12:6	31, 36
45:9	260, 267	18:7–9	260
45:11	276	20:7–18	276
45:13	260	25:9	96
49	109	25:12–14	96
49:7	174–75	26:7	102
50	109	27:6	96
50:8–9	258	30:14	103
51:1–2	192	31	269
51:9–11	107	31:3	270
52–53	109	31:7	57
53	300	31:9	92, 276
53:1	28	31:18–19	56
54	57, 60	31:20	276
54:5–10	57	31:31	278
55:1–5	66	31:33	269
56	66	31:34	271
56:1–8	58	31:35–37	56
56:6	200	33:23–26	108
56:6–7	199	33:24	65
56:7	199–209	38:31 (LXX)	278
56–66	65	38:34 (LXX)	268, 269, 271

Jeremiah (cont.)
40:14   28, 31
43:10   96

Lamentations 27, 205
3:44   205
4:12   27
4:21   108

Ezekiel   48, 55–56, 63,
             111, 268
2:3–4   278
14:14   110
14:20   110
20:33–38   55
34:23–24   109
36:22–28   55
37:11–28   108
40:46   159
42:13   159
44:15–16   159
45:1   169
45:4   159
45:13   169
48:8–9   169
48:20   169

Daniel
7   187

Hosea   57, 60, 267–68
1:5   267
2:1   276
2:2   267, 268
11:1   196, 276

Joel   260

Amos   54
3:1–2   108

3:2   48, 54
4:2   257
4:6   257
5:5   257

Jonah   31
1   66
3:4–5   34
3:5   31
3:6   34
3:7   34

Micah
7:5   31

Habakkuk   27
1:2–4   276
1:5   27
1:6–11   27, 277
1:13   276
2:9–11   277
2:15–16   277
3:3–15   151, 169
3:6   151
3:10   152
3:13–14   151

Haggai
2:23   109

Zechariah
8   272
8:23   203

Malachi
1   262
1:2–3   60, 262, 267, 294
1:3–4   261

Index of Sources 375

1:5	277	Ben Sira (Sirach/	
1:11	277	Ecclesiasticus)	24, 125, 144–69
3:24	277	1:1	145
		1:1–10	156
Tobit	115–43	1:2	145
1:10–15	117	1:3	145
1:14	142	1:4	145, 165
1:19–20	117	1:5a	148
2–4	116	1:6	145
2:1–4	118	1:9a	165
2:8	118	1:9b	145
2:10	119	1:9b–10a	146
2:11	140	1:9b–10b	145, 155, 165–66
2:11–12	141	10a	145
2:13	124	10b	145
2:14b	122	16:28	148
3:2	122	17:1–10	163
3:6	123	17:6–7	156
3:7	124	24:1–12	166
3:11	124	24:3a	147
3:16–17	124	24:4–5	166
4:1–3a	123	24:6	166
4:2	124	24:7	166
4:2–3a	123	24:8	166
4:9–10	123	24:9a	165
4:20ff.	123	33:7–12	165
4:20–21	142	33:7–15	146
5:10	134	33:7a–9b	157
6:4b–5	130	33:7b	157
6:6a	130	33:8a	159
6:6b–7	130	33:10a–12d	157
6:12	129	33:11	166
6:14–15	129	33:11a	164
12:11a	119	33:11–12	157
12:13–14	121	33:12	159, 161
12:13–14a	140	33:12a	159
12:14a	119	33:12b	159
14	116	33:12c	162
14:5–7	277, 278	33:12d	163

Ben Sira (*cont.*)

33:14–15	165
33:14a	165
33:14c	157
33:15	165
33:15a	165
39:4	163
39:17a	148
39:31	148
40:19	125
42:15–25	147
42:15–43:33	147
42:15c	147
42:16	156
42:18a	154
42:22	148
42:25b	148
43:1–12	147, 150, 157
43:2b	150
43:3–4	149
43:5ab	149
43:8c	150
43:10a	149
43:11–12	149
43:13–26	147
43:13a	151
43:13a–17b	151
43:16b–17b	148
43:17a	152
43:17c–22b	152
43:21–22	153
43:22	150
43:23–26	154
43:23a	154
43:23b	154
43:25b	154
43:26b	148
43:27–33	147
43:27a	155
43:28a	155
43:28b	155
43:28b–29a	155
43:29a	155
43:30b	155
43:30d	155
43:31ab	155
43:32a	155
43:33	165
43:33a	165
43:33ab	165
43:33b	165

Matthew

21:33–44	59

Mark

1:11	236
13	270

John

1:12–13	304
3:6	292
4:22	295, 296
8:39–59	59
10:16	349
19:17	248
19:34	346

Acts

4:12	338, 348
4:36–37	239
9:27	239
11:22–26	239
13:1–2	239
13:34	194
13:44–49	279
14:1	350
14:4	239

Index of Sources 377

15:1	274	8:33	257, 258
18:1–8	279	8:33–36	258
19:8–10	279	8:35	257, 262, 265
28:17–28	279	8:36	258, 276
		9	258, 263
Romans	60, 240, 256, 257–59, 266, 271, 274–75, 291, 294, 304, 309, 350	9–11	60, 257, 258, 259, 260, 264, 266, 269, 273, 276
		9:1	349
		9:1–5	60
1:3	274	9:1–13	291
1:16	276	9:3–5	258
2:9–10	276	9:4	258
2:9–11	206	9:4–5	260, 348, 349
2:17	276	9:6	258
2:17–24	257	9:6–9	269
2:28–29	276	9:6–18	59
2:29	269	9:6b	291, 294
3:1	349	9:7	260
3:1–2	260	9:7–13	262
3:1–9	257	9:8	291
3:3	259, 349	9:9	260
3:3–6	258	9:10ff.	294
3:8	274	9:11–12	291
3:9	276	9:12	295
4	269	9:13	261, 267, 270
4:5	24	9:17	262
5:12	279	9:17–21	263
6:1–23	274	9:20	267
8	61, 263, 264	9:20–33	259, 267
8:18	258	9:22	260, 267
8:19	257	9:24	276
8:21	257	9:25–26	267, 268
8:28–39	61	9:25–32	341
8:29	263	9:27–28	267
8:29–30	263	9:27–29	261, 269–70, 278
8:30	257, 258	9:30–33	259
8:30–31	274	9:30–10:4	257
8:32	334	9:31	258, 259

Romans (cont.)		11:27a	268, 278
9:33	259, 267	11:28	260
10	260, 267	11:28–29	60, 333
10:5–8	272	11:28–31	270
10:6–8	260	11:28b–29	62
10:9	272	11:29	337
10:12	276	11:32	257, 273, 275
10:18–21	267	11:33–36	270, 278, 347
11	61, 269, 271, 272	11:34a	278
11:1	258, 259, 268, 272	12	264
		12–15	264
11:1–5	268, 270	12:17	264
11:1–15	269, 270	12:19	264
11:1–12:39	262	13:1	264
11:2	258	13:1–7	264
11:2–4	259	13:4	257, 262, 264, 265
11:3	349		
11:4	349	13:34a	278
11:7	272	15:4	287
11:7–10	272	15:9–12	265, 275
11:10	272	15:10	265, 275
11:11–12	60	15:16	274
11:12	261, 272	15:30–32	260, 266, 279
11:14–15	261		
11:15	268	1 Corinthians	
11:17–24	270	6:9–11	274
11:20–21	60	9:20–21	275
11:20–23	266	10:1–4	268
11:23	60	10:1–13	266
11:25	258, 269, 270, 271, 272, 273, 279, 349	10:6	266
		10:13	266
		10:18	268
11:25–26	271	14:23–24	279
11:25–27	60, 265, 270, 272	14:38	349
11:25–32	261	2 Corinthians	274
11:26	258, 266, 268, 269, 273	Galatians	256, 274
11:27	267, 269, 270	3	269

3:16	274, 285
3:19	285
3:26–29	275
3:28	275
3:29	315
5:6	24
6:16	269

Ephesians
1:4	195
2:14–16	275
5:21–28	275
6:5–9	275

Philippians
3:3	269

Colossians
3:18–25	275

2 Thessalonians
2:3	278

1 Timothy
2:4–5	348
3:2	288

Hebrews
	239
11:8–11	24
11:17–18	24
12:22–24	266

James
2:21	24
2:22–24	24
2:26	24

Revelation
19:20	235
21:8	235

Ancient Near Eastern Writings/ Inscriptions

Soreg inscription	206
Enuma Elish	326
Moabite Stone line 17	70
Sabean Text RES 3945	70

POST-BIBLICAL JEWISH TEXTS

Pseudepigrapha

1 Baruch
3:6–8	278

2 Baruch 171, 186–91
1:1–9:1	186
3:5	186
5:1	186
8:2	186
14:6–7	188
14:12	188
14:18–19	188
14:19	194
15:7	188
15:7–8	189
21:11	188
21:21	187

2 Baruch (cont.)
21:24	188
21:24–25	188
29:2	197
29:2–30:5	188
40:1–3	187
40:2	187
48:19b–20	187
48:22	198
48:27	198
52:6	189
52:7	188
57:1–3	196
57:2	196
63:10	197
71:1	197
72:2–6	198
77:3	198
77:4	187
82:2	190
82:3–9	190
82:5	196
83:5	189
84:8	197
85:2	188

4 Baruch
1:5	195

1 Enoch 171–75, 192, 217, 219, 221, 228, 234
1:1–5:9	174
1:3	174
1:8	174
5:6–7	174
6–11	223
6:1–4	220
6:6	220
7:3	221
10:1–2	222
10:4–6	235
10:11	235
10:11–13	223, 224
10:20–22	227
15	224, 227, 230
15:3	225
15:8–12	225
18:15	235
21:7	235
37–71 (Book of Parables)	
39:6	174
41:2	174
45:4	192
45:4–6	174
46:2–4	174
46:4	174
46:4–8	174
47:1	174
48:1	192
48:2	174
48:7	174
48:8–10	174
48:10	174
49:2–4	174
51:1	174
51:3	174
51:5	174
52:4	174
53:6	174
58:1	174
58:3	174
60:2	174
60:8	174
60:10	174

61:4	174	6:59	184, 194, 198
62:1	174	7:11	194, 196, 198
62:11–12	174	7:20	185
62:13–15	174	7:36	235
63:1	174	7:47	185
70:3	192	8:1	196, 198
90:24	235	8:3	196
91:11	173	8:44	198, 198
91:11–17	171, 172	8:45	186
93:1–2	172	8:55	196
93:1–10	171	9:13	198
93:2	172	9:15–16	196
93:3–10	172	9:21–22	196
93:5	172	13:25–52	198
93:8	173		
93:9–10	173	Jubilees	95, 99, 109,
93:10	172, 173		131–33, 167,
			168, 172, 213,
4 Ezra	179, 181–86,		215, 221,
	194–95, 262		226–30,
3:4–27	181		235
3:12	182	2:19	195
3:13–14	182	2:19–20	167
3:15–16	262	2:20	192
3:16	195	5:11–12	227
3:28–36	181, 183	5:12	228
3:30	183	5:13–16	229
4:22–25	261	5:17–18	229
4:23	183	10:5–7	226
5:23–27	183	10:8–11	226
5:23–30	183	17:15–18	132
5:27	183	18:1–2	132
5:28–30	183	19:18	172, 196
5:30	196	25:1–12	167
6:55–59	184	30:7–10	167
6:55	184, 194		
6:56	184	2 Maccabees	
6:58	194	1:27–29	278

3 Maccabees

2:9	195

4 Maccabees

12:12	235

Psalms of Solomon 175–78, 193, 194

1	176, 183, 193
1:2–4	175
1:5	195
1:8	176
2	176
2:1–7	176
2:3–4	176
2:6	176
2:26–27	176
3:5–8	175
3:9–12	175
4:3–5	175
7:1–3	175
7:6	175
7:8	194
7:8–10	175
8	176
8:11–13	176
8:13	176
8:14–21	176
8:18–21	176
8:23–34	175
8:30	175
9	177
9:1–7	177
9:1–11	175
9:7	175
9:8–9	176, 195
9:8–11	177
9:9	195
10:1–4	175
10:4	194
10:4–8	175
10:5–8	175
12:1–6	175
12:6	175
13:6	175
13:9	175
13:10	175
14:1–5	175
14:3–5	175
14:5	175
14:6–9	175
15:6–7	276
15:6–9	175
15:10–12	175
16:15	175
17	177, 193
17:4	177
17:5	193
17:5–20	177
17:11–18	176
17:21	177
17:22–46	177
17:26–29	175
18	177
18:1–5	175
18:1–9	175
18:3–4	177, 195

Testaments of the Twelve Patriarchs

Testament of Asher

7:7	198

Testament of Job

1:5–6	108

Testament of Levi		11:1–12:13	178
10:5	195	12:4	179
13:7	278		
15:4	198	Testament of Zebulun	
		9:8	195

Testament of Moses

	178–81	
1:1–9	178	***Philo***
1:10–10:15	178	
1:12	196, 198	*De Gigantibus*
1:13	179	1:64 195
1:16	179	
1:16–17	179	*Mutatione Nominum*
1:17	179, 187	1:66 195
1:18	180	1:69 195
2	178	1:17 195
2–4	178	1:82 195
2:1	178	
2:3–10:10	179	*Quaestiones et Solutiones in Genesis*
2:6	195	2:54 223
3–7	181	
3:1–4	178	*De Sacrificiis Abelis et Caini*
3:5–4:4	178	1–4 304
4:2	180	
4:2–4	180	***Pseudo-Philo***
4:5	180	
4:5–9	178	*Liber Antiquitatum*
5:1–6:1	178	*Biblicarum* 23:2 195
6:1–9	194	
6:2–8:5	178	
9	178	***Josephus***
10	178	
10:1–2	181	*Antiquities*
10:1–10	181	14:1–79 176
10:8	180, 195	175 227
10:8–10	181	
10:11	179	*Jewish War*
11:1	179	1:117–59 176

Dead Sea Scrolls and Related Texts

1QpHab 5:4	192
1QpHab 9:12	192
1QS 3:15–16	195
1QS 3:18–26	167
1QS 4:6–14	167
1QS 8:6	192
1QS 9:14	192
4QInstruction	167
4Q70	211
4Q71	211
4Q72	211
4Q72a	211
4Q72b	211
4Q158	213
4Q252	213
4Q299 3a ii–b	167
4Q364	213
4Q365	213
4Q365 frgs.	214
4Q366	213
4Q367	213
4Q418 81 20	167
4Q418 69 ii 10	167
4Q416 1 10–13	167
4QEn^g 1 iv 12–13	192
4QpNah 3–4	176
4QpPs^a 1–2 ii 5	192
Book of Mysteries	166

Rabbinic Writings—Mishnah, Tosefta, Talmud

b. B. Bat. 15a	108
b. B. Bat. 15b	108
b. B. Bat. 16a	108
b. Ber. 17a	108
b. Sanh. 106a	108
b. Sotah 11a	108
b. Sotah 35a	108
j. Sotah 20c	108
Tosefta 3:16	201
t. Sanhedrin 6	206
t. Ber. 3:14–16	201
t. Sot. 8:7	208
Tosefta Ki–fshuta 44 line 69	207

Rabbinic Writings—Midrashic Collections

Deut. Rab. 2:4	108
Exod. Rab. 1:9	108
Gen. Rab. 19:12	108
Gen. Rab. 49:9	108
Gen. Rab. 57:4	108
Leviticus Rabbah	202–3
Lev. Rab. 1:11	201
Mekhilta, Bahodesh 5	202
Mekilta d'Rabbi Yishmael	204
Mekilta d'Rashbi	205
Pesikta de Rab Kahana	262
Pesiqta Rabbati	102
Pesiq. Rab. 29/30A:7	103
Pesiq. Rab. 47:3	108
Seder 'Olam Rab. 21	108
Sefer Vehizhir	208
Sifre Num. 42	205
Sifre Deut. 29	207
Sifre Zuta	204

Targums

Tg. Ps. 68:30	208

Moses Maimonides

The Guide of the Perplexed
1:1   328

POST-BIBLICAL CHRISTIAN TEXTS

Apophthegmata Patrum	252

Thomas Aquinas
Summa Theologica
I-II, q. 98, a. 4, c	349
I-II, q. 104, a. 2, ad 2	349
I-II, q. 98, a. 4, c	349
I-II, q. 103, a. 4, c	349
I-II, q. 104, a. 3, c	349
II-II, q. 10, a. 11	339
II-II, q. 10, a. 11, c	350
III, q. 68, a. 1, ad 1	350

Epistola ad ducissam Brabantiae
vol. 42 (ed. Leonine),
375.23–25   349

S. Thomae Aquinatis Scriptum super Sententiis
vol. 4, 67 (*In IV Sent.*
d. 1, q. 2, a. 5, qla.
3, ad 3)   350

Augustine
City of God   266
18.29	278
18.54	278

Epistle of Barnabus	239, 240, 249
7:3	241
18–20	254

1:21	328
1:26	328
1:56	328
2:30	328
2:349	328

1 Clement	237, 239, 240
5	238
10:1	238
31:3	238
42	238
44	238

Clement of Alexandria
Stromata
2:20   239

Didache   239

Eusebius
Ecclesiastical History
3.1.5.34	237
3.25.4	240
4.26.1–14	241
4.26.2	241

Gregory the Great
Moralia on Job; Preface § 5   93

Irenaeus
Adversus Haereses 3.3.1   237

Jerome
De vir. Ill. 24   241

Melito   242, 249
Peri Pascha 9   242

Origen
Homily on Genesis
8.1	244, 245
8.2	246
8.3	246
8.4	247
8.5	247
8.6	247, 248

Tertullian
De praescriptione
haereticorum 32	237
De pudicitia 20	239

Reformation and Post-Reformation Writings

Martin Luther
Luther's Works (LW)
1–8	300, 301
1:103–15	303
1:193	301
2:216–17	302
2:254–58	305
2:255	305
2:264	299
3:72–73	302
4:3–73	304
4:25–35	304
4:34–35	303
4:343	304, 305
4:345	304
4:346	304
4:347	304
4:348	304
4:349	305
4:349–50	303
4:350	304
4:351	304
4:351–52	303
4:355	305
4:366	304
4:366–67	304
4:367	305
4:368	305
5:42–50	299
5:44	299
8:199–319	304
8:319	303
9:33	305
9:63	303
10	299
11	299
23:23	304
25:80	304
33:15–295	299
35:236	301, 303
35:237	302
35:380	304
45:197–229	305
47:57–9	300
47:121–306	300
47:156–57	299

Companion Volume: Introduction to the Exegetical Writings (LW)
89	303

Martin Luthers Werke (WA)
3	299
4	299
11:314–36	305
18:600–787	299
40/3:595–682	300
40/3:683–746	300
42–44	300, 301
43:384,23–24	304
43:385,4–5	304
43:385,37–39	304

43:388,29–30	304
43:388,34–35	304
43:392,16–18	305
43:400,4	304
43:400,6–7	304
43:457–63	299
43:459	299
44:728,8–9	304
50:312–37	300
52:22–184	302
53:417–552	300
53:578–648	300
55/1	299
55/2	299
58:28–100	300

John Calvin
Institutes

2:430	327
154	327

Catechism of the Catholic Church

§1	348
§756	350
§831	348
§839	350
§840	343, 344
§846	348
§848	348

Documents of Vatican II
Ad Gentes

7	348
8	334, 340

Gaudium et Spes

22	334, 338, 341, 346

Lumen Gentium

1	334
9	334, 348
13	334, 348
14	348
16	333, 334, 348, 350
48	334

Nostra Aetate

4	333, 334, 335, 336

Index of Modern Authors

Albertz, Rainer, 72
Anderson, Gary, 3, 43, 65
Argall, Johannes, 146–47, 150–53, 158, 168, 169

Barr, James, 25, 40
Barth, Karl, 313–14, 319
Battle, John A., Jr., 267, 278
Benedict XVI, 330, 331, 333, 347
Bergsträsser, Gotthelf, 25–26, 39, 41
Brett, Mark, 79, 107, 276, 355
Brueggemann, Walter, 78, 84, 88, 353
Buber, Martin, 311, 354

Childs, Brevard, 41, 78, 85, 88
Clements, R. E., 78, 87
Clifford, Richard, 3, 21, 169
Cohen, Gershon, 261, 277
Cohen, Hermann, 319, 321–27, 328
Collins, John, 184, 185, 191, 192, 194, 196, 198
Crawford, S. W., 232, 233

Day, John, 154, 169
Dimant, Devorah, 139, 140, 141, 193, 234

Douglas, Mary, 17, 22

Ehrman, Bart D., 237, 240, 254
Eichrodt, Walther, 78, 87
Eideles, R. Shmuel, 201
Eynde, S. Van den, 141

Fishbane, Michael, 87
Fitzmyer, Joseph, 139, 140, 143, 276

Gerstenberger, E. S., 78, 88
Goldin, Judah, 204, 208
Goldingay, John, 78, 88
Greenberg, Moshe, 80, 88, 329
Grieb, A. Katherine, 88, 276
Griffiths, Paul, 266, 277
Gunkel, Hermann, 234

Ha'am, Ahad, 319
Hermisson, Hans-Jürgen, 37, 42
Heschel, Abraham Joshua, 311, 353, 354, 357
Hoffman, Yair, 86, 88

Ingeborg, Liv, 187

Jensen, Robin, 249, 255
John Paul II, 309, 330

Kahana, Menahem I., 206, 209
Kaminsky, Joel S., 3, 64, 107, 160–61, 169, 195, 196, 279, 298, 353, 358
Kaplan, Mordecai, 319
Kaufmann, Yehezkel, 324–27, 329, 356
Klein, Emma, 84
Knohl, Israel, 203, 207, 208

Levenson, Jon D., 1–3, 14–15, 21–22, 24, 40–44, 64–69, 84–85, 89, 91–92, 107–11, 115, 126, 139, 142, 145, 154, 169, 170, 191, 194, 195, 200, 207, 209, 210–11, 236, 253–55, 256, 268, 273–76, 278–79, 280, 298, 311, 314–19, 323–29
Lieberman, Saul, 201, 207, 208
Lohfink, Gerhard, 87
Lohr, Joel N., 44, 64, 65, 87
Lohse, Eduard, 37, 42
Longenecker, Bruce, 196
Longman, Tremper, III, 40

Marböck, Johannes, 146–47, 168
Meinhold, Peter, 283, 300
Milgrom, Jacob, 17, 22, 88
Moberly, Walter, 3, 37, 40, 41, 42, 93, 108
Muffs, Yochanan, 206

Neumann-Gorsolke, Ute, 19, 22
Nickelsburg, George W. E., 115, 192–95, 234–35
Niditch, Susan, 72, 86
Novick, Tzvi, 130–32, 142, 143

Olyan, Saul, 160–61, 169
Osten-Saken, Peter von der, 283, 299, 300–303

Pacifici, Ricardo, 330–31, 347
Pelikan, Jaroslav, 283, 289, 301
Perdue, Leo, 41, 88, 147–48, 158, 168, 169
Pitre, Brant, 270, 278
Pius XII, 330–31
Preuss, Horst, 41, 78, 88

Rad, Gerhard von, 22, 78, 87, 164–65, 169
Rawidowicz, Simon, 207, 209
Rendtorff, Rolf, 78, 88
Roberts, J. J. M., 40, 42
Rofé, Alexander, 232
Rosenzweig, Franz, 311, 319, 322–26

Staples, Jason, 259, 270–72, 274, 276, 278
Schäfer-Lichtenberger, Christina, 88
Schiffman, Lawrence, 58, 66, 197, 232
Seeberg, Erich, 283, 301
Skehan, Patrick, 156, 162, 163, 169
Spina, Frank, 44, 64–65
Stadelmann, Luis, 9–10, 21
Stern, Philip, 73, 86–87
Stewart-Sykes, Alistair, 242, 255
Stone, Michael, 191, 193–98, 235, 259
Stuckenbruck, Loren, 173, 191–93, 197

Tigay, Jeffrey, 71–72, 86
Tov, Emmanuel, 197, 232, 233
Tsevat, Matitiahu, 50, 65

Walke, Bruce, 78, 88
Ward, Keith, 73, 79, 82, 86
Weinfeld, Moshe, 21, 71–72, 86, 273, 274, 279
White, Hugh C., 127
Williamson, Hugh, 40, 233, 355
Wills, Lawrence, 44, 60, 64
Wright, N. T., 266, 269
Wyschogrod, Michael, 311–19, 324, 328

Zimmerli, Walther, 43, 78, 87
Zunz, Leopold, 87, 207, 209